D1625174

THE FUTURE OF
UNDERDEVELOPED COUNTRIES

The Future of Underdeveloped Countries

Political Implications of Economic Development

REVISED EDITION

By Eugene Staley

Published for the

COUNCIL ON FOREIGN RELATIONS

by

HARPER & BROTHERS

New York

1961

THE FUTURE OF UNDERDEVELOPED COUNTRIES

FOREWORD

BY STACY MAY

As the Chairman of a Study Group of the Council on Foreign Relations that held a series of meetings during 1952 dealing with the political implications of economic development, I have been asked to write a foreword to Eugene Staley's book, THE FUTURE OF UNDERDEVELOPED COUNTRIES.

The other members of the Council's study group were:

Percy W. Bidwell
Jonathan B. Bingham
Gordon R. Clapp
Harlan Cleveland
William Diebold, Jr.
William O. Douglas
James H. Drumm
George S. Franklin, Jr.
J. Kenneth Galbraith
John W. Gardner
Robert L. Garner
Arthur J. Goldberg

William L. Holland
Hugh L. Keenleyside
Edward S. Mason
Frank W. Notestein
Milo Perkins
Nelson A. Rockefeller
Walter R. Sharp
Simon D. Strauss
Phillips Talbot
Frank Tannenbaum
Ralph E. Turner
Howard Tolley

It is appropriate, I think, to start with a brief statement of the relationship between the members of this group and the volume that is now being published. That relationship may be characterized as somewhat analagous to that of the mother duck, in Hans Christian Andersen's tale, to the egg from which the Ugly Duckling was hatched.

The members of the Study Group served as a forum that afforded Dr. Staley the opportunity of trying out the ideas that are presented in his completed work through the give and take of critical discussion. Each of the participants contributed his own ideas in the course of our proceedings, which Dr. Staley incorporated into his own thinking or rejected according to his judgment of their worth.

The mature product that now is ready to soar is definitely of Dr. Staley's creation. The members of the Study Group who brooded over its period of incubation are confident that the product is a swan. Each of us, I am sure, is prepared to bask, to a degree appropriate to the relationship of foster parenthood, in such public admiration as the work may elicit. Yet I am equally sure that each member of the Study Group will subscribe to at least some of the criticisms that may be made. For no attempt was made to arrive at a consensus of opinion in the Study Group discussions; the organization, analysis and interpretation in this presentation are Dr. Staley's, and his alone; and it is inevitable that certain portions of a swan's anatomy will appear exotic, and perhaps shockingly ill-proportioned, to even the tolerantly parental eyes of those whose role at most was that of a sort of collective mother duck.

What, then, is it fitting for us to say about the launching of this work, without erring either on the side of spurious and presumptuous proprietorship or on that of ungracious and captious disinheritance?

Perhaps the dilemma can be resolved by trying to state why the Council on Foreign Relations felt that there was justification for assisting in the production of still another study in a field that, over the past five years, has been irrigated to the point of saturation by research reports and technical publications, if not by general treatises.

The Council on Foreign Relations is concerned with the core problems that affect the relationships of our Government with others. Its tripartite membership of men of affairs, government officials and academic scholars qualifies it as an agency that is especially equipped to identify the emergent problems in this field and to assist in obtaining for them the type and degree of attention that their importance to our national interest warrants—attention through general public awareness, through informed government policy, and through the focussed effort of relevant scholarship. The perception of those responsible for the guidance of the Council's activities would have been dull, indeed, if they had failed to recognize the emergence of international concern for the problem of how a dynamic upward thrust may be introduced into the economies of the so-called underdeveloped areas as an essentially new and potentially revolutionary concept in world political strategy.

As has been the case with most of the great innovations in social outlook, the "newness" of this concept is derived from compounding a number of venerable ideas into a new amalgam, welded by the heats and pressures of the current historic situation.

The concept of government initiative as an important determinant of the pattern and tempo of the economic progress of a given nation is at least as old as classical political economy although, in orthodox circles, it had fallen into neglect until revived by the harsh imperatives of the world-wide depression of the nineteen-thirties. Similarly, there is a long history of the missionary concept of transplanting the technics and procedures of modern education, medicine and agricultural and industrial production and distribution from the areas of progress to others where the formula for improving mass living levels had not been discovered. But the initiation of such effort in the past has rested largely with religious, philanthropic and business entities, and has seldom, if ever, even been considered as a serious *general* objective of any nation's foreign political policy. There have been, of course, numerous instances throughout recorded history in which one nation has sought to introduce its social, cultural, and economic institutions ino a *specific* foreign area as a concomitant of territorial conquest, or even, as in recent United States' history, as a responsible prelude to the restoration of that area's sovereignty.

The novelty in the conception of the role of economic development in international political theory that has been in process of formulation since the end of World War II rests only in part upon the increased emphasis that such problems are receiving in the foreign offices of both highly industrialized and relatively underdeveloped nations throughout the world. Equally decisive is the growing recognition of the importance to all of the establishment of economic growth trends not merely within spheres of particular national influence, but over far broader areas than could be so defined under past usages. It is fast being brought home to us that economic growth cannot be sustained in one nation of the modern world unless it is a widely shared phenomenon.

To an important degree, the urgency and the scope, as well as the immediate content, of the international development policies of all Free World nations are conditioned by the aggressive thrust of international communism which is being used as one prong of the two-tined weapon of internal subversion and external military conquest. The other prong, of course, is the armed might of Soviet imperialism. Since these weapons are being employed interchangeably and in concert, it is inevitable that all phases of the foreign policy of those nations determined to preserve democratic institutions must take cognizance of this threat.

We would have to be concerned with international development as a basic element in our foreign policy, even in the absence of the Soviet-communist drive to replace our system with theirs, because of the ever growing evidence that our economy is dependent upon foreign sources of supply and market outlets. But the threat is irrefutably present, and there is strong evidence that its major effort is focussed upon establishing its control in the underdeveloped areas which to date have proved far more vulnerable than those of relatively high industrial advancement. In a very real sense we are competing for the adherence of more than a billion people to a system that is compatible with our own survival against an attempt to attach them to a system that is dedicated to the destruction of free and democratic institutions. This is likely to prove the most important issue in international politics for many generations to come.

There is ample justification, accordingly, for a work that deals with international development as an issue of foreign policy, and that is the essential focus of the book that Eugene Staley has written. Most of the voluminous literature on development that has been published since the United States officially inaugurated a program in this field through the Act for International Development has dealt with economic and procedural aspects of the problem. Some of it has been descriptive, some technical and analytic. Much of it has been hortatory, consisting of a rather uncritical marshalling of arguments as to the necessity and virtue of one or another line of procedure with prediction of certain success if it is followed, and disaster if it is ignored; and a considerable amount has been denunciatory, rejecting the whole concept of development assistance as anything that is within either the interest or the practical competence of the governments of industrialized countries to promote.

Very little has been done to appraise the issue as one of the dominant theories in the strategy of contemporary international politics and it is as a pioneering effort in this direction that Dr. Staley's book should be judged. It presents a serious and, in many respects, imaginatively discerning analysis of why the underdeveloped areas have been selected as a primary target for communist infiltration and conquest, and how this strategy is being developed. It calls attention to the attitudes and sensitivities within the underdeveloped areas that must receive respectful regard in the framing of counter measures, since inevitably these factors will condition the chance that our efforts have of being effective. In addition it presents a record of past instances in which the successful adaptation of technics and institutions that have replaced economic stagnation with economic dynamism has produced political results so different from the peaceful and democratic order that we should like to promote as to preclude any easy complacency that there is a simple formula for success.

Eugene Staley's associates in the Study Group that served as the forum in which many of the ideas presented in this work were initially discussed can take confident, if modest, satisfaction in its publication. The modesty is impelled by the fact that the Group, as such, is not even the "author of the title." The confidence is generated by the conviction that THE FUTURE OF UNDERDEVELOPED COUNTRIES breaks new ground in exploring the problem of economic development as one of the critical foreign policy issues of our times, and one that promises to remain so for as far into the future as any of us can hope to peer.

PREFACE TO THE SECOND EDITION

Despite changes on the world scene since 1953 when the manuscript for the first edition of this book was completed, the book's central message is still valid and more relevant than ever. Briefly restated, that message is:

1. A great economic, social, and political transformation is sweeping the "underdeveloped" countries. This transformation is manifested in new aspirations and expectations, a new eagerness to plan and promote economic growth and to acquire modern technology, a challenging of age-old traditions, the rise to power of new leaders, and the emergence of new nations.

2. Economic development, which is now a major objective in practically all the less developed countries, does not automatically produce peaceful attitudes, popular and efficient self-government, or freedom of the individual spirit. Economic development is a *necessary* but not a *sufficient* condition for these good things. Economic development can provide the means either for international aggression or for peaceful cooperation, for growth of dictatorship or of democracy. It can go forward under conditions which strengthen the power of the Communist world system and bring more nations under authoritarian control or, alternatively, it can be a means of strengthening the will and ability of independent nations to resist the imposition of outside hegemony and to advance the well-being of their citizens in a setting of participative democracy and individual freedom. It can provide occasions for serious conflict between the two great power blocs, or, conceivably, for cooperation in constructive work under the auspices of an organized world community broader than either.

3. Much depends, therefore, on how economic development

takes place, under what type of leadership, with what motivations and attitudes, with how much and what kinds of external assistance, and in what sort of world economic and political environment. All this poses profoundly significant and difficult questions for policy-makers. Put most broadly, the key question is, "What can be done to make it more likely that the development of hitherto underdeveloped countries will bring both a progressive rise in the living levels of their peoples and advancement for them and for the world as a whole toward the political ideals of peace, freedom, and human dignity?"

* * *

The Council on Foreign Relations has decided that the steadily increasing importance of this subject and the continuing demand for the book justify a second edition, and that the best procedure is to reproduce the original text with a fairly extensive supplement bringing the analysis up to date. The Council has invited me, as author, to prepare such a supplement, and in it not only to survey the most important changes since the book's original publication but also to reflect on their implications for policy.

The central theme of the supplement, which constitutes Part IV in this edition, is that the case for a *world community approach* to assisting the development of underdeveloped countries has become overwhelmingly strong. I would now give much more emphasis than I did eight years ago to Chapter 3, "The Viewpoint of the World Community." Events of recent years, some aspects of which are analyzed in Part IV, as well as continuing long-term trends in weapons, technology, economics, and politics, point more and more clearly toward the necessity for a world view and world program, as contrasted with a national-interest view and bilateral programs in fostering development.

We in the United States need to rethink our national purposes in relation to development aid. Official justification for the aid program has in recent years been too negative and too narrow, too concentrated on mere defense against Communism. Certainly we and our allies must keep ourselves in a position to deter aggression, to frustrate politico-economic penetration and subversion, and to resist Communist threats or pressures. But aside from thwarting Communist purposes, what do *we* want? Can we not offer the world a big idea more charged with positive purpose and more appealing to most of the peoples of the world? Would not our own basic values be better served if we were to accentuate the positive?

A realistic United States foreign policy must have two inter-related aspects: *defensive* and *constructive*. At the defensive level, which under today's conditions means military, polit-ical, and economic defense against the Communist threat, all we can really do is buy time. How are we going to use the time that we buy? Will we use it to exert leadership toward a more viable world order so that, hopefully, defense will not always remain such an agonizingly acute problem?

In a world where rapid change is the rule, we cannot expect to buy time indefinitely and simply continue to hold the line. We must simultaneously seek to build the kind of world system in which all peoples, ourselves and others, will feel less menaced and will be able to work together to meet human needs that cut across national and ideological lines. This will have to be a world community system, and it will be workable only when it rests on loyalties to the world community much stronger than exist today. Interna-tional cooperation in economic development should be viewed as one of the principal tools for constructing such a world community system and for generating loyalties to it. The strengthening of world-wide (United Nations) develop-ment agencies should be a major aim of United States policy, not only because this is one of the best ways to get the right kind of development job done, but also because doing the development job in this way offers a means of strengthening world institutions and building world loyalties—tasks which have become essential to survival.

EUGENE STALEY

SENIOR INTERNATIONAL ECONOMIST
AND RESEARCH DIRECTOR OF THE
INTERNATIONAL INDUSTRIAL DEVELOPMENT CENTER
STANFORD RESEARCH INSTITUTE

April 1961

ACKNOWLEDGMENTS

I am grateful to the Council on Foreign Relations and to the Rockefeller Foundation for the opportunity to write this book. To Stacy May and the members of the Council's study group on "The Political Implications of Economic Development" I am indebted for helpful advice and stimulating suggestions. One who is privileged to work with a Council study group has the best of two worlds. He benefits from association with distinguished practitioners and scholars in his field, without being obligated to produce a document to which all would be willing to subscribe. Instead, he is free to express his own ideas, for which, of course, he bears sole responsibility.

I want to thank Peter J. Davies for assistance in research and Betty Ann Mitchell for help both in secretarial and research work. I am under great obligation to Ruth Savord, the Council's librarian, and her assistants and to the competent members of the Council's research staff who checked my references, read the proofs, and prepared the index. Helena Stalson, Jean Gunther, and Margaret Bowen deserve special mention. To William Diebold, Jr., and Percy W. Bidwell, who had a large part in originating the study, I am indebted for wise counsel throughout its execution and to Dr. Bidwell also for his editing of my manuscript.

E. S.

CONTENTS

PART III

DEMOCRATIC PATHS TO DEVELOPMENT

PART IV

DEVELOPMENT IN THE SIXTIES

THE FUTURE OF
UNDERDEVELOPED COUNTRIES

WORLD INCOME LEVELS

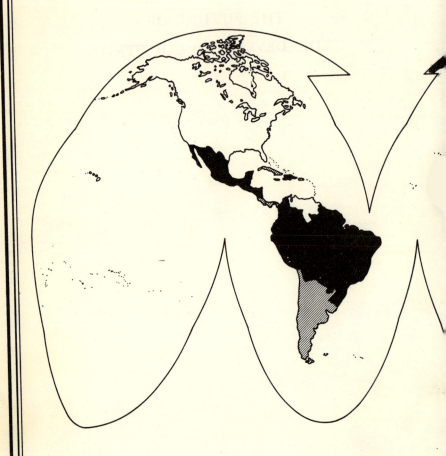

SOURCE: Mapped at Stanford Research Institute from data in Usui, Mikoto and E. E. Hagen, "World Income, 1957," Center for International Studies, M.I.T., Nov. 1959. Figures are gross national products per capita, converted to U.S. dollars by use of foreign exchange rates.

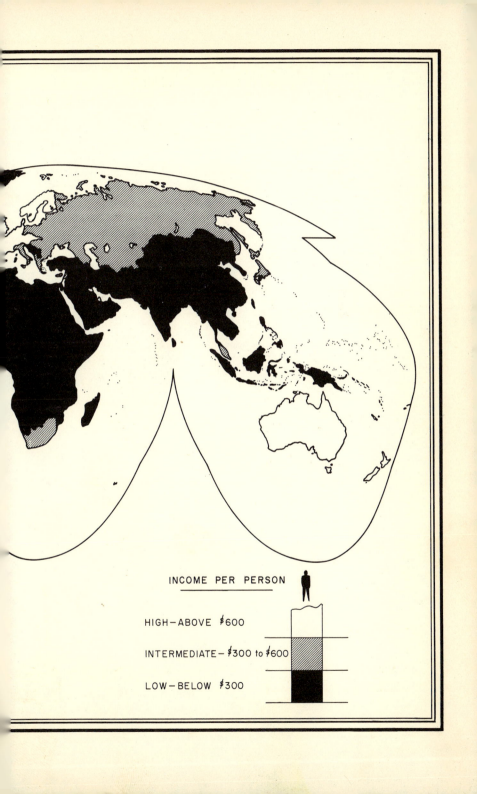

INCOME PER PERSON

HIGH—ABOVE $600

INTERMEDIATE—$300 to $600

LOW—BELOW $300

INTRODUCTION

The Western World in the last several centuries has evolved methods of production and of social organization by which it has been able to provide food, clothing, shelter, health, education, and leisure for the common man to a degree never approached by any past civilization. Along with the spectacular rise in living levels have come abolition of slavery and serfdom and an unprecedented increase in the power of ordinary people to have a say about political and economic decisions affecting themselves. This power has been made effective through representative democracy, universal opportunity for education, civil liberties, and the right of free association expressing itself in business enterprise and free trade unions and in the thousands of societies for the promotion of this or the abolition of that. The West over the centuries has made great gains in respect for the dignity and rights of the individual. The human mind and spirit have been freer than ever before to seek truth in science, philosophy, and religion. These things are true in the perspective of history even though we are only too aware today of backslidings, failures, aberrations, and abuses and of the tragic possibility that our magnificent applied science might end by destroying the whole edifice of civilization in war. It is still a fact that in the Western World over the last few centuries a greater measure of human dignity for more people has been achieved than ever before.

Peoples outside the Western World, however—and they are the great majority of mankind—have shared only in minor degree in the material and social progress of these centuries. Ancient ways of making a living and ancient poverty have remained. From the point of view of many of these peoples the West's modern development has meant mainly conquest and foreign rule. They know little of the West's home achievements in personal freedom, self-government, human dignity, and respect for individual personality. Their personal experience has often acquainted them with only the racial and cultural arrogance and contempt for "natives" shown by many Westerners. But all this is changing and is bound to continue to change.

Economic Development Vital

Today we face a new situation which poses a decisive test for Western civilization. The insulation of distance has been broken down by modern communication. The hitherto "backward" peoples are in ferment. The extreme contrasts between the modernized West and the less developed countries as to food, clothing and shelter, health and education, personal freedom and political participation are becoming less and less tenable. Either the benefits of modern civilization in living levels and human dignity will be generalized, so that they no longer will be almost exclusively enjoyed by the peoples of the West where they originated, or they will be lost even to the peoples of the West.

This is true for a combination of reasons:

1. *The material needs of industrialism.* The economic welfare and the military strength of the West depend upon maintaining the dynamism—the rising output of goods and services and rising living standards—for which the Western economy, and especially the American economy, is remarkable. This demands an increasing variety and volume of raw materials. A broad trading area, one which includes the present "underdeveloped" countries, offers the best combination of markets and resources by which to meet these growing demands at the least cost and with the least tendency to restrict the economic dynamism on which advances in prosperity and strength depend.[1] Yet the old framework of relations between the industrial West and the less developed

[1] It is worth noting that the need for raw materials and for a broad trading area arises out of the nature of industrialism and not out of impulses peculiar to profit-making capitalism. If the United States steel industry were run by commissars rather than capitalists, it would still be interested in the iron ores of Labrador, Venezuela, and Liberia. A socialist industrialism in the United States, if it produced at the rate of United States industry today, would be turning to Africa and Latin America for copper and to Asia, Africa, and Latin America for manganese and tin.

countries is no longer workable. It was built on a pattern of dominance and inferiority now stigmatized as "imperialism." There has to be a new and voluntary framework for trade and investment based on mutual respect, accommodation, and mutual benefit. This requires the rounded economic development of the less developed countries and their attainment of higher levels of living, political freedom, and respected social status.

2. *The contagion of ideas.* It would be nearly impossible for the West to continue its progress of past centuries toward human dignity if this central aspect of its civilization appeared more and more to be a peculiar trait of a stagnant or declining ideology, an island in a world of totalitarianism. Hence, it matters vitally for the main human values of Western civilization whether the non-Western world modernizes on a pattern which incorporates these values or rejects them.

3. *The specific challenge of Communism.* The Communists offer a competing system which borrows the industrial technology of the West but repudiates Western political freedom and the dignity of the individual. Communism now directs its main drive toward the underdeveloped countries. The choice of these countries between taking the Communist path or modernizing with Western aid and friendship will probably determine whether the totalitarian or the democratic way of life eventually acquires throughout the world a preponderance of economic, psychological, and military power. In other words, it will probably determine our own security and the course of world civilization.

The first major thesis of this book, therefore, is that the future of the underdeveloped countries in Asia, Africa, and parts of Europe and the Americas is a vital matter for the future of Western civilization, including, of course, the security and the way of life of the American people. Economic development of these areas in cooperation with the West is a necessary part of the conditions for Western survival and for the survival in the world of some of the West's most important contributions to human progress.

Should the Communist power bloc, however, succeed in bringing most of the underdeveloped countries into its orbit and cutting their links with us, the effect on our security would be disastrous. Also, the prestige of political freedom and individual dignity would suffer a grievous blow. Concern for economic and social progress in the lands where archaic production and chronic poverty are still the rule, symbolized by "Point Four" in American discussion, is therefore a concern that the distinctive human values which Western civilization has fostered shall remain viable in the world and viable in our own country.

If the present efforts of underdeveloped countries to develop themselves go forward with Western cooperation, then it is possible—though not certain—that a world civilization may gradually evolve in which the West's pioneering contributions to such human values as freedom, individual dignity, and material welfare are preserved and combined with the cultural heritages of non-Western peoples. The alternative, over the long run, is a real "Decline of the West."

Productivity Is Not Enough

The second major thesis of this book is that economic development of underdeveloped countries, while a *necessary* condition, is not a *sufficient* condition to insure the growth in those countries of trends favorable to human well-being and to the better world we should like to see. Not just any kind of economic development will do. Some kinds, under some circumstances, could even imperil the values that we should be most anxious to preserve and promote.

Much of the discussion about the American Point Four program seems to assume that if living levels can be raised in underdeveloped countries other good things will come automatically, such as progress in democracy, more peaceful international attitudes, and rejection of Communism. This book calls these assumptions into question. There is no simple correlation between economic development and political gains. The way economic development comes about, the pattern it takes, the auspices under which it is promoted, the world political and economic environment in which it goes forward are as important as the growth of production and consumption. Improved productivity is essential, but productivity is not enough. As a member of the Council's Study Group put it most aptly, "Economic development doesn't necessarily make nice people." Economic development does not necessarily bring either internal democracy or international attitudes that make for peace.

Development and Democracy

Americans would like to see growth in democracy along with economic growth in underdeveloped areas. We mean by democracy responsible participation of ordinary citizens in decisions affecting them, and assurances of individual rights and opportunities. The modern economic development of England, France, the United States, and some other countries was accompanied by democratic growth in this sense. In Germany and Japan, however, where the political and cultural heritage was different, a different political evolution took place along with economic development. The authoritarian political systems and social structures of these countries, while modified, were not swept away when the new production methods appeared but in many respects remained dominant. Russia offers a still different case. There a revolution against the despotism of the old regime was captured by a fanatically dedicated Communist band which pursued a policy of most vigorous economic development, but with the power of the state rather than popular welfare emerging as the dominant aim. The new Communist despotism, by making use of modern technology and industrialism, became more powerful, more pervasive, and more terrible than the old.

We cannot take it for granted that economic development in today's underdeveloped countries will follow any previous pattern, whether that of Europe, the United States, Germany, Japan, or Russia. Their cultures and social orders are very different. Their peoples are likely to respond differently to the new stimuli which are bound up with economic change. Great though the differences are among the underdeveloped countries, many of them also have important features in common. The bulk of the population lives very poorly, is uneducated, often illiterate, and most of the time politically passive. Political and economic power usually rests in a small ruling group. Politics tends to be authoritarian. Social structures are stratified, sometimes resembling those of the feudal period in European history. Nationalism is widespread and often extremely strong. Western civilization has made varying material, cultural, and intellectual impacts on different underdeveloped countries. In many of them it shows in a loose congeries of ideas in which the political ideals of democracy and economic methods of private enterprise and socialism are mixed in varying ways. In many countries intellectuals, technicians, and professional revolutionaries trained in Russia or influenced by the ideology of the Communist world movement have recently become important factors.

It is inconceivable that large-scale economic development, and particularly industrialization, can take place without bringing great changes in the political and social structures of the underdeveloped areas. Political and social change rarely takes place smoothly and easily. It is likely to involve strain, unrest, and perhaps violence. The learning of technical and industrial skills, the new discipline of factory work, the spread of a money economy in areas of subsistence farming, the growth of a managerial class and an industrial working class, urbanization, the opening up of new prospects of controlling the environment and of higher living standards, all will work to destroy the older order. The position of the ruling groups in each country will be threatened. Perhaps they will be able to adapt themselves and ride the waves of change. Perhaps the new sources of power will bring completely different groups into political leadership. In either case, the consequences are not readily predictable.

Not only are the internal political and social conditions of today's underdeveloped areas different from those prevailing in the more developed countries of the West at the time they began their economic rise, but the world setting is also different. Technology has developed enormously in the last century, revolutionizing agricultural and industrial practices, health, education, and methods of business management and social organization. There is no longer an international gold standard; there are more trade restrictions; people cannot move about the world as freely as they used to. Governments are held responsible for economic and social conditions to a much greater extent than they once were, and they have to undertake more complex tasks of administration. The United

Nations system has appeared, but without being able to bring peace and security. Instead, the tension between the Soviet world and the Western democratic world underlines and exacerbates great conflicts of ideology and power. The "field of forces" within which economic development proceeds nowadays is vastly different from that of a century or even a half-century ago, and the political and social consequences or concomitants are likely to be considerably different from those associated with any past economic development.

Development and International Politics

Large segments of the human race that for the last several centuries have been relatively weak in comparison with the West because of their technological and economic "backwardness" are now resolved to modernize their economies as rapidly as they can. Compelling reasons of enlightened self-interest, reinforced by humanitarianism, lead the West to hasten this process by making international aid of various kinds available. What new problems of international politics are likely to result from this new phase of the industrial revolution?

One thing is sure: a rise in the capacity to produce and to organize along modern lines means increased *power* for peoples that have had little power in recent times. How will they use this power?—to right old wrongs? perhaps to commit new ones at the same time?

How can the West, a comparative handful of people who have been lords of the earth thanks to their technological lead, find some new basis of accommodation with the newly-developing majority of mankind? Will Western dominance give place to dominance over the West by forces in the rest of the world that adopt Western tools without accepting the ideals and social techniques of the West related to personal freedom and human dignity? Such an outcome would be tragic not only for us Westerners but also for the other peoples of the world. This is a strong argument for unity of the West, though not unity for the purpose of a static defense of the *status quo,* whether in colonial policy or racial status or economic readjustments or the other burning issues that threaten to align the newcomers against the old hands. Realism would suggest a search for new bases of mutual respect and mutual interest on which to build cooperation between the more developed countries of the West and the advancing countries of the underdeveloped world.

If history is any guide, there is no simple, direct relation between economic development and the growth of peaceful international attitudes. Overzealous advocates of economic development sometimes give the impression that rising incomes will make nations less aggressive. The exact opposite could be argued from considerable evidence. In fact, one may reasonably raise the question: Must every large power go through an adolescent phase of aggression and empire-building, until it is checked by some combination of internal maturity and external force?

England's head start in the industrial revolution led to the growth of the British Empire. The United States expanded its boundaries along with its internal economy, and late in the nineteenth century went through a brief phase in which it carried its "manifest destiny" overseas. Germany's rapid industrial development in the last part of the nineteenth century laid the basis for Kaiser Wilhelm II's bid for a "place in the sun," thus contributing to the origins of the First World War. It was Germany's industrial might which gave Hitler the power to unleash such havoc in the Second World War. Japan, the first and thus far the aptest Eastern pupil of the industrial West, overran much of Asia before it was stopped in World War II. Soviet expansionism would not be the menace it is today were it not backed by the industrial development of the U.S.S.R.

This is not a plea for restricting economic development. The international consequences of trying to put obstacles in the way of what so many people ardently desire for such good reasons would almost certainly be disastrous. But these thoughts do suggest that it is high time we gave more sophisticated attention to the political implications, internal and international, of a movement so fraught with great consequences as that of economic modernization of the underdeveloped countries. The present study, by focusing on that problem, may contribute toward the intelligent and responsible policy-making which is needed in order to get the best and avoid the worst results from economic development.

The Outline of This Book

We cannot talk sensibly about the good or bad consequences of this or that development policy unless we have a fairly clear idea of what we want to achieve. Therefore, the first task undertaken in the following pages is to clarify the *objectives* of economic development. Part I is addressed to that problem. It explores the interests and motives of the underdeveloped countries, the United States, and the world community as they bear on development and arrives at a definition of "successful" development based on modern democratic values.

Part II is devoted to an aspect of the world political setting which has exceptional importance for economic development problems today, namely, the Communist world movement. Here we see other objectives in direct conflict with democratic objectives. Communism's main thrust is now directed toward the underdeveloped countries, as the most promising way to world dominance. From the standpoint of Western values and interests, our study of Communist strategy and tactics for seizing power in underdeveloped areas not under Communist rule, and of Communist practice in underdeveloped areas where they have gained control, is an exercise in "Know your enemy." For the Communists are pressing upon the underdeveloped areas, with great energy and skill, a formula for development which, if accepted, would defeat most of the aims we take as fundamental. The true nature of the Communist appeal to these countries is not well enough understood in the West. It is directed especially to the desire of men for status and respect, even more than to material advantage. The implications of this appeal for free world policy are important.

Part III, more than half the book, starts from the definition of successful development arrived at on the basis of democratic values in Part I. It explores key factors which will affect the prospects for attaining not only more production and better material conditions of life but also the broader political and social objectives included in that definition. Emphasis is put on the social requisites of successful development, on the necessity of building institutions as well as installing physical facilities, and on the way in which the course of development will be shaped by the world political and economic environment. A chapter on "Guidelines for United States Policy" concludes, and in a way sums up, the book. It brings the principal themes to bear on problems facing the government, the business interests, and the voluntary associations and citizens of this country in their actions related to development of underdeveloped areas abroad.

This book is addressed primarily to American readers. Hence, American interests in world development and the problems of American policy are naturally in the foreground. Other readers will find, I hope, that the view of American interests here presented is not a narrow one. Americans who read the book will do well to reflect that the United States, more than any other country, has the power and resources to influence the world situation. A tiny nation might act on a narrow, shortsighted view of its interests without doing much damage to world trends. But American decisions are such a weighty influence in those trends that we have to keep constantly in our thoughts, "What kind of world do we want to live in?" We cannot shape the world exactly to our desire, but neither can we afford to leave the big world issues for somebody else to think about.

PART I

WHAT IS SUCCESSFUL DEVELOPMENT?

Chapter 1

THE VIEWPOINT OF UNDERDEVELOPED COUNTRIES

The economy of every country is "underdeveloped" in the sense that more can be done to build up its productive power and to improve the economic well-being of its people. The term has come to be used, however, to refer—more politely than by the old word "backward"—to those countries which stand very low in relative income. The usage is loose, the distinction between more developed and less developed countries is one of degree, and there is no point in trying to be very precise in the matter. For those who like their concepts as clear as possible, however, I offer the following definition of an underdeveloped country: A country characterized (1) by mass poverty which is chronic and not the result of some temporary misfortune, and (2) by obsolete methods of production and social organization, which means that the poverty is not entirely due to poor natural resources and hence could presumably be lessened by methods already proved in other countries.

Two-thirds of the World's Population

The table on pages 16-17 classifies the countries of the world as highly developed, intermediate, or underdeveloped, mainly on the basis of the best available indexes of national income per person. The underdeveloped group includes almost all of the countries of Asia and Africa, most of Latin America, and some of Europe (see map on pp. xxii–xxiii). The total population of these countries is roughly 1,600,-000,000. Countries falling in the intermediate range include seven in Europe, five in Latin America, plus Japan, the

U.S.S.R., Israel, and the Union of South Africa. They have populations totaling about 425,000,000. The highly developed group consists entirely of countries in northwest Europe plus the United States, Canada, Australia, and New Zealand, all settled by northwest Europeans. Their population is some 375,000,000. Thus, two-thirds of the world's population of 2,400,000,000 live in underdeveloped countries, a little more than one-sixth in countries of the intermediate range, and a little less than one-sixth in highly developed countries.

The Communist bloc includes none of the highly developed countries. Several Communist countries are in the intermediate range; they have a total population of 240,000,000 (mainly the U.S.S.R.). Several are in the underdeveloped group, with a total population of 500,000,000 (mainly China). This makes 740,000,000 people in the Communist world, of whom just over two-thirds are in underdeveloped countries.

The non-Communist world is made up of the Western highly developed countries, with 375,000,000 people, a number of countries that fall in the intermediate range (several each in Europe and Latin America, two in Asia, one in southern Africa) totaling 185,000,000, and underdeveloped areas with 1,100,000,000 people. The total population of the non-Communist world is 1,660,000,000, of whom two-thirds are in underdeveloped countries.

Two facts stand out. One is the great disparity in income levels over the world. At one end of the scale are the United States and Canada with national incomes of more than $1,000 per person (in the case of the United States, more than $1,500). At the other end are the underdeveloped countries, comprising two-thirds of the world's population, where incomes average less than $150 per person.[1] According to the United Nations Statistical Office, half the people of the world live in

[1] National income figures generally include some allowance for nonmonetary income, such as home-grown food, but the value of economic activities carried on within households in less developed countries is often not fully taken into account. Also, money payments for distributive and other services increase the national incomes of the more developed countries without necessarily implying a corresponding gain in living levels. For these and other reasons, national income figures are not exactly proportionate to real living levels. There is no doubt, however, that living levels are considerably lower in the countries classed as underdeveloped than in those rated intermediate and highly developed.

countries that have per capita incomes of less than $100, some of them much less. Countries with more than $600 annual income per person include only one-tenth of the world's population. The United States alone, with slightly more than six percent of the world's population, accounted for forty percent of the world total of national income in 1950. Europe, with twenty-five percent of the population, generated another forty percent. Although Asia, Africa, and Latin America together have more than sixty-five percent of the world's population, they produced only seventeen percent of the world's national income.[2]

The other outstanding fact is political. While population is obviously not the only or even the main factor in world power and in the relative influence of nations on trends in world civilization, the sheer numbers of people in the underdeveloped countries give them a potential influence that cannot be overlooked. Their ability to make themselves heard in world affairs has already grown enormously in the last few decades. As they acquire more of the tools of modern production, higher levels of education, and more experience in modern management and government—as seems inevitable—it is likely that they will exert more and more influence on issues both of peace and of war. Given their numbers and their growing technological competence, the underdeveloped countries may in fact hold the balance of the future as between the political system and the way of life which have been evolving over several centuries in the West and the modern reversion to tyranny represented by Communism and other totalitarian systems. Whether most of these countries take a democratic or a Communist or other totalitarian path in their development is likely to determine the course of civilization on our planet.

The Revolution of Rising Expectations

The poverty of underdeveloped countries means that their people, on a broad average, have a life expectancy only about half that of the people of the highly developed countries. They suffer much of the time from malaria, dysentery,

[2] All figures are for 1950, based on the United Nations *Monthly Bulletin of Statistics*, June, 1952, pp. vii-xi and Table 54.

COUNTRIES GROUPED BY LEVEL OF ECONOMIC DEVELOPMENT [3]

A. HIGHLY DEVELOPED

Americas
Canada
United States

Europe
Belgium
Denmark
France
Germany

Netherlands
Norway
Sweden
Switzerland
United Kingdom

Oceania
Australia
New Zealand

B. INTERMEDIATE

Africa
Union of South Africa

Americas
Argentina
Chile
Cuba
Puerto Rico
Uruguay
Venezuela

Asia
Israel
Japan

Europe
Austria
Czechoslovakia
Finland
Hungary
Ireland
Italy
Poland
Portugal
Spain

Eurasia
U.S.S.R.

C. UNDERDEVELOPED

Africa
Algeria
Angola
Belgian Congo
Cameroons
Egypt
Ethiopia
French Equatorial Africa
French West Africa
Gold Coast
Kenya
Liberia
Libya
Madagascar
Morocco
Mozambique

Nigeria
Nyasaland
Northern Rhodesia
Ruanda-Urundi
Southern Rhodesia
Sudan
Sierra Leone
Tanganyika
Tunisia
Uganda

Americas
Bolivia
Brazil
British West Indies
Colombia

Americas (continued)

  Costa Rica
  Dominican Republic
  Ecuador
  El Salvador
  Guatemala
  Haiti
  Honduras
  Mexico
  Nicaragua
  Paraguay
  Peru

Asia

  Afghanistan
  Borneo
  Burma
  Ceylon
  China
  Formosa
  India
  Indo-China
  Indonesia

Asia (continued)

  Iran
  Iraq
  Jordan
  Korea
  Lebanon
  Nepal
  Malaya
  New Guinea
  Pakistan
  Philippines
  Saudi Arabia
  Syria
  Thailand
  Turkey
  Yemen

Europe

  Albania
  Bulgaria
  Greece
  Rumania
  Yugoslavia

Sources

For income data: United Nations, *Monthly Bulletin of Statistics,* June, 1952, pp. viii-ix; United Nations, Department of Economic Affairs, *National Income and Its Distribution in Under-Developed Countries* (New York: 1951. XVII.3).

For data on urbanization and occupational distribution: Food and Agriculture Organization, *Yearbook of Food and Agricultural Statistics,* 1950. Also, I wish to express thanks to the Population Division of the Bureau of Applied Social Research, Columbia University, and particularly to Dr. Hilda Hertz of the staff, for information from their comparative world surveys file on urbanization and occupational distribution, including historical data which have been of use in reaching certain judgments in Chapter 4 as well as in connection with the table above.

[3] Areas with population less than ¾ million were not included in this table.

The grouping is based mainly on per capita national income, as of 1950 or thereabouts. In Group A the estimated annual income is $450 per capita or more; in Group B, $150 to $450; in Group C, less than $150. However, degree of urbanization and proportion of the working population engaged in nonagricultural occupations were also taken into account, especially to classify countries for which income data are lacking, but also in a few instances to determine that a country should be in a lower or higher group than the one in which income estimates alone would place it. Germany was placed in Group A, although on the basis of 1950 income alone it would fall in Group B. Japan was placed in Group B, although on the basis of 1950 income alone it would fall in Group C. Venezuela was placed in Group B, although on the basis of 1950 income alone it would fall in Group A.

tuberculosis, trachoma, or other ills. They have the services of less than one-sixth as many doctors in proportion to population. Their food supply is about one-third less, measured in calories, than that of developed countries, and when account is taken of the needs of the human body for the relatively expensive "protective" foods, such as milk and meat, the extent of malnutrition is found to be very great indeed. The opportunity to attend school is limited to a small minority in most underdeveloped countries, even for the lower grades. High school, college, and professional training is even less available. Only one person in four or five, again on a broad average of underdeveloped countries, knows how to read and write. The supply of cloth for clothing, home furnishing, and other purposes is about one-fourth as great per person in underdeveloped as in highly developed countries. Nonhuman energy to supplement the labor of human beings in industry, agriculture, transport, and household tasks is less than one-twentieth as plentiful, measured in horsepower-hours per person. Incomes, on the average, are less than one-tenth as high.[4]

These disparities in living levels between underdeveloped and highly developed countries appear to have been growing wider, rather than narrowing, in recent years. According to the statistical services of the United Nations, the developed countries are not only far ahead but are pulling further ahead. Their rates of economic progress, on the whole, continue to be more rapid than those of the underdeveloped countries.

Poverty and the hunger, disease, and lack of opportunity for self-development that it implies have been the lot of the ordinary people in the underdeveloped countries for centuries past. The new thing is that now this poverty has become a source of active political discontent. Of course, no statement can be unqualifiedly true of underdeveloped countries so diverse in culture, history, and present situation as those of Asia and Latin America, Africa and Southeastern

[4] Department of State, *Point Four: Cooperative Program for Aid in the Development of Economically Underdeveloped Areas*, January, 1950; and United Nations, Department of Social Affairs, *Preliminary Report on the World Social Situation* (New York: 1952.IV.11).

Europe. (This is a caution which I shall ask the reader to apply for himself to most general statements in this book, so that I shall not have to repeat it *ad nauseam*.) But, speaking broadly, it is one of the most profoundly important political facts of the mid-twentieth century that among the people of the underdeveloped countries a ferment is at work which has already produced in some, and is bound to produce in others, irresistible demands for a stepped-up pace of economic and social change. The evidence is overwhelming.

In 1937 the then director of the International Labor Office, Harold Butler, reported on a trip to southern and eastern Asia that ". . . a great change is stirring Eastern society to its depths. The consciousness of misery has been created by the growing realisation that it is not the inescapable lot of the poor and that chances of a better life now exist. The immemorial passivity and fatalism of the Orient are beginning to yield to the desire for higher standards and the determination to acquire them." He called this "perhaps the most revolutionary movement of our revolutionary age." [5]

Testimony to the same effect by journalists and university scholars whose business it is to follow political and economic movements in the principal underdeveloped regions is emphatic and impressive. Distinguished travelers who have made soundings among leaders and peoples in underdeveloped countries, among them Wendell Willkie (*One World,* 1943) and Justice William O. Douglas (*Strange Lands and Friendly People,* 1951), have reported similarly. Justice Douglas talked with hundreds of people in the rural areas of the Middle East and found that the complaints of the peasants were specific: The absence of medical care comes first, then absence of schools. Next comes land reform; they have a passion for land ownership. Next is the desire to learn how to farm the modern way. The right to vote, to elect a representative government, to expel and punish corrupt officials are also important claims. Finally, the people of the area have a new sense of nationalism which expresses itself in many ways. "There are professional agitators who stir this brew of discontent; but the rebellious drive comes from the

[5] Harold Butler, *Problems of Industry in the East* (Geneva: International Labour Office, 1938, Studies and Reports, Series B, No. 29), pp. 65-66.

masses. I have not seen a village between the Mediterranean and the Pacific that was not stirring uneasily." [6]

Nearly all of the underdeveloped countries have within the past decade set up official agencies charged with planning and promoting economic development. Many of the plans, especially at first, were little more than dreams on paper, but now there is a noticeable trend toward sober, concrete, feasible projects. All this activity indicates a strong social demand for economic advancement.

The need for economic development, and for international assistance to hasten it, is the constant theme of spokesmen for underdeveloped countries in the economic and social organs of the United Nations and the specialized agencies.

In short, a "revolution of rising expectations," as it has been called, is sweeping the underdeveloped nations of the world. Political leaders who nowadays aspire to popular support in underdeveloped countries (and even modern dictators want popular support) must at least talk in favor of economic modernization. Failure to achieve practical, visible improvement in the lot of the ordinary people is more and more going to provoke unrest and bring political extremists to power.

Why is this happening now, not fifty years ago or fifty years hence? The answer lies chiefly in two factors: (1) the examples set by Western nations, which have proved that general poverty is not inevitable, and (2) the miracles of twentieth-century communication, through movies, the press, radio, and travel, including the travel of armies (for example, the demonstration of the fabulous American living standards by GI's on every continent in World War II). Poverty is old, but the awareness of poverty and the conviction that something can be done about it are new.

It has sometimes been maintained that happiness can be expressed as an equation:

$$\text{Happiness} = \frac{\text{Possessions}}{\text{Desires}}$$

In the Orient, until recently, the standard way to seek happiness has been to cut down on desires. The West in modern

[6] *Strange Lands and Friendly People* (New York: Harper, 1951), pp. 315-317.

times has sought happiness by increasing possessions. There can be no doubt that the ascetic philosophy of the East is losing ground to the activist philosophy of the West. In many Eastern communities the most respected person formerly was the man who withdrew from society, but abnegation is no longer held in such high esteem. The man who tries to better his community and himself is gaining respect.

It is worth stressing that the social stirrings in underdeveloped countries are basically a reflection of the revolutionary technological and economic progress of the Western world, and in considerable part reflect Western ideals. The Soviet revolution and the work of Communist agitators and organizers, however, are influencing the form which discontent takes. Communists turn the discontent to their own purposes and use it to seize power where they can. But revolutionary economic, social, and political changes would be under way in the underdeveloped countries today had there never been a Moscow or a Communist.

Political and Psychological Motives

It is my conviction that in the United States discussion of the driving forces behind the new demands for economic development generally pays too exclusive attention to desires for more food, clothing, health, and education and neglects the motives that may be labeled political and psychological. These motives are just as strong as desires for improved economic well-being, and in many underdeveloped countries they are even more decisive in their immediate effects on attitudes and government policies.

Factors in the demand for economic modernization in underdeveloped countries, other than the desire to overcome poverty, include:

1. The desire of new, self-conscious nationalisms to attain or preserve independence, and to be free of foreign political or economic dominance, real or imagined.

2. The desire for the means of national defense and security. In some cases there may be an unavowed or latent desire for expansion at the expense of neighbors.

3. The desire for national and personal respect, status, prestige, and importance in the world, which experience

shows not to be readily accorded to "backward," weak countries or their citizens.

The historical decision to modernize Japan and the activity of the Japanese state in promoting that country's extraordinarily rapid development were determined by men much less concerned with popular welfare than with military power. At first they sought military power in order to resist foreign encroachment, later to realize Japan's own ambitions for expansion.

Turkey under Mustapha Kemal Ataturk turned to modern methods, but not in order that the ordinary citizen could have more food and health services. The main impulse was to make Turkey strong.

Of course, state policy in most countries is more concerned today than formerly with economic well-being for the citizens. Even so, considerations like national power for defense or offense and psychological imponderables, such as a respected and important position in the world, have by no means lost their compelling force. An Indian economist, after describing traditional social obstacles which impede economic development, writes that the "most important" factor at work to break through barriers is "the wave of national feeling that is sweeping the backward areas of the world. Nationalism is everywhere associated with a twofold objective. Firstly, to be able to order one's own affairs, and secondly, to attain a position of dignity and importance in the community of nations." [7]

The lesson that a country with backward technology and a poor economy is militarily weak and politically uninfluential has not been lost upon the leaders of today's underdeveloped countries. Many have only recently gained political independence or still aspire to attain it, and one of the strongest compulsions for economic development is the desire to build up economic power as a foundation for independence.

Ambition for a respected status in the world must not be underrated among the driving forces behind economic development programs. Many, perhaps most, of the present-day leaders of underdeveloped countries have known in bitter

[7] D. R. Gadgil, "Pre-conditions of Economic Development," *Indian Economic Review*, February, 1952, pp. 17-18.

personal experience the humiliation of "colored" peoples exposed to the arrogance of some members of the white race. In some areas there are resentful memories of the social discrimination that characterized the old colonialism—clubs for the white rulers only, no "natives" allowed—and of other tokens of inferiority and exploitation. These things, which Westerners tend to forget, combine with conditions of appalling human need and the passions of new nationalisms to produce attitudes and demands which would hardly be human if they were always sweetly reasonable. As a Pakistani put it, "We want freedom from contempt."

Prestige is involved in development, as well as living levels, independence, and security. The experience of an international agency in one of the Latin American countries is not uncommon: when the organization's engineers were asked to advise on construction of a steel mill they showed how to design one that would cost about 12 million dollars, but the country's representatives wanted a much larger and more complex one to cost about 80 millions. Prestige, not economic calculation, was the ruling factor. There is a strong feeling, not entirely rational but powerful none the less, which associates export of raw materials and import of manufactured goods with "colonial" status. Sensitive national pride rebels against the thought that raw materials producers are "hewers of wood and drawers of water" for the industrially advanced countries. Here is one of the roots of the demand for industrialization, as distinct from the improvements in the efficiency of agriculture and commerce which in some circumstances may be more immediately helpful in a country's economic advancement.

The Communists, who are supposed to be economic determinists, have played most adeptly on these "noneconomic" motives in their practical work as agitators in underdeveloped countries, as we shall see in Part II. Much of Western policy, on the other hand, even of the enlightened sort which concerns itself with technical and economic assistance, shows too little appreciation of the psychological and political realities, tending to assume that all realities must be economic. A sort of third-hand Marxism makes us suppose that if people are discontented it must be because they are hungry.

Hunger is certainly a factor in underdeveloped countries, but other desires also motivate human beings and act very powerfully on politics in these countries, as elsewhere. A crude economic interpretation of political attitudes is almost always wrong.

Where political-psychological motivations come into conflict with desires for better economic well-being, the priority of the political is generally rather clear. Does Iran want more to get maximum income from its oil industry or to satisfy nationalistic emotions by ending foreign management? Could one imagine an Indonesian patriot agreeing that it would be better to go back to Dutch rule, supposing it could be proved that this would surely advance living levels for the people (which no patriot would be willing to suppose in the first place)? Debates on economic development in the United Nations are marked by reiterated assertions from spokesmen of underdeveloped countries that, while they need financial help for their projects on a much larger scale than has been forthcoming, they are determined that no loans or investments or grants shall be a means of infringing on their national freedom. Burma has refused on political grounds proffered American aid which it badly needs.

Societies in Motion

The new nationalisms of the underdeveloped countries and their passion for equality, respect, and status, like their new awareness of poverty, have some of their roots in the West's own cultural contributions. The ideas and ideals which produced the struggles for parliamentary rule in Britain, the American Declaration of Independence, the liberty, equality, fraternity, and the rights of man of the French Revolution, and the national unifications of Germany and Italy are now at work in new places. Not only mechanical inventions like radio, the airplane, and improved roads are having their impact on underdeveloped countries; so are social inventions like the free public school, universal suffrage, business corporations, trade unions, and social insurance. In lands with different cultural settings and historical backgrounds, where recent relations with the West have been tinged with inferiority and resentment, the effects of these cultural borrowings are not readily predictable.

Also available and being borrowed in some places are social inventions of the Communists, such as new strategy and tactics in revolution, comprehensive five-year plans, and methods of rule by police and propaganda. What the end results will be no one can tell, though we may be sure they will be important not only for the people of these countries but also for us.

The underdeveloped countries are in motion, and economic modernization of some kind, accompanied by drastic social and political changes as well, is on the way in practically all of them, though at different speeds and in a variety of directions. This does not mean that the resistance to change, which has kept some of these countries static for centuries, has entirely disappeared. The inertia of long-established habits and institutions is still a very important fact. So is the open or secret opposition of powerful individuals and groups that fear to lose their present privileged positions. In countries experiencing a strong cultural impact from outside there is always a struggle between the two kinds of response distinguished by Arnold Toynbee: (1) flexible adaptation, in which portions of the outside culture are taken over, and (2) "zealotism," a defense against change by resort to rigid and fanatical orthodoxy. Zealotism still plays a role in some areas, for example in Arab countries and among certain African peoples. But the impact of the industrial revolution has now become so overwhelming that few of the underdeveloped countries are likely to delay for long their switch to the more feasible response of adaptation.

As a measure of the changed climate of opinion in most underdeveloped countries we may recall that in China only about a century ago the first railway had to be torn up because of popular opposition; people threw their bodies in front of the engine. Conservatives of that day opposed the establishment of schools to teach the youth of China science and technology. Still further back, Emperor Ch'ien Lung had sent the famous message to Britain's King George III: "Our Celestial Empire possesses all things in prolific abundance, and lacks no product within its own borders; there

is no need to import the manufactures of outside barbarians."
The technical assistance officials of the United States or the
United Nations would be much surprised to receive a com-
munication in this tenor from any government today!

Chapter 2

THE VIEWPOINT OF THE UNITED STATES

It is declared to be the policy of the United States to aid the efforts of the peoples of economically underdeveloped areas to develop their resources and improve their working and living conditions by encouraging the exchange of technical knowledge and skills and the flow of investment capital . . .

This declaration was adopted by Congress in the Act for International Development of 1950.

Viewed in historical perspective this is a remarkable policy. It has not been usual for governments of nations in positions of technological leadership to go out of their way to spread technical knowledge and skills abroad. The attitude of Colbert, the French statesman who served Louis XIV, has probably been more common. In 1679 he learned that the Spanish Ambassador had hired four master silk-makers and a number of workers to go from France to Spain to establish silk manufacture. Colbert thereupon ordered an official at Rouen to clap the would-be emigrants in jail, to "provide scantily for their nourishment," and especially to keep the masters in jail a long time, "so as to prevent other Frenchmen from taking the same road and transporting manufactures out of the kingdom." [1]

The United States is committed to a policy of technical and economic assistance in order to encourage the development of underdeveloped areas. Is such a policy solidly rooted

[1] Charles Woolsey Cole, *Colbert and a Century of French Mercantilism* (New York: Columbia University Press, 1939), Vol. II, pp. 140-141.

in the national interest of the American people? Or is it a result of passing sentiments or temporary circumstances? What are the goals or objectives of economic development as seen from the American viewpoint?

Other economically advanced countries of the free world besides the United States are cooperating with underdeveloped countries in their development programs. The analysis of American interests and motives which follows will apply in part, but only in part, to these other countries of the more developed group.

Aims and Realities

There is some danger, in an analysis which concentrates on the American interest, of subtly conveying certain impressions that are not intended. Therefore, let me make the following points explicit at the outset: To say that America has a strong national interest in the development of underdeveloped countries is not to say that America can determine whether or not they develop, or what course they will take if they do. Nor does it imply that America can, or should, do the development job for them. Here, as in Part I generally, we are talking about *aims,* and the interests which should determine aims. The conditions that will have to be met before desirable aims can be achieved is the subject of Part III. It will be apparent there that the internal changes which an underdeveloped country must undergo to attain substantial development are both drastic and difficult. If the people of a particular country do not have what it takes in leadership and will to rebuild old institutions and to do the plain hard work that successful development requires, then there is not much that the United States or any international agency can do about it. More than ninety-five percent of what gets done in improving conditions in underdeveloped countries will have to be done by local people.

Part III will also bring out that there are things a powerful, wealthy, and technologically advanced country like the United States can do, directly or indirectly, to help the development process along, or to help create conditions in which it is more likely to take a desirable course than might otherwise be the case. In some circumstances our influence may even be decisive, in the sense that it could tip the scales. Hence, we need to be aware of our vital interest in the outcome, and we need to act realistically to use our influence accordingly. But the main responsibility for the future of the underdeveloped countries rests with the underdeveloped countries themselves. This we must recognize, and so must they.

BACKGROUND OF AMERICAN POLICY

Precursors of Point Four

The United States policy of helping underdeveloped countries to improve their economic productivity has roots which go back considerably before President Truman's "Point Four" address in 1949. Missionaries and philanthropic foundations had for a long time operated hospitals and schools abroad and carried on vocational and agricultural education. Many American business firms operating in underdeveloped areas actively promoted the technical and business training of local people. The American government from time to time had been lending technicians from the Department of Agriculture or the Geological Survey or other agencies to help an underdeveloped country meet some special problem. Though not a member of the League of Nations, the United States in the late thirties was cooperating more and more closely with the League's activities in humanitarian and scientific fields. Just before the outbreak of World War II a League committee under Mr. Bruce of Australia reported, with American encouragement, a plan for associating the United States and other nonmembers in an expanded economic and social program.

It was in Latin American relations, however, just before and during World War II that the characteristic elements of what later became the Point Four program began to be shaped into a definite pattern. Important innovations were worked out under the leadership of the Office of Inter-American Affairs headed by Nelson Rockefeller. Notable was the organization of grass roots work for the improvement of health, education, and productive skills in various Latin American countries under jointly administered and jointly financed commissions known as *Servicios*. The following interests of the United States motivated these pre-Point Four measures in Latin America:

1. A desire to strengthen the Good Neighbor Policy, with its broad political objectives of friendly cooperation in the Americas.

2. The need to offset the threat to the strategic interests of the United States posed by the danger of Nazi penetration.

3. The wartime need for the cooperation of the Latin American countries in supplying raw materials.

Wartime Discussion and Postwar Policies

At the same time that these practical patterns in technical and economic aid were being established in Latin America, discussion of postwar policies was going on in the United States. The views on economic development expressed by United States officials, and also the unofficial views put forward by leaders of opinion-forming groups, interpreted the economic and political interests of the United States in ways that strongly favored economic improvement in the underdeveloped areas.

This point is important because it has sometimes been implied that American interest in the progress of these areas would not exist but for the struggle between the Soviet Union and the United States. The facts refute this thesis. At a time when high hopes were entertained for postwar friendship with the Soviet Union, long before the disillusion which ushered in the epoch of "cold war," American policy was definitely headed toward world-wide technical and economic cooperation for the development of underdeveloped areas.[2] The Soviet threat has vastly increased the urgency of American interests in the development of underdeveloped countries. For the time being at least, it has shifted the emphasis among those interests. But the interests were already there and were being perceived.

[2] I speak with conviction because I had occasion in 1943 to make a rather comprehensive survey of official and unofficial statements indicative of attitudes in the United States toward postwar economic development. This was reported, with a number of quotations, in Eugene Staley, *World Economic Development: Effects on Advanced Industrial Countries* (Montreal: International Labour Office, 1944, Studies and Reports, Series B, No. 36), pp. 15-21.

The third of President Franklin D. Roosevelt's "Four Freedoms," enunciated in 1941, was "Freedom from want ... everywhere in the world." He more than once elaborated on the advantages to America of encouraging other peoples to raise their productivity, their living standards, and their purchasing power. It would mean greater safety from attack and from war and would encourage the development of democracy, he told a press conference in 1942. In answer to those who feared that America might be hurt economically by the growth of competition abroad, Mr. Roosevelt recalled how the economic rise of the South had increased its buying power for Northern goods. "The same thing that was done for the South," he stressed, "could be done for nations; and it would help them and us." [3] His message to Congress of January 11, 1944, declared that "Freedom from fear is eternally linked with freedom from want."

There were many statements favorable to postwar development abroad from American leaders of opinion, including Wendell L. Willkie, Republican candidate for the presidency in 1940, the Postwar Committee of the National Association of Manufacturers, industrial leaders such as Henry J. Kaiser, and leaders of both the American Federation of Labor and the Congress of Industrial Organizations. These statements showed wide agreement that it would be in the American national interest as well as good for the world to help other peoples to help themselves by raising their capacity to produce.

Practical application of this doctrine was seen at the end of the war in United States action for emergency relief and rehabilitation measures in war-torn countries, through the United Nations Relief and Rehabilitation Administration and in other ways, and in the leading role which the United States took in the establishment of international agencies active in development, such as the Food and Agriculture Organization, the International Bank for Reconstruction and Development, the World Health Organization, and the economic organs of the United Nations itself. The Marshall Plan came in 1947 as a response to an emergency situation in Europe. Though not primarily concerned with underde-

[3] *New York Times,* November 25, 1942.

veloped areas, it was a landmark in the evolution of American policy on economic aid; its effectiveness in hastening the economic revival and political stabilization of Europe encouraged Americans to consider a similar use of economic resources to attain economic and political objectives elsewhere.

Since 1949

This was the background for President Harry S. Truman's inaugural address of January 20, 1949, which launched the latest and most important phase of United States policy toward economic development. President Truman laid down a foreign policy program of four points, of which the last was: *"Fourth,* we must embark on a bold new program for making the benefits of our scientific advances and industrial progress available for the improvement and growth of underdeveloped areas." He appealed to these interests of the American people in justifying "Point Four":

Concern for human misery,
Better use of the world's human and natural resources, which would lead to expansion of commerce,
Increasing the chances for world peace,
Progress of democratic government.

When Congress in 1950 passed the Act for International Development, and thus opened the way for practical application of the Point Four program, it adopted the following official statement of motives:

The peoples of the United States and other nations have a common interest in the freedom and in the economic and social progress of all peoples. Such progress can further the secure growth of democratic ways of life, the expansion of mutually beneficial commerce, the development of international understanding and good will, and the maintenance of world peace.[4]

Meanwhile, the tension between the Communist world and the non-Communist world had continued to mount. In June, 1950, the Communist-dominated North Korean government launched its attack on South Korea. The United

4 U. S. Congress (81st), Public Law 535, Section 402 (a).

States government and the majority of the United Nations took the position that this flagrant aggression must be resisted. Since the United States had rapidly reduced its armed forces after World War II while the Communist bloc had remained heavily armed, the Korean war and the tension that it signified made a major rearmament effort necessary. In this setting Congress passed the Mutual Security Act of 1951, declaring the purpose of the Act to be:

> . . . to maintain the security and to promote the foreign policy of the United States by authorizing military, economic, and technical assistance to friendly countries to strengthen the mutual security and individual and collective defenses of the free world, to develop their resources in the interest of their security and independence and the national interest of the United States and to facilitate the effective participation of these countries in the United Nations system for collective security. The purpose of . . . the Act for International Development . . . shall hereafter be deemed to include this purpose.[5]

President Dwight D. Eisenhower in a speech of April 16, 1953, called upon the Soviet Union to show its devotion to peace by deeds rather than words and outlined a program for political settlement and disarmament which would bring opportunity for "a new kind of war," a "declared total war, not upon any human enemy but upon the brute forces of poverty and need."

This government is ready to ask its people to join with all nations in devoting a substantial percentage of the savings achieved by disarmament to a fund for world aid and reconstruction. The purposes of this great work would be to help other peoples to develop the undeveloped areas of the world, to stimulate profitable and fair world trade, to assist all peoples to know the blessings of productive freedom.

The monuments to this new kind of war would be these: roads and schools, hospitals and homes, food and health.

We are ready, in short, to dedicate our strength to serving the *needs*, rather than the *fears*, of the world.[6]

---

[5] U. S. Congress (82nd), Public Law 165, Section 2.

[6] "The Chance for Peace," *Department of State Bulletin*, April 27, 1953, p. 602.

Public Opinion

The American people appear to be overwhelmingly in sympathy with the general aims of "Point Four" and with President Eisenhower's proposed "new kind of war . . . upon the brute forces of poverty and need." Most of the important opinion-forming groups are favorable—organized labor, the National Association of Manufacturers, church groups, farm organizations, and the various groups that especially concern themselves with international problems. There are inevitably differences of emphasis and different views about the methods that should be used. In some quarters there is enthusiasm for what has been done thus far, and considerable skepticism in others. There is a segment of opinion, which in the old days would have been called "isolationist," that takes a dim view of Point Four, as of the United Nations, or the North Atlantic alliance, and everything international.

Public opinion polls have indicated that American voters approve the Point Four idea—decisively among those who had heard of it, less decisively among those who had not. One such survey in 1951 found that 32 percent had heard of the Point Four program and 68 percent had not. Of those who *had*, 62 percent favored it, 25 percent opposed, and 13 percent did not know. Of those who *had not* previously heard of it, 41 percent favored it when the interviewer explained, 33 percent opposed, and 26 percent did not know. The best educated and the well-to-do are strongest for Point Four. Thus, 68 percent of those who had been to college thought the plan worth while, but only 33 percent of those who had not gone beyond the eighth grade. Sixty percent of the upper-middle income group favored Point Four, but only 39 percent of the lowest income group. Sixty-six percent of the professional people were for it, but only 39 percent of the farmers. There were, of course, many more "don't knows" among the less educated, lower income groups and the farmers. The crucial factor, it would seem, is amount of information on world affairs.[7]

Will the present American commitment to aid in eco-

[7] Elmo Roper, CBS Radio Network, "Where the People Stand," November 25, 1951.

nomic development of underdeveloped areas be lasting? Will it be implemented by vigorous action, public and private, and by substantial funds for grants in aid, loans, and investment? No one can prophesy with assurance on this score. We can, however, analyze the variety of interests and motivating factors which have combined to produce present policy and which may sustain it in the future. Such an analysis reveals that the policy has a broad and substantial base.

The American Interest in Development

The American national interest which it is proposed to analyze below is the interest of the American people, of the American community. It is not the interest of some abstraction like "the state" or "the nation" presumed to exist above and apart from the people. It is not an interest in glory and aggrandizement, nor is it exclusively an interest in power politics and balance of power, though the tough realities of the world situation and our imperative interest in security make it essential to give power considerations their due. It includes moral interests as well as power interests. The American national interest is a pluralistic interest, a bundle of interests, as broad and multifarious as the interests of the people that make up a democratic society.[8]

Analysis of American interests and motives as they bear on development abroad should help us in our relations with the underdeveloped countries. If we Americans on our side and they on their side understand *why* the United States wants to see them productive and prosperous, both unfounded suspicious and certain kinds of false hopes may be lessened. Agreed cooperation for mutual advantage creates a

[8] It is necessary to say this because a concept of national interest is current among some political scientists which, in my view, is in conflict with democratic political theory and the American tradition. If adopted generally, it would inject into American thinking some of the very elements that led to tragic results for the people of Germany and other countries of the Old World. I agree with Thomas I. Cook and Malcolm Moos that America should continue to reject the old European concept of the state, and the idea of a nation as a real super-being. Instead of "statism," our concept of the state as an instrumentality of the people, and of international relations as more than state relations, offers a better approach to world problems. See their article, "The American Idea of International Interest," *American Political Science Review*, March, 1953, pp. 38-44.

healthier situation than one built around a concept of the United States as a rich uncle handing out gifts in the grand manner, or as an imperialist ordering other people around, or as a sucker to be imposed upon.

American interests in economic development will be discussed under the headings: general political interests, special political interests, economic interests, and humanitarian interests. The order of treatment does not imply order of importance. There can be no *single* order of importance. Motives that rank highest with one group in our citizenship will rank lowest with another. A vital consideration at one time and place may be insignificant at another. What we are doing here is to lay out the whole range of American interests and motives, and perhaps the most important thing to note about them is their wide variety.

GENERAL POLITICAL INTERESTS

The Kind of World We Want to Live In

The shrinking of the world under the influence of modern technology has changed the outlook of the American people. Isolation is no longer possible. Furthermore, the rise of the United States to first rank in wealth and power means that what it does or fails to do may determine which way things go in the world. We are faced with the problem of what kind of world we want to live in and what we are going to do about it, for no other nation is in a position to act as effectively as we.

This question, "What kind of world do we want to live in?" is the key to the long-range political interests of the United States in economic development of underdeveloped areas. Political interests are of two sorts:

1. An interest in internal political trends, particularly in the progress and stability of free institutions.

2. An interest in international attitudes which affect the chances of war or peace, the security of ourselves and our allies, and the possibility of eventually developing a more friendly atmosphere among nations.

Interest in Internal Political Trends

When it took weeks or months to travel between America and most of Asia, Africa, or Latin America, these areas were not only remote in distance but also in the impact of their events on us. The case is very different today. No nation—at least no nation that allows free communication—can insulate itself from the contagion of political ideas. Should that large majority of the human race which lives in underdeveloped countries turn to totalitarian ways for meeting its problems, the blow to the prestige of free institutions could not fail to affect the outlook for freedom in the United States itself. Americans have long believed, and with more reason today than ever, that our own institutions are in danger in a world where freedom does not flourish.

This does not mean that it is in the American interest to impose, or try to impose, our particular pattern of representative government or a replica of our free enterprise system on other countries. It would be naïve to think that the political and economic institutions which we have selected and molded over a century and a half to suit our conditions and our temperaments could be successfully transplanted into a very different cultural background without substantial modifications, or that they would work the way they do here. Hybrid corn developed for Iowa is not suitable for Mexico; it was necessary for the plant breeders to start afresh to select traits adapted to Mexican conditions. The aim was the same, namely a higher-yielding corn, but the answers best suited to the two different situations were not identical. This principle applies even more strongly to social institutions. However, the fundamental principles which had to be followed in Mexico to develop a suitable hybrid corn were the same as elsewhere. We shall later be insisting that there are some fundamentals that any country wanting real economic and social advancement must reckon with.

The true American interest is in the results. There will inevitably be diverse ways in which different nations go about achieving these results. Good results from our point of view, considering the kind of world we want to live in, would include government that is responsive to the needs of the people and reasonably stable, an economic system that produces and distributes the goods, and a social organization and attitudes that tend to advance the dignity, initiative, and individual freedom of man. In some underdeveloped countries political leaders are striving for these very things, through governments or political movements that, though non-Communist, seem to many Americans too "socialistic," or too different in other ways from our experience and preferences. Are they really moving toward desirable goals, in different ways made necessary by their circumstances, or are they far off the beam? These problems abound with complexities, and even if we agree on broad principles that underlie the American national interest it is not easy to be sure just how the principles should apply in concrete cases.

While we must not jump to the conclusion that anything different from our way is harmful to our interest, the prospect for getting the kind of world we want to live in is diminished and American interest is harmed wherever the future of freedom is foreclosed by systems which exalt the state above the citizens, suppress free communications, and trample on civil liberties. Nowadays Communism is the most dangerous of such systems. Without attempting to impose our own system, and admitting that there is room for a great diversity of forms which qualify as free institutions, we should have no hesitation in asserting our interest that no one else shall impose a less tolerant system and thus whittle down the area of the world within which the people can choose freedom.

Interest in International Attitudes

It is obvious that conflicts, aggressions, alliances, and shifts of power positions in the less developed parts of the world are no longer purely local matters. Some of the underdeveloped regions have an extremely high strategic value, because of their position or their resources or both. The Middle East is one such region. The peace and security of the United States is from now on closely tied to the currents of change in these regions.

We have already quoted the legislative declaration in the Act for International Development which asserts the common interest of the peoples of the United States and other nations in the freedom and the economic and social progress of all peoples and which sets as objectives "the secure growth of democratic ways of life" and "the development of international understanding and good will, and the maintenance of world peace."

Former Secretary of State Dean Acheson, discussing "the heart of our real interest in the Point Four Program," spoke of the American faith that representative and responsible government is more deeply in accord with man's nature than any other system of government and that it contributes toward world peace. "We have an interest, therefore, in the development of representative and responsible governments in the world, since it creates an environment in which we can live peacefully and continue to develop our own society. This is the central purpose of our whole foreign policy." Continuing, the Secretary spoke of the crisscrossing of two revolutionary movements in our time: the revolution of technology, and the revolution worked by the contagious ideas of liberty represented in our Declaration of Independence and our Bill of Rights. If, by the Point Four program, we can help people not only to develop their resources, "but to develop the culture that suits them and fits their needs, and to fulfill their aspirations for responsible and more representative government," then these revolutionary forces can be constructively channeled and will contribute to world peace. "If not, the world will continue to be swept by the rip tides of conflict." [9]

A United States spokesman in the United Nations General Assembly explained that American citizens are convinced "that only through economic and social improvement can the world achieve those conditions under which free governments can be maintained, unrest decreased and war banished. They are convinced that the only solid foundation on which we can build security is world-wide economic advancement." [10]

[9] "What is Point Four?" *Department of State Bulletin*, February 4, 1952, p. 157.

[10] Mike J. Mansfield, *Department of State Bulletin*, December 17, 1951, p. 989.

I can confirm, from following the discussions and pronouncements of many opinion-forming groups in the United States on the subject, that the long-term political interests described in the foregoing quotations play an important role in motivating American attitudes toward development. This is true on the unofficial as well as the official level.

SPECIAL POLITICAL INTERESTS

Strengthening the Free World against Communism

The American nation has a positive interest in doing what it can to shape the world so that the climate will be more favorable for our own free institutions and for our peace and security. Growing out of this we also have a negative interest: to stop any movement of tyranny and aggression which assumes the proportions of a world menace. In its day the Nazi-Fascist movement became such a menace. Our interest, under the impact of events, led us to join in defeating this bid for world power. Now the balance of forces has shifted. While "the totalitarianism of the right" is still alive in some parts of the world, the "totalitarianism of the left"—that is, Communism—is at this moment in history by far the most powerful and virulent menace to free institutions and the most aggressive threat to the peace and security of free nations.

In these circumstances, the need to meet the Communist threat has become a major, urgent motivation of American foreign policy, including policy toward economic development. The underdeveloped countries are special targets of Communist conquest, as we shall see in Part II. The methods that the Communist leaders use in their determination to impose their system on the rest of the world are a skillful combination of political subversion with armed force. Both are applied from inside and outside the country under attack, the exact combination depending on the situation as diagnosed by the leaders of the Communist world movement. To meet and defeat the two-pronged Communist thrust, American interest requires strengthening of the non-Communist world in two respects:

1. Against political subversion. This means helping un-

derdeveloped countries to meet their urgent economic and social problems and to attain their reasonable political aspirations, in order that there may be less of the discontent which Communist parties know so well how to exploit.

2. Against armed attack. This requires the strengthening of local non-Communist military forces where the danger of armed attack by Communist forces from inside or outside the country is acute. Further, it requires building up the over-all military capacity of the free world to promote the common strength and security of all its members. Free world military capacity can be increased by expanding the production of the strategic raw materials available in underdeveloped countries. Also, in an atomic age, the wider the spread of defense-related industries through the free world the better.

A joint report of the Committee on Foreign Relations and the Committee on the Armed Services of the Senate thus characterized the objectives of the American Mutual Security Program in the Near East and Africa:

First, discouragement of aggression; second, protection against subversion from within; third, strengthening the will of the people in this area to resist aggression and to encourage them in their efforts to achieve stability and progress; and fourth, removal of sources of dissidence and unrest.

Referring to Asia and the Pacific the same report said: "This is the principal underprivileged area of the world and therefore is especially susceptible to the blandishments of false Communist promises and propaganda. Satisfying of the more urgent basic needs of these people is therefore vital to the security of the area and constitutes a fundamental part of American foreign policy." [11]

The Committee on Foreign Affairs of the House of Representatives linked the security of the United States to economic development of underdeveloped areas in these ways:

(1) The hope of preventing another world war lies in making ourselves and our friends strong;

(2) This will require the maximum development and utiliza-

[11] U. S. Congress (82nd), *Mutual Security Act of 1951*, Report No. 703 of the Senate Committee on Foreign Relations and Committee on Armed Services on H. R. 5113 (Washington, August 27, 1951), pp. 26, 29-30.

tion of the resources of the entire free independent world through international cooperation;

(3) The strength which will come from the collective efforts of this combination will far exceed the strengths of the separate national components.[12]

The same committee stated as an objective of the United States in such regions, besides developing military strength, "the creation of social and economic conditions that will permit the growth and survival of non-Communist political institutions under which the people can feel that the fulfillment of their basic needs and aspirations is being effectively sought by their own free governments." The Economic Report of the President added in January, 1952:

Chronic poverty now affects the ability of some of these countries to maintain independence in the face of threatened aggression or subversion. This calls for a demonstration—by positive and sustained action by the free nations as a whole—that the economic aspirations of underdeveloped countries can best be realized in association with the rest of the free world.[13]

ECONOMIC INTERESTS

Interest in an Expanding World Economy

National policy responds not so directly to the "real" economic interests of a country as to what policy-makers and influential groups *think* those interests to be. Nowadays America's real economic interests are strongly on the side of encouraging the economic development of underdeveloped countries and, fortunately, the most influential opinion groups also see it that way, on the whole. There are always some people, of course, who take the old mercantilistic view of trade and prosperity and, like Colbert, think it harmful to us that the arts of manufacture should go "out of the kingdom." But the more enlightened view of America's broad economic interest in the general growth of world production prevails. This does not preclude conflicts in American policy, of which we shall have more to say in later chapters, particularly the

---

[12] U. S. Congress (82nd), *Mutual Security Act of 1951*, Report No. 872 of the House Committee on Foreign Affairs on H. R. 5113 (Washington, August 14, 1951), p. 6.

[13] Text from *Department of State Bulletin*, February 4, 1952, p. 183.

conflict between a general desire to have an expanding world economy with increasing investment and trade and the resistance of particular groups to imports which they regard as competitive.

The tradition of the expanding frontier and the "bigger and better" motivation in the American temperament predispose Americans to look favorably on world economic development. There is less disposition than in European countries to think of markets as fixed in size, more to think of them as expansible. Some of the characteristic credos of American business are that there is more to be gained by a low markup and a high turnover than the opposite; that business grows with the prosperity of its customers; and that high wages, expanding mass markets, higher living standards, and good business go together. These beliefs, which Americans feel to have been justified by results here at home, make it seem sound common sense and enlightened self-interest to help the people of underdeveloped countries to produce more and thereby to get ahead.

A rather typical statement of the positive view is this from the National Association of Manufacturers:

Sound economic progress not only makes other countries better neighbors; it makes them better customers and suppliers. As their productivity rises, their ability to supply us with the goods and raw materials which we need, will be increased. As their living standards are raised, and the earning power of the countries and their nationals is increased, they will provide expanded markets for the goods we want to sell. In this way, the entire world economy and the economy of the United States will be strengthened.[14]

This statement could be matched, as to general doctrine, from organized labor, farmers, and other important groups. Congress declared in the Act for International Development of 1950 that the policy of the United States is to aid the development efforts of the peoples of economically underdeveloped areas where such aid "can effectively and constructively contribute to raising standards of living, creating new sources

[14] National Association of Manufacturers, *The Bold New Plan*, Economic Policy Division Series, No. 11 (New York: May, 1949), p. 2.

of wealth, increasing productivity and expanding purchasing power." [15]

Industrialization and Trade

In its early days the United States was an importer of manufactured goods and an exporter of raw materials and foodstuffs. Nowadays it imports mainly raw materials and exports mainly manufactures. Does this mean that the economic interest of the United States is to restrict the development of manufactures abroad and hence to oppose the industrialization of underdeveloped areas? Not at all. Experience shows that, where trade channels are not unreasonably blocked, the very countries which produce the most manufactured goods for themselves are the best customers for the manufactured goods of other countries. [16] This is not a paradox, but a straightforward consequence of the fact that those who can produce more have higher incomes and therefore can buy more. Highly industrialized Canada to the north, with only 15 million people, buys almost as much from the United States as ten times as many people in the Latin American republics to the south, mostly nonindustrialized.

Economic development of underdeveloped areas does, of course, produce new competition for some of the established industries of the more developed countries. At the same time, it produces new opportunities. In this respect it is like technological change. In fact, economic development of underdeveloped countries is a form of technological change. Which effect—the new competition or the new opportunities—will predominate in its impact on the economy of an industrially advanced country will depend on many factors in each case, the most important being the economic adaptability of the advanced country. If its business leaders are alert they will shift production progressively toward those lines for which the new demands and increased purchasing power of

[15] U. S. Congress (81st), Public Law 535, Section 403 (a).
[16] The classic study on this point is that of Folke Hilgerdt: League of Nations, Economic, Financial and Transit Department, *Industrialization and Foreign Trade* (Princeton: 1945.II.A.10). See also Part II of the study which I did for the International Labour Office, *World Economic Development*, cited. This stresses the need for economic adaptability on the part of the more developed countries as new countries develop.

developing areas are expanding the market, and progressively out of those lines where the dominant effect is new competition. Then the advanced country will usually find that economic progress abroad means rising benefits from trade, employment at better wages, and general gain in income and living levels. If, however, the advanced economy is inflexible and insists, in effect, on trying to produce and sell the same old products in the same old markets, it will probably find itself in trouble.

The American economy rates high in adaptability. We specialize in technological progress and have learned to make the adjustments which new machines and new processes in industry, agriculture, and commerce continually require.

There is another reason why America is in a peculiarly good position to benefit from the new trade opportunities created by successful economic development abroad with only a minimum of disturbance from the new competition. A high proportion of the goods which United States producers offer on the world market are of kinds for which the demand is especially stimulated by economic growth. They are goods needed in development, like trucks and electrical equipment, or goods which are purchased in much larger volume by people with moderate to high incomes than by impoverished people, goods like refrigerators, radios, vacuum cleaners, and passenger automobiles. Some years ago I had occasion to write that "The United States is probably in a better position than any other trading nation to gain expanded markets as a result of rapid economic development and rising income levels in the rest of the world. . . . Its 'comparative advantage' in world trade is a dynamic advantage, which has its greatest scope when the trend of development and income is sharply upward. Thus, it so happens that the country whose governmental policies and business decisions will have the greatest influence in determining whether or not there will be vigorous economic development throughout the world is also the country whose export trade prospects are most favourably influenced by world economic development." [17]

This fact may contribute to awkward problems of international economic equilibrium, meaning the chronic "dollar

[17] Eugene Staley, *World Economic Development*, cited, pp. 151-152.

shortage," but the present point is that it makes world economic development attractive from the point of view of the immediate interests of American business and labor as well as on the long-term view. Some other countries will have more difficult adjustments to make.

Economic Stability

An expanding world economy is also in the economic interest of the United States because such an environment would make it easier to maintain a high level of economic activity here and in friendly countries.

Let us assume that the present arms build-up achieves its object of strengthening the military power of the free world sufficiently to discourage a Soviet attack, and that we pass into a period of less feverish tension. Our military aid to foreign allies would decline, as would the domestic expenditure on arms and arms facilities. It is impossible to say now how much difficulty the United States economy might encounter immediately and over the next decade or two in maintaining a high enough level of aggregate demand to call forth a continuously high level of production and employment. The decisive factor will certainly be internal adjustments in consumption, savings, and investment. The American domestic economy is so large in relation to the rest of the world economy that investments of American capital in underdeveloped countries, even in much larger volume than can now be anticipated, could hardly be a controlling factor in American prosperity or depression. Nevertheless, it remains true that our adjustment to decreased arms expenditure would be easier in a world environment of economic growth than in one where the underdeveloped countries were not making progress or where they were successively slipping away from our trading area into the Soviet orbit. (In this latter case, however, the arms race would hardly be slackening, so the problem we are discussing might not arise.)

A widespread misinterpretation of American motives, which the Communists do all they can to foster, is that a chronic "crisis of capitalism" forces the United States to find foreign outlets for its "surplus production" or else face business collapse and breadlines for workers. The Marshall Plan and now aid to underdeveloped countries are supposed to have been expressions of this economic compulsion to keep a sick capitalism tottering along. The truth is that when the Marshall Plan was first debated and adopted, and again in the program of economic aid to underdeveloped countries which got under way during the Korean rearmament period, the United States made foreign aid available in spite of scarcities and shortages (not surpluses) and in the face of inflationary pressure (not depression). At some future time, perhaps in the near future, the advantage of a heavy outflow of foreign investment in stimulating production and employment at home may become a significant factor in American policy. To date it has not been a major influence in governmental or business decisions, let alone the controlling one.

Economic Health of Western Europe and Japan

A matter of great economic as well as political interest to the United States is the outlook for the economies of Western Europe and Japan. We are so interested in the stability and strength of these countries that the American taxpayer has been making up their international deficits. Naturally, the United States would like to see them permanently self-supporting.

It is hard to see how they can be self-supporting at a satisfactory level of living except in an environment of world economic growth in which rapid progress of the underdeveloped countries would be a central feature. Expanded purchases of European and Japanese goods by the underdeveloped countries, as part of the development process, would help the former to increase their exports and enable them to pay for needed imports of foodstuffs and raw materials. If, at the same time, the underdeveloped countries could supply more raw and semifinished materials for export, Western Europe and Japan would be able to import larger quantities from nondollar sources. United States raw materials shortages would also be eased. These considerations add to the economic interest of the United States in encouraging a flow of capital (especially dollars) into the underdeveloped countries, thus promoting their rapid economic growth. They also argue for a policy which will not tie the supply of capital funds to purchases of equipment but will instead encourage the revival of a multilateral system of trade and investment. In other words, it is in the American interest that some of the proceeds of dollar loans, investments, or grants be used by the borrower to buy equipment in Japan and Europe. The dollars would eventually come back to pay for Japanese and European purchases in the United States.

Raw Materials Needs

The dynamic nature of the American economy gives the United States a strong interest in the expansion of the world output of raw materials. This interest becomes vital when we add to it the need for building up the defensive strength of the non-Communist world to forestall aggression. Most of the best sources of additional raw materials are in underdeveloped countries, but it is unlikely that we can count on a large and steady flow from these sources unless general, rounded economic development to meet the needs and aspirations of these countries proceeds along with raw materials development.[18] Hence the United States has another major motive for concerning itself with economic development of underdeveloped areas.

The United States is now a large net importer of raw materials. According to the President's Materials Policy Commission (Paley Commission) our materials deficit in 1950—the amount by which the value of production of raw materials fell short of consumption—was 9 percent. In the important field of metals the deficit was much greater. By 1975, the Commission believes, we may need to import about 20 percent of a total materials consumption, which, if past growth rates are maintained, will be 50 or 60 percent greater than in 1950. When we consider the needs of the rest of the non-Communist world, the problem becomes still larger. Western Europe's demand is expected to increase by somewhat less than half by 1975, that of Canada, Australia, New Zealand, and Japan, rather more than half. Percentagewise, the demands of the underdeveloped countries will probably increase most of all, but the volume they will require will still be small compared to the totals used by the more industrialized coun-

[18] See on this point Chapter 15.

tries. For the free world as a whole, the Commission estimates that the total volume of materials required may be two-thirds to three-quarters greater than the volume used in 1950.[19]

The following "impressive facts" as to the dependence of the American economy upon underdeveloped areas for industrial raw materials were stressed by the International Development Advisory Board (Nelson Rockefeller, Chairman) in its report to the President in 1951: The United States, with only 6 percent of the world's population and 7 percent of its area, accounts for roughly half of the whole world's industrial output. But it produces only about a third of the world's annual output of the fifteen basic minerals. ". . . virtually all of our natural rubber, manganese (upon which the manufacture of steel depends), chromium, and tin, as well as a quarter of our zinc and copper and a third or more of our lead and aluminum, come from abroad, mostly from the underdeveloped areas. This is also true of the largest part of our uranium ore." "How long," the report asks, "could the United States maintain its place as a producer of more than half of the world's industrial output if forced to depend on its own material supplies?" [20]

Where can the United States, the other industrial countries, and the many countries that want to become industrialized find the added raw materials (especially minerals) that will be essential to their dynamic growth? Those who have given expert study to these problems say that the sources best suited for expansion are in the Near East, South and Southeast Asia, Africa, and Latin America—that is, the underdeveloped countries. The known and inferred reserves of important minerals in these parts of the world are large enough and of sufficiently high grade to meet free world requirements for at least the next twenty-five years with little or no increase in real costs. But this will be possible only if these areas remain accessible and if local conditions are not too unfavorable to attract the large amounts of capital and

[19] President's Materials Policy Commission, *Resources for Freedom*, A Report to the President (Washington: U. S. Government Printing Office, 1952), Vol. I, pp. 2, 11-12, 59.

[20] International Development Advisory Board, *Partners in Progress* (Washington: 1951), pp. 4-5, 51.

the technical skills and equipment which, for at least the next few decades, would have to come largely from the industrially advanced countries.

The industrially advanced countries, says the President's Materials Policy Commission, are looking increasingly to the less developed countries to help meet their expanding needs for materials. On the other hand, the less developed countries want diversified development which will advance their economies and improve the conditions of life for their people. "This set of circumstances could, if approached with statesmanship, lead to great benefits to the underdeveloped countries and to the entire free world." Specifically, "The more advanced nations could export the tools of growth to the less developed areas. The less developed nations could expand their exports of materials as a rich source of foreign exchange, and by attracting capital and management skills, could accelerate their economic growth and improve their living standards." [21]

The United States can look to other potential sources of expansion in raw materials supply besides the underdeveloped countries. The most important is new technological development, such as oil from shale, new methods of handling low-grade ores, substitution of plastics for metals, materials-savings engineering, harnessing of solar energy, and so on. If the needed increases in raw materials supplies cannot be had from the underdeveloped areas or, because of conditions in those areas, can be had only at excessive cost, the search for alternatives will proceed with the aid of an extremely inventive and resourceful modern technology. Sometimes the substitutes worked out under the stimulus of necessity are actually better and less costly than the traditional materials. Generally, however, the scarcity and high price of a preferred material will lead to a somewhat more costly and less satisfactory substitution. The cumulative effect of many instances of rising raw materials costs would certainly act as a drag on the further development of productivity and living levels in the United States and other industrial areas. For this reason we have a great economic interest in working cooperatively with

[21] President's Materials Policy Commission, cited, pp. 59, 12.

the underdeveloped countries to meet both their needs for general development and our needs for materials.

Strategy of Raw Materials

When we turn to the economics of defense, the American national interest in a friendly arrangement with underdeveloped countries so as to mobilize their materials resources for the strengthening of the free world may fairly be called a "vital" interest—one on which our very survival as a free people may depend. Mobilization for defense requires an especially rapid build-up of industrial power. Delay may spell defeat. Hence, as compared with the more leisurely conditions of peaceful economy, there is less time for working out of raw materials bottlenecks by substitution and by the invention of new techniques.

Three-quarters of the imported "critical materials" which are considered of sufficient military importance to be included in the United States stockpile program come from the underdeveloped areas. "The loss of any of these materials, through aggression, subversion, or economic or social collapse, would be the equivalent of a grave military set-back." [22]

The Soviet Union has a generally strong position in reserves of militarily important materials, but it also has significant deficiencies. One of them is oil. In 1951 when the dispute over Iranian nationalization of oil operations led to the shutting down of the largest refinery in the world at Abadan, the loss of oil to the Western world was considerable. But it was made up by an increased flow from other sources in a surprisingly short time. A Soviet political or military success in Iran which would make Iranian oil available after a few years to the Soviet military machine would have a much more serious effect. Some estimates are that Iranian oil would strengthen the Soviet situation in this vital military material by 60 or 70 percent. The free world cannot afford to lose the crucial materials of the underdeveloped countries, and even less can it afford to have them come under the sway of the Soviet Union.

[22] International Development Advisory Board, *Partners in Progress*, cited, p. 46.

HUMANITARIAN INTERESTS

The jump from raw materials and military strategy to humanitarianism may seem abrupt. If so, it merely points up the true diversity of motives and interests back of American attitudes on development.

"Only by helping the least fortunate of its members to help themselves can the human family achieve the decent, satisfying life that is the right of all people." Thus President Truman in his original Point Four address appealed to feelings of human brotherhood as one of many arguments for the "bold new program." The same note has been struck repeatedly, by the former administration ("The only war we seek is the good old fight against man's ancient enemies—poverty, disease, hunger, and illiteracy") and by the new administration ("We are ready, in short, to dedicate our strength to serving the needs, rather than the fears, of the world"). There is abundant evidence that this appeal to basic human kindness evokes a strongly favorable response from American public opinion and that it is a genuine and powerful factor in the American policy toward underdeveloped areas.

Among opinion-forming groups in the American democracy, the churches have rallied with enthusiasm to the Point Four program. They stress, as might be expected, the humanitarian motive:

As Christians in a Christian nation, we submit we have a duty to our fellow human beings of whatever color or creed—a duty that makes the well-being of other people a matter of deepest concern to us. We dislike knowing that more than half the people of the world go to sleep each night hungry and rise each morning with no ray of hope for better days to cheer their drab existence. We dislike the envy with which other people view our plenty. We are uncomfortable with the knowledge that we could help them and we have not. We know, furthermore, that, when we help other areas, we invariably increase our own security and opportunity.[23]

[23] Statement of Delbert E. Replogle, American Friends Service Committee. U. S. Congress (81st), *Act for International Development, Hearings* on H. R. 5615, 6026, 6834, 6835, 7346, House Committee on Foreign Affairs (Washington, 1950), p. 401.

But church groups are not the only ones that show a humanitarian concern. The CIO, for example, has issued literature for its members on Point Four which appeals in popular style to practically all the motivations discussed in this chapter, and the appeal to human sympathy is by no means least.[24] Farm organizations and farm publications have shown a lively interest in Point Four, especially in connection with agricultural improvement. American farm people seem to respond readily with a fellow feeling for farmers in underdeveloped areas. When they hear that families are struggling to make a living from the soil without steel plows or improved seeds or modern insecticides, their reaction is, "By all means, let's help them to get these things." It is not uncommon for American 4-H Clubs of farm boys and girls to carry on private, voluntary projects for aiding farmers in some underdeveloped area.

Organized humanitarianism has long figured in the international contacts of the American people. Examples are: mission hospitals and schools around the world, voluntary popular subscriptions for disaster relief after a flood on the Yangtze River or an earthquake in Japan, the notable achievements in international health and education over many years by American private foundations, and ready support from the public for emergency relief, both private and governmental, after World Wars I and II.

Two new elements have conspired to channel humanitarian impulses into economic development. One is the vast improvement in travel and communication. This has made Americans much more aware than ever before of the lives and problems of people in underdeveloped areas. The other is the extraordinary technological progress of the twentieth century. "For the first time in history, humanity possesses the knowledge and the skill to relieve the suffering of these people," as President Truman said in his Point Four address.

Alleged humanitarian motives are, of course, sometimes a cover for other less avowed motives. But in this instance, so far as opinion-forming groups in America are concerned, it

[24] Congress of Industrial Organizations, Department of Education and Research, *Point 4: Helping People to Help Themselves*, Pamphlet No. 199, reprinted from *Economic Outlook*, November, 1951.

would be my judgment (and there is no way of proving or disproving this) that the reverse is probably more true. That is, a considerable amount of genuine humanitarian sentiment is dressed up in "hard-headed" arguments because, in some circles at least, people are fearful of seeming to do good for its own sake. At the same time, the humanitarian interest is only one element in a composite. American farmers, for example, not only have a fellow feeling for farmers elsewhere, but they also believe that sending better seeds is one way to combat Communism. It is the *combination* of motivating forces, including humanitarianism and many other types of national interest, which explains current American concern for the development of underdeveloped countries and which suggests that this concern is likely to be more than temporary.

Chapter 3

THE VIEWPOINT OF THE WORLD
COMMUNITY

Until modern times, few men identified themselves with
the interests of a nation. They could think in terms of a tribe
or a city-state or a principality, but the idea of a "national interest" would have seemed remote and unrealistic. With the
improvement of communications and the rise of nation-
states, national armies, and national economic policies, the
"national interest" became a paramount reality.

Now we are well along into a still later epoch of human
affairs, one of unavoidable world interdependence on a world
basis, though not always of friendly cooperation. Thanks to
modern communication and transport, no part of the world
is now very far from any other by radio, airliner, or bomber.
The whole trend of science and technology is such as to make
it practically certain (barring catastrophe which would wreck
civilization as we know it) that each succeeding decade will
see peoples brought closer together, whether for friendly exchange of ideas and goods and joint collaboration or for hostile interchange of deadly explosives.

In these circumstances the idea of a common interest of
human beings which transcends local and national interests
has been gaining ground. Many men in underdeveloped
countries and advanced countries alike have begun to think
of themselves as citizens not only of their own countries but
also of the world. The growth of international organization,
especially the development of the United Nations and its
specialized agencies, has begun to provide centers for the
crystallization of this wider common interest and to give it
instrumentalities for practical action.

We must take into account, therefore, not only the motivating factors which impel the separate countries of the underdeveloped group and of the industrially advanced group to discover a national interest in carrying on or assisting economic development, but also the motivating factors which produce a world community interest in economic development.

The common interests which men have as members of a world community are not likely to be adequately evaluated by adding up the interests they perceive when they think as members of separate nations. As a practical matter, even the true interest of each nation can be found only by supplementing national thinking with a broader approach. A major part of the national interest of the American people in economic development is to shape "the kind of world we want to live in." That kind of world can become reality only as we and other peoples think of the common interests of the world community as part of our own interests.

Commitments of the United Nations

The United Nations Charter pledges members to take joint and separate action: "With a view to the creation of conditions of stability and well-being which are necessary for peaceful and friendly relations among nations . . ." In this connection "the United Nations shall promote: . . . higher standards of living, full employment, and conditions of economic and social progress and development . . ." [1] The charters of the specialized agencies and numerous resolutions of United Nations organs amplify and reinforce this formal statement of the common interests of the peoples of the world in economic development.

Between 1946 and 1948 the Secretary-General of the United Nations, following the directives in the Charter, initiated a small but significant program of technical assistance. For the first time a concerted effort was made by a world body to pool human knowledge and experience and make it available to all governments upon request for the advancement of

[1] Article 55.

their countries' economies.[2] A great stimulus was given to this international movement by President Truman's enunciation of the Point Four doctrine in 1949. The United States wisely decided to channel part of the "bold new program" through United Nations agencies, and United Nations development work entered a period of rapid expansion. The "Expanded Program of Technical Assistance" was set up with a specially contributed fund of approximately twenty million dollars, of which the United States pledged twelve million (sixty percent) on the understanding that other countries would contribute the rest. This fund was used to operate the newly organized Technical Assistance Administration of the United Nations and to support technical assistance projects of the specialized agencies, such as the Food and Agriculture Organization of the United Nations, the World Health Organization, the International Labor Organization, and the United Nations Educational, Scientific and Cultural Organization.

No phase of the activities of the United Nations has met with more general approval by governments and peoples than this. The view has often been expressed that in promoting economic and social development the United Nations is able to make a positive approach, one which stimulates the constructive imaginations of men, and that this is not only good in itself but necessary to the attainment of all its other goals.

Common Values of Mankind

The broad, common interest of the world community on which the United Nations program is founded might be put this way: to create opportunities for as many as possible of the world's people to live a good life. Notions of what constitutes a good life vary. Are there any wants or "goal-values" common to all mankind?

One surely is improved material livelihood. Some people have made a virtue of necessity, but experience shows that very few anywhere in the world deliberately prefer poverty.

[2] See H. L. Keenleyside, "Administrative Problems of the Technical Assistance Administration," *Canadian Journal of Economics and Political Science,* August, 1952, pp. 347 ff.

A second is freedom for the human spirit. Perhaps the universality of this want may be doubted, in view of the past and present willingness of many men to subordinate their wills to authoritarian governments and religions or to rigid customs. On the other hand, many have risked torture and death for freedom. Is it not in rejection of slavery and in the quest for a free society where men can work together voluntarily on a basis of mutual respect that we see the most characteristically human traits, or at any rate the best hope for progress in civilization? If abject poverty can be conquered and life be made less insecure for the majority of people in the world, it is reasonable to suppose that more and more of them will want the benefits and responsibilities of freedom.

A third is security and peace. Whatever be the views of dictators who would not shrink from aggressive force to spread their doctrines and power, no one can doubt that the overwhelming mass of mankind would like to be rid of war and to live out their lives in peace.

For each of these objectives economic development of the underdeveloped areas is an essential condition. It is not, however, a sufficient condition for any of them, since economic advancement does not of itself guarantee the kind of society and government which will bring a wide distribution of economic goods, or freedom, or security and peace.

Material Livelihood

An elementary common purpose, and therefore a basic interest of the world community, is to promote those material and social conditions of production which can make it possible for all peoples to have the means for a decent human existence. People who live in squalor, undernourishment, disease, and ignorance are not able to develop to the full their creative human capacities. They are handicapped in attaining the full dignity of man.

From the world community viewpoint, poverty, disease, and ignorance have to be regarded as contagious. No part of the community will be safe from their effects so long as they exist on a large scale anywhere. Economic well-being, health, and enlightenment are also contagious. The world community interest, of course, is to spread these good sorts of contagion.

A world environment of economic growth would make most of the particular economic maladjustments that plague the world easier to solve. In general, expansion in one area helps to induce expansion in others. Old debts and old disputes weigh less heavily in a growing economy. Economic progress brings some upsets, some displacements from jobs and loss of former markets, but when the trend is upward there are new opportunities opening, and growing wealth makes possible community action to facilitate adjustment and to relieve temporary distress.

"Enlightened self-interest on the part of the great industrial and commercial powers," says Hugh L. Keenleyside, Director-General of the United Nations Technical Assistance Administration, "is obviously the most potent factor in the initiation and support" of international programs designed to raise levels of livelihood. "Progress in the underdeveloped world can yield colossal dividends to those in a position to take advantage of its expanding markets. . . . But it is also true that the most active, convinced, and persistent support for the international programme of mutual aid comes from men and women in all countries who are activated by motives of good will and by instincts of humanity; from individuals who are unwilling to see their fellow human beings live one day longer than is necessary in conditions of ignorance, hunger, disease, and injustice; from those who realize that as long as anyone, anywhere, unnecessarily suffers, no one can be truly free." [3]

Wasted Human Talent

A factor that is not often noted could be extremely significant in the long run in reinforcing the "contagion" of better living levels and better cultural opportunities as underdeveloped areas advance. The unprecedented growth of productivity in the West in modern times has been immensely aided by discoveries in science and their application in constantly improving technology. The progress of science and technology depends in part on the number of trained scientists,

[3] Same, pp. 356-357.

the number of laboratories and institutes and experiment stations, and the interchange of ideas and information. At present, two-thirds of the people in the world live under conditions in which they not only make little use of modern science and technology but are practically excluded from making any contribution to it. An illiterate peasant may have been born with a remarkable brain, but he will never contribute to the further working out of Einstein's equations, or to the discovery of a better germicide.

There is every reason to assume that the quality of the human talent which is latent in the 1,600,000,000 people of underdeveloped areas is no less, on the average, than that of their fellow members of the species *homo sapiens* in the modernized countries. Yet only the latter have lately been contributing to scientific discovery and technological invention. As the economic level rises in the underdeveloped countries, as health improves, as elementary education spreads, as the means expand for supporting universities and research institutes and industrial laboratories, and as exceptionally gifted individuals discovered in the lower schools get opportunities to go on for higher education, we can expect scientific, technical, and other contributions to culture to come in larger volume from today's underdeveloped areas.

Modern science owes much to mathematical inventions which came from India and the Near East (Arabic numbers, algebra). China produced printing and gunpowder before these ideas appeared in the West. Perhaps even more important, many of the contributions which the world acknowledges as greatest in human relations and religion have come from leaders like Hammurabi, Confucius, Plato, Buddha, and Jesus of Nazareth. They appeared among peoples whose descendants today are prevented by economic and educational handicaps from making a full contribution to current cultural developments. The *human talent* that is going to waste in the underdeveloped countries is the greatest untapped resource in the world.

Freedom for the Human Spirit

Abject poverty, disease, and ignorance retard the full development of the human spirit just as they often cripple the body. It may be taken as a fundamental interest of the world community to free the spirit of man, so far as possible, from all such handicaps. This obviously requires economic development. But the human spirit can also be bound and broken by various kinds of social traditions and by despotic government. Through millennia man has managed to climb slowly away from the brutish. An important aspect of that climb has been the achievement here and there, always imperfectly, of free, voluntary cooperation among self-respecting and respected individuals. This is our ideal of democratic society and democratic government. The enduring aspirations of the human spirit validate this ideal and make its fuller achievement one of the major interests of the world community.

There is a direct connection between progress toward such ideals and economic development. Surveying the experience of mankind with democratic government, the historian Carl Becker concluded that democracy is in a certain sense a social luxury. At best it is a delicate and precarious adventure which depends for its success not only on the validity of certain assumptions about the capacities and virtues of men, but also on the presence of "certain material and intellectual conditions favorable to the exercise of these capacities and virtues." Among the material conditions he listed ease of communication, a certain measure of economic security, and a high enough level of subsistence so that people generally can have access to education. In modern times, says Becker, democratic institutions have been most successful in new countries such as the United States, Canada, and Australia where the conditions of life have been easy for the people, and in European countries more or less in proportion to their prosperity. Indeed, there has been a close correlation between the development of modern industry and the emergence of democratic institutions. When prosperity disappears, democracy works less well, and "Democracy does not flourish in communities on the verge of destitution." [4]

After a period in the nineteenth and early twentieth centuries, when it appeared that the ideals of free society and democratic government were making steady progress in the

[4] Carl L. Becker, *Modern Democracy* (New Haven: Yale University Press, 1941), p. 12.

world, militant movements of relapse toward tyranny appeared—Fascism, Nazism, and Communism. At present it is Communism that offers the most immediate threat to the world community's interest in freedom. It is backed by formidable armed might. It has introduced a new form of imperialism, just when the older forms were retreating. It has proved itself particularly adept at foisting itself upon underdeveloped countries, exploiting all discontents in the effort to seize power. It has shown itself still more adept at the throttling of the free human spirit, once it has seized power, by highly developed techniques of mass propaganda, by preventing access to truth, and by the terror of the police state.

This immediate menace to freedom concerns the whole world community. The defense against it has to be a combination of armed strength, to forestall military aggression, and economic and social improvement, to show that better conditions can be brought about by free cooperation than by giving totalitarians the uncontrolled power which they demand. This argues strongly, because of political, economic, and strategic factors that have already been examined, for giving high priority to economic development of underdeveloped areas as an essential part of the world's quest for freedom of the human spirit.

Security and Peace

The United Nations has gone further along the road of world-wide collective security against aggression than has ever been possible before. But there is still a great gap between the present attainment and what has to be achieved before the world community can feel secure. Economic development of underdeveloped areas has an important relation to this problem. A Chilean statesman, Hernán Santa Cruz, put the matter clearly during the 1951 session of the United Nations General Assembly:

The United Nations had taken up arms, he said, to repel aggression and to vindicate collective security. The main burden was being carried by Western countries whose spiritual concepts and material interests were those most seriously threatened. The Western countries needed the material and moral support of all peace-loving nations. For if they did not receive raw materials from the other countries they could not physically resist, and without moral support the collective struggle against aggression in the name of principle would degenerate into a mere fight in defense of political and economic interests.

In view of these facts, he continued, it was important to recognize that millions of human beings, ninety percent of the Asian, African, and Latin American peoples, were indifferent to that struggle. The fact that some of their leaders had supported the United Nations cause was of secondary importance. It was indispensable to gain the support of the masses, without which the cooperation of governments would prove illusory. And the common man in the underdeveloped areas would only support the United Nations and its great work of collective security if he were convinced that its action was part of a universal undertaking, the object of which was to secure peace, individual freedom, and the self-determination of peoples, and also to provide him with a decent standard of living and material and social progress. Until it was understood by leaders of great nations that the true battle must be fought in the mind of each of those millions in the backward countries, the cause of the United Nations would continue to be in peril and its final triumph would be uncertain.[5]

A hundred years ago Friedrich List argued that a universal union of nations and freedom of trade would be possible only when all had reached an advanced stage of industrial development.[6] Looking ahead today, the prospects for attaining a really durable world peace, essential for the preservation of civilization itself in this era of increasingly effective

[5] Paraphrase from United Nations, General Assembly, Second Committee, *Official Records*, Sixth Session, 147th Meeting, November 20, 1951, p. 11.

[6] "A universal republic (in the sense of Henry IV. and of the Abbé St. Pierre), i.e. a union of the nations of the earth whereby they recognise the same conditions of right among themselves and renounce self-redress, can only be realised if a large number of nationalities attain to as nearly the same degree as possible of industry and civilisation, political cultivation, and power. Only with the gradual formation of this union can free trade be developed, only as a result of this union can it confer on all nations the same great advantages which are now experienced by those provinces and states which are politically united."
Friedrich List, *The National System of Political Economy*, translated by Sampson S. Lloyd (London: Longmans, 1904), p. 103.

science, are ultimately dependent on the chances of establishing some form of world government and having it function effectively. Yet the outlook for world government on a basis compatible with our democratic ideals is definitely clouded, in addition to all other obstacles, by the problem of the underdeveloped areas. The fact that half the people of the world even today cannot read or write is itself an obstacle of no mean proportions. So long as today's great disparity in productive capacity and wealth persists in the world, the more prosperous countries would undoubtedly fear the use of genuine legislative powers in a world government on behalf of "share the wealth" movements, and troublesome questions like freedom of migration would be insoluble.

Americans are familiar with the doctrine enunciated by President Lincoln that a nation cannot exist half slave and half free. In a world as closely linked as modern technology has made the world of the twentieth century, such a contrast of living standards as is manifested in the comparative luxury of a few countries and the grinding poverty of many others is a constant source of disunity and instability. Our world cannot remain permanently half wealthy and half miserable.

Unless there is an urgent and well-supported effort to accelerate the economic development of the less advanced areas, the discontents caused by the gap between rich areas and poor areas will increase. The gap itself has been growing wider. Former Secretary-General Trygve Lie, alluding to this fact when opening one of the sessions of the United Nations Economic and Social Council, called it "a very serious, a very dangerous trend." Bold measures are needed, he said, to lessen the disparity of living standards by raising those of the peoples who live in poverty. Asking whether this can be done in the face of current armaments programs, he answered, "it can be done if there is sufficient understanding of the essential place of such an expanded program in the effort to win security from world-wide war and chaos, and . . . it must be done if the world is to avoid disaster." [7]

[7] Opening meeting of the 12th Session of the Economic and Social Council, Santiago, Chile, February 20, 1951.

Chapter 4

A GLANCE AT HISTORY

In current discussions of economic development the easy assumption is too often made that, if only the production of underdeveloped countries can be increased, not only will the people be materially better off but democracy, peace, and other good things will follow almost automatically. One of the tasks of this book is to challenge such assumptions.

Economic development does not always bring wholly desirable results, especially in the political sphere. There is no simple uniformity in past cases, certainly no one-to-one relation, between economic growth and either a democratic internal development or a peaceful disposition toward the world. This will become apparent in the present chapter.

The purpose in developing this thesis is to lay the basis for a more sophisticated view of the political implications and problems of development. It is no part of our purpose to suggest that because there is danger as well as promise connected with the processes of economic development we should go slow on development or oppose it. Rather, the argument is that the very uncertainty about the political outcome of economic development which a realistic view of history gives us should inspire a healthy respect for the obstacles and pitfalls and a more intelligent effort to avoid them.

An analogy will make the position clear. A century ago parties of pioneers were crossing the Sierra Nevadas in their wagon trains to get to California. Some were caught in the mountains by the early onset of winter snows. There was peril ahead, but greater peril in turning back, and the greatest peril of all in staying where they were. In such a situation the fact that a scouting party reports not merely the smiling plains which can be seen in the distance but also the intervening precipices and ravines does not counsel inaction but, rather, more intense action combined with careful planning and alertness.

It is not a paradox to maintain that the only hope for democratic progress and durable peace in the modern world is by way of raising the economic level of underdeveloped countries, and at the same time to recognize that this necessary process is not an easy one, that its outcome is uncertain, and that economic development will create many political and social disturbances, the consequences of which we cannot confidently predict.

POLITICAL CONCOMITANTS OF ECONOMIC DEVELOPMENT

Thirteen countries have raised their economies to the "highly developed" level as judged by income per person and the other criteria used in preparing the table on pages 16-17. Nine of these are in Europe: Belgium, Denmark, France, Germany, the Netherlands, Norway, Sweden, Switzerland, and the United Kingdom. Four are areas of European settlement overseas: Canada, the United States, Australia, and New Zealand.

In addition, special interest attaches to two countries on the "intermediate" list: Japan and the U.S.S.R. Though their income levels per person are not high enough to put them in the "highly developed" group, both have had spectacular industrial growth, and both have attained great political power.

Let us glance at the history of these fifteen countries, noting in each case the *political concomitants of economic development*. Along with economic growth, was there progress in democratic society and government and in individual freedoms? Internationally, did these countries become more peaceful and easier to live with, or more aggressive and expansive? Note that we are talking of *concomitants* of economic development, political changes that took place at the same time or shortly before or after the economic changes. Without further analysis we cannot affirm that these are either consequences or causes of economic development.

Great Britain

In Britain, which pioneered the modern industrial economy, economic development was a long, gradual process extending over centuries. The enclosure movement was continuous from at least the thirteenth century and reached its
climax in the eighteenth century. This movement transformed the medieval village, with its commons, its arable
land cut into strips, its predominantly subsistence farming,
and its rule of custom into a modern, capitalistic, rural organization with compact farms and technically improved commercial agriculture. Innovations in commerce and mechanical inventions in industry for the most part came gradually,
though toward the end of the eighteenth century the steam
engine and its application in power-driven machinery for factories introduced an era of spectacular change known as "the
industrial revolution." Industrial growth and urbanization
were rapid during the nineteenth century, and there appears
to have been a special spurt in the decades immediately following 1850. Not long after the middle of the century the
United Kingdom had reached a stage of development which,
as measured by such indicators as occupational distribution
and urbanism, would put it in our category of "highly developed" economies.

On the political side, there was a correspondingly gradual
development, also over centuries. In general, the trend was
toward broader diffusion of political power, greater participation by more people in the processes of government, greater
freedom for the individual, the wearing away of old class distinctions, and a more democratic equality of opportunity,
wealth, and respect. Well into the nineteenth century England continued to be governed by an aristocratic rural class,
but with increasing pressure from new commercial and industrial groups. The franchise was extended in 1832 to town
property-holders, but not to the majority of workers in industry and agriculture until 1867 and 1884. Also late in the
nineteenth century or early in the twentieth came universal,
free, public education, the rising power of trade unions, continued decline in the power of the House of Lords, and systems of income and inheritance taxation and of public wel-

fare and social security which broadened the distribution of income.

Internationally, Britain's economic advance gradually put it in the forefront of military and political affairs. As the world's most thoroughly industrialized country it was the world's greatest power during much of the nineteenth century. Territorial expansion, culminating in the greatest empire the world has ever seen, accompanied rising power. But Britain's use of great international power was tempered by liberalism and humanitarianism. It did not turn militaristic or idolize power. The chapter it wrote in the long history of empire is, comparatively speaking, a creditable one, especially as the chapter is ending with a policy of preparing colonies for self-government.

The United States and British Commonwealth Countries

The four non-European countries on our "highly developed" list are Canada, the United States, Australia, and New Zealand. All are heritors of Britain's political pioneering in representative government, the common law, individual liberty, and related ideas. Their economic growth has been accompanied by growth in democracy. The influence of "the frontier," which in these countries meant not the boundary of a hostile nation but the challenge and opportunity of great expanses of new land open for settlement, helped to produce an even stronger growth of individual initiative and more leveling of class distinctions than in the Old World. It should be noted, however, that this democratic social effect depended not merely on resources and the availability of land, but also on traditions and policies, manifested in such measures as the Homestead Act (1862) in the United States, which encouraged individual family-sized farms. In Latin America there was also plenty of land, but the laws and customs converted much of the available land into great estates. Russia, also, has had plenty of land without advancing in democracy.

In their external relations, Canada, Australia, and New Zealand have been too small to be much tempted toward aggressive expansionism. They have not been militaristic. Neither has the United States. The United States, in the course of economic development, and expansion over a thinly-held continent, was not always considerate of its neighbors. Around the turn of the century it showed symptoms of extending its "manifest destiny" further and acquired some territory overseas, later to release it voluntarily. Preoccupied until recently with internal development, the United States now finds itself, somewhat unwillingly, thrust into a position of leadership in world affairs, in large part because internal development has given it enormous economic and political power. The use of American power has not been to subjugate other peoples; on the whole, both our government and our private economic interests have taken the course of cooperating freely with other free nations. The propaganda about "American imperialism" has a hollow ring to those who can look at facts fairmindedly.

The Low Countries

Like Britain, the Netherlands and Belgium have a history of a gradually growing and changing agriculture, commerce, and industry from the time of the Middle Ages. In the nineteenth century they followed Britain's lead into the modern phase of machine industry. Again like Britain, their internal political institutions have evolved in the direction of freedom and democracy, and in the period when the West had a vast superiority in power each acquired an overseas empire, one mainly in the East Indies, the other in Central Africa.

Switzerland and Scandinavia

Switzerland, Denmark, Norway, and Sweden are all small countries whose modern economic development has been characterized by a broad distribution of wealth and power, well-functioning democratic government, and a citizenship that is virile and self-reliant but at the same time able to cooperate for common ends. None of these countries in recent times has been aggressive toward its neighbors or has cultivated a swashbuckling, militaristic spirit. True, they are small countries and therefore relatively weak; but not all small countries have been peacefully inclined—in the Balkans, for example.

France

In the 1780's France was nearly 85 percent peasant. It was far behind Britain in economic progress and was ruled by a decadent aristocracy of nobles and clergy. The convulsion of the French revolution and its Napoleonic aftermath was necessary to break the hold of medieval survivals and, by reforms in land tenure, government, and social outlook, to release energies for development. Even so, a modern industrial economy was slow in evolving. "The transformation accomplished in a century was in many ways less complete than that which Germany experienced in the forty years after 1871." [1] Politically there were ups and downs, but the ideals of "liberty, equality, fraternity" on the whole guided France's political evolution.

An external political result of the explosive turn away from the old regime was the trouble which the wars and conquests of France's postrevolutionary dictator, Napoleon I, made for Europe. France had lost in war to Britain, or sold to the United States, its eighteenth-century claims in North America, but with the general expansion of Western colonialism in the late nineteenth century it acquired a considerable empire in Asia and Africa.

Germany

Germany is one of the most interesting cases. "All the forces tending towards industrialism and urbanisation had struck Germany at once," says Clapham. "She began the century with no highly developed urban life. . . . Down to the forties she went through no industrial revolution. . . . Then, crowding fast on one another in two generations, came the railways; the abolition of the last remains of medieval economic restriction after 1848; the expansion of the Zollverein . . . ; the creation of a modern financial and banking system . . . ; the great steel inventions; the swift, cheap, glorious and exhilarating achievement of national union; and the period of electricity, overseas expansion and world policy." [2]

[1] J. H. Clapham, *The Economic Development of France and Germany, 1815–1914* (Cambridge: Cambridge University Press, 4th ed., 1936), p. 53.
[2] Same, pp. 279-280.

Here is the rapid catching-up of an important "under-developed" area. For Germany was underdeveloped by comparison with Britain and some other Western European countries that were leaders in the industrial revolution. By economic tests Germany's development in the nineteenth and early twentieth centuries was surely a successful one, and in some other ways too. Great contributions to science and technology came out of Germany. But if one applies political tests of success the outcome can hardly be called good.

While Germany was catching up and even forging ahead in industry, science, and technology, it also made considerable changes in its political institutions and social attitudes. Some were in the direction of a more liberal, democratic society. But there remained in Germany, more strongly than in other countries of northwestern Europe, vestiges of the old feudal institutions, notably the great estates of the *Junkers* in East Prussia and the authoritarian, hierarchical, militaristic outlook which this group personified. Internally, these traits continued to be reflected in Germany's social institutions as well as in the government itself. Externally they contributed in some measure, through the expansionism of Kaiser Wilhelm II and of Hitler, to the tragedy of two world wars. But there is room for unlimited debate on how much blame to apportion to Germany's aggressiveness and how much to other factors in the world situation.

Japan

Even more instructive is the case of Japan. That country had already gone through the preliminary stage of transition from an agrarian to a mercantile economy before Commodore Perry's arrival in 1853. Even certain lines of manufacturing industry, though without power-driven machinery, were fairly well developed.[3] In 1868 came the restoration of the Emperor. Then followed unification of the nation, with the abolition of feudalism and the pensioning of the professional warrior class, the Samurai. The old policy of deliberate isolation was reversed, and missions were sent abroad to col-

[3] G. B. Sansom, *The Western World and Japan* (New York: Knopf, 1950), p. 498.

lect Western ideas. Modernization was viewed by those in authority as the only way to make Japan strong enough to stand up against the encroachments of nations whose technological lead gave them vastly superior military power.

There followed the most rapid transformation and growth of a "backward" economy which the world had seen up to that time. In the narrow sense of more production, swift rise of industry and trade, and creation of an industrialized base for national power, Japan's economic development was highly successful. Even by the test of average living levels it was moderately successful, though the burst of population growth which accompanied modernization was a serious handicap in this respect and remains a grave problem for present-day Japan.

The political concomitants of this development have not been happy for the Japanese people or for the world. Many Western political forms were adopted, education was fostered, and illiteracy fell to a low level. Also, many Japanese learned to understand and appreciate the liberal political and social institutions that had developed in the West. Yet the Japanese state on the whole produced loyal subjects rather than free citizens; the old tradition of the warrior caste carried over into the extraordinary influence of the military in modern Japan; the peasants made relatively little progress; and while a very active and energetic modern business class developed, old cultural traditions showed their influence in this field, too, in the dominance of great family combinations, the *Zaibatsu*.

When economic development gave it power, Japan embarked on ambitious plans of expansion, built a colonial empire in Korea, Formosa, and Manchuria, overran a large part of eastern Asia, attacked the United States at Pearl Harbor, and came to disastrous defeat in World War II.

Veblen on Germany and Japan

Thorstein Veblen in *Imperial Germany and the Industrial Revolution* [4] explained Germany's political behavior on the ground that, unlike Britain, Germany had suddenly taken over modern industrial technology without having gone

[4] New York: Viking, 1939. Originally published 1915.

through a long period of evolving popular political and social institutions. Thus it combined in a politically dangerous mixture the old feudal ideas of hierarchic authority, fealty, and war-mindedness and a modern industrialized basis for power.

Japan is a more extreme case of the same sort. Veblen also wrote an essay on Japan in 1915, which in some respects reads like a prophecy of the country's later actions.[5] Japan, he said, has acquired the modern industrial arts without as yet having had time to experience the disintegration of the feudal "Spirit of Old Japan" which is the chief asset of the state as a warlike power. "It is, hitherto, only in respect of its material ways and means, its technological equipment and information, that the 'New Japan' differs from the old." This anachronistic combination of modern, technical means with the medieval spirit of servile solidarity, Veblen continued, gives Japan a great opportunity for imperial aggrandizement. "It is the present high efficiency of the Japanese, an efficiency which may be formulated as an exceptionally wide margin between cost of production and output of military force—it is this that makes Japan formidable in the eyes of her western competitors for imperial honors, and in substance it is this on which the Japanese masters of political intrigue rest their sanguine hopes of empire."

But, Veblen held, the modern industrial arts in time would change the spirit of Japan. Commercialism, pecuniary standards of value, and demands for better living standards, all of which have appeared with modern industry in the West, would also result from industrialization in Japan. If Japan's new-found efficiency is to serve the purposes of imperial aggrandizement it must be turned to account before industrialization has too far corrupted the old spirit, "which should, humanly speaking, mean that Japan must strike, if at all, within the effective lifetime of the generation that is now coming to maturity."

Veblen's analysis of the political implications of installing modern production methods while social and political ideals

---

[5] Thorstein Veblen, "The Opportunity of Japan," in *Essays in Our Changing Order* (New York: Viking, 1934), pp. 251, 265. Article reprinted from *The Journal of Race Development*, Vol. VI, July, 1915.

remain dominated by earlier culture-patterns is most suggestive. His notion, however, that life under conditions imposed by the modern industrial arts (necessitating internal and external communication, popular education, and intelligence) will inevitably produce the mental outlook and the principles of conduct and ethical values which have grown up in the modern West, must be viewed more skeptically today than when he wrote. We have seen the rise of modern totalitarian states which have managed to combine industrialism with a political system where government is still "an autonomous co-optative bureaucracy" as Veblen said of Japan, and where the people are still "the government's chattels, to be bred, fed, trained, and consumed as the shrewd economy of dynastic politics may best require."

We must be wary of an exaggerated or one-way concept of the influence of material conditions of life on ideals, ethical values, habits of thought, and social and political institutions. Contrary to the dogmas of economic determinists, values, habits, and institutions shape the material ways and conditions of life as much as they are shaped by them. Also, we cannot afford to ignore the demonstrated capacity of new totalitarian techniques to make industrial production compatible with servitude, and even to use "liberal" institutions like public schools and trade unions to enslave rather than to liberate.

Factors That Influenced Japan's Course

From the first, says G. B. Sansom, the leaders of modern Japan thought of their main task and duty as "the rapid organization of national strength." [6] Also, "it is clear enough that ultimate expansionist designs were harboured by most of the leaders of the Restoration . . ." [7]

The urge to expand which was latent in Japanese ideals and institutions received additional support from outside influences, such as the behavior of the Western powers during their late nineteenth-century surge of imperialism. The trend toward economic nationalism in the world, especially in the 1930's, gave Japanese expansionists the excuse that

[6] G. B. Sansom, cited, p. 347.
[7] Same, p. 333.

they must conquer a "co-prosperity sphere" in order to get "access to raw materials and markets."

One of the most powerful early factors favoring antidemocratic, chauvinist, and warlike tendencies in Japan was the national sense of humiliation inflicted by the "unequal treaties." [8] Similar feelings were kept alive, long after the treaties were revised, by racial discriminations embodied in foreign immigration, citizenship, and land laws, most notably in the United States. The depths to which this rankled in Japanese national feelings is almost unbelievable to those who have not looked into the question. The drive for status and for a respected position among the nations of the world was powerful with rulers and people alike. Resentment over the unequal treaties was such that, according to Sansom, "The problem of securing new treaties on a footing of equality with other powers overshadowed all other problems and influenced not only foreign but also domestic policy" until revision was accomplished in 1894. The accompanying outburst of antiforeign sentiment "imprinted a special character upon the future relations of Japan with foreign countries. It can even be argued, though not proved, that they started Japanese policy, both domestic and foreign, upon a course that it would otherwise not have taken." The government resisted agitation for popular rights not only because of a natural authoritarian bias but also because it thought the security and independence of the country to be at stake, and "there are indications that the Japanese people were more enthusiastic for national prestige than for a share in domestic policy." [9]

Japan's cultural heritage was not one to make easy the adoption of democratic ideas. It is significant that when the Japanese came to translate Western laws and political literature they found nothing in their language for "popular rights," and a term had to be invented. "Indeed, not only in its laws but in its customs the social system of Japan was penetrated by the idea of duties to the exclusion of the idea

---

[8] Treaties negotiated by the Western powers with a weak Japan in the 1850's placed foreigners residing in Japan under the jurisdiction of their own consular courts (extraterritoriality) and fixed the Japanese customs tariff at very low rates.

[9] Same, pp. 291, 359.

of rights." [10] Much has been made of the German influence on Japanese political development, but in the informed view of G. B. Sansom Japanese tradition was the controlling factor. The Japanese found much useful material in German history and political thought because they felt at home in a German atmosphere. "Both had an autocratic and warlike tradition, a strong monarchy, a powerful conservative ruling class (samurai and junker) and a determination to make up for lost time by building up national strength at the expense of civil liberties." German methods of administration, military organization, and economic control did not require important deviations from traditional Japanese principles, whereas English, French, or American practice in these matters would have brought a radical change in Japanese life. There was diligent study and ardent advocacy in Japan of responsible parliamentary government and individual freedom. Yet the liberals lost, and their failure "can be summarized by saying that Japan was not ready for democracy. Her past history was against it . . ." Sansom continues, ". . . there was force in the argument, with which those in power repeatedly countered pleas for an immediate grant of popular rights, that it was too soon to pass the conduct of affairs into inexperienced hands. The liberal reply was: 'Yes, it is true that democratic institutions were the result of centuries of evolution in Europe. But that is also true of modern science and art and machinery, as well as of political forms. Would you have us abstain from the use of steam or electricity until we have gone through all the stages that ended in their discovery?' This was an ingenious retort, but it raises without answering the whole question of cultural relationships between East and West, for history so far has shown that machines will enter where ideas cannot penetrate." [11]

Russia

Consider finally the political concomitants of economic development in Russia. The freeing of the serfs came in the 1860's, and shortly afterwards railroad-building began to

[10] Same, pp. 311, 446.
[11] Same, pp. 363-364, 355.

gather pace. A great spurt of industrial growth started in the middle eighties, was interrupted by depression, war and civil strife after 1900, and then resumed until the outbreak of World War I in 1914. The Tsarist government actively promoted industry, especially in the early part of this period, by its railroad-building activities (which were strongly influenced by military policy) and in other ways. Its attention was centered on basic industrial materials and machinery rather than consumer goods industries. In 1914 Russia had a partly modernized economy in a state of highly unbalanced development. It was a country of great contrasts. The industry which existed in the Petersburg and Moscow districts and in the south was very modern, equipped with up-to-date German and English machines and often staffed by German and English managers and engineers. Large factories where the work force numbered more than a thousand people employed nearly a half of all factory workers. At the same time, only 15 percent of the Russian people lived in towns. In the countryside primitive peasant agriculture existed alongside landlords' estates, some of which were run on model large-scale lines. Tsarist absolutism had been only a little modified by concessions to democratic demands, and the aristocracy enjoyed their privileges with slight concern for the condition of the people.

The revolution of 1917, provoked by the oppressions and inefficiency of the old regime and the strains of war, at first was under moderate leadership aiming at democratic reforms. Then it was captured by Lenin and his Communist Party. The first decade was marked by "war Communism," economic breakdown, and revival under a "New Economic Policy" which temporarily permitted private enterprise. Then the Communist regime launched the country upon a series of five-year plans under which it built up industry, especially heavy industry, at an extremely rapid rate and revolutionized the organization of agriculture by forcing the peasants into collective farms and state farms. Economic development in this case has been accompanied by the growth of a political despotism more oppressive to individual freedom than even that of the Tsars, and much more menacing to the rest of the world.

Alexander Gerschenkron, speculating on the historical background which made it possible for the Communist tyranny to establish itself, asserts that "The Soviet government can be properly described as a product of the country's economic backwardness. Had serfdom been abolished by Catherine the Great or at the time of the Decembrists' uprising in 1825, the peasant discontent, the driving force and the earnest of success of the Russian Revolution, would never have assumed disastrous proportions, while the economic development of the country would have proceeded in a much more gradual fashion. If anything is a 'grounded historical assumption,' this would seem to be one: the delayed industrial revolution was responsible for a political revolution in the course of which the power fell in the hands of a dictatorial government to which in the long run the vast majority of the population was opposed." Gerschenkron concludes that Soviet experience teaches the formidable dangers in our time from the existence of economic backwardness. "The paramount lesson of the twentieth century is that the problems of backward nations are not exclusively their own. They are just as much problems of the advanced countries. It is not only Russia but the whole world that pays the price for the failure to emancipate the Russian peasants and to embark upon industrialization policies at an early time. Advanced countries cannot afford to ignore economic backwardness." [12]

I would add that this example also shows the menace to the rest of the world of political and social backwardness. Surely the delay in Russia, as compared with Western Europe, in overcoming absolutism in government and religion was one of the reasons for delay in economic progress, as well as vice versa. Russian Communism can be regarded as, in no small measure, a projection into the industrial age of the authoritarian outlook of Tsarist society. As in Germany and Japan, industrial techniques were adopted in Russia without a groundwork of democratic institutions. A new order in industry was grafted onto an old order in political and social

---

[12] Alexander Gerschenkron, "Economic Backwardness in Historical Perspective," in Bert F. Hoselitz, ed., *The Progress of Underdeveloped Areas* (Chicago: University of Chicago Press, 1952), pp. 27-29.

relations, and the result was a more efficient internal oppression and a more menacing external imperialism.

QUESTIONS AND INTERPRETATIONS

The one conclusion which we can draw with certainty from this survey of the political concomitants of economic development is that there is no simple correlation between economic development and democracy or peacefulness. In a number of cases economic development has seemed to spring out of, and in turn to foster, an increasing freedom of the human spirit, greater respect for the dignity of the individual, and more democratic government. But in other cases economic development has been pushed through by determined oligarchies ruling without much reference to the consent of the governed and even with totalitarian ruthlessness, while freedom and individual dignity have made halting progress or moved backward. In their international behavior, countries in process of development or having reached substantial development have likewise shown extreme variation—all the way from a peaceful and cooperative disposition to expansionism and deliberately planned aggression. Quite clearly there are many other factors at work besides the common factor of modernization of production methods, and it is impossible to predict from the mere fact of economic development what sort of political trend will appear. "Economic development doesn't necessarily make nice people."

Difficulties in Learning from History

When I began research for this study I planned to draw rather heavily on the histories of countries that have undergone modern economic development in order to discover what relations might exist between economic development on the one hand and political concomitants on the other and to evaluate the factors of greatest evident importance in determining the nature of these relationships. I did do a fair amount of historical reading and study for this purpose. But the results were largely negative or inconclusive, for several reasons that are not without interest.

In the first place, the number of cases that can be examined (that is, the number of countries that have become advanced, modern economies) is small, while the complexity of the human relations involved in these problems is so great that the number of factors at play must be very large—cultural heritage, resources, climate, timing and pattern of development, and so on. One can reach no very positive conclusions on a scientific basis about the apparent influence of multiple factors when there are only a few cases to examine. For example, it would not be valid to conclude from ten or fifteen cases that political democracy promotes or retards economic development or is promoted or retarded by it, when all the cases that might be cited pro or con are complicated by a dozen other factors whose degree of influence in each case may have been important but cannot be precisely evaluated.

In the second place, it soon became evident—and we shall return to this point below—that the nature of the interrelations between political and economic changes *is itself changing*. It is doubtful how much we can learn about present and future relationships from experiences of fifty, one hundred, or two hundred years ago. In other words, the time factor adds one more important variable, and a complex one, to the multiplicity of other variables that have to be taken into account when we try to understand the reasons for the observed political concomitants of economic development. An economic change which encouraged one sort of political trend in Europe in 1850 may have quite a different political meaning in Asia or Africa or Latin America in 1920, and still another in 1960. The climate of ideas is different, technology is different, the state of development of other countries is different, and people who know what has happened *since* 1850 have a different understanding of and reaction to events than the people who had to react in 1850.

In the third place, I found that the economic historians, and historians in general, have for the most part not made their studies and written their reports in ways that answer the questions to which I needed answers. There has been little systematic attention to the political consequences and prerequisites of economic development. What has been done is on a country-by-country basis and is not in a form that lends itself readily to cross-country comparisons. But without cross-country comparisons one is generalizing from single cases. It is often remarked that each generation has to rework history to bring the experience of the past to bear on its own problems. Today, the tremendous interest in economic development and the need for guidance not merely on its more narrow economic aspects but also on its broad political and cultural implications should send our historical experts back to their sources with some urgent new questions. This is true despite what has been said above about the difficulty of reaching scientifically based and presently applicable conclusions on these complex and changing problems. After all, we do act all the time on assumptions that certain kinds of measures are likely to have certain kinds of effects, and these assumptions come in one way or another out of what we think we know about past experience. More careful study of a broader range of experience should give us a better basis on which to set up our working assumptions.

History, though it cannot give us the answers to present perplexities in the form of a simple set of cause and effect relations, can make three important contributions: It can make us aware of the unreality of overly simple formulas, like the assumption that economic development will automatically promote democracy and international cooperation. It can call attention to possible obstacles and pitfalls in the development process. It can suggest intelligent questions and hypotheses to bring to the study of current materials and current problems. I hope that the specialists who are equipped to do so will give us more studies of the dynamic process of economic development and its interrelation with political and cultural change in a variety of countries, and also that some of them will undertake cross-country comparisons.

The Time Factor

If we compare the political concomitants of economic development in countries where economic modernization came early and gradually with those in countries where economic modernization came later and more suddenly (because technology could be borrowed from the early-comers), some contrasts emerge which are rather striking. From the point of view of democratic ideals they are disturbing.

In the group of early-comers are Britain, the Low Countries, France, and the overseas areas—Canada, the United States, Australia, and New Zealand, which from this point of view can be regarded as extensions of the political and economic evolution that had long been going on in Britain. In the group of late-comers are Japan and Russia. Somewhere between are the Scandinavian countries, Switzerland, and Germany.

In the early-comer, gradual group the political concomitants are distinctly on the side of personal and intellectual freedom and democracy. In the late-comer, sudden-development group, authoritarianism in society and government are prominent features. Now, there are many other factors at play in these cases besides the timing and the suddenness of the modernization process. Also, there are still more recent cases of development now under way in which a definite effort is being made to combine quick progress with democratic methods, with the outcome necessarily unknown until some time in the future. Turkey, after an initial period of dictatorial modernization, now manifests democratic trends of considerable vitality. In many other countries large and small, from India to Puerto Rico, development problems are being confronted under leadership imbued with a genuinely democratic spirit. I do not suggest that there is any historical "law" which makes late and quick modernization inevitably authoritarian.

But how can we explain the greater disposition toward freedom among the early-comers than the late-comers? One hypothesis which fits the facts is the following: It took a considerable degree of individual and intellectual freedom to make possible the invention and initial growth of the modern industrial system, including modern science and all that goes with it. That is why modern economy *originated* in the countries of the West where political and social freedoms were gradually growing after the Middle Ages, and why economic development and democratic political development tended to reinforce each other. But once industrialism has been invented and demonstrated, it can be *taken over* and deliberately installed in unfree environments which could not have created it in the first place. In fact, an authoritarian society and government have certain advantages in organizing the quick transformations which are required for rapid installation of the new production methods. These methods may even be carried to further technical perfection in an authoritarian atmosphere which would have stifled the early pioneering inventiveness. And the modern methods of production may be used quite effectively to provide a powerful economic base for despotic, totalitarian systems. The leaders of these systems have developed special social inventions which adjust despotism to modern technology—such inventions as the twentieth-century police state and the skilled manipulation of mass communication and all kinds of psychological pressure to control men's minds.

In the early days development *had* to take place in an atmosphere of growing freedom, otherwise the basic innovations in science, technology, and business would not have been made. Nowadays we are dealing in the underdeveloped countries with a quite different kind of economic development which, in its first phase, is a development by borrowing ideas from abroad. The political atmosphere in which this process takes place can be *either* authoritarian or democratic.

All this poses serious problems for democracy. The modern communication of ideas has created insistent demands for quick economic development, which, as we shall see more clearly in Part III, is inevitably associated with sudden transformations in social institutions as well as adoption of machines and accumulation of capital. Is the democratic outlook which originated modern production methods compatible with their quick transfer to societies where they have not been an indigenous growth? The problem of converting a country under pressure from premodern to modern economy is analogous in some respects to the problem of converting from peace economy to war economy, though the transformations go much deeper. In the conversion to war economy even the most steadfast democracies recognize the need for an amount of authoritarianism and government direction which is not acceptable under other circumstances. Can democracy develop techniques which will enable it to compete in effectiveness with authoritarian methods during the *catching-up phase* of development? Can it at the same time foster the democratic spirit? Perhaps community development programs of the type being tried in India, adult education programs and agricultural extension work, international technical assistance in administration and in management, new ways of encouraging private enterprise to take hold, and some of the other devices now being tested in international aid programs will point the way. Veblen held that Japan could use modern industrialism for imperial aggrandizement only while the rising expectations of the population and the influence of new modes of thinking lagged behind. One recent writer has applied this line of thought to current situations as follows: "The development of industry is a boon for a country only if there is a concomitant creation of mass purchasing power, dispersion of incomes, improvements in health, education, and productivity, orderly promotion of trade unions and collective bargaining, and the maintenance of civil liberties and the rule of law." [13]

Development and Aggression

Another sobering reflection inspired by our historical cases is that, if we exclude the small countries which are less tempted, there is a practically perfect record of advance in economic and technological efficiency being used at some stage to support one type or another of aggressive outward thrusts. Effective economic development in any country means a rise in national *power*, unless all the country's neighbors are developing at least as rapidly. Must every country of considerable size which modernizes its economy become expansive? Clearly, the world setting in which development goes forward, as well as the particular cultural background of each country, will go far toward determining the answer to this question. This is another respect in which the time factor is very important, for the field of forces in which Britain emerged as the first, and for a time the only, industrial state is very different from the situation today. A world characterized both by a deep split between the Soviet bloc and the

[13] Henry William Spiegel, *The Brazilian Economy* (Philadelphia: Blakiston, 1949), pp. vii-viii.

West and by strong efforts to establish a working collective security system is in some respects less favorable, but in other respects more favorable, to the peaceful accomplishment of economic growth than the former world setting in which there were many separate national power units.

Common Elements in High Development

Suppose we look for common characteristics among the countries which to date have reached the highest level of economic development as measured by national income per person. These are the thirteen countries of our "highly developed" group in the table on pages 16-17. Japan and Russia are not included, for they fall in the intermediate income group.

All are in the temperate zone. This is also true of Japan and Russia and nearly all, but not quite all, the other countries of the intermediate group. Is climate a fundamental determinant of economic activity, perhaps through its physiological effects on human energy, as some have contended? May the interconnecting factors, whatever they are, between climatic zones and levels of development also be changing through time? For example, the remarkable burst of scientific discovery and technological invention of the last several centuries has been almost entirely in and for temperate-zone conditions. Now that more scientific and technological skill is being turned to tropical medicine, tropical agriculture, and the many other aspects of human adaptation to a tropical environment, may there not be a profound change in the making? These are fascinating considerations to which we shall have occasion to revert later.

Culturally, all the countries of the "highly developed" group belong to the Greek-Roman-Christian tradition which we call Western Civilization. But not all the countries of distinctly Western heritage are in the highly developed group, only those of northern and western Europe. All of them are predominantly Protestant countries, with two exceptions, Belgium and France. France has long been known as anticlerical, and its population statistics for the past century suggest that, on social matters like birth control, the influence of the Church is weak. Economic historians have often traced a significant relation between the spirit of the Protestant Reformation and the rise of modern trade, investment, science, popular education, freedom of thought ,individual initiative, and other components of economic progress. These interrelations are complex, however. Simple association gives us no firm ground for asserting what is cause and what is effect.

All the "highly developed" countries, with qualifications for Germany, have attained their advanced economic levels as comparatively free societies under comparatively democratic governments. Also, all of our "highly developed" countries owe a large part of their progress to the initiative of private enterprise. At present they are all "mixed systems" in which the government and public corporations have taken on many important economic functions but in which individuals and private corporations manage most of production and trade. Some of them have had, or now have, avowedly "socialist" governments and others have strong socialist parties, but in all cases this is democratic evolutionary socialism of the sort represented by the British Labor Party and not the antidemocratic, revolutionary Communist brand of socialism.

It is noteworthy that, directly contrary to the confident expectations of Marx and Engels and to the conclusions of allegedly "scientific" Marxist political economy, not a single one of these highly developed countries where modern industrial capitalism has had the longest and fullest development has been the scene of a "proletarian revolution." Communism has been able to take hold only in less developed countries. More will be said on this in Chapter 6.

FACTORS AFFECTING THE POLITICAL OUTCOME

We return to the theme of this chapter: economic development does not produce uniform political results. We are not able to predict with assurance what the political outcome may be in a given country when development starts. Experience in past cases and the knowledge that social scientists have acquired about the working of human institutions do, however, point to the importance of factors which may be grouped under three headings: (1) the cultural heritage with which a country embarks on economic modernization, (2) the world environment which impinges on it during the development process, and (3) the pattern of development, that is, the choices that are made as to what kinds of development are to be sought and what measures are to be used to promote development.

Cultural Heritage

The cultural heritage that each country brings to economic modernization is different from every other. Some traits may be favorable to the development of modern productive efficiency, and to the beneficent use of modern production in the service of democratic and peaceful ideals, others unfavorable. It may be that certain traits which facilitate the quick taking-over of modern industrial technique, like the authoritarian nature of Japanese society, also endanger democracy and peace. Some underdeveloped countries—for example, portions of Indonesia—appear to have at the local level a deeply-rooted tradition of community cooperation and democratic social relations. Such a cultural heritage, if it can be adapted to modern production methods without being perverted in the process, might influence the political and social outcome of modernization much more favorably than did the feudalistic, hierarchical, warrior heritage of Japan. The problems will be different in each cultural environment. The worst mistake we can make is to neglect these cultural differences in thinking about problems of development.

It is easy to slip into the tacit assumption, which no one would defend if he stopped to think about it, that today's underdeveloped countries come to economic modernization with the same heritage of social institutions, social structure, social skills, purposes, and ethics as Britain and other Western countries had when they modernized. That is the assumption implied in the notion that introducing similar mechanical techniques of production will foster similar political and social results, such as growth of democracy. In Britain and most of the West there was a long evolution of economic, political, and social institutions prior to, and in a very real sense preparing the way for, the industrial revolution. Late-comers can skip that long preparatory stage which gave time for gradual shaping of social institutions and values and for the rise of middle classes. Nowadays it is possible, by technological borrowing, to graft up-to-date production methods on outdated systems of social institutions and values. In some cases the graft may not "take," for certain kinds of social institutions and values are not compatible with efficient modern production. In other cases, the outcome may be productive efficiency that is harnessed to political and social purposes which oppress rather than free people, and which lead to war rather than to better living conditions.

World Environment

The world environment in which economic development goes forward also influences the political outcome. "The times" have changed and will continue to change with respect to such important influences as the accumulated store of technology on which underdeveloped countries can draw, the world economic setting as regards possibilities for trade and for obtaining capital from abroad, and the world political and social atmosphere. Times differ with respect to the degree of nationalistic fervor, of militarism, of imperial expansionism in the air, and with respect to the relative prestige of democratic and authoritarian systems.

It is possible now for development to take place at a much more rapid pace than in the past. In general, the later the start of a modernization movement the greater the world store of technological knowledge and experience which can be taken over. The late-comer is also relatively free from the vested interests of large investment in recently outmoded equipment, such as power plants and railway equipment of vintage 1920, and can select the latest techniques.

Another very significant change is that peoples and governments are much more conscious of economic development nowadays, and the old process of more or less automatic, unplanned development under the leadership of private enterprisers is now supplemented and in some cases superseded by deliberate, planned, and politically directed development. There has been a world-wide shift in social values, so that the amount of approval bestowed today upon thrift, profits, and business success is less than in the days of nineteenth-century Western development, while a higher rating is given to welfare, social security, and equality of income.[14]

A warning offered by Japan's case would seem to be valid today despite changing times. The world environment can, without anyone's intending it, weight the scales in favor of internal political and social forces that stand for authoritarianism, militarism, super-patriotism, and ultimately external aggression. The cultural heritage of Japan predisposed it to these trends. Yet there were times in that country's history when the internal balance of forces seemed to be moving toward the ultimate victory of the new liberal, democratic ideas brought from the West—that is, by the more healthy part of the Western impact. A little more weight on that side of the scale at crucial moments might have changed the course of history. The unfavorable world factors we have noted were four:

(1) The inferior status imposed on Japan by the "unequal treaties" and by discrimination against Japanese abroad in such matters as immigration and citizenship. Both gave a basic emotional advantage to the antiforeign, antidemocratic, militaristic forces. Conservatives deliberately played on these emotions to help shape educational policy toward the inculcation of authoritarian loyalty and Emperor-worship, and to help establish constitutional practices favoring absolutism and militarism. Experience in other countries shows that the Japanese people were not unique in wanting to be proud of their country more than they wanted to have a share in its government. To impose on any country a status of inferiority appears to be one of the surest ways to promote within it antidemocratic, aggressive, and fanatic movements.

(2) The bad example set by the Western powers as respects aggression and conquest of empire. At the end of the

[14] Henry C. Wallich has called attention to these differences in social values as between the "production-oriented," entrepreneurial economies of former days and the "consumption-oriented," directed or managed economies characteristic both of developed and underdeveloped countries today. His paper, presented at a conference organized by the Social Science Research Council in 1952, has since appeared in the *Proceedings of the Third Conference of Central Bank Technicians of the American Continent* (Havana: Banco Nacional de Cuba, 1953).

nineteenth and early in the twentieth centuries imperial conquest was "being done" in the best international circles. There was considerable evidence that respect, territory, and other rewards go to strong, aggressive nations and that "might makes right."

(3) The collapse of the free world economy following 1929, and the rise of tariffs, quotas, exchange controls, and other national barriers to trade. It seemed to many that Japan's vital need for materials and markets to support its growing population could not be satisfied by peaceful trade.

(4) The absence of an effective system of collective security. The leading members of the League of Nations and the United States were unwilling to resist aggression by force when tested by Japan's militarists in Manchuria in 1931. Mussolini and Hitler got away with similar provocations. Isolationist sentiment in the United States expressed itself in "neutrality" legislation in the 1930's, and Europe's hopes for peace took the course of "appeasement." It is not strange that in such an international environment the Japanese advocates of using their newly-developed industrial power for militaristic expansion had their way.

Patterns of Development

Finally, we would expect the political outcome of the development process to be influenced by the pattern of development, that is, by the choices that are made between initial emphasis on heavy industry or light industry, industrial centralization or decentralization, broad community development or narrow concentration on material output, and by the types of social institutions that are relied upon for capital formation, education, and the other tasks of modernization.

These problems will occupy us more extensively in Part III, where the central question will be: What can be done by leadership dedicated to democratic and peaceful ideals to guide the processes of economic development toward desirable political and social ends? Before turning to that question, however, we shall sum up the objectives which are to be taken in this study as valid goals of development policy (Chapter 5). Then it will be advisable to examine in some detail the strategy and tactics of the most active opposition, the Communist movement in underdeveloped countries, and the implications of Communist opposition for free world policy (Part II).

Chapter 5

DEFINING THE OBJECTIVES

In Chapters 1, 2, and 3 we examined the motivations for economic development from the viewpoints of underdeveloped countries, the United States, and the world community. Chapter 4, by a brief survey of past cases, has brought us the sobering realization that the political and social outcome of the development process is uncertain and not always good. Economic development can be successful in the narrow sense —that is, it can bring a substantial increase in a country's capacity to produce—without being fully reflected in better living conditions for the majority of people or without being successful in terms of those human values that lead us to prefer democratic and peaceful societies to oligarchic, authoritarian, and warlike ones.

The test of a development program ought to be its effects on human beings directly and indirectly affected by it. What are the human values that we should have in view in order to be able to appraise intelligently the different kinds of economic, social, and political change that may come with economic development and to say, with reason, that this would be good and that bad? These values can best be expressed as basic human wants or desires, and I have drawn up the following list of wants that seem relevant to the problem of defining objectives for economic development. Others would no doubt choose a different emphasis, or vary the phrasing. Also, the wants as stated here admittedly reflect the liberal, Western cultural tradition. But they are by no means exclusive to that tradition. There is strong evidence that the great majority of men and women in today's world, in other cultural traditions as well as in that of the West, would regard these "basic human wants" as recognizably their own—*if* they had a chance to learn about them and to express a choice. And it is the fact that so many people have learned about them and about the possibility of meeting them more fully that has caused the revolution in people's expectations referred to in Chapter 1.

BASIC HUMAN WANTS

A person wants:

An Adequate Living—"enough" food, clothing, housing, health services, educational opportunities, leisure time, and acceptable working conditions. Adequacy here is a relative idea, of course, and depends on what people know about how much others have of these good things, and what changes for the better they are led to believe are possible.

A Sense of Security—reasonable assurance of personal safety and of stability in essential life conditions, including freedom from violence and from terror and from interruption of the flow of livelihood values. Security values are interfered with by despotic governments, by wars, and by famines and economic depressions.

A Sense of Freedom and Participation—shared power, that is, opportunity for effective participation in decision-making by people whose lives are affected by the decisions. This includes local self-rule in so far as it is compatible with order and welfare, individual freedoms, and absence of tremendous or rigid inequalities in the distribution of wealth, power, and respect. These are the values served by systems of representative self-government, civil liberties, and measures for broadening the distribution of wealth and income and overcoming barriers of race, caste, education, or other social obstacles to equality of opportunity.

Creative Opportunities—opportunities and stimuli for making the most of human capacity; personal fulfillment, creative expression in the arts and sciences and in individual and community accomplishments. Economic progress, security, and democratic freedom and participation may not be all that is needed for a high level of human creativity, but at least they provide a useful foundation.

A Sense of Belonging—fellow feeling, social incentives that emphasize love and cooperation more than hate and conflict, a sense of solidarity in small and large communities, the sharing of aspirations, purposes, and faith which give meaning to life. These are values stressed by many of the great religions, and they are among the roots of democratic ideals.

A Sense of Purpose—a feeling that one's life is heading somewhere, confidence in and affirmation of life, a meaningful integration of all the values to which a person or a society holds. This has been the special province of religions, and in this sense Communism is a religion, too. A faith which gives a sense of purpose can be fanatic, intolerant, and destructive of the other life values, or can powerfully support and reinforce them.

All these basic human wants, or values, can be summed up in the Western, Christian idea of "the dignity of man." All of them are associated with the desires of the individual human being; the desires of groups or the State are thus subordinated to the ultimate desires of the individual.

With these basic wants as a background, it is clear that not just any kind of economic development will promote human dignity.

Economic development in the narrow sense is a *necessary* but not a *sufficient* condition for the results we want. In other words, it makes a difference how economic development takes place, what sort of development it is, and what ends it serves.

When the term *successful development* is used in this book, the reader should understand it to mean something more than economic growth or even than rising living levels for the average man. It will mean economic development of such a character, and associated with such political and social developments, as to provide a greater measure of these basic human values to the people directly affected and to the world. Translated into economic, political, and social terms, *successful development* will be taken to mean:

Within the Developing Country

1. Higher levels of production and real income, widely shared.

2. Progress in democratic self-government, reasonably sta-

ble and at the same time responsive to the needs and wishes of the people.

3. Growth of democratic social relations, including broadly shared freedoms, opportunities for self-development, and respect for individual personality.

4. Less vulnerability to Communism and other totalitarianisms, by reason of the foregoing.

In External Relations

1. Growth of attitudes that make for a more peaceful world, and for freedom both from external oppression and from use of power to oppress others.

2. Growth of mutually beneficial international trade and investment.

3. Strengthening of the over-all resources of the free world and the collective defense capacity of free peoples against any aggression.

Successful development as so defined, it is submitted, will simultaneously serve the interests of the people of the underdeveloped countries, of the United States and the other economically advanced countries, and of the world community.

Be it noted that successful development is a *multi-valued* goal. That is, achievement cannot be adequately measured in terms of any single economic, social, or political accomplishment or in terms of the advancement of any single human value. Man is not just an economic man or a political man or a religious man, but all of these in combination and more. This raises problems, for pursuit of several aims simultaneously means that at times the requirements for one objective may conflict with those for another. Is a somewhat faster increase of production worth a somewhat less equal distribution of income, or a somewhat more authoritarian government? There is no easy answer to such questions. Problems of this sort are characteristic of human affairs. The best we can do is to be aware of them and try to encourage the people who decide them to weigh the alternatives intelligently.

PART II

THE COMMUNIST PATH TO DEVELOPMENT

INTRODUCTION

The seizure of power by Communist parties in underdeveloped countries and the application of their formula for development would mean the defeat of most of the objectives we have defined in Part I. Communism is not the only danger to successful development of underdeveloped countries, but it is certainly the most active menace at the moment. The precise nature of the menace needs to be more clearly understood both by Americans and by potential victims in underdeveloped countries. A sound maxim is "Know your enemy." Therefore, Part II is devoted to Communist doctrine, strategy, and practice as applied to underdeveloped countries.

In the deliberate, skillful, and highly organized campaign now being waged by the world Communist movement for control of the underdeveloped countries, there is at stake the political allegiance of the majority of the world's peoples, the vast potential resources of their homelands, and, ultimately, the fate of the United States and of our most cherished ideals of human freedom. Yet most of us here in America have very inexact ideas of what the Communists are up to in underdeveloped areas and how they are going about it. Nothing like the powerful Communist movement of today existed when Britain and Western Europe, the United States, Japan, and even Russia changed over to modern industrialism. The Communist movement is at one and the same time: (1) an arm of the Soviet state, backed by the military, economic, and propaganda resources of the Soviet Union to the extent that seems expedient to the Soviet rulers; (2) a set of national Communist parties, each using in its own country techniques elaborately worked out and tested in other countries for the purpose of mobilizing discontent and ultimately seizing power; and (3) a world view, a quasi-religion, which gives its adherents a pleasant sense of certainty about all the puzzles of history and a vocation or calling to which they dedicate their lives. It would certainly be impossible to make a correct estimate of the political implications of economic development anywhere in the underdeveloped world today without giving attention to this new factor.

In the chapters that follow I have had to sacrifice much concrete evidence for the sake of brevity. The reader will either have to trust my generalizations or go to the sources himself. We are beginning to get competent social science studies which illuminate the doctrinal development of Communism in relation to underdeveloped areas, the strategy and tactics of Communist parties in particular localities, and the Communist ways of using certain issues, such as agrarian unrest. I hope that someone will soon undertake a comprehensive analysis of Communist relations to underdeveloped areas, more thorough than has been possible in this study, and will publish a necessarily rather lengthy book on the subject. The importance of the topic can hardly be overrated.

Communist leaders think in terms of "strategy and tactics," for they have a clear, military-like goal in all non-Communist countries: seizure of power. They put more weight on "correct theory" than do statesmen of democratic countries, for they believe that in Marxism-Leninism they have a science of human society which makes possible the prediction and, within limits, the engineering of the course of history. "The strength of Marxist-Leninist theory," Stalin said, "consists in the fact that it enables the Party to orient itself in a situation, to grasp the internal connection of surrounding events, to foresee the course of events and to discern not only how and when events are developing in the present but also how and when they must develop in the future." [1] If we want to meet Communist methods effectively we must try to understand in what light their theory leads them to view "the internal connection of surrounding events" in the underdeveloped countries. Chapter 6 undertakes this task, which also amounts to sketching the grand strategy of Communism toward under-

[1] Stalin's *History of the All-Union Communist Party,* first published 1938, as quoted by Historicus in "Stalin on Revolution," *Foreign Affairs,* January, 1949, p. 177.

developed areas from the time of Marx to the time of Mao Tse-tung.

Chapter 7 then surveys Communist methods of agitation, organization, and propaganda in underdeveloped countries. Included is a brief account of the Communist line toward United Nations assistance for underdeveloped areas and toward the Point Four program of the United States.

Chapter 8 sketches Communist practice in underdeveloped areas that have come under their rule.

Finally, Chapter 9 discusses the implications of the Communist challenge in underdeveloped areas for the policy of the United States and the free world. Have we been underestimating the enemy? Are we proceeding on correct assumptions about what it is that makes people go Communist in underdeveloped countries? Have we properly evaluated both the politico-economic and the military prongs of the attack and achieved the best possible balance in our countereffort?

Chapter 6

COMMUNISM TURNS TO UNDERDEVELOPED AREAS

A century ago Marx and Engels wrote in the *Communist Manifesto* a forecast of the supposedly inexorable fate of capitalism. They based it on what they saw or thought they saw in Britain and Western Europe, the economically most advanced areas of the mid-nineteenth century.

Prophecy and Reality

"Society as a whole is more and more splitting up into two great hostile camps," they wrote. In one camp they saw the bourgeoisie or owners of capital, in the other the proletariat or workers. The bourgeoisie were destined to become fewer and richer as big capitalists destroyed little capitalists, while the proletariat would grow more and more numerous, at the same time sinking deeper into misery. At length the proletariat would rise in violent revolution, seize power, overthrow the system of private property, and open the way to a new proletarian society. "Let the ruling classes tremble at a Communistic revolution. The proletarians have nothing to lose but their chains."

Not some accident, but the "inner contradictions" of capitalism in its advanced stages would bring this result. The "immanent laws" of capitalistic production, which would make the rich richer and fewer, the poor poorer and more numerous, were briefly sketched in the *Manifesto* and then worked out in great detail in Marx's huge volumes on *Capital*. It allegedly follows from these laws that, "in proportion as capital accumulates, the lot of the labourer . . . must grow worse. . . . Accumulation of wealth at one pole is, therefore, at the same time accumulation of misery, agony of toil, slavery, ignorance, brutality, mental degradation, at the opposite pole . . ." Again, "Along with the constantly diminishing number of the magnates of capital . . . grows the mass of misery, oppression, slavery, degradation, exploitation; but with this too grows the revolt of the working-class. . . . The knell of capitalist private property sounds. The expropriators are expropriated." [1]

Marxists have always prided themselves on their allegedly "scientific" analysis of historical forces. Stalin's boast that this gives the Communist Party the ability to foresee the course of events was quoted on page 100. Here was a major prediction, not peripheral but central to Marx's whole system, about the inevitable polarization of society in advanced capitalism and the coming in advanced capitalist countries of proletarian revolution. What has in fact happened?

1. Polarization of society. Instead of the rich growing richer and the poor poorer, the outstanding social fact in the economically developed countries of Western Europe, North America, and Australasia has been the rise of a broad, middle-income group. There has been a general advance in wealth and well-being widely distributed among the population. International wars have brought suffering and privations, but this is quite a different thing from the allegedly inexorable laws of capitalist production which Marx described.

2. Proletarian revolution. There has not been a single case anywhere in the world of a proletarian revolution in an industrially advanced, capitalist country. Seizure of power in the name of the proletariat first occurred in a relatively backward area, Russia, then in the satellite countries of Eastern Europe under the shadow of the Red Army, and then in the most backward country of all, China.

What Defeated Marx's Predictions?

Few questions are more important for us to reflect on in connection with the political outlook for underdeveloped

[1] Karl Marx, *Capital: A Critical Analysis of Capitalist Production,* translated from the third German edition by Samuel Moore and Edward Aveling; edited by Frederick Engels. A reprint of the edition of 1889 (London: George Allen and Unwin Ltd., 1946), pp. 661, 788-789.

countries than this: What defeated Marx's confident prediction about the course of development in the early-comers to industrialization—that is in today's advanced capitalist countries? I suggest that the answer lies along two lines: (1) rapid advance in technology, combined with voluntary population control, which brought great increases in per capita production and consumption, and (2) the adaptability of societies built on individual freedom and popular government, especially in broadening the distribution of income, power, and respect, avoiding rigid class lines, and creating a great middle class.

Neither Marx nor most of his contemporaries foresaw the enormous increase in the wealth-producing capacity of mankind which came with the progress of science and technology in the last half of the nineteenth and the first half of the twentieth centuries. This made it possible in countries of advancing technology to have a progressively rising level of income and increased leisure for all, not merely luxury for a small élite and poverty for the masses, as in most previous societies. When Marx formulated his theories the influence of the railroad, the steamship, and the telegraph were only beginning to be felt in practical economic improvement. These would enormously increase the productivity of human labor by extending interregional and international trade—for example, by making the wheat areas of North America and other continents accessible in world-wide exchange. Still in the future were such tremendous advances in material technology as electric motors, internal combustion engines, automobiles and airplanes, electronic equipment, and modern metallurgy. Also to come were equally important advances in social technology or in combinations of social and material techniques, as in control of contagious diseases, scientific farming promoted by agricultural experiment stations and extension services, assembly lines producing for a mass market supported by high wages, mass distribution through department stores, chain stores, and supermarkets, the professionalization of management, cost accounting, and modern concepts of personnel administration and human relations in industry.

More production may not mean more per person if population growth is unchecked. In the latter part of the nineteenth century and especially in the twentieth century the small-family pattern spread rapidly in the economically advanced countries. It was facilitated by improved contraceptive techniques, but the fundamental impulse came from rising living standards, the desire to get ahead, to give one's children a better education, and the influence of urbanization on modes of living. Thus the industrialized peoples of the West moved toward a population balance combining lower death rates with lower birth rates. Family limitation removed the dilemma which Malthus posed for nineteenth-century thinkers, namely, that the attempt to provide higher incomes for the masses would simply result in more people surviving until population growth was checked by famine, pestilence, or war. Thus the "iron law of wages" limiting labor to a mere subsistence was broken, and the pressure of surplus population, a source for Marx's "industrial reserve-army" of unemployed and degraded workers, was relaxed.

Self-Correcting Capacity of Free Society

The fundamental blunder of Marx—the blunder which vitiated his forecast for the course of development in the advanced countries of nineteenth-century capitalism—was his underestimate of the self-correcting, self-adjusting capacity of societies which permit a considerable degree of individual freedom and initiative, and in which government is responsible to the people in free elections. Marxist dogma assumes that class lines are rigid. Furthermore, it asserts, in the face of many facts to the contrary, that no class ever gives up its power without a (violent) struggle. In the Western world of the late nineteenth and early twentieth centuries, where educational opportunities were becoming more and more widely available, where men were free to start projects on their own or to organize with their fellows, and where every man's vote came to count equally in choosing the government, these dogmas proved ridiculously untrue. Under these conditions economic and social changes of very great moment took place by evolution rather than revolution.

In a setting of individual freedom, where new resources were becoming available by expanding technology, employers had to bid against each other for labor. Over the long pull they had to increase wages progressively in accordance with the rise in productivity of labor. Trade union organization enormously increased the bargaining power of labor, not only in relation to wages and working conditions and numerous fringe benefits, but also in ability to demand respect and dignified treatment. The system of political democracy in which each man and woman has a vote that counts as much as any other has had an influence on the sharing of the product of society which Marx, with his dogma of the "class" control of the state, completely failed to take into account. How could the "bourgeois" state, by hypothesis under the thumb of the capitalists, enact steeply graduated income taxes and inheritance taxes, minimum wage laws, social insurance to meet the hazards of accident, unemployment, ill health, and old age? Yet the political system of Western "capitalist" democracy has in every economically advanced country produced such laws and many more.

In consequence of all this, and quite contrary to Marxist theory, the gap between rich and poor has narrowed in the countries of advanced industrial capitalism. Abject poverty, instead of being the lot of increasing masses of people, is on the way to being eliminated. Many wage earners and farmers enjoy luxuries which would be the envy of aristocrats of other times or other countries. The "proletarians" now have much more to lose than their chains!

Changes in Britain and America

Marx and Engels based many of their theories on conditions in Britain around the middle of the nineteenth century. This was before universal suffrage (after the Reform Bill of 1832 but before that of 1867). It was before trade unions had become powerful, before a national school system offered universal educational opportunity, before steeply graduated income taxes and social security. According to J. H. Huizinga, writing on "The Bloodless Revolution," even the wealthiest in present-day Britain "must make do with a net income which—at least in fiscal theory—is at most some 12 to 15 times that of the coalminer; in 1900 . . . this differential lay somewhere between 1,500 and 2,000. That is the measure of the economic revolution which has come over Britain." Until the twentieth century the British state contented itself with a levy on even the highest incomes of no more than 2 to 3 percent. In 1913 the figure had risen to 8 percent, in 1919 to 51, in 1939 to 78, and in 1945 to 94 percent. A multimillionaire with a money income of £100,000 in 1950 had a post-tax purchasing power of £2,097, as against £91,700 in 1913.[2]

The social distance between the different classes in British society has also been markedly lessened. Disraeli wrote in one of his novels: "An impassable gulf divided the Rich from the Poor . . . the Privileged and the People formed two nations, governed by different laws, influenced by different manners, with no thoughts or sympathies in common, with an innate inability of mutual comprehension." [3] He would hardly write that of Britain today. It has been one of the strengths of Britain that it has time and again renewed its governing class. Even the British peerage is not exceptionally old; most of its titles are said to have been created within the last fifty years. The two Labor Party governments after World War II created eighty peers, among them a miner's son, a former shop assistant, and a union secretary who was once a newsboy and a teacher.

In America, of course, the fluidity of classes has been even greater. Marx's prophecy of wealth accumulating at one pole and misery at the other has been belied by the economic and political forces of a free society. Careful studies of income distribution sponsored by the National Bureau of Economic Research reveal a trend in the last few decades toward more equal sharing, described by the Director of the Bureau as "a transformation that has been carried out peacefully and gradually, but which may already be counted as one of the great social revolutions of history." [4] Politically installed reforms from the "Square Deal" of Theodore Roosevelt through the "New Freedom" of Woodrow Wilson and the "New Deal" of Franklin D. Roosevelt helped to keep the

[2] J. H. Huizinga, "The Bloodless Revolution," *Fortnightly*, April, 1952, pp. 255-261.

[3] Quoted by Huizinga, same, p. 256.

[4] Arthur F. Burns, *Looking Forward*, Thirty-First Annual Report of the National Bureau of Economic Research (New York, May, 1951), pp. 3-4.

American system acceptable and thus to forestall the revolutionaries, even while evoking strong opposition from the conservatives. Political and trade union pressures and the great willingness of American business to make innovations produced a modern, socially responsible type of capitalism in America which bears hardly a shadow of resemblance to the Marx-Engels picture.

Evolution vs. Revolution

Revolution is one of those confusing words which we use in two quite different senses. Revolution in the first sense means a change of great scope and significance, especially a rapid change. Thus we speak of "the industrial revolution," a "revolution" in the practice of medicine, and the "revolutionary" social changes which the impact of modern technology brings to an underdeveloped country. Revolution in the second sense means an overturn of existing authority by unlawful and usually violent means, with connotations of street barricades, arbitrary executions, and forcible suppression of opposition views. Under the methods of individual freedom and popular government, immense and momentous economic and social changes have taken place in the more highly developed countries of Western capitalism since Marx wrote—changes which certainly add up to revolution in the first sense. They have come about gradually by an accumulation of thousands of small changes. This flexibility and adjustability has made revolution in the second sense unnecessary. This is the main reason why Marx's prophecy has failed.

Britain, the United States, and the other countries of Western democracy where economic development has reached an advanced level cannot claim to have solved all their economic and social problems. But they can point to great constructive achievements, and above all to a *method* of social change by freedom and democracy. Instead of two great hostile camps, the Western democracies have produced hundreds of overlapping and crisscrossing political and social groups which have bargained and struggled by democratic means and arrived at consensus and compromise. Marx never imagined that. Is it possible that by similar means Marxists can be proved wrong again in today's underdeveloped countries?

THE SHIFT TO UNDERDEVELOPED AREAS

"Old Testament" Marxism, as expounded in the writings of Marx himself, assigned no significant role in the revolutionary struggle to the economically underdeveloped areas. From Marx's scattered references to the "backward" areas we gather that capitalist industrialism is at work remaking these areas in its own image. But it was taken for granted that the central drama in the conflict between capital and labor—bourgeoisie and proletariat—would be enacted in capitalism's original home.[5] The "New Testament" apostles of Marxism, from Lenin to Stalin and Mao, have given greater and greater attention to underdeveloped areas both in action and in theory.

Lenin did not wait for Russia to become a mature capitalist country and to generate by Marx's "immanent laws" the polarized situations which, according to Old Testament Marxism, would make it ripe for revolution. He seized power in one of the least developed countries of Europe. He did so by using a core of hardened, disciplined, professional revolutionaries and playing on any handy discontent to manipulate mass support. Both the core of revolutionaries and the mass discontent arose out of political absolutism and the abuses of a precapitalist, preindustrialist past compounded by the stresses of war. The rather primitive capitalist-industrialism which had developed in Tsarist Russia had not had time to mature, and had not remolded Russian society and Russian social and political ideas. Experience elsewhere suggests that had it done so Russia would not have become the first Communist state. Marxist revolutionaries were successful not *in spite of* Russia's economic, social, and political backwardness but *because* of it.

Stalin's successes in expanding the Soviet Union and the Communist bloc were almost exclusively in underdeveloped areas. Such countries as Poland, Hungary, Rumania, and Albania which went Communist after the Second World War

[5] Benjamin I. Schwartz, *Chinese Communism and the Rise of Mao* (Cambridge: Harvard University Press, 1951), pp. 7-8.

were at a low level of economic development. Czechoslovakia was more highly developed, but the special pressures on this country next door to the Soviet Union make the reason for the exception obvious. It had nothing to do with Marx's "immanent laws" of capitalist development. In all these countries internal conditions were only part of the forces which turned them Communist, and probably not the most significant part. More decisive was the external pressure from the Soviet Union, through the Red Army and in other ways. Communist regimes in the Soviet-occupied zones of Austria and Germany were, of course, even less the product of internal conditions.

Mao in China achieved the greatest Communist success since the Russian revolution, and he had only a moderate amount of material aid from the Soviet Union. In this case internal factors of discontent were controlling. It is significant that this happened not in a mature capitalist country but in one of the world's most underdeveloped areas.

Communist Hopes for the Future

Communists continue to prophesy a "revolutionary crisis" for the United States, Britain, and the other highly developed countries which have hitherto proved invulnerable. But it is evident that the more realistic hopes of the Communists, and the greatest danger spots for the non-Communist world, are nowadays in underdeveloped areas—such countries as Korea, Indo-China, Malaya, Indonesia, Burma, India, Iran, and Guatemala. The two countries of Western Europe where Comunism has been a real threat are Italy and France. It is significant that Italy cannot be grouped among the economically advanced countries, and that both Italy and France have lagged behind in technological and managerial progress and social reforms. They have "maintained rigidities and cleavages favoring the class warfare approach of the Communists." [6]

Only in underdeveloped countries have Communist revolutionaries been able to seize and hold power, exception

[6] Mario Einaudi, "The Sources of Communist Strength in Western Europe," in Mario Einaudi, Jean-Marie Domenach, and Aldo Garosci, *Communism in Western Europe* (Ithaca: Cornell University Press, 1951), p. 7.

made for a few areas within the Soviet military sphere, and the Communist threat today is greatest in underdeveloped countries. One might say that events are proving the original Marxist forecasts about capitalism and the reaction of people to it to be correct where capitalism is not very far developed, as in the mid-nineteenth-century Britain that Marx knew and underdeveloped areas today, but incorrect where development has gone further. Even this would be conceding too much to a fundamentally false theory, however. Marx claimed to expound the necessary laws of capitalist *development*. Capitalism simply has not developed the way his laws said it would.

Where modernization of production is only in its beginning stages, where the evils of impersonal commercialism and the machine have appeared but productivity has not yet risen enough to provide a good standard of living for all, where the gap between rich and poor is immense and perhaps still expanding, where inequalities of educational opportunity keep many talented people ignorant or frustrated in the use of their talents, where business leadership is primitively ruthless and exploitative, where there is little professionalism in management and little sense of community responsibility in business, where government responds mainly to the demands of a privileged class and public administration is inefficient and corrupt—in such circumstances the Communists find their opportunity. Here is the best market for their stock-in-trade of class hatred, subversive organization, and the doctrine that progress can come only by revolution and dictatorship. The circumstances listed above come nearer to describing the Britain and Western Europe which Marx knew, and, by the same token, the underdeveloped countries of today, than the countries where development has gone further.

Revolutionary Marxism is a disease of modern industrial society. But it is a disease of childhood, mainly, rather than of maturity. Countries in early stages of modernization—the underdeveloped countries of today—are the most vulnerable. The impact of a new commercial and industrial culture breaks down the old pattern of life and the old social system. Only gradually can the society find the necessary new adjustments and learn to operate satisfactorily a more complex and dynamic modern system. The period of transition gives the Communists, with their tactics of hatred and force, their deceptively simple solutions, and their skill at using a dedicated minority to manipulate mass discontent, a ready opening.

UNDERDEVELOPED AREAS IN MODERN COMMUNIST STRATEGY

The capital-labor conflict within nations was the center of attention for Marx. Modern Communists dramatize class conflicts on a "one world" stage befitting the twentieth century. They portray the conflicts as exploited nations vs. exploiting nations, not merely local labor vs. local capitalist exploiters. For Marx, the more developed countries were the center of attention and the immediate revolutionary hope, with the underdeveloped countries waiting in the background. Lenin, Stalin, and Mao have nearly reversed this emphasis. They see a world system of "capitalist imperialism," to be attacked at its "weak links" in the underdeveloped countries.

To throw light on the strategic thinking of Communist leadership today we shall sketch first its view of the relations between the industrially advanced countries of the West and the underdeveloped countries, then its view of the struggles within the underdeveloped countries, and finally its view of the effects of the Soviet revolution and the growth of Soviet power on the underdeveloped countries and the role they can play in strengthening Soviet power.

Theory of Economic Imperialism

Lenin's *Imperialism—The Last Stage of Capitalism*, written in exile just before the Russian revolution, is the foundation of present-day Communist views on this subject. Lenin claimed that capitalism inevitably develops into "monopoly capitalism" and that the great capitalist monopolies, supported by national governments which do the bidding of the capitalists, engage in a ruthless scramble for markets and raw materials. This leads to a division of the world into empires and spheres of influence. The capitalist exploiters oppress dependent peoples, and also weak nations that are nominally independent, for the sake of profits. They also fight each other—that is, they get their governments to fight each other—over the division of the plunder. Thus capitalism in modern Leninist doctrine is responsible not only for the colonial and semicolonial rule of one people over another but also for wars between major powers.

It follows that, according to the Communists, nothing effective can be done about the evils of imperialism and war except through the revolutionary overthrow of capitalism. Just as Marx had argued that "immanent laws" of capitalist development make the rich richer and the poor poorer until there comes the final revolutionary smash-up, so Lenin argued that imperialistic oppression of less advanced peoples and international war are built-in features of capitalism. He strongly criticized Karl Kautsky, from whom he had borrowed some features of his doctrine, for suggesting that imperialism may be merely a *policy* of imperialistic nations instead of a *necessary phase* of capitalist development. In 1947 the prominent Soviet economist, Eugene Varga, who had been a major expounder of Lenin's theory of imperialism, was disciplined for "errors" in his book, *Changes in the Economy of Capitalism Resulting from the Second World War*. In it he had suggested that some underdeveloped areas may be acquiring a degree of economic and political independence from the "imperialist powers." Britain may become a debtor instead of a creditor of India, as Varga pointed out, but in the orthodox Communist view there can be no "organic" change in the relations of "imperialism" unless there is a Communist-approved revolution. Have not Lenin and Stalin said so?

Lenin's doctrine of imperialism and war will not stand comparison with the facts on any objective, scientific basis. As a description and prophecy of events in the real world, it is as false as Marx's earlier inevitable laws showing that the rich must get richer and the poor poorer under capitalism. The topic is too large to be treated here,[7] but three points especially pertinent to our study will be mentioned:

[7] An excellent brief confrontation of the Leninist theory with the factual evidence is in a series of lectures by Lionel Robbins, *The Economic Causes of War* (London: Jonathan Cape, 1939), especially Chapter III, "The Marxian Theory Tested."

1. Detailed investigations fail to support the Leninist view that it is primarily the interests of capitalist financiers which drag their governments into imperialism and war. In cold fact, capitalist financiers have just as often tried to restrain their governments from dangerously aggressive political ventures abroad. They have often been attacked for their "internationalism" and timidity by chauvinists who desired nationalistic expansion. Foreign investments have more frequently and more dangerously been involved in international conflict as instruments of aggressive diplomacy than as its instigators.[8]

2. The rule of one people over another, either by conquest and colonial government or by one-sided economic arrangements, is not something peculiar to the capitalist epoch. Neither is war. Within the capitalist epoch itself, there is no factual ground for asserting that only the more highly developed capitalist countries—in their "last" or "monopoly" or "finance capital" stage—build empires or attempt economic imperialism or engage in wars, or that imperialism and war are more characteristic of such countries than of the more primitive capitalist countries or the noncapitalist countries.

Spain and Portugal fought to acquire great empires and to dispute each other's access to overseas wealth. Italy and Russia in the late nineteenth and early twentieth centuries, though poor countries, certainly not in an advanced stage of

---

[8] Jacob Viner has made notable contributions to the scientific study of the interrelations of finance and diplomacy. See especially his articles, "Political Aspects of International Finance," *Journal of Business of the University of Chicago*, April and July, 1928; "International Finance and Balance of Power Diplomacy, 1880–1914" and "Peace as an Economic Problem" reprinted in his *International Economics* (Glencoe, Ill.: Free Press, 1951), pp. 49-85 and 247-267. Viner studied mainly the diplomatic aspects of loans to governments. As a student of his, I undertook at his suggestion a similar investigation of the political significance of foreign investments other than loans to governments, including investments for the development of business enterprises, mines, railroads, plantations, etc. This was published as: Eugene Staley, *War and the Private Investor: A Study in the Relations of International Politics and International Private Investment* (Garden City: Doubleday, 1935). See also in this field of study: Herbert Feis, *Europe, The World's Banker, 1870–1914* (New Haven: Yale University Press, 1930); William L. Langer, *The Diplomacy of Imperialism, 1890–1902* (New York: Knopf, 1935); R. G. Hawtrey, *Economic Aspects of Sovereignty* (London: Longmans, 1930; 2nd ed., 1952).

capitalist maturity and without any "surplus" capital pressing for investment abroad, expanded to the limits of their power. The Soviet Union, where no capitalism of any kind exists to exert pressures for expansion, has certainly shown a disposition to impose its rule on other peoples. Its trade and investment relations with the Soviet republics of Central Asia and with East European satellites are flagrant examples of just the sort of thing Communists call "economic imperialism" in capitalist countries.

On the other hand, the United States, at the height of its economic and military power, freed the Philippines, and its Point Four program—despite Communist propaganda efforts to picture it as "economic imperialism"—aids underdeveloped countries to become more independent. India and Pakistan have become self-governing and fully equal parts of the British Commonwealth of Nations. Indonesia is free from Dutch rule. Britain's African colonies are taking unprecedented steps toward self-rule. The mandate system of the League of Nations and the trustee system of the United Nations mark the advance of the idea of international responsibility for peoples requiring tutelage. Through the forum of the United Nations, small and weak countries are exercising a greater influence than before. Underdeveloped countries nowadays impose stringent requirements on foreign capital and enterprise; the days are past when local wishes can be brushed aside by outside "economic imperialists." Technical assistance is available to underdeveloped countries from the United States and from the United Nations and its specialized agencies, but only at their request, not by imposition.

All in all, and quite contrary to the Leninist view of the relation between advanced capitalism and imperialism, we are now in an epoch of "de-imperialism"—except for the rising imperialism of the Soviet Union and its Communist bloc!

3. It is an article of faith with Communists that the advanced industrial countries of the capitalist world depend on "exploitation" of less developed areas for their prosperity and that capitalist trade and investment pay off more or less in proportion as the other countries are kept poverty-stricken and "exploited." This is akin to Marx's false view that cap-

italists make the most profits when they pay the lowest wages to labor, because they get "surplus value" from the "exploitation" of underpaid labor. Modern, progressive capitalism, especially that of mid-twentieth-century America, operates on a quite contrary principle, namely, that high wages create mass purchasing power which makes possible a mass-production economy in which profits come from a large volume of efficient operations. Similarly, the accepted view in America today is that the best markets are in prosperous, technologically advanced, high-income countries. Poor countries are poor customers. Also, as for raw materials supplies, experience with such countries as Canada demonstrates that efficient, modernized methods of production using skilled and self-respecting labor in a country thoroughly capable of managing its own political and business affairs are at least as sound a way to get the raw materials of modern industry as the method of relying on low-paid, unskilled labor under foreign political and economic domination in a so-called "backward" country. The Communist dogma that advanced capitalist countries are vitally dependent for markets and raw materials on an "economic imperialism" that maintains poverty, backwardness, and political weakness in the underdeveloped areas will not stand rational examination.

Despite its falsity as a scientific theory, Lenin's doctrine of imperialism has a huge emotional appeal in underdeveloped countries. It touches on enough half-truths and provides enough easy answers on emotionally charged issues to serve as a convenient mythology and a dramatic framework for propaganda. Some of its main elements are accepted almost as self-evident truths even in anti-Communist circles in many underdeveloped countries. It brings to a focus and turns against the industrialized West a multitude of resentments stemming from unequal treatment and abuse by Western people in the past, and from today's flaming nationalisms and new awareness of poverty.

It is highly significant, as will be brought out later, that it was the "anti-imperialist" aspect of Communist doctrine which first interested young Chinese intellectuals in the early 1920's and produced the first converts who, in the person of Mao Tse-tung and others, provided leadership for a movement that was destined to conquer China thirty years later.[9]

By-passing the Capitalist Stage

As everywhere, Communists see the economic, social, and political problems of underdeveloped countries in terms of class struggle. But they hold that underdeveloped countries have a relatively primitive class structure, as did Western Europe before the rise of modern capitalism. For this reason, Communists formerly thought that these "backward" countries would have to go through a capitalist stage in order to evolve factories and a working class and to break down the old institutions—generally called "feudal" in Communist writings—before they would become ripe for proletarian revolution and be ready at length to adopt the "higher" forms of social relationship which Communists envisage. Now it is held that, largely because of the support which the Soviet Union can give to the Communist Party as the "vanguard of the proletariat" of these countries, they can skip the capitalist stage and proceed at once from pre-industrial society to revolutionary transformations under Communist leadership.

Communist doctrine holds that the growth of national self-consciousness and the achievement of national independence are the first order of business in the present stage of development of most of the underdeveloped countries. These "tasks" were performed earlier in the Western democracies under "bourgeois" guidance, along with capitalist development of the economy and establishment of parliamentary institutions and civil liberties. Nowadays, however, the historical forces making for nationalism and the enormous emotional drives behind the new nationalisms can, in the Communist view, be turned against Western capitalism. Communists, therefore, must at this stage ally themselves with "national liberation" movements.

Communist strategy sets up two main targets for the class struggle in underdeveloped countries: (1) foreign exploiters, the "imperialists"; and (2) domestic exploiters, principally landowners and related "feudal" or "semifeudal" classes,

[9] Benjamin I. Schwartz, cited, pp. 21-27.

since underdeveloped countries are overwhelmingly agricultural and rural. Featured targets in the first group are at one time and place the British, at others the Japanese, at others the French, the Dutch, and nowadays practically everywhere the Americans, who are pictured as either urging and directing the other "imperialists" or alternatively maneuvering to wrest power and profit from them. The domestic exploiters are both the absentee landlords and the more wealthy peasants who rent land or hire workers, together with local moneylenders. The Chinese Communist Party, for example, has from time to time set up arbitrary definitions by which to distinguish "rich peasants," "middle peasants," and "poor peasants," in order to intensify class consciousness and make it easier to manipulate one class against another for Communist purposes in the villages.

The Communist analysis of the social forces at work not only couples local with foreign "exploiters" but, playing up to the strong passions of nationalism, generally makes the "imperialist" the arch villain. Mao Tse-tung wrote in 1939 that the chief enemies of the Chinese revolution were "none other than imperialism and semi-feudalism, in other words, foreign bourgeoisie and the Chinese land-owning class, because these two classes are oppressing and retarding the development of the Chinese society. They conspire hand in hand to oppress the Chinese people; and as imperialistic oppressions are the severest, imperialists then are the most deadly enemy of the Chinese people." [10]

Once the Communist Party has seized and consolidated power in an underdeveloped country it is confronted (according to its doctrine and strategy) with an enormous task: the task of telescoping into a comparatively brief period of intense social transformation the numerous and profound changes in economic, social, and political structure and behavior which in the earlier industrialized countries had been accomplished during generations of gradual development. They must achieve not only those shifts in attitudes, skills, and habits which have characteristically been achieved

[10] Mao Tse-tung, *The Chinese Revolution and the Communist Party of China* (New York: Committee for a Democratic Far Eastern Policy, no publication date), p. 8. Mao's statement was written in 1939.

by "bourgeois-democratic" societies, but at the same time proceed with the vigorous promotion of transformations into the "higher" forms of social organization for which the Soviet Union is the model. The Chinese Communists under Mao, having consolidated their power over the mainland, have been proceeding with utmost vigor, according to accounts which filter out, with such "social tasks" as weakening the traditional hold of the Chinese family on the loyalties of its members, improving the network of roads and railroads and preparing for industrialization, building an efficient state apparatus and training the necessary "cadres" for all sorts of political and economic administration, breaking the traditions of private ownership in industry and commerce and substituting state-managed operation, and reorganizing agricultural and rural life with a view to the ultimate extension of collective and state farming systems. The problem of Communist leadership is to push the pace of these transformations as rapidly as possible, without arousing more opposition at any one time than can be successfully handled by the apparatus of propaganda and suppression. The theory of "New Democracy" is especially designed to meet this need for proceeding by stages. (See pages 140-141, Chapter 7.)

Underdeveloped Countries and Soviet World Revolution

It is not possible even to summarize here the enormous mass of doctrinal discussion, analysis of particular areas, and strategic directives which Communists have devoted to underdeveloped areas since Lenin and the Russian revolution, or to recount the successful and unsuccessful actions they have taken. Four propositions of utmost significance for this study stand out and will be briefly illustrated below. In the view of those who direct the world Communist movement:

1. Underdeveloped countries have become the weakest links in the world system of capitalism which it is the Communist aim to overthrow and to conquer.

2. Since these countries have very little modern industry, class conflicts of bourgeoisie and proletariat are not mature, and the revolutionary struggle is first and foremost for "na-

tional liberation," to throw off the political and economic yoke of the "capitalist imperialists." Communists should encourage and assist such struggles wherever they can be used as a means of weakening the capitalist enemy.

3. A determined Communist Party can seize power in a "backward" country and proceed directly to transform its society, skipping the stage of capitalism.

4. The resources of the underdeveloped countries, if they can be captured by the Communist movement, will bring an enormous and perhaps decisive shift in the strategic balance of forces, strengthening the Soviet Union and weakening the West for the final showdown.

In the doctrine of Lenin, Stalin, and Mao, revolution in one country is only a stage toward world revolution. The great "historical problem" of the Russian revolution, said Lenin, is "the necessity of calling forth an international revolution, of traversing the path from our strictly national revolution to the world revolution." [11] Stalin in his *Problems of Leninism*, which has long been and still remains one of the main textbooks for all faithful Communists, says:

The victory of Socialism in one country is not a self-sufficient task. The revolution which has been victorious in one country must regard itself not as a self-sufficient entity, but as an aid, a means *for* hastening the victory of the proletariat in all countries. For the victory of the revolution in one country, in the present case Russia, is . . . the beginning of and the groundwork for world revolution.[12]

In speeches and writings Mao has consistently spoken of the Chinese Communist revolution as part of a world movement. There can be no reasonable doubt that world revolution and world conquest are active aims of the leaders of the Communist movement. Policies of "socialism in one country" have to be regarded as temporary expedients for gathering power, and statements favoring "peaceful coexistence" of Communism and capitalism as maneuvers to throw the enemy off guard or to play for time.

[11] V. I. Lenin, *Selected Works* (New York: International Publishers, 1943), Vol. VII, p. 288.

[12] J. Stalin, *Problems of Leninism* (Moscow: Foreign Languages Publishing House, 11th ed., 1940), p. 113.

Lenin saw the great masses of people in the underdeveloped countries as potential allies in world revolution. In the "colonial" countries, he told the Communist International in 1921, ". . . millions and hundreds of millions, in fact the overwhelming majority of the population of the globe, are now coming forward as independent, active, revolutionary factors. It is perfectly clear that in the impending battles in the world revolution, the movement of the majority of the population of the globe, which at first is directed towards national liberation, will turn against capitalism and imperialism and will, perhaps, play a much more revolutionary part than we expect." [13]

The Sixth World Congress of the Communist International in 1928 gave particular attention to "the revolutionary movement in the colonies." Its report, constituting a guide to Communist forces all over the world, pictured the struggles against "imperialist slavery" as "a most powerful auxiliary force of the Socialist world revolution. The colonial countries at the present time constitute for world imperialism the most dangerous sector of their front." [14]

Short-Circuiting Historical Processes

The same report stressed the changed situation for the underdeveloped countries, brought about by the existence of a strong revolutionary center in the Soviet Union and a strong world Communist movement. Despite the immaturity of social relationships in these countries taken by themselves, this "creates for the toiling masses of the people of China, India and all other colonial and semi-colonial countries, the possibility of an independent, free, economic and cultural development, *avoiding the stage of the domination of the capitalist system* or even the development of capitalist relations in general." [15]

Normal historical processes can be shortened and the capitalist stage skipped, according to Communist theory, because

[13] *Selected Works,* cited, Vol. IX, pp. 228-229.
[14] *Theses on the Revolutionary Movement in the Colonies and Semi-Colonies,* resolution of the Sixth World Congress, Communist International, 1928, in *International Press Correspondence,* Vol. 8, No. 88, December 12, 1928, p. 1661.
[15] Same.

the Soviet Union exists. The Soviet Union serves, in Stalin's words, as an "open center of the world revolutionary movement" around which revolutionary movements even in countries that would otherwise not be ripe for a proletarian revolution can rally and organize. This gives Communism a doctrinal foundation for forcible Sovietization of underdeveloped countries.

Lenin's technique for seizure of power—a disciplined, revolutionary élite, the Communist Party, manipulating mass discontent—has been so perfected in its application to less developed countries that the "vanguard of the proletariat" can take over where practically no proletariat exists and then, *after* acquiring power, proceed to create industry and a proletariat as called for by Marxism. This is what happened in China where Mao got his mass support from peasants, not from city workers. The Soviet Union aids and foments such movements in underdeveloped countries in many ways: by a world-wide propaganda barrage, by sending trained revolutionaries, by bringing local leaders to the Soviet Union for revolutionary training, by supplying funds, and by brandishing in the background and on appropriate occasions the might of the Soviet Union and its satellites. It is clear from Soviet action in eastern and southeastern Europe, Korea, and from episodes in Spain, Greece, and Iran, that the only restraint on intervention to support Communist revolution is fear of starting a large-scale war. Soviet thinking does not hold that agitation, propaganda, and peaceful organization by themselves are enough to bring about a successful Communist revolution, and Soviet leaders have from the start visualized the use of military power created in one Communist country to support Communism elsewhere.

Strengthening Soviet Power

Not only can the Soviet Union and the Communist bloc aid revolutionary movements in underdeveloped countries, but revolutionary movements in underdeveloped countries can greatly strengthen the power position of the Soviet Union and the Communist bloc. Soviet power can be increased either by (1) subtracting from the resources of the capitalist enemy, or (2) adding to the resources of the Soviet bloc.

The first is accomplished to some degree by almost any civil disturbance, unrest, guerrilla activity, or colonial revolt which hampers production in mines, plantations, or factories, interrupts the flow of trade by which the industrial countries of the capitalist world acquire raw materials, or forces the "imperialist" power to engage in expensive military or police action which is also likely to antagonize local sentiment. Indo-China and Malaya are examples of Communist gains by this method.

It must be emphasized that Communist support of "national liberation" movements is for a definite, strategic, power purpose, and not because Communists believe in national independence. Stalin made this plain in his *Problems of Leninism:* "This does not mean, of course, that the proletariat must support *every* national movement, . . . support must be given to such national movements as tend to weaken, to overthrow imperialism. . . . The question of the rights of nations . . . is a part of the general problem of the proletarian revolution, subordinate to the whole . . ." [16] In plain language this means that Stalin regarded national independence movements as good where they weaken the non-Communist world and bad where they might weaken Soviet power.

While Soviet power can be strengthened *relatively* by any revolutionary movements which disorganize the relations between the underdeveloped countries and the industrially advanced countries of the non-Communist world, it is strengthened still more wherever Communist forces are successful in putting themselves at the head of a revolutionary movement, seizing power, and thus bringing a new satellite into the Soviet economic, political, and military system. In this manner underdeveloped countries can be transformed, in Stalin's phrase, "from a reserve of the imperialist bourgeoisie into a reserve of the revolutionary proletariat . . ." [17] This has been accomplished in eastern and southeastern Europe and in China. Such shifts from the non-Communist to the Communist world mean a loss to the former and a gain to the latter of (1) manpower, (2) raw materials, (3) strategic position, and

[16] J. Stalin, *Problems of Leninism*, cited, p. 52.
[17] Same.

(4) the important intangibles of power such as prestige and the desire of hesitant nations to join the winning side.

China's prodigal use of manpower on behalf of world Communist aims in Korea illustrates the Soviet profit in the manpower field as a result of the accession of an underdeveloped country to its bloc.

With respect to raw materials, Communist China has undoubtedly strengthened the Soviet strategic position in such minerals as antimony and tungsten. The Soviet bloc would be greatly benefited from a military viewpoint if it could acquire the tin, rubber, and petroleum of Indo-China, Malaya, Indonesia, and adjacent areas, or the oil of Iran. It is thought by some that the Soviet decision to precipitate a coup in Czechoslovakia in 1948 was decisively influenced by the important uranium resources in that country.

Strategic position gives many underdeveloped countries enormous importance in the struggle of the Soviet Union for world power. Control of Egypt, for example, or internal disturbances there which might interfere with traffic in the Suez Canal, would obviously be greatly to the Kremlin's advantage.

As for the intangibles of power, a shift from the non-Communist to the Communist world of a great country like India, or successively of a group of countries like Indo-China, Indonesia, Thailand, and Burma, coming on top of the Communist success in China, would promote a "wave of the future" psychology which Soviet propagandists could use very effectively.

CONCLUSIONS

An essential part of Communist strategy for world conquest is to nourish the idea of inevitable class conflict not only *within* nations, as Marxists have always done, but also as *between* nations at different levels of economic development. Since Lenin, Communists have lost no opportunity to portray the underdeveloped countries as "exploited" and the non-Communist industrial countries as "exploiters"—"capitalist-imperialist exploiters." They see an inevitable "contradiction" and a fatal weakness in the fact that the non-Communist world contains poverty-stricken nations along with wealthy nations. This is analogous to the fatal weakness that Marx thought he saw in the contrast of rich and poor people within the countries of nineteenth-century capitalism and the allegedly inevitable tendency for this contrast to increase.

Marx's forecast of doom for the advanced capitalist countries failed because the system proved more adaptive than he had thought. These countries remedied some of their most serious social weaknesses by democratic, evolutionary means. The position of the poor improved because of advances in technology, expansion in trade, voluntary population control, general education, and the wider distribution of income, respect, and power brought about by the working in a free society of such institutions as the right to vote and the right to organize trade unions.

The great question now is: Can the same sort of thing happen on a world scale? Can transformations take place in underdeveloped countries so that they become the abodes, not of poverty, misery, and despair shameful to the modern world, but of progressive, hopeful, educated, healthy, and prosperous people? Can the remnants of the colonial system and the scars of resentment from the rule of one people over another be superseded by international aid and mutual respect and cooperation? Can such momentous transformations take place along with progress in political democracy and personal freedom? Can they take place rapidly enough so that discontented peoples do not turn in despair to the Communist nostrum? Can they take place at the same time that the non-Communist world maintains a military defense adequate to discourage Communist strategists from trying to expand their system by armed force?

If the answer to these questions is "no," then the tide of Communist totalitarianism and the new form of imperialism centering in Moscow and Peking may flood very far indeed. By engulfing one after another of the less developed countries the world Communist movement could eventually subject the United States and the other economically advanced countries of Western civilization to mounting pressure until perhaps it conquered them by encirclement and isolation where other means have failed. On the other hand, achievement of genuine economic and social advance in the underdeveloped countries, with the aid and cooperation of the economically advanced countries of the non-Communist world, would give enormous support to the strength and prestige of free institutions everywhere.

Chapter 7

COMMUNIST TACTICS AND PROPAGANDA IN UNDERDEVELOPED AREAS

The Communist aim is power, total power. This is the key to understanding Communist strategy and tactics in underdeveloped countries, as elsewhere. The power of the Soviet Union comes first, because that is regarded as the great bastion for Communist movements everywhere. Sometimes the prospects of a local Communist party have to be sacrificed for the sake of overriding Soviet interests. For example, the Communist Party of India took a great loss in prestige by suspending its anti-British "national liberation" line and advocating cooperation in the war effort after 1941, because the Soviet Union was for the time being an ally of Britain. Except for this qualification, the aim of Communist parties in underdeveloped countries is seizure of power, by whatever means may be most effective.

Technique for Seizing Power

For this reason, Communist demands and promises are *tactical*, not programmatic. That is, they indicate what the Party thinks will help it win power in a given situation, not what it intends to do if it gets power. An ordinary political party in the democratic tradition puts forward its program and tries to win adherents on that basis. Not so a revolutionary party. The revolution, meaning seizure of power by the Communist Party, is the focus of efforts. What looks like a substantive program to the uninitiated—demands for national independence, land reform, tax changes, rights of racial and cultural minorities, and so on—are in the view of Communist Party leaders merely the tactics most likely to help them gain power. The hard core of insiders, the "vanguard," knows the long-term aims. The stated program and the agitational "line" of the moment are the bait deemed most effective to bring these manipulators the mass backing they need.

The historic contribution of Lenin, which made modern Communism out of Marxism, was a technique of seizing power. The Leninist formula is:

1. A dedicated, disciplined, trained, élite corps of professional and semiprofessional revolutionaries—the Party.

2. Mass support, rallied around any popular discontent, organized, cemented, and manipulated by the Party for its purposes.

Mao Tse-tung added to this formula a number of elements especially designed for the most underdeveloped countries, like China. The success of the Chinese Communist Party has given his methods enormous prestige among Communists in other underdeveloped areas, especially in Asia. Mao's most important innovations are these:

1. Building up to seizure of power from a purely peasant base. Communists had previously held that city workers, the proletariat, would provide the motive power for their revolution. In the 1920's Chinese Communists under Kremlin guidance failed dismally in their efforts to build up Party strength around the workers of the few Chinese cities where there were modern industries. Then Mao, in an isolated rural area, began to have success playing on peasant grievances and building up a Party army and a state within a state. Two decades later it was a rurally based Communist movement and a peasant army which finally conquered the cities and for the first time annexed a "proletariat" in the traditional Marxist sense of that term. This has measureless practical implications for the future of other underdeveloped countries, since peasants form the great bulk of their populations.

2. Establishing a territorial base, with a Party army and a Communist state within a state. Mao set up a Red Army and a Chinese Soviet in an inaccessible part of south-central China. In the 1930's the armies of Chiang Kai-shek at length forced him to shift, by the famous "long march" over a route of thousands of miles, to the Yenan region in northwest

China. From here the Chinese Communists, now calling their army a "People's Army" and their government a "People's Government," gradually extended their military and civil power, skillfully using guerrilla tactics both against the Japanese during the war with Japan and against the Nationalist government of China. A combination of military and political warfare enabled them to spread the Communist zone like a spot of oil until it covered all the mainland of China.

3. A lengthened version of united front tactics known as "New Democracy." This was useful to disarm opposition during the rise to power, and continues to be valuable during the period of consolidation of power and stage-by-stage remolding of Chinese society. The device is so important, especially in view of signs that we may be entering a period when the Communist tactical line throughout the world will be "softer," that we shall return to it later in this chapter.

The Zigzag Path

In planning their mass manipulations, Communist strategists try to analyze the social forces, internal and external, operating in a given region or country at a given time. Their thinking is "dialectical." That is, they think in terms of stages of revolutionary development, each demanding different actions and different agitational slogans. It is important that the West and non-Communist leaders in underdeveloped countries should understand this and realize that it makes Communist methods extremely flexible while their end remains undeviatingly the same: seizure of total power.

The greatest danger to the unwary comes in those situations where the Communists find it expedient to talk of mutual accommodation, united fronts, and peaceful coexistence of Communism and capitalism. There are indications today that a new, more conciliatory phase may be in the making. It would be shortsighted to regard this as a sign of lessening danger of Communist conquest in underdeveloped countries.

Lenin and Stalin time and again taught their followers that they must move forward whenever possible but recognize that there are times when resistance will develop and when the best expedient is to hold all gains and appear to subside for a while so that resistance will weaken, and then move forward again. Said Lenin, "The strictest loyalty to the ideas of Communism must be combined with the ability to make all the necessary practical compromises, to 'tack,' to make agreements, zigzags, retreats, and so on . . ." [1] Again, "The task of a truly revolutionary party is . . . to be able *throughout all compromises,* when they are unavoidable, to remain true to its revolutionary purpose." [2] Stalin has added: "It is not for nothing that the proverb says 'An obliging bear is more dangerous than an enemy.' " [3]

WAYS TO POWER

Exploitation of Every Conflict

"The Party must utilize every conflict, however insignificant, between the workers and the capitalists in the factories, between the peasants and the landlords in the villages, between the soldiers and the officers in the army, deepening and sharpening these class clashes in order to mobilize the widest masses of workers and peasants and to win them over to its side." This directive from the Sixth Congress of the Comintern, 1928, is tirelessly applied by Communists in underdeveloped countries today. They use to the nth degree the old political principle that it is generally easier to rouse mass support against something than for something, and particularly against some person or group on whom responsibility can be pinned for popular woes.

They take pains to find out what local people are most discontented about. Then they blame all these evils on the existing government and its Western "imperialist" friends and promise that the victory of Communism will remedy matters. In Thailand an embassy of the Soviet Union was established in 1948 with a staff of sixty, subsequently increased to some two hundred. One of their main occupations seemed to be to find out grievances and aspirations, through persons familiar with local language and customs. This knowledge was used to guide the apparatus of propa-

---

1 Lenin, *Selected Works,* cited, Vol. X, p. 138.
2 Same, Vol. VI, p. 208.
3 J. Stalin, *Problems of Leninism,* cited, p. 254.

ganda and agitation at their command, including, of course, local Communists and groups they might be able to infiltrate or influence.[4]

In the Middle East, Justice William O. Douglas observed the Communist appeal in travels which took him to cities, villages, and remote tribal areas. Communist propaganda exploits the news of the day, he says, charges Britain and the United States with designs on every nation in the region, represents the Soviets as the forces of good, America and Britain and all non-Communist governments as the forces of evil, and identifies Communism with every minority cause and every nationalist ambition. The atheistic side of Communism is played down among these very religious peoples, so much so that some who preach Communism by word of mouth even identify it with the Koran. Local Communists do not talk about the system they hope to install, but purport to stand only for honesty in government, land reform, rationing of food, elimination of unemployment, education for the masses, and a rising level of living.[5]

Almost any situation of conflict and discontent can be turned to account by the Communists. In India they not only try to use the passions of nationalism against the West but also the passions of sectionalism against the Nehru government. The issue of "linguistic states" arouses deep feelings and creates almost insoluble problems for the government, so the Communist Party's manifesto promises not only to set up such units but to grant them "wide powers including the right of self-determination, and create a united India by voluntary consent."[6] We shall note the Communist record on self-determination in the next chapter.

In Africa, of course, the burning issue of racial conflict is made to order for Communist manipulation. This is not to say that Communists are the cause of unrest in Africa, but they are trying to inject their leadership and give dissatisfactions and resentments a revolutionary turn.

Of all Communist agitational themes in underdeveloped

[4] See the article by Anthony E. Sokol, "American Dilemmas in Southeast Asia," *Pacific Spectator*, Spring, 1952, pp. 225-242.

[5] William O. Douglas, cited, pp. 1-5.

[6] *Indian Press Digests*, Vol. I, No. 1, March, 1952, pp. 103-106.

countries, the most universal and insistent, by far, are appeals to (1) sentiments of nationalism against the West, and (2) agrarian discontent against landowners and governments. This reflects Communist analysis which holds that the revolutionary stage in which most underdeveloped countries find themselves is one of revolt against "imperialism" and "feudalism."

The Anti-Imperialist, National-Liberation Theme

Closing the nineteenth congress of the All-Union Communist Party in 1952, Stalin once more called upon Communist parties throughout the world to pick up "the banner of national independence and national sovereignty," which he said the bourgeoisie had thrown overboard.[7]

Communists have profited by nationalist resentment in Iran against the Anglo-Iranian Oil Company, helping to whip it into a frenzy and to turn it also against America. In Indo-China the Communist-led Vietminh got most of its political strength from espousing demands for faster progress toward national freedom than the French were willing to grant. Communist leaders in North Africa and in other African areas under European rule obviously hope that in time they will be able to put themselves at the head of similar revolts. In Chile and Guatemala Communists have directed much of their agitation against foreign enterprises, mainly North American, which bulk large in the economies of these countries.

The anti-imperialist theme was a major factor in the origin and in the triumph of the second most important Communist party in the world. It is most significant that, as Benjamin Schwartz brings out in *Chinese Communism and the Rise of Mao,*[8] the Chinese Party was founded by men who became Communist largely out of nationalist reaction against the treatment of China by the Great Powers. Communism took root in China in the early 1920's with the conversion of Li Ta-chao and Ch'en Tu-hsiu. These two Chinese professors carried with them into the Communist camp a whole host of students, many of whom later became promi-

---

[7] *New York Times,* October 15, 1952.
[8] Benjamin I. Schwartz, cited.

nent. Among them was Mao Tse-tung, who at that time lived on the fringes of academic life as a library employee of Li. The crucial period in their conversion was 1919–1920, the period of the "May 4th movement" in which the fires of nationalism smoldering among China's student elements finally burst into flame. The weakness of the Chinese government in the face of pressure from Japan and the betrayal of Wilsonian idealism at the Versailles Peace Conference, especially in the matter of Shantung, were sparks which ignited boycotts and demonstrations. The fact that Lenin had an interpretation of imperialism which provided a starkly melodramatic explanation of the humiliating situation in which countries like China found themselves appealed strongly to the politically articulate intelligentsia. It brought Li, Ch'en, and the other intellectual founders of Chinese Communism into the Party. And, Schwartz adds, acceptance of the Leninist theory became so widespread in China that, even in circles far removed from the Communist Party, wherever imperialism was discussed the Leninist interpretation came to be taken for granted.[9]

Anti-imperialism was given top billing by the Chinese Communist leaders in the course of their Party's rise to power. We have already quoted Mao on the subject (page 118). In their judgment, it must have been an effective slogan. Its use may be illustrated from a propaganda booklet prepared by a representative of the Comintern in China and issued in 1937. The booklet leads off with anti-imperialism:

China is a semi-colonial country, and it is this that determines her position. The international imperialists are rending the living body of China and trampling upon the national sentiments of this great people. The international imperialists are subjecting the vast millions of the Chinese toilers to ruthless exploitation and are dooming them to poverty and starvation.

It goes on to say that the "international imperialists" have seized the key economic positions in China, including the important factories, railroads, and water and air transport

[9] "Whether living experience will ever teach the Chinese Communists to doubt the Leninist theory that imperialism is a phenomenon peculiar to a certain stage of 'capitalism' is a question which only the future and their own interests can decide." Same, p. 204.

systems. They control the financial life of the country, the customs and the salt monopoly. They rule over the so-called leased territories wrested from China by force. They are masters in the foreign concessions and settlements. They maintain their garrisons on Chinese soil. They enforce the system of extraterritoriality under which foreigners are not subject to Chinese law. The masses of the Chinese people are being made into nationally degraded, semicolonial slaves. High rents to the landlords, the burden of military imposts and taxation, and high usurer's interest are then connected to "imperialist" bondage and exploitation. The Communist Party of China is presented as the leader of the "national liberation movement" for "the complete economic and political independence of their country." [10]

It hardly need be added that the Communists' devotion to slogans of nationalism and their readiness to attack any outside political or economic influence as imperialism are strictly limited to non-Communist countries. National independence, like freedom of speech, fair trials, and free elections, are, in the Communist view, bourgeois ideals which Communists can and should make into agitational weapons where it serves their interest in the period of struggle for power. But once the Communist Party has firm control, the situation passes into a new historical stage where all such bourgeois ideas are counterrevolutionary and notions of local self-determination on vital matters of politics and economics are ruthlessly suppressed as "nationalist deviations."

The Agrarian Reform Theme

Second only to the national-liberation, anti-imperialist theme in Communist agitation in underdeveloped countries is the theme of land reform, coupled with attacks against landlords, moneylenders, middlemen, and the other traditional targets of resentment in a peasant, village economy.

In the underdeveloped countries of Asia, the Middle East, Africa, and Latin America the overwhelming majority of the people, as many as four-fifths of them, live on the land. Land

[10] P. Miff, *Heroic China: Fifteen Years of the Communist Party of China* (New York: Workers Library Publishers, 1937), pp. 5-8.

ownership is not only a source of income; particularly where it has become concentrated it is also the main basis for political power and social prestige. Social tensions and discontents generally center on the desire to own land, on the share of the crop taken by the landlord, or on the bondage of usury into which peasants fall where rates on crop loans run as high as 100 percent a year or even more, as happens in some areas. The rural social structure in many underdeveloped countries is undergoing changes roughly corresponding to those which took place in Western Europe from the end of the Middle Ages to the middle of the nineteenth century. This is what Communists mean when their strategic directives call for leading the struggle against "feudal and semi-feudal" conditions.

In India "Land to the Tiller" is one of the main Communist slogans. The Party demands immediate confiscation and redistribution rather than the reform measures of the Nehru government, which proceed gradually by land purchase. In the Philippines, the abuses of absentee landlordism and other peasant discontents have been the mainstay of the Communist-led Hukbalahap movement. In Iran, Egypt, and throughout the Middle East Communists continually play on the miseries of the peasants, emphasizing the startling contrast between their abject poverty and the ostentatious luxury of the small clique of landowning families that, at least until lately, have had undisputed rule. In Guatemala, Communist agitation and advice has been apparent in local land reform programs.

We have already noted that in China, proving ground for so much of Communist policy in underdeveloped areas, Mao was able to use agrarian discontent to build the peasant mass support on which the Communist Party at length rose to power. The failure of the Nationalist government to take effective measures to meet demands for agrarian reform, until far too late, was one of the main sources of its weakness in the face of the Communist political and military attack. Mao stated his agrarian strategy in 1934 as: "to depend upon the hired farm hands and poor peasants, to ally with the middle peasants, to check the rich peasants, and to annihilate the landlords." [11] Later, when circumstances called for a united front against Japan, the flexibility of Communist tactics showed itself in a much more tolerant attitude toward "class enemies," and there were many reassuring stories out of Yenan about the way in which all patriotic persons, even landlords, were working together. Still later, when the Communists had completed their conquest of the mainland, the class struggle was intensified once more in the villages. But Mao has been more astute and gradual than were the Russian Communists in his reshaping of agriculture and rural life.

Just as the "national liberation" appeal in the mouths of Communists is fundamentally fraudulent, because their ultimate program is antinationalist, so their slogan of "Land for the Tillers" is a transitional device only, designed to gain power. It is reported—from India, for example—that information filtering through about collectivization in Russia and Eastern Europe has had a disquieting effect on peasant leaders and is to some extent undermining the Communist Party's influence with rural people.

Insurrection and a People's Army

Military and political means are united in Communist practice. Their tactics, even where the Party makes a vigorous parliamentary fight, are normally directed to preparing the way for insurrection.

Success in China has given great prestige to an expedient particularly adapted to underdeveloped countries having weak governments and poor communication to remote or inaccessible areas. This is the building of a regional military base with a Communist state within a state supported by its own Red Army or "People's Army." Communist leaders have become experts in guerrilla tactics, and technical knowledge in this field gained in one country is quickly transmitted to the Communist parties of other countries.

Communist guerrilla forces nearly succeeded in taking over Greece; only large amounts of American military equip-

[11] *Report to the Second All-China Soviet Congress,* January 22, 1934, as quoted in Conrad Brandt, Benjamin Schwartz, and John K. Fairbank, *A Documentary History of Chinese Communism* (Cambridge: Harvard University Press, 1952), p. 235.

ment and technical and economic aid finally turned the tide against them. A Communist-led peasant uprising in the Philippines at the end of World War II made a strong bid to convert the war against the Japanese into a civil war. In Indo-China the Communist-led Vietminh has succeeded in ruling a portion of the country and in carrying on a bitter military and political war. Communist-led guerrilla bands in Malaya, making sallies from jungle fastnesses, kept the country for years in a general state of insecurity and demoralization. By terrorizing workers on estates and in mines, they endeavored to interrupt the production of rubber, tin, and other materials supplied to the West. In Burma, three separate Communist groups, the strongest loyal to Moscow and one of the others passing as "Trotskyite," were at one time holed up in the jungles or mountains, carrying on agitation against the government and raiding communications.

In India at one period Communists seized local power in several areas, established camps and formed guerrilla detachments, took over village organizations, expropriated landlords, and had high hopes of making Hyderabad an "Indian Yenan" from which to march on New Delhi. These hopes were dashed in the autumn of 1948 when the government drove the Communists out of Hyderabad City.[12]

Sabotaging Parliamentary Democracy and Democratic Reform

A fundamental aim of all Communist tactics is to make it appear that Communist rule is the only alternative to existing bad conditions. If they succeed in this, they have won more than half the battle.

In China, when a progressive, patriotic Chinese became fed up with the inefficiency and corruption of the Nationalist government he was likely to feel that he had no other place to turn than to the Communist camp. There was no strong democratic opposition party, only the revolutionary alternative offered by the Communists. Ironically, even evils which are many times worse under a Communist regime may make converts for them. For example, violations of civil liberties and abuses by the Nationalist government's secret police led

[12] Ruth Fischer, "The Indian Communist Party," *Far Eastern Survey*, June, 1953, p. 81.

to incidents in Chinese universities which made many intellectuals willing to cooperate passively, at least, with the
Communists.

While Communists magnify and denounce every unpopular or corrupt or inefficient action of non-Communist governments in underdeveloped countries, they also do their
utmost to prevent these governments from acting effectively,
and they especially try to sabotage reforms. They know that
democratic reform is the greatest enemy of revolution. When
the reform-minded Shah of Iran undertook a large program
of land distribution, thus confronting one of the basic evils
of Iran, obstacles were put in his way both by the big landowners and by the Communists. The latter advised the peasants not to take land on the proposed twenty-five-year payment plan in the Shah's program, because under Communist
leadership they would soon get it for nothing.[13]

When Communists succeed in getting elected to legislative bodies in non-Communist underdeveloped countries,
they act in the manner directed by the long-standing instruc-
tions of the French Communist Party: "Those elected must
make purely demonstrative proposals, conceived not with a
view to their adoption, but for propaganda and agitation."[14]
They are adept at tactics designed to sabotage the legislative
process and generally to impede the working of parliamentary democracy. Newly-established representative governments such as that of India face enormous problems with
scanty resources in money, personnel, and tradition. The
Communists contrive, by injecting confusion and distraction
and by combining with any dissident faction, to make these
problems even more difficult. We have mentioned the passionate issue of "linguistic states." In the spring of 1952 a
small group of three Communist members in the state legislature of Patiala and Punjab States Union was able to bring
about the fall of the Congress Party ministry by joining with
the Akali Party, a Sikh faction that wants a separate province
speaking the Punjabi language. The same technique was be-

[13] See the illuminating dispatches by Albion Ross to the *New York Times*,
especially January 28 and July 13, 1952.
[14] Jean-Marie Domenach, "The French Communist Party," in Einaudi,
Domenach, and Garosci, cited, p. 120.

ing applied in the Madras state legislature where another united front also threatened to outnumber the majority party.[15]

Communists are often aided by the weakness or malfeasance of governments in power. It is easy to sit outside, however, and criticize. It is extremely difficult for the governments of underdeveloped countries, especially those that are relatively new, inexperienced, and lacking in resources, to meet the expertly calculated disruptive tactics that Communist groups are well schooled in using.

THE TACTICS OF THE UNITED FRONT

Temporary alliance with other groups and parties is a standard technique for Communists on the road to total power. Such alliances do not represent a genuine attempt on their part to establish a common will by a mutual process of give and take. They are not democrats imbued with the idea of consensus. Their alliances are always maneuvers along the necessarily zigzag path toward the unchangeable revolutionary goal of absolute power for the Party.

At some times and places it seems to the Party leadership that their ends are best served by a policy of bold and unremitting attack. In such circumstances they denounce in the most vituperative terms all non-Communist leaders and parties, especially parties of economic and social reform. Then the world situation or the local situation may change, or the interpretation of it by high Communist authority changes, and the Party may decide that it is time for a temporary relaxation of pressure. Such a maneuver is designed to throw the "enemy" off guard, to check the military, political, or economic unification of anti-Communist groups or nations, and to permit quiet preparation for the next thrust when some crisis or confusion or other weakness of the opposition offers a favorable opportunity. In such a phase of Party policy, Communists and their friends will proclaim their undying devotion to "united front" cooperation among all "progressive" groups. They will seek alliance with non-Communist reform movements, though the hard-core Communists still privately regard democratic re-

[15] *New York Times*, April 19, 1952.

formers as their deadliest enemies, since reform undermines revolution. However, by demanding more than can be accomplished and by insinuating Party "cadres" into positions of leadership, they hope to be able to capture nonrevolutionary reform movements and divert them to revolutionary purposes.

From 1947–48 through 1952 the tough, hard-driving policy seemed to be in the ascendant. Recently, even before the death of Stalin and still more clearly since, there have been signs of a major shift toward the softer policy and the united front maneuvers that served Communist purposes in the 1930's and early 1940's. As early as the fall of 1952 a new "national front" policy was reported from Indonesia under which Communists were seeking to spread their influence through a broader association with non-Communist groups and individuals, "shunning provocative independent activity, attempting to play the role of patriotic nationalists and social reformers." [16] The danger of ultimate Communist conquest may well be made greater in Indonesia, and in such other crucial countries as India, if provocative methods which have tended to consolidate the opposition to Communism give way to the united front tactics of deception. There is some ground for hope that ruses which have been used repeatedly in various countries may have lost some of their power to mislead. But people are often not well informed on what has happened abroad. That is why it is so important that there should be a realistic understanding of Communist doctrine, strategy, and tactics among the leaders both of underdeveloped countries and of the Western world, and it is one reason why I am devoting so much attention to the subject in this book.

"New Democracy"—Mao's Contribution

The Indian Communist Party has announced that its aim is to set up a government of "democratic parties, groups and individuals, representing workers, peasants, the middle classes and national capitalists . . ." [17] Ho Chi Minh's Com-

[16] *New York Times*, September 26, 1952, dispatch from Jakarta by Tillman Durdin.
[17] *Indian Press Digests*, Vol. I, No. 1, March, 1952, p. 103.

munist-dominated Vietminh in Indo-China claims to be a national united front comprising all classes, parties, and races banded together to oust the French oppressors. Class warfare and the transformation of society on Communist lines are postponed until later. Meanwhile, "the national bourgeoisie must be encouraged, assisted and guided in their undertakings, so as to contribute to the development of the national economy. The right of the patriotic land-lords to collect rent in accordance with the law must be encouraged." [18]

This is the application in other countries of Mao's policy of "New Democracy." Mao used united front maneuvers with great effect in winning China for Communism. He also extended the united front idea into a theory of *stages* in class struggle particularly designed for underdeveloped countries. This strategic concept makes allowance for the fact that Communists in underdeveloped countries are likely to find it expedient to ally themselves over a considerable period of time—but still temporarily—with nonproletarian classes. Communists may even gain by allying themselves with some elements of the local bourgeoisie and other class enemies, in order to concentrate on foreign "imperialists" and consolidate their own power.

The New Democracy idea has great advantages: (1) It lulls to sleep many potential opposition elements, future victims, during the period of conquest of power. Also, it bemuses opinion abroad, which was strikingly true of much American opinion respecting Chinese Communism some years ago and continues to be true of much opinion in India and other parts of Asia even today. (2) In the period of con-solidation of power, when the Communist parties are carry-ing out the enormous "tasks" of social transformation that they set for themselves where they acquire power, the New Democracy idea lets the job be undertaken in successive steps, without arousing too much opposition at one time. It encourages private production to continue until the Com-munist leadership is prepared with its plans for state pro-duction and is ready to liquidate the old system.

[18] Quoted by Morris Watnick, "The Appeal of Communism to the Under-developed Peoples," in Bert F. Hoselitz, cited, p. 170.

Mao expounded his ideas in 1940 in his tract, *On the New Democracy*. The advanced form of Soviet proletarian dictatorship will be established ultimately, but during a certain historical period it is not practicable for the "colonial and semi-colonial" countries, he said. The existence of the Soviet Union makes it possible for the bourgeois revolution to take place in these countries under the auspices of the proletariat (meaning the Communist Party). The "new democratic republic" is the political form appropriate to this transition period. It is necessary, but definitely transitional, therefore temporary.

Such a new democratic republic differs, on the one hand, from the old, western-type bourgeois-democratic republics that are under the dictatorship of the bourgeoisie; that kind of republic is out of date; it differs, on the other hand, from the newest, Soviet-style republic, which is under proletarian dictatorship. This kind of republic has already arisen in the Soviet Union and will be established in every country. It will no doubt be the final form of control for the completion of the nation and of government power in all progressive countries. Nevertheless, in a certain historical period, the Soviet-style republic cannot be fittingly put into practice in colonial and semi-colonial countries, the state form of which must be of a third form, namely, that of the new democratic republic. Being the state form of a certain historical period, it is a transitional form; but it is all the same an inevitable and necessary form of state.[19]

In the early 1930's Mao set up a Soviet in the Communist-controlled region of China. Later this was superseded by the broader, "new democratic" form of a People's Assembly. This body included not only Communists but also representatives of other parties, and at times even landlords and private businessmen were permitted in it. During the Yenan period in World War II the famous system of "thirds" prevailed by which the Communist Party voluntarily restricted the number of its own members in the People's Assembly to one-third of the total. This disarmed democratic opposition and made excellent propaganda among people abroad who were not yet well acquainted with Communist methods.

[19] Mao Tse-tung, "On the New Democracy" (January 19, 1940), in Brandt, Schwartz, and Fairbank, cited, p. 267.

But it did not risk any loss of substantial control, for fundamental decisions were made in any case by the Communist Party machinery, not by the apparent machinery of government.

The exposition of New Democracy by Communist leaders is couched in terms which are likely to have a reassuring meaning to non-Communists unfamiliar with the jargon of the movement, especially to wishful thinkers who are quick to read their own ideals of social improvement and their own interpretations of the length of the "transitional" period into Communist pronouncements. But the basic strategy and the double meanings are well understood by the hard core of party workers.

An example is Mao's explanation of the meaning of dictatorship in the *Dictatorship of the People's Democracy* (1949). Experience shows, he says, that for China to get ahead *reactionaries* must be deprived of the right to voice their opinion. Only *the people* will have the right to voice their opinions. Who are the people? At the current stage in China, says Mao, they are the working class, the peasant class, the petty bourgeoisie and the national bourgeoisie, under the leadership of the working class and the Communist Party. The reactionaries, the "lackeys of imperialism," are the landlord class, the bureaucratic capitalist class, and the Kuomintang. Dictatorship is necessary in order to crush the reactionaries, but "the democratic system must be realized among the people, granting them freedom of speech, assembly, and association," and also the right to vote. Since the Communist Party defines from time to time "the people" and determines whether any particular individual is one of the people or a "reactionary," and since freedom of speech, assembly, association, and the right to vote under a Communist regime consist only in freedom to support the plans of the regime, Mao's formula disguises despotism in the verbal trappings of democracy.

Brandt, Schwartz, and Fairbank in their *Documentary History of Chinese Communism* say that in the realm of political power the theories of the New Democracy and even of the People's Democratic Dictatorship seem no longer to correspond to any reality in Communist China. "In the realm of economic relations, however, they still reflect the régime's policy of maintaining private property in land and a sector of privately owned industry. We have every reason to credit Mao's sincerity when he tells us that in view of China's feeble industrial development, China must still 'utilize all urban and rural factors of capitalism which are beneficial.' " This is analogous to a phase in the history of the Soviet Union. Under Lenin's New Economic Policy (1921–27) the Communist Party "monopolized political power but granted the peasantry and the nepmen a certain limited economic function." [20]

THE PARTY LINE ON INTERNATIONAL DEVELOPMENT AID

In the United Nations

The Soviet Union joined in the unanimous vote of the United Nations General Assembly (November 16, 1949) which authorized an Expanded Program of Technical Assistance. Its representative warned, however, that differing concepts of what constitutes technical aid lay behind the unanimity, and that it remained to be seen which concepts would triumph.

On the proposal of the United States, the United Nations program has been financed by voluntary pledges of member nations, in addition to their regular contributions to the organization. The United States has contributed approximately 60 percent of the total. The Soviet Union and the other Communist countries made no pledge or contribution in the early years of the program. They did, however, use the debates on development problems to offer a great deal of advice to underdeveloped countries, to attack the motives of the United States and other Western countries, and to reiterate the standard Communist propaganda themes.

In a meeting of the Economic and Social Council on July 15, 1953, the Soviet delegate offered a contribution of four million rubles—the equivalent of one million dollars at the official rate of exchange—to the U.N. Technical Assistance Program. He also pointedly said that the offer included Soviet experts. The most obvious use of a ruble contribution

[20] Same, p. 448.

would be to pay their salaries. If one could assume that this offer represents a change of heart—a genuine concern to help underdeveloped countries advance in ways of their own choice and a willingness to cooperate in the true spirit of United Nations aid—then it might signal the dawn of a better era in international affairs. Everything we know of Communist strategy and tactics warns us, however, that, pending overwhelming proof to the contrary, the offer of participation in technical assistance has to be regarded as another maneuver, a "peace offensive" calculated to confuse the opponents of Communism, to place Communist technicians in underdeveloped countries, and ultimately to help achieve the Communist aim of complete power. Whether by astute timing or by accident, the Soviet offer of aid coincided with a trend in Congress which sharply reduced the American contribution to the United Nations program.

The Soviet Union is not a member of most of the specialized agencies of the United Nations which, in their regular activities or as part of the U.N. expanded program of technical assistance, aid underdeveloped countries. Thus, it contributes nothing through the International Bank or the Monetary Fund, the Food and Agriculture Organization, the International Labor Organization, UNESCO, or the World Health Organization.

In United Nations debates on economic development the major aims of the Communist bloc have been to show that the Soviet Union is the true friend of the underdeveloped countries and to portray the United States and the Western nations as imperialist exploiters who subordinate the interests of the poorer countries to their own greedy and aggressive ambitions. The Communists profess great concern for the independence and well-being of the underdeveloped countries and offer many observations, among which the following themes are typical:

1. Independence. In order to be independent of the economic, political, and military pressures of the "imperialists," underdeveloped countries must control their own resources and bring about speedy industrialization. Their great danger

is from the interference of the Western powers, particularly the United States.

2. *Foreign capital.* Foreign capital can, no doubt, be used for economic development, but it is essential to guard against "exploitation" and loss of independence. Hence strong restrictions on private foreign investors are urged.

3. *Local capital.* Underdeveloped countries should mobilize local resources by redistributing the national income and controlling their internal economies and foreign transactions.

4. *Industrialization.* Industrialization is practically synonymous with economic development and is necessary to the achievement of economic and political independence. Heavy industry, in particular, is the key to the economic development of underdeveloped countries.

5. *Improvement of agriculture.* Rural reforms, and especially land reform, are necessary to bring more equal distribution of the benefits of economic development and to promote well-being.

6. *Soviet assistance.* The spokesmen of Eastern European satellites have told United Nations bodies of the splendid technical assistance they get from the Soviet Union. Even the representatives of Czechoslovakia, a country generally considered at least as advanced technically as Russia, have joined in this.

The speeches of the Soviet bloc in the United Nations attribute United States support of international aid programs and its own Point Four program to such motives as:

1. A desire for taking over the underdeveloped countries as "de facto colonies."

2. A desire for strategic raw materials and military bases, as part of a "warmongering" policy.

3. A desire to prevent the underdeveloped countries from industrializing, for fear of their competition with American industries, and in order to keep these countries as economic dependencies supplying raw materials to the United States.

4. A desire to find adequate markets and outlets for investment capital, in a futile effort to escape the inevitable breakdown of capitalism.

5. A desire for exorbitant profits to benefit American

"monopolists" and "Wall Street," portrayed as the manipulators behind all American action.

The Communist bloc repeatedly warns the representatives of underdeveloped countries that the United States is bound to have a bad depression which will pull others down with it in general collapse. The peril to raw materials countries is especially stressed. The Soviet bloc also hammers on the theme that rearmament of the West is adding to the suffering and economic instability of the world, impeding the development of underdeveloped areas, and setting the stage for economic collapse. They assert that the standard of living of the non-Communist world is continually going down, that underdeveloped countries are worse off today than before, and will continue to be worse off so long as they trust the United States.

Attacks on Point Four

The general line of Communist attack on the United States Point Four program is already evident from what has been said. These themes reverberate around the world in the drumfire of propaganda from the Communist press and radio, in the agitation of Communist Party workers, and also in the news and interpretations given by the Party press and radio, and by organizations and individuals that they are able to inspire or influence. It is amazing, and for an American disquieting, to see the extent to which these opinions that the Communists are trying to spread are also found in non-Communist organs in underdeveloped areas, for example, in the Peronista press of Latin America and nationalist organs of Asia and the Middle East. Sometimes Communists have picked up popular prejudices useful to their propaganda and given them further circulation. In other cases ideas originally of Communist manufacture have caught on and spread. It works both ways.

A few concrete examples will give the characteristic flavor of Communist propaganda against American activities, governmental and private, in underdeveloped countries:

Shortly after President Truman's Point Four address of January, 1949, *Pravda* claimed that the "new Truman plan" was arousing the greatest anxiety among the old colonial powers, which understood very well what it meant. The American Department of Agriculture was already making experiments with rubber in Peru and Brazil, "dominating these countries as if they were its own colonies." The main part of the program would come with the export of American capital, making use of the experience of American businessmen in such well-known colonial concerns as the United Fruit Company, "which controls a whole series of Latin American countries, and 'Aramco' (the American Oil Company), which exercises undivided rule in Saudi Arabia." Naturally, in the United States system, "not the smallest place is left . . . for the sovereignty of the governments of the economically backward countries, but that troubles Wall Street least of all." Wall Street's gradual advance upon colonies considered the property of other colonial powers, illustrated by American business expansion in British and French spheres, "drives the old plunderers into a state of frenzy which they restrain with difficulty." [21]

New Times shortly afterward presented a horrifying picture of the condition of workers employed by Aramco in Saudi Arabia. It should be said, as a preface to this propaganda gem, that in the view of competent and unprejudiced observers this American enterprise has shown an extraordinary alertness to the interests and sensibilities of the Saudi Arabians and has done much to win their good will by providing its employees with a standard of housing, health care, educational opportunities, and opportunity for advancement far above the usual level in the region. But the *New Times* writer speaks of the "wretched company barracks" of Aramco workers and says that the old custom of punishment by the cutting off of hands is still in force, except that now it is done by a cleaver kept in the Aramco hospital and American surgeons afterwards sew up the stumps! [22]

Izvestia, reporting a session of the United Nations Economic Commission for Asia and the Far East, distorts a report of a working group on industrial development by as-

[21] Yu Zhukov, "New American Colonial 'Business'," *Pravda* (Moscow), February 21, 1949. (Translated in *Current Digest of the Soviet Press*, Vol. I, No. 8, p. 39.)

[22] V. Lutsky, "America's New Plan of Colonial Expansion," *New Times* (Moscow), March 2, 1949.

serting that "the report guides the economies of the Asiatic countries along the path of agricultural development, with a view to keeping those countries as sources of raw materials for industrially developed countries." The United States representative is alleged to have "categorically objected to the development of heavy industry in the Far Eastern countries." He is said to have recommended instead an expanded output of raw materials and agricultural products, which would "fully accord with the U.S. course toward economic expansion in the Asiatic countries, regarded as sources of cheap raw materials and manpower and as a sphere for the investment of American finance and industrial capital."

All these facts attest that the imperialist powers, headed by the U.S.A. and Britain, are impeding in every way the economic and political development of the colonial and dependent countries, with the intention of keeping them agrarian dependents of the metropolitan countries, supplying the latter with raw materials . . .

Unmasking the policies of the imperialist countries, the U.S.S.R. delegation in the Economic Commission defended principles of economic development of the Far Eastern countries which would guarantee, not in words, but in deed, the national independence, sovereignty and genuine equal rights of the Asiatic peoples. The industrial development of the Far Eastern countries would proceed along the lines of the creation of national industries, primarily heavy industry, which would further the attainment by the Asiatic countries of economic independence and a high standard of living.[23]

A question and answer column in another Soviet organ carried a query from two puzzled readers who wanted to know "what the American plan for 'aid' to backward countries consists of and what are its aims." The answer explained that the struggle of the imperialists for markets has become more acute in Asia, Africa, and elsewhere. The Marshall Plan for the enslavement of Western Europe was not able to stave off the impending crisis of American capitalism for any length of time. Therefore, U. S. ruling circles began a feverish search for methods of winning new markets. One re-

[23] "The Colonial Policy of the Imperialists in Asia," *Izvestia* (Moscow), March 6, 1949. (Translated in *Current Digest of the Soviet Press*, Vol. I, No. 9, pp. 22-23.)

sult was the plan for so-called "aid" to backward countries. Economic and technical missions of every sort, "that is, intelligence units" will be sent to backward countries. Their task will be "to explore the weak spots in the economic and political positions of the English, French, Dutch, and other colonizers, to determine the most profitable fields for the investment of American capital, to remove the obstacles in the way of its advancement, and to win the native authorities and local bourgeoisie over to their side. In short—to prepare for the economic intervention of Wall Street." In this way, the author says, "American businessmen count on attaining two objectives: to ease the blows of the crisis as much as possible and simultaneously to seize the colonies of their 'junior partners.' " This plan "inevitably arouses, on the one hand, an even greater aggravation of the controversies and internecine struggle within the imperialist camp, and on the other, the insurmountable resistance of the peoples in colonial and dependent countries who are defending their liberty and independence." [24]

The interest of American private organizations in population problems and the birth control activities of Mrs. Margaret Sanger and others have been made the subjects of Communist propaganda stories. The "infamous theory of the earth's 'overpopulation' " is tied in with "human sterilization," and in this connection "the American obscurantists are particularly concerned about the densely populated countries in Asia and the Far East, considering them testing grounds for their inhuman experiments." Finally, "A direct link exists between human sterilization, the lynching of Negroes and the waging of germ warfare in Korea. All these reflect the cannibalistic policy of the American pretenders to world domination." [25]

Communist radio broadcasts assert that "oil and bases are the two words which epitomize U. S. policy in the Near and Middle East, which is camouflaged by the cloak of aid and

[24] V. Ivanov, "What is the American Plan for 'Aid' to Backward Countries?" *Trud* (Moscow), August 6, 1949. *(Soviet Press Translations*, February 1, 1950, pp. 76-78.)

[25] O. Skalkin and A. Filippov, "Designs and Deeds of American Neo-Malthusians," *Pravda* (Moscow), November 20, 1952. (Translated in *Current Digest of the Soviet Press*, Vol. IV, No. 47, p. 23.)

concern for the well-being of the people." On the pretext
of "so-called aid" U. S. agents have been striving to penetrate the Iranian economy. The implication of constant references of this sort is that "so-called U. S. technicians" are
really spies and military planners. The mission to Iran from
the International Bank for Reconstruction and Development was fiercely attacked on the ground that it "did not
represent any world bank, but was merely a group of spies
for the British and American oil companies . . . their vain
purpose was to give Iranian oil to the American and British
imperialists by any possible hook or crook."

Other broadcasts claim that "the real wage of the Iraqi
worker today is 8 times lower than that of 1939," because
of the "Anglo-American imperialists" who for twenty years
have been piling up profits and increasing their capital by a
merciless exploitation. "The workers now have reached an
unbearable degree of poverty and depravity." In Indonesia,
according to the Soviet radio, "More and more national
enterprises are forced to close down by foreign competition,
causing unemployment among hundreds of thousands of
Indonesians. In the Malang area alone, 90 percent of the
national enterprises have to close down." Indonesia, it is
claimed, has been forced to export its strategic materials at
low prices set by Americans. In this connection American
pressure to prevent shipments to Soviet bloc countries is frequently denounced.

In Brazil, according to the Soviet radio, "The railways . . .
are overloaded with raw materials of war for the United
States, while in the heart of the country as a result of the
shortage of transport facilities, foodstuffs are rotting when
they are desperately needed by millions of Brazilian workers." United States Point Four technicians in Paraguay have
"advised the government to invest money in industries
needed by America's military plans," and devaluation of the
currency has made it easy for "Yankee monopolies to get
cotton, timber, meat, etc. for ludicrous sums." Paraguay's
dependence on the United States is said to be increasing, and
"the country is now on the border of national catastrophe."

These Communist broadcasts also proclaim that the "progressive people of the world" are rising against the "im-

perialists." According to the Albanian radio, "the working people, led by the Communist parties, are carrying out their war for liberation and freedom and against American domination," and a Chinese Communist broadcast said:

We oppose . . . the so-called "economic aid" qualified by political restrictions. We stand for help to underdeveloped countries on the basis of genuine equality and mutual benefits so as to enable them to utilize their own supplies and resources freely and by self determination. By so doing, they can achieve economic development and raise the living standard of their people through real aid from advanced states.

Finally, a sample of what we may expect in carefully planned and concerted attacks on Point Four programs in the field comes from India. In the summer of 1952 India's Communist Party began a coordinated campaign of village parades and posters against the Indian government's community development program, which is being aided by the American government and by the Ford Foundation. The posters said "Go Home Americans." The Communists centered their opening attacks on the three thousand Indians who were being trained as field workers. Reports reaching New Delhi said Communist agents were circulating tales in the villages "that the trainees actually were spies sent into the villages to seek out hidden grain which the government intended to seize; that the Ford Foundation intended to enslave the Indian people; that India evicted the British, but the Americans would be much harder to drop." An Indian official stated that the Communist campaign "is an obvious effort to smash any program which might raise the living standards of the Indian people and wean them safely away from Communism." [26]

[26] *Christian Science Monitor,* July 2, 1952.

Chapter 8

PRACTICE IN COMMUNIST-
CONTROLLED AREAS

Despite the "iron curtain" and the fog of propaganda pro and con, we do have some opportunity—unfortunately very imperfect—to observe Communist practices and results in underdeveloped areas where they are in control. Communists rule underdeveloped areas in Soviet Central Asia, in the satellite countries of southeastern Europe, in North Korea, and in China.

It is important that we should not overlook Communist relations with their own underdeveloped areas for two reasons: (1) The rapid rate of certain kinds of development, especially industrialization, in some of these areas has made a big impression in other underdeveloped countries, even among anti-Communists. This is one of the main strengths of the Communist appeal to those who are impatient with the pace of change in their own countries. (2) It is illuminating to compare Communist practices with their slogans, such as "National Liberation" and "Land to the Tillers."

The information presented below will have to be sketchy and imperfect. A study bringing together all that can be learned from scattered sources about common patterns of action in Communist-ruled underdeveloped areas would be very useful, and I hope someone or some group will undertake it. It would enable people in underdeveloped areas to see Communist methods in perspective, including both the achievements and the human costs. It would show us in the West what "the competition" offers to underdeveloped countries, aside from slogans.

National Self-Determination

Though Communist doctrine and propaganda directed at non-Communist areas put great emphasis on "national liberation" and "anti-imperialism," the record of actual practice in Communist underdeveloped areas is quite contrary to these ideals. Soviet nationalities policy has turned from an early liberal tendency to one which reflects a new type of imperialism and colonialism that is rising in the world as the older "capitalist" types are receding. During and after World War II minority peoples totaling millions were removed to distant parts of the Soviet Union and destroyed as nations.

Before the Russian revolution Lenin proclaimed "the right of self-determination for nations forming part of the state," and this was specifically interpreted to include the right of secession. Stalin, who served as Commissar of Nationalities under Lenin, in 1917 drew up a Report on the National Question in which he explicitly stated that "The oppressed nations forming part of Russia must be allowed to decide for themselves whether they wish to remain part of the Russian state or to separate and to form an independent state." Similar promises were held out to the seminomadic Moslem peoples of Central Asia east of the Caspian Sea by Communist leaders who urged them to overthrow the imperial regime of the Tsar and their local rulers.

Once the Communists were in power, however, they began to qualify the self-determination principle and to refuse to apply it in practice. Three reasons seem to have been controlling. They bear a remarkable resemblance to reasons heard a half-century ago in the heyday of "capitalist imperialism."

The first was the importance to the Soviet economy of the raw materials of Central Asia. In 1920 Zinoviev said, "but we cannot do without the petroleum of Azerbaijan or the cotton of Turkestan. We take these products which are necessary for us, not as the former exploiters, but as older brothers bearing the torch of civilization." [1]

[1] Alfred Cobban, *National Self-Determination* (New York: Oxford University Press, 1945), pp. 107-108. Cobban cites on this point W. R. Batesell's *Soviet Rule in Russia.*

The second was strategic: the desire to control the border regions leading to India and the Orient, the fear of encirclement by hostile powers, and the military need for resources. Stalin said in 1920, "Central Russia, that hearth of world revolution, cannot hold out long without the assistance of the border regions, which abound in raw materials, fuel, and foodstuffs. The border regions of Russia in their turn are inevitably doomed to imperialist bondage without the political, military, and organizational support of more developed Central Russia." [2]

The third was ideological: the need to present to the world a picture of united revolutionary progress. Though claiming to stand on the principle of voluntary union of many nationalities, the Soviet leaders could not afford to let any of these outlying dependent areas actually secede.

In consequence, movements with considerable popular support which declared for autonomy in Central Asia were ruthlessly suppressed by the Red Army. Little is known today about the true feelings of the people of the area after a quarter-century of Sovietization, but Party purges for "nationalist deviations" and denunciations by Communist leaders of "bourgeois nationalism," religious attitudes, and "feudal survivals" in the region suggest that desires for more local freedom have not been entirely suppressed. [3] The fate of Moslem peoples and institutions in this area deserves study by Moslem nationalists of the Middle East who are aroused against the imperialism of the West. [4]

It is instructive to note how Communist doctrine reconciled denials of national self-determination and local autonomy with the previous slogans. First, the right of self-determination was held to be the right of the *proletariat*, not of any "reactionary" or "exploiting" classes or their lackeys and dupes. [5] The Communist Party, being the vanguard of the

<hr />

[2] Joseph Stalin, *Marxism and the National Question* (New York: International Publishers, republished 1942), p. 76.

[3] *New York Times*, May 23, 1952, dispatch by C. L. Sulzberger.

[4] They will find much food for thought in the pertinent sections of the book by Walter Kolarz, *Russia and Her Colonies* (London: George Philip & Sons, 1952).

[5] See V. I. Lenin, *Collected Works* (New York: International Publishers, 1927), Vol. XIX, pp. 47-60.

proletariat, speaks with the authentic voice of the proletariat, and Communist leaders also determine who, at a given time and place, are to be considered reactionaries. Thus, in Turkestan local soviets consisting mainly of Russian railway workers were recognized as the spokesmen for the proletariat. Moslem religious movements which had the sympathy of the great bulk of the people were written off as expressions of hostile class interests, as were all demands for autonomy. Second, in the words of Stalin, "There are occasions when the right of self-determination conflicts with the other, the higher right—the right of a working class that has assumed power to consolidate its power. In such cases—this must be said bluntly—the right of self-determination cannot and must not serve as an obstacle to the exercise by the working class of its right to dictatorship." [6] The authentic voice of "the working class," of course, is the Communist Party.

Economic Imperialism

The Communist governments of Bulgaria, Rumania, Albania, Hungary, Czechoslovakia, and Poland are rather clearly subservient in all important matters of policy to decisions made in Moscow. This includes matters of economic policy, such as the nature and pace of development, agricultural collectivization, and trade relations with the Soviet Union and other Communist countries. When Tito in Yugoslavia insisted that the Yugoslav Communist Party would make some of its own decisions, the bitter denunciations and the pressures, internal and external, by which Moscow sought to re-establish its dominance underlined the true nature of the new imperialism that it has imposed on formerly independent nations in Eastern Europe. Whether China, in view of its size, its distance, its peculiar problems, and the fact that its Communist Party came to power with relatively little material aid from the Soviet Union, will have more freedom of action is a question for the future. Also, the Kremlin may have learned something from Tito's revolt and may be more flexible in its dealings with China.

In Eastern Europe, Moscow's economic control is implemented through:

[6] *Marxism and the National Question,* cited, p. 158.

(1) Joint Soviet-satellite corporations controlling basic resources and industries, with key management positions in the hands of Soviet representatives, although the Soviet share in the enterprises often consists of former German assets or other items representing no real investment by the Soviet Union.

(2) Economic treaties and trade agreements by which the economies of the satellite countries are geared to the Soviet economy, directed along lines that suit Soviet purposes, and often exploited by trading terms decidedly to the advantage of the Soviet Union.

(3) An influx of Russian technicians, military men, and secret police.

(4) The fundamental all-pervasive policy direction of the Communist Party.

Soviet Central Asia has been developed as an integral part of the Soviet economic system. The forced expansion of cotton cultivation in this area to supply the U.S.S.R. is the sort of thing regularly denounced by Communists as "economic imperialism" when practiced in milder form elsewhere—for example, by the French in North Africa. Certainly the local peoples "have not been the arbiters of this development or of the price they had to pay." As one student of Central Asian areas concludes, "The Soviet system does not offer economic nationalism to its constituent units. Whether this is a desirable, or even possible, method of economic growth for underdeveloped territories is another question, but for those countries which desire economic nationalism, the example of Uzbekistan and Kazakhstan does not supply the model." [7]

Land and the Peasant

In agriculture the Communist pattern is rather clearly standardized. It starts with redistribution of land, favoring the poorer peasants at the expense of richer peasants and large landowners, followed, as soon as Communist power is sufficiently consolidated, by enforced collectivization. The first wins peasant support, the second antagonizes and dis-

[7] M. Holdsworth, "Soviet Central Asia, 1917–1940," *Soviet Studies*, January, 1952, p. 276.

illusions the peasants. But by then it is too late for them to resist effectively.

David Mitrany [8] has pulled together the threads of Communist theory and practice on this problem. Until the Communist Party has succeeded in seizing and consolidating power, the peasant must be wooed as an ally of the proletariat. This calls for Communist programs of land reform which make the maximum of demagogic appeal to the immediate interests of discontented rural populations, while concealing ultimate aims that would antagonize them. Once victory has been attained, however, as Lenin said long ago, "it would be ridiculous to speak of the unity of will of the proletariat and of the peasantry, of democratic rule. . . . Then we shall have to think of the Socialist, of the proletarian dictatorship." [9] Agriculture, like industry, must be based on large-scale mechanized production. The duty of the Communists is to transform the peasant, despite his "backward" preference for private land ownership and independent work, into a collective worker or industrial proletarian.

This was the strategy applied in the Soviet Union. In the Communist satellite states of Eastern Europe a similar pattern has emerged, but more rapidly. Once political opposition had been destroyed, the policy "alternated between concessions intended to 'soften' the peasants and drastic steps for bringing them to heel. As in Russia, there was no clear and continuous line of policy one way or the other: the line was played out or reeled in sharply as the tactics of the moment seemed to demand." [10] At first, the poorer peasants were usually assisted in taking over the land of large estates and of the richer peasants (Kulaks). The process was carried through rapidly without a considered plan or the possibility of proper distribution and registration. There followed a period of free economic activity comparable to the NEP period in Russia; the peasants were left to try to squeeze a living out of the much too small units they had received. Then came a sharp turn to the relentless drive for abolition

[8] *Marx Against the Peasant* (Chapel Hill: University of North Carolina Press, 1951).

[9] Same, p. 23, quoting Lenin, "Two Tactics of Social-Democracy in the Democratic Revolution" (in Russian, 1905), London, 1935.

[10] Same, p. 171.

of private property, nationalization of all industry, and collectivization of all agriculture. ". . . in Russia it took some twenty years of trial and hesitations before the policy of collectivizing agriculture was brought to a head, whereas in the eastern countries the decisive turn came only three to four years after the peasants had been endowed with land." [11]

In Eastern Europe, as in the Soviet Union, tractor stations and machine shops and state-run "cooperative" granaries and mills have been established, ostensibly to serve the peasants but also to collect and supervise their production. Such information as is available in the outside world indicates that everywhere the Communist measures have antagonized the peasants, particularly the more skillful and prosperous ones who are likely to be the best producers, but who must be ruined under the Communist concept of class war. Communist doctrine holds that replacement of tiny peasant enterprises by large collective farms should result in increased output and reduced cost. Experience in the Soviet Union casts doubt on this thesis. According to Naum Jasny, who has devoted much attention to the problem, "the savings in productivity per man attained by mechanization and large-scale output are offset or overcompensated by the labor used on administration, supervision, and guards, and by the naturally smaller intensity of work for the kolkhozy [collective farm] than in the enterprises of the individual peasants." Jasny compares the collective farmer to the Russian serfs before 1861. While the landowner in the old days did not pay the serf for his labor, he asked for less labor and allowed the serf several times more land for his own use. He finds that the same negative effects on labor productivity which were brought about by serfdom are observable in the collectives. [12]

In North Korea one of the first acts of the Communist government was to confiscate all farm lands of landlords, without payment, and to announce that the land would be given free to the tenants. The farmers later were disillusioned when they found that their "ownership" depended on com-

---

[11] Same, p. 183.

[12] Naum Jasny, "The Plight of the Collective Farms," *Journal of Farm Economics*. May, 1948, p. 313.

plete obedience to the Communist Party and that, in place of rent, taxes and contributions to "voluntary patriotic rice collections" took 50 percent or more of their total crop.[13]

In China the Communist government has announced virtual completion of a land redistribution program under the slogan "Land to the Tillers." The property of landlords has been confiscated by the state and divided among small farmers. This is being followed by the organization of recipients of land into peasants' associations, labor mutual-aid teams, and cooperatives, apparently as the first step on the road to Soviet-style collective farming. Mao said in 1949 that "Without the socialization of agriculture, there will be no complete and consolidated socialism." But he indicated at the same time that the peasant problem must be approached gradually. "Judging by the experience of the Soviet Union, it requires a very long time and careful work to attain the socialization of agriculture." Only when the regime has built up "a powerful industry" will it be able to push agriculture to the "higher" stage.[14] Communist organs claim that the land reform has generated enthusiasm among peasants and brought an increase of production. According to refugees leaving China, the state, as the new landlord, has increased taxes and levies to such an extent that many farmers find themselves worse off than under their old landlords. There is considerable evidence that the Chinese Communists have lost much of the popular support they once had among the peasants.

Promoting Industrial Development

Communist practice as well as Communist doctrine stresses the development of industry, and especially heavy, large-scale industry. The rate of industrial growth in most of the Communist-controlled areas is remarkably high.

The methods have been ruthless. Human rights and human values have been disregarded. The results of the enlarged output to date have been mainly to increase the military capacity and the power of the Soviet state, while the

[13] See C. Clyde Mitchell, *Land Reform in Asia—A Case Study* (Washington: National Planning Association, Planning Pamphlet No. 78, February, 1952), p. 18.

[14] Mao Tse-tung, "On the People's Democratic Dictatorship" (July 1, 1949), in Brandt, Schwartz, and Fairbank, cited, p. 458.

benefits received by the mass of the people, in terms of consumption goods, housing, and the like, have not been nearly in proportion to the hard work and sacrifices imposed upon them. But unquestionably Communists do install "the industrial revolution" at a terrific tempo. The appeal of this fact to impatient modernizers among the intelligentsia of underdeveloped countries is something we in the West dare not underrate. Nor can we afford to overlook the economic and political power which phenomenal rates of industrial growth are giving to Communist areas.

In the Soviet Union itself industrial output rose from the beginning of the five-year plans in 1928 through the 1930's at an average rate of about 15 percent annually.[15] The corresponding industrial growth rate in prerevolutionary Russia from 1885 to 1913 was 5.7 percent annually, though in the decade of the 1890's it was 8 percent.[16] United States industrial output in the rapid expansion after the Civil War grew at rates which exceeded 10 percent annually for some nondepression periods, but the over-all rate in the late nineteenth century was closer to 5 percent.[17] Germany's industrial growth rates in the late decades of the nineteenth century were around 5 percent, Sweden's 6 to nearly 10 percent, and Japan's about 8.6 percent from 1907 to 1913.[18]

Thus, Soviet industrial development has been extremely rapid by any standards, even allowing for the advantage of

[15] This seems to be the consensus among outside experts, after allowance for an upward bias in Soviet statistics. Alexander Gerschenkron estimated Soviet industrial growth between 1928 and 1938 at 14 to 16 percent annually for all industry and perhaps 15 to 17 percent for large-scale industry. ("The Rate of Industrial Growth in Russia Since 1885," *Journal of Economic History*, Supplement VII, 1947, pp. 144-174.) Donald R. Hodgman, in a recent thorough study which derives a new "value added" index for Soviet industrial production, arrives at an annual average growth rate of 15.7 percent for the period 1927/28–1937, 4.7 percent for 1937–1940 when military preparations were interfering, and 20.5 percent for postwar reconstruction in 1946–1950. For the entire period 1927/28–1950, war years and all, his index shows a growth rate of 8.9 percent annually. See "Industrial Production," in Abram Bergson, ed., *Soviet Economic Growth: Conditions and Perspectives* (Evanston, Ill.: Row, 1953), p. 242.

[16] Alexander Gerschenkron, "The Rate of Industrial Growth in Russia Since 1885," cited, p. 146.

[17] Same; see also the chapter by Norman M. Kaplan, "Capital Formation and Allocation," in Abram Bergson, ed., cited, pp. 37-87.

[18] Alexander Gerschenkron, "The Rate of Industrial Growth in Russia Since 1885," cited, p. 156.

late-comers in taking over technology already developed elsewhere. It is especially impressive when looked at from the perspective of underdeveloped countries that are striving to initiate industrial growth. The impressiveness in their eyes is all the greater because of a widespread tendency to identify *industrial* growth uncritically with general economic growth and to forget that both industrial growth and general economic growth can occur without necessarily being translated into a proportionate advance in the real incomes of consumers.

Soviet national product as a whole has certainly grown much less rapidly than industrial output, for agriculture has lagged badly. Calculations of Soviet national income and its growth rates are beset with great conceptual and statistical difficulties. Gregory Grossman in a recent paper concludes that Soviet national income grew from 1928 to 1937 at about 6.5 to 7 percent annually, and at about the same rate in 1948–1950. Perhaps this figure is too low; some other students of the subject feel that further inquiry is in order. Nevertheless, it is a very high growth rate for national income, though not entirely unprecedented. Japan seems to have attained comparable rates from 1914 to 1937. The American gross national product, in constant prices, rose at an average annual rate of just under 3 percent between 1929 and 1950.[19] We badly need more work which will permit international comparisons of growth rates in national income, total and per capita. Systematic information on comparative rates of advance in *consumers'* real income is especially important, and is almost entirely lacking.

The Soviet Union has attained its extremely high rates of industrial growth, it appears, in part by neglecting "social overhead" investment in housing, various urban facilities, and perhaps transportation. Also, consumers' welfare has been treated as definitely secondary to the quickest possible industrial expansion. Norman M. Kaplan concludes, in a careful comparison of investment in the Soviet Union and the United States (the U. S. data covering the last part of the nineteenth century and the first half of the twentieth), that

[19] Gregory Grossman, "National Income," in Abram Bergson, ed., cited, pp. 1-23, and comments by other members of the symposium.

"the greater rate of increase of industrial output in the USSR has been due, basically, *not* to differences in USSR-United States rates of investment, but rather to differences in the *direction* of investment." The rather surprising fact emerges from his study that "the United States and Soviet rates of investment (excluding war and depression years) have been virtually identical." [20] This refers to *gross* investment as a percentage of national product. *Net* investment in the Soviet Union has been at a higher rate than in the United States when one allows for higher depreciation on the older capital equipment of the United States. The Soviet Union has had a far higher ratio of industrial to total investment than the United States. Furthermore, it has invested more in heavy, metal-working industries and less in consumer goods industries. Housing investment in the U.S.S.R. was only 8 to 10 percent of total investment between 1928 and 1945; after World War II it went up to 16.9 percent for 1946–1950, and to 18.2 percent for 1951. In the United States, housing construction took 26 percent of total investment in 1880–1912, 24.6 percent in 1920–1929, 13.5 percent in 1930–1940, and 26.2 percent in 1950. [21]

Comparative Rates of Growth

Peter Wiles in a recent article stresses the sobering thought that "by whatever other criteria economies may be judged, Communism is at any rate beating 'capitalism,' whether in the form of laissez-faire or of the welfare state, in its rate of growth." He adds that "Only in wartime do capitalist systems show comparable rates of growth: that is, when they cease to be capitalist and borrow many of the vices and virtues of centralized Communist planning." Communist regimes are able to impose very high rates of saving and investment, and they overcome institutional obstacles to economic expansion by force. There is no consumers' sovereignty, no bargaining power in the hands of labor, little concern for vested interests, individual freedom, or popular well-being. In consequence, the Kremlin is in a position to

[20] Norman M. Kaplan, "Capital Formation and Allocation," cited, pp. 80, 40.
[21] Same, pp. 61-63. See also observations by Gregory Grossman, Joseph A. Kershaw, and Oleg Hoeffding, pp. 16, 295, and 326 of the same volume.

"make truthful propaganda among the free but backward nations about the rate of its economic progress. It may also make a serious bid to capture the world markets by dumping, for if the Soviet Union can save it can also have an export surplus. This will make no small impression upon Asians, Africans and Latin Americans. It can even run a genuine Marshall Plan of its own, and infiltrate the poor free countries with technicians and managers." [22]

Soviet organizations are now inviting people from other Asian areas to visit showplaces in Soviet Central Asia. Some Americans, among the few outsiders who have seen the area, feel that the economic developments which can be shown are quite impressive. They fear that the Communists, while continuing to conceal facts that might reveal undesirable features of their system, will be able to gain considerable prestige in this way, especially if comparable non-Communist areas are not making much progress.

Warren Wilhelm, in a study of economic development in Soviet Central Asia during the decade 1928–1937, estimates that the output of local industries rose 9.5 times in ten years. It must be remembered that this expansion was from a very small base. In agriculture, cotton output expanded about 2.9 times in the decade, with the help of irrigation and other improvements. This made the Soviet Union approximately self-sufficient in cotton. Wilhelm's study leads him to believe that the total output of the region, agricultural and industrial, increased during the decade by more than 2.6 times and that output per person was at least doubled. "It is quite possible that such a rate of increase in agriculture and industry combined has never been attained in any other region of equal size."

The capital investment required for this increase in output was not obtained by depressing living standards in the area; neither was there any large net inflow of capital from the rest of the Soviet Union. The great increase in the cotton crop, for which the Soviet Union provided a guaranteed and unlimited market, offset most, perhaps even all, of the investment goods and consumer goods shipped into the region from Russia. Much of the needed capital came from plowing back local increases of production. Because of the previous technological backwardness, these increases could be large, once better technology was applied. Another factor was the organization of underemployed labor for the building of capital goods, such as irrigation works, without decreasing the output of food and other consumer goods.[23]

The satellite countries of Eastern Europe all have their Five-Year Plans. With 1938 as 100 the targets set for industrial output in Bulgaria and Czechoslovakia were 293 and 213, respectively, by 1953; in Hungary, 393 by 1954; and in Poland, Rumania, and Eastern Germany 428, 302, and 234, respectively, by 1955. Albania, starting from an especially low level, was to attain an industrial output figure of 1200 by 1955.[24]

"The Kremlin presents itself to the conquered," says K. M. Smogorzewski in an anti-Communist comment on the industrial revolution taking place in Eastern Europe, "as a liberator who cares for the well-being of the liberated and fulfills their dreams of industrialization, enabling them to reduce the overpopulation of the countryside and to increase their national income." It has encouraged, however, only such types of industrialization as suit its own purposes, especially the development of heavy industry, producing steel, tractors, and fertilizers, guns, tanks, and explosives. "The satellite nations look on at this industrialization of their country with mixed feelings. Naturally, they welcome the fact that it is being carried out so speedily, and that their depressed areas are disappearing. At the same time they are aware of being ruthlessly exploited, that big brother is taking not only the coal they extract and the steel they produce, but also a great proportion of their food and clothing. Official propaganda seeks to comfort them with statements that the national income of their respective countries is increasing. Statistically this is true, but the increases are immediately reinvested, additional sums of money are squeezed out of the

[23] Warren Wilhelm, "Soviet Central Asia: Development of a Backward Area," *Foreign Policy Reports,* February 1, 1950, pp. 218-227.

[24] K. M. Smogorzewski, "European Robots," *Fortnightly,* May, 1952, pp. 298-306.

population by yearly compulsory loans and fewer consumer goods than before the 1939–45 war are purchasable for actual wages." [25]

The Chinese Communists, even during the long period in the rural hinterland while they were building to power on a peasant base, never for a moment renounced the aim, "which lies at the very heart of the Marxist-Leninist-Stalinist world view," of converting China into an industrialized state.[26] In 1949, while the Communists were completing their conquest of the mainland, one of their leaders stated that the goal of the industrialization program would be "to increase the proportion of industrial production from about 10 percent in the total national income to between 30 to 40 percent in ten to fifteen years." A first five-year plan of economic construction, stressing industrialization, started in 1953.

Popular Well-Being

Increase of industrial output is one thing, improvement in the living standards of the people another. In the first place, agriculture has lagged in Communist areas. In the second place, Communist methods do not seem to be conducive to the most efficient production, either by management or by labor. In the third place, the all-powerful state continues to direct production primarily for the sake of strength and strategy in promoting world revolution and very secondarily for popular welfare.

Trends in real income of workers, farmers, and others in the Soviet areas are extremely difficult to assess with any confidence or objectivity, because basic data are suppressed. Hence, wide gaps often exist between Communist claims and anti-Communist criticisms.

It appears that per capita real income in Soviet Central Asia has risen substantially, so that the area has caught up with other parts of the Soviet Union. In the satellite countries of Eastern Europe there may have been some rise in the general level of consumption as compared to prewar, though the situation for individuals varies greatly as between the favored and the persecuted groups. In the Soviet Union it-

[25] Same.
[26] Brandt, Schwartz, and Fairbank, cited, p. 442.

self the latest trends and plans suggest that more goods may be available for popular consumption, although the general level of living by Western standards remains low and in such an important item as housing is wretched. In China it is much too early to know what effects Communist policy is having or may eventually have on the level of living of the people.

In Soviet Central Asia the number of doctors and teachers has been greatly increased. Communist governments everywhere put much stress on mass education and on opportunities for technical training. The modern, industrialized, power state does not keep its subjects illiterate and untrained, as did the old-time despotisms. On the other hand, the system of education in a Communist state does not aim to produce inquiring minds or self-reliant citizens, but reliable workers and Party members who will carry out obediently and with enthusiasm the tasks determined for them. However, we must not forget that in underdeveloped areas where the masses have never known educational opportunities the chance to go to school at all, to get a technical education, and to have a part in the transformation of one's country opens exciting new vistas for many people, especially the young.

There must be many intangibles in any estimate of popular well-being. We cannot afford to overlook the capacity of the Communists, at least in the early stages, to generate a great surge of enthusiasm and a new sense of participation among important segments of the population, especially young people and persons to whom the revolution offers a sudden prospect of improvement in status. But there is also evidence that this enthusiasm wears thin after some years and has to be sustained more and more by the synthetic methods of propaganda monopoly and by the police state.

The blackest part of the record in Communist-controlled countries is the ruthless disregard for all the human values summed up in the word freedom. Forced labor has become an established part of the Soviet system of production, and apparently well authenticated estimates place the number in slave labor camps at many millions. Evidence submitted in 1952 to the United Nations Committee on Forced Labor showed the system rapidly on the increase in the satellite states of Eastern Europe. The same trend appears in Communist China.[27]

Trade unions under a Communist regime become instruments by which the totalitarian state directs its workers, not free associations to defend their interests. The myth of the "worker's state" and a "worker's paradise" under Communist control cannot stand up to facts; instead, Communist methods transform the worker into a semiserf.

Terrible suffering is inflicted on innocent people labeled class enemies, including the peasants who resist collectivization. No honest, independent thinking is permitted, even for scientists in such a field as genetics, let alone on political and economic subjects. The terror of the secret police and the forced confession overhang even faithful Party workers.

The Challenge

When we compare Communist propaganda with Communist practice in underdeveloped areas under their control the fraudulent nature of some of their leading slogans, like "National Liberation" and "Land to the Tillers," stands revealed.

In other respects, especially industrialization, they show accomplishments that must give our side pause, both because of the consequent rise in Communist military strength and because of the appeal the accomplishments may have for half-informed people in underdeveloped countries. We must remember that Soviet accomplishments look quite different viewed from an extremely underdeveloped country and

[27] In May, 1953, a special Committee on Forced Labor set up by the United Nations and the International Labor Organization submitted its final report on an investigation extending over twenty months. The Committee was chaired by Sir Ramaswami Mudaliar, of India, and members were Paal Berg, former President of the Norwegian Supreme Court, and Enrique Garcia Sayan, former Foreign Minister of Peru. The Committee found that forced labor both for political purposes and economic purposes existed in the Soviet Union and in various Soviet satellites. In the Soviet Union, "these measures seem to be applied on a large scale . . . constituting an important element in the economy of the country." The report declared that a system of forced labor used as an instrument of political coercion "is, by its very nature and attributes, a violation of the fundamental rights of the human person as guaranteed by the Charter of the United Nations and proclaimed in the Universal Declaration of Human Rights." See United Nations, Ad Hoc Committee on Forced Labour, *Report*, Supplement No. 13, *Official Records*, Sixteenth Session, Economic and Social Council. International Labour Office, Studies and Reports (New Series), No. 36 (Geneva: 1953), pp. 98, 125.

viewed from America. Living standards in the Soviet Union, low to us, are high to them. Freedoms that we prize may seem less important to them, because of lack of understanding, an acute sense of present miseries and frustrations, or resentment against past denials of freedom. It would be disastrous to the West should the conviction gradually grow among the advocates of economic modernization in underdeveloped countries that "The Communists may use rough methods, but they are the ones that get things done."

Unquestionably the rate of industrial growth, and doubtless also the over-all rate of real investment in all forms of productive capital (as a percentage of national income), has been greater in Communist underdeveloped areas than in non-Communist underdeveloped areas. It cannot be denied that the ruthless methods of Communism do work, in the narrow sense of removing obstacles to economic growth, mobilizing investment, and putting through an industrial revolution. In this respect as in others we must not underestimate Communist capabilities.

Two problems arise for the West out of the Communist record in the underdeveloped areas which they control. One is to see that the truth about what happens to people and to national freedom under Communist regimes gets known in underdeveloped countries. The other is to help underdeveloped countries in the free world to develop with reasonable rapidity. Speed is not everything. Leaders in most underdeveloped countries are intelligent enough to appreciate that the forced-draft methods of the Communists, though they have produced impressive rates of industrialization, do this at very great cost in human terms. Solid economic and social progress that really benefits the people and endures takes time. Nevertheless, this truth must not be allowed to become an excuse for feeble action. To let it appear that Communists get rapid results in economic development while underdeveloped countries of the free world struggle along ineffectively would be tragic. If the comparison between the Communist world and the free world is put in terms of advancement of human well-being, *and if the resources of the West are really brought to bear on the development problem,* then the Communist challenge can be met successfully.

Chapter 9

IMPLICATIONS FOR FREE WORLD POLICY

What can our examination of Communist aims and methods teach us about the most effective ways to resist Communism in underdeveloped areas?

The first lesson is that the free world cannot afford to underestimate *either* the military *or* the politico-economic aspects of the Communist threat. The methods on which the world Communist movement relies to detach underdeveloped areas from the free world and add them to the Soviet bloc are a blend of outside pressure and internal subversion in which military and political means are two sides of the same coin.

Military pressure is exerted on underdeveloped countries, where circumstances permit, both from the outside and from the inside. The outside pressure is based on the military power of the Soviet Union and the Communist bloc; the world has seen examples in Eastern Europe and in Korea. The internal pressure takes the form of insurrections and the development of a regionally based army and a Communist state within a state, as in Mao's successful operations in China.

The politico-economic pressure is also external and internal. From the outside, the world-wide Communist propaganda apparatus lays down a barrage. The Soviet Union, with support from its satellites, advances the Communist cause on the diplomatic front. Internally, the local Communist Party plays on every discontent and alternately denounces democratic reform movements or tries to capture them under a fraudulent united front.

Mistakes to Be Avoided

There are two equally dangerous mistakes to be avoided in our thinking on how to resist the Communist attack. In the first place we should not assume that if countries are internally sound, if the majority of people feel that economic and social conditions are improving and that political grievances can be righted through established channels, then they need not fear Communism. This assumption overlooks the fact that the leaders of world Communism will have no hesitation in imposing the Communist yoke by force of arms, from inside or outside or both, if the situation seems to them propitious.

We must avoid also the assumption that tanks and guns, military assistance missions, and military pacts can by themselves stop the inroads of Communism. The flaw in this theory is well illustrated by what happened in China, where whole divisions of American-equipped and American-trained Nationalist troops went over to the Communists. They are past masters at organizing mass discontent and using it as a steppingstone to power. They know that the minds of men control the direction in which guns are pointed.

Under present circumstances the United States is more likely to make the second mistake than the first. This has not always been true. Right after the Second World War wishful thinking about the hoped-for peaceful intentions of the Soviet Union, combined with the natural disinclination of free peoples to devote their young men and their national substance to war preparations, produced a dangerous disarmament of the United States and its allies. At the same time the hard-bitten players of power politics in the Kremlin maintained and augmented their forces. But this period has passed, and the rearmament of the free world, since the lesson provided by Communist aggression in Korea, has improved the military position of our side. Very likely, therefore, in the years just ahead Communism will rely even more on politico-economic means of struggle, and the *relative* importance of politico-economic measures will increase both for us and for them.

Weaknesses in Nonmilitary Defense

In the struggle for men's minds and hearts and imaginations, the United States and its allies have begun to show more awareness. The best indications of this are the Point Four program and the various United Nations programs for cooperation with underdeveloped countries. But there are two major weaknesses in the United States politico-economic defense against Communist attempts to turn the underdeveloped majority of mankind from our side to theirs. One relates to the quantity of our effort, the other to its quality.

The first weakness is that our effort in this field is not nearly large enough. It is not large enough in relation to the Communist effort that we are trying to counter. And it is not large enough in proportion to the expenditures of manpower and money that are going into the purely military side of defense. Those who determine American policy—and this has been even more true of Congress and the people than of the executive branch—still seem to lack a realistic understanding of the means on which Communism relies to capture the underdeveloped countries. Appropriations for Point Four, for international information activities, and for related efforts to do something concrete to resist Soviet infiltration into "weak link" areas are niggardly as compared with the cost of our military establishment and our military assistance to friendly nations. Yet our flank could be turned by Communist politico-economic victories in any of a half-dozen areas. A single major defection of this sort from the free world could cost us more in strategic position, extra military equipment required to redress the balance, potential raw materials supplies, and prestige than we have spent on our whole program of politico-economic defense in underdeveloped areas to date. When there is an "economy" drive in Congress it generally seems to be assumed that the way to serve the national interest is to cut much more drastically on programs of economic and technical assistance and international information activities than in the other phases of our defense effort. This is folly. Such thinking certainly needs to be revised.

The second major weakness is our failure thus far to adjust the content and thrust of our defense against Communism in underdeveloped areas accurately and boldly enough to the real demands of the situation. Much of what the United States has been doing in this field, especially since the Point Four program has got well under way, is excellent. But there are more things that we could be doing, and there are some shifts of emphasis within the program which a truer understanding of the nature of the Communist danger in underdeveloped areas would suggest. This is the theme to which the rest of this chapter will be devoted.

SUSCEPTIBILITY TO COMMUNISM

Communism is a disease of society. It is social ill-health when people turn to doctrines of bitter, unremitting class struggle, bloody revolution, irresponsible rule by power-hungry conspirators, and suppression of personal and group freedoms under a totalitarian system of police terror and mass propaganda. To combat Communism we need to understand as much as possible of its "etiology," as the medical scientist would say—that is, where and how it develops, the causative agents and carriers, and environmental conditions that favor it. Our study leads to certain conclusions in this field that are very important and not entirely in line with views generally heard in the United States.

In the first place, experience has shown that the more advanced industrial countries of the West are not really very susceptible to Communism. It is the countries just started on the road to modernization, like Russia in 1917 and China in 1949, that are most likely to succumb. Communism, as we have said, is a disease more devastating in the infancy and childhood of modern industrial societies than in their maturity.

In underdeveloped countries the impact of modern industrial culture, acting through powerful external and internal forces, breaks down old patterns of life and old social systems and inspires new wants. Only gradually can the society find the necessary new adjustments and learn to operate satisfactorily a more complex and dynamic modern system. It is in this transitional period, betwixt the old and the new, that the Communists with their deceptively simple solutions and their tactics of hatred and force have their best opening.

In the second place, the countries and the districts within countries which are at the very bottom in economic well-being and education are not necessarily the places most susceptible to Communism. In fact, a case can be made for the generalization that discontent is most active and most likely to provide a soil for Communist agitation sometime *after* an economic advance has started.

It may be that the most dangerous decades, in the sense of vulnerability to Communist subversion, are those after a country has begun to stir out of the centuries-old conditions of ignorance but before it has attained a living level within the "range of toleration" determined by modern standards. This is the situation of most of the underdeveloped areas today.

Material progress is often presented as an almost sure-fire antidote to Communism. This is too simple. The truth, as we have stated before, is that material progress is a *necessary* but not a *sufficient* condition for preventing the Communist infection. We return to this point and to other essential conditions below.

In the third place, those segments of the population of underdeveloped countries most susceptible to Communism are not the abjectly miserable and hopeless, but rather those who have made at least a start on the ladder of economic advancement and either found their personal ambitions frustrated or had their social consciences aroused by the misery around them. It is from the ranks of the relatively well-to-do intelligentsia, not peasants or manual workers, that the key recruits come. They are the active agents, the carriers of Communism. It is they who supply the nucleus of Party members, the "vanguard" in Communist terminology, who in turn manipulate the masses. The masses may be subject to manipulation because of a great variety of discontents, economic and noneconomic. It is not inevitable that these discontents should take the highly specific form of Communism, with its support of a power-hungry group fanatically dedicated to a specific doctrine and to unwavering support of the Soviet Union. Rather, this is a consequence of the effective work of the "vanguard." These points have a very important bearing on our problems of policy and appear to be less well understood than they deserve to be. We shall therefore look further at the sources of Communist strength in underdeveloped countries, with special reference to: (1) the active agents, and (2) the mass base.

Recruits from the Intelligentsia [1]

The most active agents in the Communist triumph in Russia were the Marxist-trained Russian intelligentsia: Lenin, Trotsky, Radek, Bukharin, and the rest. Hundreds of Russian students had been living in Zurich, Munich, Vienna, Heidelberg, and Paris, waiting for the "revolutionary situation." When the "call of history" came they helped to transfer to Russia the Messianic doctrine of modern Marxism and to turn the Russian revolution away from the pattern of Western liberal democracy, which might well have been the tendency without the determined Bolshevik leadership, into the Communist pattern.

The Chinese Communist Party during its rise to power was an élite corps, and, in the words of Morris Watnick, "the entire history of the party" from its founding by Li and Ch'en to Mao and Liu "is virtually an unbroken record of a party controlled by intellectuals." A careful study has been made by Robert C. North of the background of Kuomintang and Communist leaders. "In both parties, the leaders have been drawn most frequently from a relatively thin upper layer of the Chinese population. In both parties these men were often the sons of landlords, merchants, scholars, or officials, and they usually came from parts of China where Western influence had first penetrated and where the penetration itself was most vigorous. All of them had higher educations, and most of them had studied abroad. . . . The majority were alienated intellectuals, men and women whose Western educations isolated them from the main currents of Chinese society. In the chaos of modern China, these persons

[1] I want to acknowledge my indebtedness to the authors of two excellent articles on which I have drawn freely in this section: Eduard Heimann, "Marxism and Underdeveloped Countries," *Social Research*, September, 1952, pp. 322-345; Morris Watnick, "The Appeal of Communism to the Underdeveloped Peoples," in Bert F. Hoselitz, cited, pp. 152-172.

became full-time professional politicians specializing, for the most part, in military violence or in party administration." [2]

In India, of 139 delegates at the first all-Indian Congress of the Communist Party in 1943, 86 were members of professional and intellectual groups. One of the great sources of Communist converts is the frustration of students who, on acquiring a liberal arts education with little practical training, find good jobs almost impossible to obtain. Thousands of recent graduates earn no more than $8 or $10 a month.[3] The Communist advance in Madras and Travancore seems to have owed much of its vigor to leftist movements among middle-class students who then made themselves available to go out and campaign among the people.

The Communist parties of Indo-China, Thailand, Burma, Malaya, and Indonesia all show a heavy preponderance of journalists, lawyers, and teachers among the top leadership. Communists are especially active in organizing or attempting to gain control of trade unions. The roster of top trade union leaders attending the congress at Peking in 1949 sponsored by the Communist-dominated World Federation of Trade Unions shows that many of the newborn unions of Southeast Asia are being guided by professionals with no direct experience in the occupations concerned.

In the Near East, says a survey of Communism in that area, "Young men, industrial workers, intellectuals, and pseudo-intellectuals, teachers, students, journalists, and litterateurs, government workers, a few army men and others, with a real or fancied interest in reform, have formed the professional cadres and filled the ranks of the fellow travelers, joined by malcontents with a chronic grudge against any government in power." [4]

[2] Robert C. North, with the collaboration of Ithiel de Sola Pool, *Kuomintang and Chinese Communist Elites* (Stanford: Stanford University Press, Hoover Institute Studies, 1952), p. 46.

[3] The Indian Government, according to former Ambassador Chester Bowles, is keenly aware of this problem. Volunteer groups are being organized for road-building and other construction work during vacation periods, and it is planned to recruit some 60 thousand young men and women within the next few years as village workers to carry on the rapidly expanding community development program. Chester Bowles, "New India," *Foreign Affairs*, October, 1952, pp. 90-91.

[4] U. S. Congress (80th), "Communism in the Near East," Supplement III, Part B of *The Strategy and Tactics of World Communism*, Report of Sub-

One of the great political dangers created by the loss of revenue following oil nationalization in Iran was that the government might have to make wholesale cuts in the ranks of the civil service. This would put many educated or semi-educated persons into the street. "It is this group that has shown itself to date to be most receptive to Communist propaganda," wrote Albion Ross to the *New York Times*. His dispatches from other trouble spots in the region reveal a similar pattern. For example, in Iraq where Communists succeeded in engineering a student demonstration into an anti-U. S. and antigovernment riot, "Dissatisfied intellectuals have provided the most important leadership for seditious forces. . . . The Lawyers Association, for example, provided the center from which outright seditious elements worked, and newspapers accounted for a considerable part of the unrest . . ." [5]

The leaders of world Communism, despite their idolization of the proletariat, were quick to recognize that in practice the point of entry to underdeveloped countries lay through comparatively privileged, intellectually trained people. This was clearly stated in 1928 by the Comintern Congress in its important directive on revolutionary strategy in the "colonies and semi-colonies":

Experience has shown that, in the majority of colonial and semi-colonial countries, an important if not a predominant part of the Party ranks in the first stage of the movement is recruited from the petty bourgeoisie and, in particular, from the revolutionarily inclined intelligentsia, very frequently students. It frequently happens that these elements enter the Party because they see in it the most decisive enemy of imperialism . . . [6]

There are good sociological reasons for this. The new intelligentsia in underdeveloped countries—doctors, lawyers, teachers, engineers, journalists, civil servants—by their very existence are symptoms of cultural ferment and disintegration of an old order. They represent Western ways of thinking

committee No. 5, House Foreign Affairs Committee (Committee print, Washington, 1948), p. 12.

[5] *New York Times*, September 28, November 28, November 29, 1952.

[6] *Theses on the Revolutionary Movement in the Colonies and Semi-Colonies,* cited, p. 1670.

quite foreign to the traditional mentality. "They are stran-
gers in their own countries;" as Eduard Heimann says, "what
they stand for, however wholesome and necessary, is in un-
resolved conflict with their own backgrounds." [7]

The West has provided most of the stimulus which
brought this nonconforming intelligentsia into being, by
its communications network, by opportunities for schooling,
by its books and magazines, its trade and investments. In
areas under Western colonial rule, or even in independent
areas where Western large-scale enterprises have dominated
the modern sector of the economy, the West also created
situations in which members of this intelligentsia could
never rise to the very top. Many were condemned to a form
of déclassé existence, as Morris Watnick puts it, between the
masses of their own people and foreign rulers. Furthermore,
the educational system in most areas has tended to train
technicians, lawyers, and other groups of professional workers in numbers beyond the capacity of the local economy
to give them jobs. The result is "a rootless intellectual proletariat possessing no real economic base in an independent
native middle-class."

Where the economy is not developing rapidly, this intellectual proletariat lacks jobs, hope, and constructive, challenging tasks. Communist doctrine offers an explanation for
their frustrations and the ills of their country. The explanation is full of large abstractions and theories which appeal
to the trained or half-trained mind. Above all, the Communists offer a vision, and a dynamic role of leadership for
the intelligentsia in the regeneration of their own country.
Much of the Communist offer turns out to be fraudulent, as
we know. But what does our side offer as an alternative?
These people must have constructive tasks, a sense of participation in moving events that promise to bring about the
transformation and betterment of their country. No less important for the intellectual type of person whose role is crucial in these problems, they must have a sounder theory
of history and of human progress than that offered by the
Communists.

[7] Eduard Heimann, cited, p. 338.

Vanguard and Mass Base

The key to the transformation of Marxism from a doctrine designed for the most developed countries (but unsuccessful there) to a powerful force in underdeveloped countries is Lenin's strategy of the "vanguard." A dedicated élite, having true knowledge of the inevitable course of history, can guide the people to salvation, whether the people like it or not. It is almost theocratic. The goal is a proletarian man, the mass man modeled on the machine and produced by a society based on large-scale industry and universal mechanization. It has proved actually easier for the vanguard to get control and to move in dictatorial fashion toward this goal in preindustrial than in industrial countries. There need be no proletariat at all to begin with. This skipping of stages renounces certain advantages of "maturity," from the Communist viewpoint, but, as Eduard Heimann says, avoids the obstacles raised by the unwillingness of the proletarians themselves in the industrially advanced countries to be led by the vanguard.

The first Communist job in an underdeveloped country is to recruit a vanguard. Members of the intelligentsia are the best prospects, for the reasons just stated. Also, it takes people with some education to provide the top leadership and the intermediate "cadres" which plan the Party tactics, launch the propaganda drives, organize the unions, the youth groups, the military formations, and publish the Party organs, infiltrate press and radio and schools, and so on.

But the vanguard, in order to get power, has to achieve a "mass base" which it can manipulate in demonstrations and riots, count on for the election of Communist candidates, or use as a source of recruits and supplies for an insurrectionary "people's army." Here is where mass discontents enter the picture. Our emphasis on the role of the Party vanguard and the intelligentsia from which it is generally drawn is not intended to play down the equally important factor of the *conditions* which make it possible for a determined Communist nucleus to rally enough support to make a serious bid for power. Among these conditions are poverty and a new awareness that something can be done about it;

abuses of tenancy and usury in rural areas; popular ignorance; unjust, ineffective, or corrupt government; famine or unemployment; and hurt pride and a sense of grievance against foreigners. To recur to the disease analogy, the setting up of a Communist Party nucleus is like the lodgment of a disease germ in the system, but how far it spreads depends much on the health and vigor of the system.

Mass discontent, however, does not necessarily take the form of Communism. If it did, the outlook for the underdeveloped areas would be gloomy indeed. Everywhere there is a strong demand for change—for "revolution" in the sense of deep-going transformation of economic, social, and political life. Revolution in this sense is already in full course; it is inevitable. What is not inevitable is that the ongoing revolutions should be seized and steered by Communist parties taking orders and support from Moscow or Peking.

In a very real sense the problem of the Communist vanguard in most underdeveloped countries is not to *start* a revolution but to *capture* the revolution that is already under way. The problem of the West is to help the underdeveloped countries to help themselves so that they can carry through their fundamental changes without subservience to anybody, ourselves included, and without the terrific sacrifice of human values that Communism demands. Measures of prevention, to be successful, should be directed both at the fundamental conditions that create mass discontent and also at the conditions that make the intelligentsia of these countries susceptible of recruitment as active agents. To the latter, especially, inspiring ideas are as important as bread.

Measures of prevention include: (1) progress in status, including satisfaction of the strong nationalist urges sweeping underdeveloped countries; (2) economic progress, bringing visible improvements in living conditions; and (3) progress in democratic techniques and ideals, to assist in the development of strong non-Communist parties capable of rallying popular support to democratic government.

PROGRESS IN STATUS

One impression stands out from a study of the doctrinal writings of Communists, their strategic directives for underdeveloped countries, their propaganda in underdeveloped areas and in the United Nations, and their activities in key underdeveloped countries. *In their attempts to influence the peoples of underdeveloped countries the Communists put great emphasis, I would say even chief emphasis, on appeals not to the material wants of man but rather to the human desire for status, equality, freedom from domination or oppression, especially domination by foreigners.* The thing they talk about most where underdeveloped areas are concerned is conveyed by such constantly reiterated words as "imperialism," "imperialists," "colonial," "semicolonial." Of course, they also denounce local landlords, moneylenders, and any other groups against which mass discontent can be organized. But even the local targets are characteristically presented as tools—the favorite expressions are "lackeys" and "running-dogs"—of foreign "imperialists."

The Stomachs and the Minds of Men

"Stomach Communism" is perhaps a useful phrase to get across part of the truth about the conditions which make people susceptible to Communism. But the Communists themselves, despite their doctrines of economic determinism, do not act on the assumption that people are mainly interested in their own material advancement.

"The spread of Communism through Asia," says Charles Malik, a philosopher-statesman who represents Lebanon in the United Nations and who is one of the most perceptive friends of democracy, "is often explained simply as the inevitable result of the terrible poverty and misery afflicting so great a part of that continent. Banish this hunger and need (it is so often argued) and Communism could be erased. This analysis is almost as false as it is brisk. In fact it is notable that so wrong a theory could be so popular. Precisely such theories themselves contribute enormously to Communism's spread, for they help blind the West to true perception of the forces it must face and rout." [8]

Consider the fact, says Mr. Malik, that in India "Communism has made *least* progress among the most destitute— the scores of millions of untouchables and aborigines. . . .

[8] Charles Malik, "From a Friend of the West," *Life*, March 31, 1952, p. 53.

Communism cannot be labeled the direct, automatic result of a people's want or suffering. Nothing so complex as Communism could have so starkly simple an origin. There is no political compulsion that inexorably converts plain *want*—the lack of either security or equality—into Marxist ideology. Hunger *alone* does not make Communists: they are made by belief—dedicated, fanatic belief."

Nationalism and Self-respect

What the West must seek to grasp, Mr. Malik holds, is that "the causes for the spread of Communism and the reasons for its appeal are exceedingly complex" and that "its retreat cannot be forced by . . . mere material and economic uplift." When he turns to the factors that make Asia susceptible to the anti-Western appeals of the Communists he begins, significantly, with a political idea exported by the West to Asia: nationalism. "Europe has taught the world that no greater disgrace can befall one people than to be politically subject to another. . . . the important fact is that the Communist movement is identifying itself with resurgent nationalism in Asia." This is done for ulterior motives, but often with powerful effects.[9]

In the competition for the minds of men in underdeveloped countries our side suffers from certain heritages of the past and from the (fortunately lessening) extent to which certain evils and blunders and resentments of an older era continue in the present. It is almost unbelievable to those who have not had personal experience of it how deeply the Western rule over subject peoples has scored the minds of the intelligentsia in Asia and the Middle East. Similar tendencies are now manifest in Africa. The underlying trend is probably favorable to the West. Contrary to the teachings of Lenin, the latest stage in the development of "capitalist" relations to underdeveloped areas is "de-imperialism" rather than more imperialism. The West is steadily moving—sometimes with good grace and sometimes with bad—toward the substitution of mutuality, respect, free negotiation, and co-operation within world institutions for dominance, arrogance, and imposition. The new Communist imperialism,

[9] Same, pp. 53-54.

on the other hand, has now placed enough peoples under its rule so that onlookers in the underdeveloped countries can see for themselves and be aware of the fraud in Communist slogans.

But the wounds to self-respect inflicted by the West in the past have created deep resentments and long-lasting suspicions. Sensitive reporters such as James A. Michener tell us that the resentment arises probably as much from being made to feel inferior socially as from political rule. Clubs restricted to white foreigners contributed to that feeling. And all through the Orient he found that the discrimination against colored people in the United States does inestimable damage in sustaining a perverted concept of America which Communists are adept at turning to their purposes.[10]

The Task of America and the Free World

The great significance of all this for American policy is not yet well enough understood in this country. Some of its implications will occupy us further in Part III.

The task of America and the free world in combatting the Communist thrust toward underdeveloped countries is more than a problem of military defense or of helping them to build up their capacity to produce and hence their material well-being, though both these things are certainly important. We have to show these people that in fact the non-Communist world offers them more than does the Communist world in genuine progress toward the ideals of equal status with other peoples, national self-determination, self-rule, and respect. To win this phase of the struggle with Communism we must:

1. Eliminate as fast as we can the remaining real justifications for complaint against our own actions and those of our partners in the free world. This means living up to free world ideals. Fortunately for us, our ideals and the trend of our practice are in the right direction.

2. Let the truth be known. We need a much more vigorous and extensive public relations program to counteract the false picture which Communists present of American

[10] James A. Michener, *The Voice of Asia* (New York: Random House, 1951).

purposes and to provide people in the underdeveloped countries with information on which they can form their own truer picture.

If we want the peoples of the underdeveloped countries on our side, and we do, we must also show them that the West is their most effective help in their struggle to catch up with modern progress in production and thereby to emerge from conditions of poverty, disease, and ignorance. The masses of people will be impressed by practical results that they can see in their own villages and towns. The crucial group of intelligentsia will react both to their enlarged personal opportunities and to ideas, such as the presence or absence of a dynamic program, the independence and honor of their country, and to facts comparing their country's progress with that of others, particularly those in the Communist sphere.

Establishing an Upward Trend

Probably it is true that the *level* of economic well-being in a country is less important than the *trend and prospect* in determining its susceptibility to Communism. At least we must hope so and act on this assumption. If a country has to reach a living level like that of Western Europe before it can establish a fair degree of immunity to the politico-economic attack of Communism, then the outlook is indeed grim. Economic development to such levels is likely to be, with the best of efforts and luck, a matter of many decades if not of generations. This is particularly true of some of the largest and most crucial of the underdeveloped countries, such as India. The Marshall Plan in Europe could bring quick results because its problem was to revive already developed economies. Economic development of underdeveloped areas is a time-consuming process, for people must be trained, habits of work and social organization must be changed, capital must be accumulated and equipment installed, and tendencies to excessive population growth must be brought under control. It is not possible to attain a modern living standard in two or three or five or ten years. What is possible, and vitally necessary for the future of freedom in the world, is to establish an upward trend, a well-founded feeling that things are getting better, that there is progress.

America and the other industrially advanced countries of the free world are much better equipped than the Soviet Union and the Communist bloc to provide effective technical and economic assistance for development. We must not neglect that advantage. Communist propaganda, of course, claims that America and the West want to retard the economic progress of underdeveloped countries and especially to prevent their industrialization. At the same time it paints a glowing picture of economic and industrial development in the Soviet sphere, exaggerating actual accomplishments and neglecting to mention ruthlessly imposed sacrifices, terror, forced labor, and the failure of most of the increased output to filter through to the people. The best counter to such Communist agitation is a combination of more effective practical help and better public relations in underdeveloped countries.

The Distribution of Economic Gains

It makes a great difference to us how the results of economic progress in underdeveloped countries are shared. This is true both from the point of view of our long-range objectives in promoting development (see Chapter 5) and from the point of view of the narrower problem under discussion in this chapter, namely, how to prevent Communism.

It would not advance our purposes if a few privileged people in each underdeveloped country got most of the new wealth and income from better farming methods and modern factories, while the level of living of the great majority rose hardly at all. Recognition of this fact leads us directly into some very knotty problems. What should be the attitude of the United States, as a friendy outside power aiding in modernization, toward internal reform in underdeveloped countries? In the absence of rather drastic reforms there is a great risk in many of these countries that our technical and economic help will either be ineffective or actually contribute to widening the gap between the haves and the have-nots, with the result that the country would be more susceptible to Communism than before. But, on the other hand, there is a risk in seeming to want to impose our own economic and social ideas by intervening in the domestic affairs of sovereign countries. These matters, too, are discussed in Part III.

Agrarian reform is an area in which this dilemma is particularly acute. In preindustrial countries land ownership is usually the key to economic wealth, social position, and political power. Archaic land systems are a serious obstacle in many countries to the increase of production, as well as a fertile source of discontent. The Communists, as we have noted, make the landlord class a major target, generally coupled with "imperialists." Promises of agrarian reform have been effective in swinging peasants to the support of their insurrectionary armies. The issue is one which the United States cannot afford to neglect. It would be a needless tragedy if the Communists were to win on this issue, because their ultimate aim—as distinguished from their slogans—is one that the peasants themselves find unattractive. On agrarian reform questions the United States is in a strong position. Our rural tradition is against the estate system which plagues some underdeveloped countries. Moreover, techniques practiced in this country for advancing the welfare of farm people through research, education, extension services, and voluntary cooperation are proving applicable, with modifications, of course, to underdeveloped countries. As we shall see in Chapter 12, the United States has effectively seized the initiative on agrarian issues in international forums, thereby undercutting, to some extent, one of the leading Communist appeals.

PROGRESS IN DEMOCRATIC TECHNIQUES AND IDEALS

The Soviet Union promotes Communist movements in underdeveloped areas by a form of *technical assistance:* assistance in methods of manipulating human relations, a specialized, Communist type of social technology or human engineering. It has been well said that:

The contribution of Moscow to Chinese Communism, then, was its ideology, the system of planning for strategy and tactics, the schooling supplied in Moscow to the leading cadres of young Chinese Communists. This provided the skill, the art, the technique by which to exploit the motives of progressive movements, the black art of having a military force without a formal government, the turning of collaboration with larger groups into the use of those groups for Communist ends, the finesse by which to espouse what many desire without compromising the drive for power. In short it was the modern technique of revolution, the know-how of the politics of violence, made adaptable to China partly by Moscow and partly by native Chinese Communists like Mao Tse-tung.[11]

American technical assistance concentrates largely, though not exclusively, on the know-how of controlling the material environment: how to grow better corn or rice, how to build roads, how to survey and use mineral wealth, how to control disease. Our assistance is rendered by agreement with recognized governments. Soviet technical assistance, by contrast, is focused mainly on a certain system of know-how for controlling human relationships: how to discover and intensify class conflicts, how to use these conflicts and all sorts of discontents to build mass support for a revolutionary party, how to organize guerrilla warfare and insurrection, how to seize power and consolidate it. This type of assistance is rendered to dissident movements in the non-Communist countries which are conspiring to overthrow their own governments and which are bound by a superior loyalty to the Soviet Union.

Communism's main export to underdeveloped countries is thus a certain technique of human relations, a formula offered them as the allegedly best means for correcting injustices and making economic and cultural progress. Does not this suggest that a most important aspect of free world defense against Communism in underdeveloped areas is to make it known that there are *better* techniques of human improvement—what we call democratic techniques—and to offer much more assistance in installing them and adapting them to special local needs?

Democratic Know-How

To some degree our Point Four program is already doing this, for example, when we assist in training programs for

---

[11] "Communism in China," Supplement III, Part C of *The Strategy and Tactics of World Communism*, cited, p. 17.

teachers and agricultural extension workers and when we
hold international seminars on problems of land tenure. The
United Nations technical assistance program is now devoting much attention to the extremely important problem of
improving public administration in underdeveloped countries. All this is to the good. The effort devoted to the hu-
man-relations side of technical assistance should be intensified and the subject matter covered should be expanded.
This is true not merely from the standpoint of countering
the Communist drive but also because successful economic
development depends, as we are now beginning to learn, as
much on better social technology as on better mechanical
technology.

The technologies of "advanced" and "underdeveloped"
countries differ not merely in how crops are grown, how
metals are used, and how goods are made and transported,
but just as strikingly in how enterprises are organized and
managed, how public affairs are administered, how private
associations like trade unions and farm cooperatives are set
up and run, and how the conditions are created for an informed and responsible citizen-participation in local and
national affairs. The vital importance of social technology
and social institutions in the development efforts of underdeveloped countries will be further discussed in Part III.

Democratic skills and ideals in human relationships were
not invented overnight. They represent a body of know-how
that was as difficult to come by in human experience as the
know-how of steam engines and electronics. The Communists offer a highly specialized social technology which they
claim to be the best, or the only, road to economic and social advancement. The free world must not be hesitant about
making known the democratic alternatives and must not neglect to show how democratic social technology can be adapted
to the needs of underdeveloped countries—in theory and in
practical demonstration.

This is not a plea to impose the American system of economics and politics on the underdeveloped countries. It does
not suggest that they adopt our ways unchanged, for democratic social technology offers wide flexibility and variety.
Within the broad principles that constitute its essence, par-

ticular adaptations have often been made in the past and will have to be made in the future to suit the traditions of different peoples and to fit their circumstances and problems. There is no reason to think that the particular adaptation which we have found best in the United States, or which the British or the Danes or the Australians have worked out in their countries, would be best for the Iranians or the Indonesians or the Bolivians, either in general pattern or in details.

Contrasts in Social Technology

There are, however, certain fundamentals which mark off the social technology of democracy from the social technology of Communism, and it is these that we should stress.

Communism tells how to change a society by intensifying and enlarging class conflict, breaking society into hostile groups, seizing power by force, and imposing the will of a small, self-appointed élite which plays off one group against another and combines propaganda with terror to remold men and institutions into a prescribed pattern. Democracy tells how to change a society by consent, collaboration, working out of conflicts through spread of mutual understanding and compromise, lessening of class barriers and group hostilities, achievement of consensus, encouragement of individual and group initiative and free association, helping men to seek human dignity and full expression of human potentialities in a diversity of growth, not according to one pattern.

Democracy builds its social technology around a conception of the proper relation between man and the state which is basically and irreconcilably different from that of Communism. Democracy aims to disperse political power among many groups and to create a situation where tyranny and exploitation by any one group need be only temporary because it can be broken at the polls. Communism aims to concentrate political power in one group, nominally the proletarian class, but really the small clique supposed to represent the vanguard of that class. Once this happens, there is no way to regain freedom under the Communist system except by violent revolution.

Democratic peoples believe in the tolerance of one political

party for another, that the party in power is on probation
only, that opposition is needed. Communists suppress all
other parties, try to build up the myth that the Communist
Party is always right, ruthlessly rooting out any signs of opposition. Democracies can tolerate many different solutions
for social and economic problems. Some democrats are avowed
socialists, like the democratic-socialist parties of Northern
and Western Europe and Australasia; others hold more
closely to capitalism. Americans are committed to no panacea.
"We can have a T.V.A. in Tennessee or on the Columbia without nationalizing all the enterprises along Main Street." [12]

The fatal concentration of Communism on the notion of
class struggle has caused it to build its theory and practice
of human relationships largely on hatred. It is remarkable
the extent to which Communist appeals, even in countries
where Communists are firmly in power, run in negative
terms: *against* the imperialists, the landlords, the kulaks, the
left and right deviationists, the class enemies, and the targets
of such campaigns as those selected for the "Five-Anti Movement" in Communist China. A textbook for elementary
schoolteachers in the Soviet Union instructs them:

> The pupils of the Soviet school must realize that the feeling
> of Soviet patriotism is saturated with irreconcilable hatred
> towards the enemies of socialist society. Hatred gives birth to
> class revolutionary vigilance and creates a feeling of irreconcil-
> ability towards the class enemy; the weakening of such vigilance
> undermines the cause of the socialist revolution. It is necessary
> to learn, not only to hate the enemy but also to struggle with
> him, in time to unmask him, and finally, if he does not sur-
> render, to destroy him. [13]

Now, no realist would affirm that democracy as practiced
in the United States or elsewhere in the West is a pure mani-
festation of brotherly love and good will toward men. Political and social struggles in the democracies, too, sometimes

[12] William O. Douglas, "Dialectic Materialism," a chapter in Frederick
Ungar, ed., *What's Right with America* (New York: Ungar, 1952), p. 105.
I have drawn freely on this excellent statement by Justice Douglas of the dif-
ferences between Communism and democracy.

[13] As quoted from a Soviet textbook in the diary of Frank Rounds, Jr.,
formerly of the U. S. Embassy staff in Moscow, "Eighteen Months Inside
Russia," *U. S. News and World Report*, November 28, 1952, p. 98.

invoke appeals to hate and fear. But it is important to compare ideals with ideals and practices with practices. The great, recognized expounders of democratic ideals stress the appeal to the reasoned intelligence and good will of the citizen. The deliberate fostering of hate and fear for political ends occurs, but it is a violation of democratic ideals. It is, however, a central part of Communist ideals, as expounded by the recognized leaders of Communism. If practices are to be compared, on the other hand, aberrations in America and other democratic countries from the democratic ideal, manifested in assaults on freedom of individual thought, racial and religious bigotry, and the like, are small by comparison with the totalitarian suppression of individuality, the terror, forced labor, liquidation of millions of "class enemies," and similar regular practices of the Communist system.

Need for Ideas and Ideals

The issue really boils down to this: revolution, in the broad sense of fundamental economic, social, and political change, is already under way in the underdeveloped countries. They are rapidly taking over our mechanical technology. Where are they going to get the basic ideas, the social technology and social ideals, that will shape these revolutions?

One observer, speaking specifically of Iran, notes a "curious inversion." He says that the Point Four program and the Voice of America seem to present the materialistic view supposedly characteristic of Marxism. The Moscow radio, on the other hand, "strikes the chords that awakened the American colonists and the people of France to rise and assert their natural and human dignity." Should we not dwell more on free elections, equality before the law, integrity in office, and other political concepts which are as significant in the larger view as tractors or DDT? [14]

Former Ambassador Chester Bowles has urged that we try to give the Indian people a much clearer picture of the United States and of our great democratic tradition than they have been getting. We do not make friends by boasting of our material comforts. It is especially important for us

[14] Elgin Groseclose, "Point Four: A Good Idea Gone Wrong," *U.S.A.* (National Association of Manufacturers, August, 1952), p. 20.

that India understand our concept that every individual is important, that governments exist for him, not he to serve the state. Also, many Indians think of us in terms of nineteenth-century capitalism, with its sweatshop wages, disregard for the health and welfare of workers, and emphasis on speculative short-term profits. They know hardly anything of the dynamic, socially conscious American private enterprise system of today.[15]

An Indian statesman and industrialist summed it up this way: "empty minds and souls provide as good a breeding ground for communism as empty stomachs." He added, "There is no country in the world today so well placed to lead the social revolution in Asia as the United States. Unfortunately while you feed the body, you starve the mind and soul." Among the qualities the United States might well share with the East, he said, were love of freedom, belief in the dignity of labor, the spirit of adventure, generosity, and a world-sized mind. "It is time we heard more about these aspects of your life and less about the number of your automobiles and television sets. The world needs your technicians, your engineers and chemists, but it also needs your teachers, your labor leaders, your social workers, your philosophers."[16]

SUMMARY AND CONCLUSIONS

Revolutionary Marxism has failed in the West. Today its power in Western countries "is only a reflex derived from its victories in Russia and China; without moral and material support from there it would not have a chance."[17] But modern Marxism, in the form of Soviet Communism, continues to menace the West with a powerful attack which is at the same time military and politico-economic. The main thrust of that attack has shifted to the underdeveloped countries, and Communist leaders have developed special strategy and tactics which they confidently hope will bring these

[15] "The Partnership Must Not Fail," *Department of State Bulletin*, February 4, 1952, pp. 163, 166.

[16] M. R. Masani, in a speech to the Convocation on Science and Human Values, Mount Holyoke College, as reported in the *New York Times*, October 5, 1952.

[17] Eduard Heimann, cited, p. 322.

countries into their camp. This is an integral part of the Communist plan for world conquest. They see in it the means of attacking "capitalist imperialism"—what we call the free world—in its weakest links.

Under which of the two competing systems of life are the underdeveloped areas to be modernized, that of Communism or that of democracy? The issue is terribly important for the future of mankind. For at some point the areas now underdeveloped are likely to hold the balance of power between the two.

Communist seizure of power in underdeveloped countries adds important sources of raw materials needed both in peace and in war to the power-base of the Soviet Union and its bloc, at the same time subtracting them from the resources of the free world. The manpower of such countries also becomes available for service in Communist armies, and the highly strategic location of some of them across routes of communication important in peace and war enhances the importance of the struggle for their allegiance. Furthermore, free institutions can hardly be maintained in isolation, and our whole way of life might be defeated without a direct attack on this country if we were to stand idly by while great segments of the world turned one by one to the Soviet bloc.

The Communists have certain advantages in their approach to underdeveloped areas. Resentments left over from the Western rule of subject peoples under a system which now belongs to the past, though remnants of it remain to be liquidated, favor the Communists. Also, Communism seems to offer a quicker solution to economic and social problems of development because it can rely on direct, forcible methods, by-passing the difficult problems of human freedom. It provides a dramatic theory of history and human progress which offers an especially great role to frustrated members of the new intelligentsia in underdeveloped countries, and it provides expertly constructed strategy and tactics by which to mobilize the mass discontents that are bound to exist in areas of poverty, political weakness, and rapid social change.

The West also has certain advantages in dealing with the underdeveloped areas. First, the actual practice of Communism as it has gradually come to light in the Soviet Union and other areas in the Communist bloc is removing much of the early glamor from Communist visions and promises. The revolution has "gone sour" in many ways, as Philip Mosely puts it. The agricultural revolution with its forced collectivization has given the peasants very little while demanding a great deal from them. Soviet industrial development has not led to decisive improvements in the general standard of living but has continued to build for state power with expectations of popular well-being more and more deferred. The Communist cultural revolution has spread literacy and opportunities but has enforced dead uniformity and throttled free discussion. The Communist nationality policy has turned from the early liberal one to dispersal and destruction of some nationality groups on Soviet soil.[18] The fraud in united front tactics and its "new democracy" variant has been exposed repeatedly.

Second, the Western democracies have shown a capacity to learn from experience and have been mending their ways on some matters of prime importance to underdeveloped countries. The colonial system and attitudes associated with it are on the way out. Though race prejudice and discrimination are still problems in the United States, we can honestly point to actions and trends for the better. The United Nations and its specialized agencies have demonstrated promising patterns of action for replacing the old relations of dominance and subservience by international methods that preserve respect while providing needed assistance. The level of information on the problems and aspirations of the underdeveloped countries is rising. Public opinion has rallied in an encouraging way to the Point Four concept in the United States. Field techniques and a corps of experienced personnel for technical and economic assistance are developing rapidly. We are becoming more aware that not only material means of production but also assistance in democratic techniques and in the great ideas and ideals of democracy are needed if economic development is to reinforce and not undermine political freedom. Finally, there can be no doubt

18 Philip E. Mosely, "Soviet Policy and the Revolutions in Asia," *The Annals of the American Academy of Political and Social Science*, July, 1951, pp. 97-98.

that the resources in capital and technical skill which the West can bring to the problem of development, if it has the will to do so, are vastly greater than the comparable resources of the Soviet bloc.

These advantages are great enough so that intelligent statesmanship should be able to make them decisive in favor of a democratic rather than the Communist path to development in most parts of the underdeveloped world.

PART III

DEMOCRATIC PATHS TO DEVELOPMENT

INTRODUCTION

Part III explores the problems of *democratic* development. It emphasizes the difficulties and uncertainties that have to be met if the majority of the world's peoples in presently underdeveloped areas are to make their way to economic efficiency *and human dignity*. The reader is already acquainted with the vast issues that turn on the outcome, both for them and for us in the West.

This study is primarily directed at the *political* implications of economic development. The economic problems of development have been more often dealt with by other writers, and it is not our main concern to elucidate them. On the other hand, we cannot entirely leave aside the central economic problems of building up production in a low-productivity country, such as reorganization of agriculture and industry, capital formation, and raising the skills of labor and management. Successful democratic development cannot take place without substantial growth in economic productivity. In fact, much of our discussion of political implications can be organized around these central economic problems. But when we discuss them it will be with a view to: (1) the *political requisites* for meeting the economic problems effectively and in ways compatible with democratic objectives, and (2) the *political consequences* of meeting them in some ways as compared with others or of failing to meet them.

"Political," it should be said, means more than governmental. It has to do with all aspects of the distribution and use of power in society. The emergence of new institutions by which men organize their relations to each other and the reshaping of old ones, as well as the rise and fall of élites who steer these institutions, are the fundamental features of the internal political changes tied in with economic development.

Both internal and international influences on development are important to our analysis, as are the internal and international consequences. Whether or not a country will successfully move along a democratic path to development depends on elements in its own culture and on the interplay with them of influences from the world environment. The interactions are so complex that the safest conclusion in any particular case is that we cannot be sure what is going to happen when development gets under way. Nevertheless, decisions do have to be made, by leaders in underdeveloped countries and by outsiders whose actions or inactions have a bearing on the outcome. They have to act on some working assumption about the most likely results of changing this or that in the internal situation or bringing in this or that influence from outside. This justifies our attempt to discover some of the relations that seem most significant, even while we recognize that any analysis of such a complex web of mutually conditioned factors is bound to be an oversimplification. Our object is to make what progress we can in understanding the big problems that the peoples of underdeveloped areas and of the whole free world are up against when they try to combine swift economic transformation with democratic aims.

Chapter 10

POLITICAL AND SOCIAL REQUISITES

Everybody knows that if the underdeveloped countries are to overcome their chronic poverty they must acquire tools, fertilizers, roads, factories, power stations, and the other mechanical or material appurtenances of modern production. Less appreciated, at least until recently, has been the necessity for far-reaching *social* changes. "Social" in this context means all aspects of the relations of human beings to each other—political, as in government decisions and government administration; economic, including systems of land ownership and use, organization of production, marketing, and finance; and patterns of family life, education, and the ideals or values that determine what people strive for.

The Communists have been more aware than most of the rest of us that modernizing production means changing the relations of people in society, and this has been one of the sources of their strength. They apply this knowledge in their perverted and ruthless way to sweep away a great many outworn social relations in regions that fall under their control —"the social debris of centuries." Their ruthlessness appeals to some impatient people in underdeveloped countries who have been frustrated by the social obstacles to development. It does "get things done" in a hurry. Our side has to be equally aware of the necessity for deep social changes as a part of economic modernization, but the democratic problem is to find means of stimulating and guiding those changes without sacrificing human dignity, the good which makes development a good thing.

For successful development as we mean it in this book two things are necessary:

1. A substantial and continued economic advance. Economic development must "take," or become "self-generating."

2. A social and political outcome which produces self-reliant citizenship in a free society, stable and responsive democratic government, and cooperation with other free peoples.

The first is not possible in the typical underdeveloped country without such drastic changes in economic and general social relations that "economic transformation" is in some ways a more descriptive term than "economic growth." [1] And if the changes are limited to those (considerable in themselves) required merely for increase of production, the result could be a social and political monstrosity. As we know, a modern industrial economy can be created without creating a democratic society or one inclined toward peaceful international cooperation. All through our exploration of the political and social requisites for successful development, therefore, we shall be concerned *both* with the requisites for a modern level of production and the requisites for a desirable kind of socio-political development.

DEVELOPMENT: A PROBLEM IN SOCIAL CHANGE

An economist writing in a professional journal some years ago defined economic development as essentially the accumulation of capital. I do not believe anyone in touch with the concrete problems of underdeveloped countries and with the experiences gained in the United States Point Four program and in United Nations technical assistance would make that mistake today. Capital accumulation is important, but the real core of the development process is what happens in men's minds, especially in their habits and organization for working together. Even if we want to center attention on capital, the key questions, as we shall note in a later chapter, relate to capital *formation*, which is a social process.

Economic development is a whole complex of interdependent changes manifested simultaneously in the physical environment (new roads, buildings, harbors, machines, im-

[1] Unless in thinking of growth one thinks of such processes as the transformation of the caterpillar into the butterfly.

plements, chemicals), in the forms of association by which men live and work (growth of cities, changes in government, factory organization, business corporations, banking, readjustments in land tenure, family practices, even religion), and in the skills, habits, and thought-patterns of millions of individuals (literacy, technical specializations, respect for scientific methods, ambition, the idea of progress). To pick out any one aspect of this interdependent complex and center attention on it involves a considerable danger of wrong analysis, out of which ineffective or even harmful policies may spring. If we must simplify, we are least likely to go wrong when we think of economic development as a massive problem in human education and social readjustment and only secondarily a problem in equipment.

This is true even if we confine our attention to the problem of bringing about a radical increase in the output of goods and services. It is doubly true for the political and social aims expressed in our definition of successful development (Chapter 5). If capital investment and material technology are pushed energetically in an underdeveloped country while little or no attention is given to deliberate promotion of appropriate social and psychological change—that is, to the more specifically *human* side of development—the result is likely to be either a failure of the development process to "take" and become "self-generating" or creation of a menace to the free world.

Social Obstacles to Development

"Development is a state of mind," says Robert L. Garner, whose experience as vice president of the International Bank for Reconstruction and Development has given him firsthand knowledge of these problems in a great number of countries. "People have to develop themselves before they can change their physical environment and this is a slow process. . . . It involves changes in relations between classes and races. It requires improvement of governmental organization and operations; the extension of social institutions, schools, courts, and health services. These things take much longer than the building of factories and railroads and dams.

. . . Habits of thought and of conduct are the most stubborn obstacles to development . . ." [2]

The industrial system is not a piece of machinery which can be uncrated and set going successfully in the political and social environments characteristic of preindustrial society. Tractors can, of course, be shipped to Anatolia or Thailand, and from the purely mechanical point of view they can be made to work there as well as anywhere else. But to use them well for advancement in popular well-being requires a revolution in thinking, as well as the learning of mechanical skills. The economic productivity of the tractor depends on having a large market for the crops it helps to produce, and this in turn demands drastic departures from the traditional system of local trading. In some regions tractors may be quite impracticable, pending new social arrangements, because land is owned in tiny, separate patches. In other places they may give large landholders the incentive and the economic power to displace small proprietors and tenants. The new equipment may disrupt traditional ways of livelihood in villages before people are able or willing to establish new types of employment and new ways of living in the growing towns and cities.

Thus, because of social obstacles which represent essentially habitual ways of thinking and acting, a machine which has been a great boon to small as well as large farmers in the United States and to American consumers of farm products may be of little use, or actually harmful, in certain situations not uncommon in underdeveloped countries, unless a difficult series of social readjustments is carried out at the same time. The same is true of other machines, and of collections of machines in factories.

Natural Resources and the Human Factor

Natural resources are, of course, essential as a basis for any economic development. Yet a comparison of the basic resources in soil, water, minerals, forests, and so on in the economically advanced parts of the world with those in the

---

[2] As quoted with approval by the International Development Advisory Board, *Guidelines for Point 4* (Washington: June 5, 1952), p. 3. The Board advises the President of the United States on the Point Four program.

underdeveloped areas, where people live in poverty, suggests that the difference in economic level must depend to a considerable degree on other things than differences in these resources. It would be hard to maintain that the soil, water, minerals, etc. of England, Australia, Denmark, and Switzerland are so superior to the corresponding resources of the Philippine Islands, Indonesia, Burma, Iran, and Bolivia as to account for the tremendous differences in their economic levels. Many an underdeveloped country, though not every one, seems well enough endowed by nature to be described as "a rich land inhabited by poor people."

There does seem to be one type of natural resource that is highly correlated with level of development; that is climate. Every modern, economically advanced country lies in the temperate zone, though not every country in the temperate zone is economically advanced. A belt around the world at the equator, between the Tropic of Cancer and the Tropic of Capricorn, contains not a single highly developed country. It is fascinating to speculate about the reasons for this. Geographers and others have long debated the influence of climate on human activity, but it is still a matter on which our scientific understanding is very inadequate. Perhaps when some fraction of the scientific research that has been lavished on the agriculture, industries. and living problems of the temperate zones in the last few centuries has been devoted to mastering the problems of the tropics these areas will yield a much better living to their inhabitants. An exploratory study is now under way at the Council on Foreign Relations by which it is hoped to clarify this set of problems.

To account for the fact that some countries have remained underdeveloped while others have forged ahead we must talk in human terms. Is the answer to be found in hereditary, that is, racial differences? The scientific evidence is strongly against any notion that the spectacular technical and economic achievements of the Western European peoples in modern times are a reflection of some special biological superiority. When the ancestors of the Western European peoples were still primitives, those of many of the peoples whose countries now belong to the underdeveloped group were leaders in human progress—the Greeks, the Chinese, the Iranians, the Indians, the Egyptians.

The human factors which make the difference between economically advanced and underdeveloped countries are not biological; they are *cultural*—using this word in the broad sense in which the social scientist speaks of cultural or social change. What we really need to know in order to be able to promote successful economic development is what elements in the culture of a people are essential to or conducive to such advance, what other elements are obstacles, and whether it is possible to change some of these key elements in the desired direction by deliberate policy—if so, how?

These questions are not easy to answer. In fact, we had better admit candidly that the processes by which cultural change takes place are so complex and the various influences which may shape it in one direction or the other are so numerous and so imperfectly understood that any conclusions we reach have to be strictly tentative. The field of deliberate economic development is one in which we are learning rapidly by experience, and we should be able to test and retest what we think we know.

Having said this, however, the other side of the picture is that practical administrators who have been dealing with these problems, and social scientists who have been studying them, have already learned a great deal. There are in many matters good grounds for choosing one approach rather than another to accomplish given ends. It would be an excessive humility which would withhold from decision-making influence the knowledge of those who are aware of the complex social problems involved in development. That knowledge is already several steps beyond the unsophisticated view which sees development mainly as a problem in mechanical engineering and finance.

Common Cultural Characteristics

Underdeveloped areas have many characteristics in common, despite vast differences in heritage and all manner of local peculiarities. As one reads the reports of economic survey missions sent to underdeveloped countries by the International Bank for Reconstruction and Development, the United Nations Technical Assistance Administration, agencies of the United States government and other governments, engineering firms, and foundations, many key paragraphs seem almost interchangeable. For example, practically all such reports imply more or less delicately, and some say frankly, that a great obstacle to development is ineffective, untrained, incompetent, and usually corrupt public administration. Again, the search for centers of private business initiative and capital formation repeatedly leads to observations like this:

The investments of the wealthy are largely in land, revenue-producing real estate, or relatively small privately-controlled businesses. Trained for generations as traders and merchants, they do not seem to have confidence in long-term investments, and the practice of investing in the shares of enterprises controlled by others is practically non-existent. A sense of responsibility, normal to those answerable for the safety and the gainful employment of the investments of others, such as is common to the managements of western industrial enterprises, has not been developed. An unfortunate corollary of this is laxness in fulfillment of legal obligations such as the payment of income and other taxes. Failure to collect taxes from those best able to pay places an unfair burden upon the remainder of the community.[3]

Business enterprises generally operate on the principle of a high profit margin on low turnover rather than low margin on high turnover. Little use is made of the tools of modern management, such as cost accounting, personnel departments, and modern marketing. Other comments in these reports generally describe the lack of even elementary educational opportunities for most of the people, lack of vocational training, lack of effective agricultural extension services or research applied to agriculture and industry. They find that social tradition among educated people tends to insulate them from the practical activities that build up an economy, making even a man with engineering training, for

[3] This happens to be from the Overseas Consultants, Inc., *Report on Seven Year Development Plan for the Plan Organization of the Imperial Government of Iran* (New York: Overseas Consultants, Inc., 1949), Vol. I, p. 4. Similar passages appear in reports on many different countries.

example, loath to don overalls and get in close on a job.
The list could be expanded.

Social Obstacles Illustrated in Cuba

The Mission to Cuba of the International Bank in 1950
concluded that the chief obstacles to Cuba's further development were deficiencies in what it called "the organizing factors." [4] These deficiencies are probably no more striking than
those in many other underdeveloped countries, but it may
nevertheless be instructive to use the Cuban situation as a
specific example of a general condition.

Cuba has excellent natural resources and a location and
political relations which give it favored access to the huge
United States market. It has a substantial body of technical
personnel and of labor accustomed to industrial processes.
When the sugar market is good it has a large source of income and foreign exchange. Certainly in the decade before
1950 Cuba's development had not been held back by shortage of potential capital or foreign exchange, or by inability
to finance government services. Yet there had been relatively
little development of new industry for a generation, and income per person, instead of showing a progressively upward
trend, had simply fluctuated with the world market for sugar.
Meanwhile, mechanization in agriculture and growth of population had helped to add chronic unemployment to severe seasonal and cyclical unemployment in this unstable
economy.

What was holding the economy back? Many *social* factors.
Public administration was ineffective and often corrupt. The
nation received much less than full value for monies invested in public works. These lacked a coherent plan related
to development needs and were often left incomplete because of a change in administration. A mass of overly rigid
labor regulations, erratically and politically administered,
acted as a drag on enterprise, new and old. Like many other
countries, Cuba has tried to legislate modern standards of

[4] *Report on Cuba: Findings and Recommendations of an Economic and
Technical Mission*, organized by the International Bank for Reconstruction
and Development in collaboration with the Government of Cuba (Washington: International Bank for Reconstruction and Development, 1951), especially Chapter 4. The author served as chief economist with this mission.

social security without building up the productivity to sustain them. Agricultural experiment and extension services, mining and other resource surveys, vocational training, current information on economic and social trends, and other potential aids to economic expansion were inadequate and poorly supported. The tax system was cumbersome and unjust, unnecessarily discouraging constructive initiative. One of the greatest tragedies was the public school system. The comparatively excellent system of elementary education, installed fifty years ago by the American army after the war of liberation from Spain, still ranked a quarter of a century ago as one of the best in Latin America. Since then it had been weakened and demoralized by maladministration and large-scale misappropriation of funds.

Private owners, investors, and managers, whose functions in a private enterprise economy are to be enterprising and to organize production efficiently, in Cuba had been as deficient in their field as the government in its field. The quality of management was low, with outstanding exceptions. There were no schools of business management, only some university courses designed to train accountants. The great sugar industry, with plenty of money at its disposal, had devoted insignificant sums to research and development, though the benefits that would come from new products and diversification have long been apparent. Men with money preferred to put it into apartment houses in Havana or New York stocks or even to hoard it rather than to build up new business ventures. There was more speculation than investment. Commerce and manufacturing mostly followed the old pattern of high markups, low turnover, limited markets. Personnel management, with outstanding exceptions, was 25 to 50 years behind modern practice. This fact, the lack of competent and responsible trade union leadership, the sense of insecurity resulting from an unstable economy, and the lingering resentment in the ranks of labor over past abuses were largely responsible for the extremely bad labor relations which were probably the major obstacle to industrial development.

Thus Cuba, though far enough along to be in our "intermediate" rather than the "underdeveloped" group (see the table on pp. 16-17), stays on dead center. Its problems are like those of many other underdeveloped or partially developed countries. Though it has ample resources and opportunities, it is caught in a mesh of vicious circles. It could cut its way out if somehow improvement could be brought about in the organizing factors—government, business leadership, labor leadership—and if there could be a stronger sense of social cohesiveness and civic responsibility throughout the community. Here we are at the heart of the social problems of economic development.

Social Classes and Individual Deviants

The social obstacles to development are tenacious because they are deeply imbedded in habits of millions of individuals, in the accepted social arrangements we call institutions, and in the system of values by which people decide that some things are good and others bad, some more important and others less important. Also, in underdeveloped countries relatively small groups of privileged people often enjoy exceptional wealth, political power, and prestige under the old system. They are likewise privileged as respects health and education and hence possess more than average energy and social skills by which to influence events. Yet this group, because of its relative comfort and its fear that any substantial economic and social changes might undermine its position, is likely to be apathetic, if not actively hostile, to many of the measures required for economic modernization.

While this last is true and important and for some countries can hardly be overstressed, still, for the generality of underdeveloped countries, I think it can be overstressed. Blaming every lack of dynamism on a small "reactionary" minority hides the true depth and complexity of economic and cultural change. It neglects the natural conservatism in the great majority of the people in any country where the economy has long been static and the culture traditional rather than scientific or technological. And it neglects the permeation of portions of the old élite in many countries by modern ideas, often through sons who acquire a Western education or are otherwise shaken loose from tradition. Many acquire loyalties to their nation, or perhaps to humanity, stronger than their loyalties to the supposed interests of their class. The phenomenon of a Franklin D. Roosevelt—patrician-born but giving leadership to causes distinctly unpopular among patricians as a class—is frequent enough to be highly significant in social change.

Also the impact of ideas, education, and economic activities from outside tends to break down class barriers and to offer new avenues to success for individuals outside the hitherto privileged groups. The notion that social origin determines a man's political views, and especially his attitudes toward the changes requisite for successful economic development, no doubt has a good deal of validity in terms of statistical averages, but in any society where new ideas have begun to percolate there are bound to be a considerable number of individual deviants, mutants, who do not follow the average pattern. It is precisely these individuals who are the key to social and economic change.

We are dealing here with something absolutely vital to the *democratic* method of surmounting the social obstacles which block economic development. Once we cast our picture of society into the rigid class mold we have surrendered to the totalitarian enemy. For if you assume that people cannot be taught, induced, persuaded to change as *individuals,* then you are on the way to the Communist formula of social change through liquidating various kinds of "reactionaries" *as a class.*

SOCIAL TECHNOLOGY

The key to greater productivity and higher living levels in underdeveloped countries has often been described as a wider application of modern scientific and technical knowledge. International programs of aid to underdeveloped countries have been built around technical assistance.

What is this "modern technology" that the underdeveloped countries lack and the economically advanced countries have? It will be contended here that our customary concept of technology is faulty and misleading because it centers on the mechanical or physical side, which will here be called *material technology,* and leaves out what we shall call *social technology.* The upward surge of production in the modern

West and the lead of the United States in productivity today are as much due to advances in social technology as in
material technology. Material technology could never have
forged ahead the way it did except in combination with social
inventions such as civil rights, representative government,
universities, free public schools, joint-stock companies, fed-
eralism, the idea of the mass market, and so on. The needs
of underdeveloped countries for better techniques are as
great in the social as in the mechanical field. This is a fact
which has quickly and overwhelmingly forced itself on the
attention of those concerned with international technical
assistance.

Experience has shown that technical assistance, if it is
really to foster development that "takes," needs to be concerned even more with the social know-how of public administration, business management, and agricultural extension work than with the know-how of mechanical and
chemical engineering. And if we want technical assistance to
promote "successful" development as defined in Chapter
5—a more complicated problem than merely raising productivity—then aid that helps underdeveloped countries to acquire the social and political skills and to build the institutions necessary in a democratic society is still more vital.
Concretely, this means modern methods of business management, public administration, constructive types of trade
union leadership, the techniques of a free and responsible
press, and ways of arriving at a democratic consensus through
political parties, elections, and responsible governments.

Material technology is visibly expressed in artifacts we
call "fixed capital"—like the tanks, pipes, and instruments
that embody the know-how which goes into a modern oil
refinery. But the equipment will not work for long without
men who have an understanding of it. The real essence,
even of material technology, is in men's minds. This is one
of the reasons why machines can be set down in an underdeveloped country in perfect condition and still not work
the way they did where they came from.

Social technology gets embodied in social institutions,
which are the "fixed capital" of men's social relations. For
example, certain techniques of organizing and controlling

behavior are embodied in the family, government, armed forces, business firms, trade unions, and churches. At times the social techniques may change while the outward embodiment remains apparently the same but really operates differently. Also, just as a modern machine may be installed in an underdeveloped country but operate poorly or simply rust until local people acquire necessary know-how, so it is with a modern social institution. A civil service, or a modern business corporation, or a bank, or the latest model in parliamentary government may be installed, in form at least, in a country where social technology, like material technology, is "backward." But it will operate poorly and figuratively rust and break down in the absence of know-how, practice, and accessory institutions. Furthermore, neither modern machines nor modern social institutions will work in an underdeveloped country until enough people with enough influence want them to work. This is the question of will or social values to which we return later.

What Kind of Social Technology?

Technology, whether material or social, is a *means* and can be made to serve good or bad *ends*. Social technology in the West has developed under the shaping influence of a set of social values which gives a high place to the worth of each individual and therefore prizes the democratic ideals of personal freedom, equal opportunity, and government by consent. There are many types of social technology in the world, among them some based on quite different notions of what values are most important. The underdeveloped countries themselves bring a varied heritage in social technology, as in material technology, to the threshold of modernization. They cannot raise their economic levels substantially without changing their social technologies as well as their material technologies. What will be the direction of those changes and the nature of the new social techniques and institutions that they evolve? The answer will be different in different countries, and the nature of the answer will go far to determine both the internal and the external political consequences of economic development.

As Part II brought out, the Communist movement offers

the underdeveloped countries a ready-made social technology which would effect a rapid transition from the old order to the machine age under the ruthless rule of a "vanguard." This variety of social technology idealizes the mass man, fashioned in a rigid mold of conformity in the image of the machine itself. Its techniques are techniques for manipulating men to obtain the results decided upon by the manipulators. This is the key to the difference between Communist or other totalitarian social technologies and the social technologies suited to democratic values.

Democratic social technology defeats its own aims if it becomes merely a means of manipulating other people. It has to contrive ways by which the initiative of individuals can be released, not merely to serve predetermined ends but to participate intelligently and effectively in the choice of ends. This difference of attitude runs all through the institutions in which the social techniques of democracy and of totalitarianism, respectively, are embodied. Both have trade unions, but democratic trade unions are a means by which workers can express their own grievances and aspirations, whereas trade unions in totalitarian countries are among the means by which the state-employer manipulates the workers. Both aim at universal education, but democratic education is designed to encourage each person to think for himself and to play a free, cooperative role as a citizen, while totalitarian education is designed to inculcate, besides technical skills, certain prescribed dogmas and the habit of conformity. Both have adult discussion groups. In democratic countries they are a means of bringing out divergent views and seeking a voluntary area of agreement. In totalitarian countries—especially "New China" where this instrument is being widely used for mass indoctrination—the right answers are predetermined, and the whole process is set up to bring almost irresistible group pressures on recalcitrants.

There is a danger that changes in social technology, social institutions, and social values will lag behind changes in material technology and equipment. "It is an old maxim in sociology that it is fairly easy to induce a primitive to substitute a steel plow for a wooden plow, but it is difficult to get him to change his institutions of marriage, family, and religion." [5] In Japan, textile machinery replaced the spinning wheel and artillery the samurai sword more rapidly than modern ideas replaced traditional ideas concerning the status of women or the role of the fighting man in the state.[6] Such a cultural lag could make economic development abortive or give it a bad political and social outcome. The other danger is that the social technology, institutions, and values of the Communists may be forced on people, with all that this implies for human values and for world politics.

The United States and other Western nations have much to offer the underdeveloped countries in the field of democratic social technology. Social technology and institutions, however, are even less capable than material technology and equipment of being transferred successfully without substantial modification from one environment to another. What we can contribute in such important fields as government and administration, business management and industrial relations, education, community cooperation, and the like is a set of fundamental attitudes suited to the ends of human freedom and dignity, and a great wealth and variety of experience. Underdeveloped countries will have to work out their own applications and make their own choices.

THE WILL TO DEVELOP

Beyond both material and social technology is an intangible something which we may call "the will to develop." We do not understand this very well, especially why it appears at one place and time and not another. Yet there is no doubt that a key question in economic development is, "What will the people of the country do for themselves?" Motivation is the important thing. Unless something happens to change motivations, a static economy will not turn into a dynamic economy, and an economic development movement, if somehow started, perhaps with outside aid, will not become self-generating.

[5] Clyde V. Kiser, *Annals of the New York Academy of Sciences*, Vol. 54, Art. 5, May 2, 1952, p. 762.
[6] W. W. Lockwood, Jr., in an unpublished study on Japan which I have had the advantage of consulting.

What brings changes in basic motivations and stimulates the will to develop? To what extent is it (1) possible and (2) justifiable to influence these things from outside, since they touch directly the fundamental values or preferences of people with respect to their way of life? When fundamental values start shifting, as they obviously are doing in many underdeveloped countries today, what can be done to shape the change so that the result is a dynamic free society, not dynamic totalitarianism? I do not have the answers to these questions, though a few thoughts and hypotheses will be suggested below. This is another of the important areas where men concerned with practical programs need to cultivate a reflective awareness of what is involved and where social scientists, by their research, may be able to make a crucial contribution to the understanding and guidance of the development process.

In the West the will to develop was a decentralized will. It was manifested in the initiative of individuals and private groups. Governments performed important tasks in the development process, but they did not provide the motive power; on the whole they were more pushed by the society than pushing it. The will to develop grew in the West along with the weakening of old feudal loyalties, changes in land systems and the rise of towns and cities, the rise of individualism and representative democracy, the Protestant Reformation in religion, the inquiring mind in science, the inventive mind in technology, and the enterprising, innovating spirit in business.

In the later cases of development, the will or motive power has been much more centralized. Governments have had much more to do with initiating the process. They have borrowed ideas and technology from abroad and have deliberately persuaded or in some cases forced their people to accept the innovations.

Japan suddenly acquired a will to develop in the late nineteenth century. The impact of the West, dramatized in Commodore Perry's visit, touched it off, but unquestionably the modernization of Japan was undertaken and carried through by the Japanese themselves. Japan, after deliberately insulating herself from foreign contacts for centuries, decided to adopt the industrial methods of the West and did so. This rapid turnabout and the effectiveness with which the new decision could be carried through were made possible by the hierarchical structure and centralized loyalties of Japanese society. The Japanese government pushed and guided the development process—for example, by sending missions abroad to bring back techniques in many fields of material and social technology, and by founding new industries, often turning them over later to private management. But the government did not have to do it all. Development quickly became self-generating and predominantly private. The motivations of the élite who made the key decisions and carried out the modernization program were mainly political and military. They saw that the only way to save Japan from humiliating subservience to better armed foreigners was to modernize, and their central aim was military strength. Japan's will to develop was not stimulated primarily by a desire for economic well-being, at least not in the democratic sense of improving the well-being of the common man.

In Turkey, Mustapha Kemal Ataturk was able to crystallize and direct a social movement powerful enough to impose radical changes in direct defiance of the strong conservative force of religion. The change was symbolized by abolition of the fez, enforced adoption of Western dress, transposing the language to the Latin alphabet, and starting industries. This was done through dictatorship. Ataturk and his group provided the will. The changes "took," and now democratic values and practices seem to be emerging rather strongly in Turkey. Ataturk's motivation, like that of the Japanese leaders, was primarily to make his country strong so it could be independent. He cared very little about shoes for the peasants. Even today the strong patriotism of the Turks and their determination to defend Turkey against a possible attack from the Soviet Union seem to be the primary explanation for the energy they are putting into economic development. There are signs, however, that the desire for better living is beginning to percolate to the villages and may become more and more influential in shaping Turkish policy.

In the Soviet Union and the other Communist-ruled countries the will to develop, along lines predetermined by the Party, is supplied by the Party élite. The Party undertakes to guide the masses and to infuse them with enthusiasm by propaganda, terror, and force. But this is also combined with genuine opportunities for education, jobs, and a sense of participation in the upbuilding of the country.

In India the responsibilities of independence seem to have given added impetus to the will to develop. Here is a case, the most important in the underdeveloped world, where an enlightened political leadership which believes strongly in the democratic values is striving with great intelligence but in the face of tremendous handicaps to lead, not drive, the people toward a better future. Can these leaders, faced with mass misery and ignorance, inspire and channel the will of the people so as to bring about the drastic changes that have to be made; or will they be defeated by inertia or swept aside by a tidal wave of heedless demands for the shortcuts advertised by the Communists? This is one of the great questions of unfolding history.

Puerto Rico in the last decade has shown a will to develop, under political leadership inspired by a concern for popular well-being and adhering to democratic values. Mexico, Burma, Israel, and other countries might be cited, all with different histories and cultures and in different ways showing enough individual and collective ambition to break out of old ruts.

Willing the Ends and the Means

The will to develop is in essence a matter of what individuals and social groups *want*, and *whether they want it badly enough to be willing to change their old ways of doing things* and to work hard at installing the new. This will may be based, as we have seen, on the individual ambitions of people scattered all through a society, on the driving force of a few, on the desire of an élite or of people generally for national strength and independence, on a widespread social demand for improvement in living conditions, or on some mixture of these. A mere desire for more of the good things of life which others are known to enjoy is not enough to produce development. People must be willing to undertake, or at least to accept, important changes in the way they make their living, in their attitudes toward investment, taxes, and countless other things, even some of their religious and family traditions.

If an economy is to become dynamic, both the élite who are the key people in various aspects of economic, political, and social life and the masses of people have to be willing to face change. But nearly everyone has vested interests in the old ways of doing things. Sometimes the habits of daily routine are the strongest vested interests of all. It is not uncommon in underdeveloped countries, as we have noted, for a relatively small privileged group to constitute at one and the same time the élite of wealth, of political power, of education, and of social prestige. This élite may block economic development by being apathetic (there being no other leadership), by actively opposing the whole idea of development, or more probably by giving lip service to development "in principle" while actively opposing the essential means. On the other hand, if the existing élite or strong segments of it decide that modernization is the thing, the resulting change-over may be very rapid. This seems to be what happened in Japan. It may also be rapid when the old élite is completely replaced by a new élite, as in the Soviet Union and other countries where the Communists have seized power. In general, the will to develop may arise through: (1) conversion of the old élite, or portions of it; (2) replacement of the old élite by new leaders; or (3) a combination of the two. The third is the usual democratic alternative.

Most observers nowadays hold that the more responsive a government is to the wishes of the masses of ordinary people the more ardent it is likely to be for economic progress. But we have to be careful not to oversimplify. True, a government sensitive mainly to the views of large landowners who are satisfied with the old system is unlikely to press a development program vigorously. The views and influence of the military, intellectuals and students, religious leaders, peasants, commercial groups, and industrialists and workers, where some industry already exists, will not be uniform from country to country. Among the mass of the population the demand for betterment may be latent rather than active. A characteristic of ordinary people in a static society is likely to be inertia. Even when stirrings have begun and the people are becoming conscious that better food, health, education, and other good things are possible, as is the case in most underdeveloped countries today, they may will the *ends* without willing the *means*. Popular pressures have forced some governments to pass laws raising wages and at the same time restricting mechanization. Once a development program gets down to concrete changes it encounters the conservatism of habit, intertwined with all sorts of family and religious and other sanctions. It takes leadership to give form and direction to the rather vague aspirations of the masses and turn them into a definite program. Whether mass aspirations crystallize into constructive or destructive programs depends on the kind of leadership.

THE CAPACITY TO COOPERATE

The ability of groups of people to cooperate, a sense of civic responsibility, and a certain minimum of honesty and integrity in public office and private business dealings seem to be among the characteristics which differentiate countries that have moved ahead rapidly in economic development from others which have remained stagnant. These are intangible factors, but they help to explain why development "takes" in one place and not in another.

Obstacles which interfere with social cohesion include barriers of prejudice—caste, race, and class—and intense loyalty to family as opposed to broader civic loyalties. This last has been characteristic of China and in lesser degree of Latin America and other parts of the underdeveloped world. A social scientist has suggested that the strongly "family-oriented" social structure of traditional China, contrasting with Japan where loyalty to the feudal hierarchy took clear precedence over loyalty to one's family, is the main explanation for the fact that China took to modern industrialism less readily than Japan.[7] Japan had a basis which China

---

[7] Marion J. Levy, Jr., "Contrasting Factors in the Modernization of China and Japan," *Economic Development and Cultural Change,* October, 1953, pp. 161-197.

lacked for effective public administration and business organization, and for reshaping the life of the country without a breakdown of social control.

A modern economy requires large-scale organization, and it makes people interdependent over large areas in ways unknown to a preindustrial society. Personal and family loyalties are not enough. Obligations have to be fulfilled between individuals who have perhaps never seen each other. "Let the buyer beware" is no basis for mass marketing. A credit system depends on good faith. Individualism must not be so extreme as to prevent teamwork, including teamwork in large organizations—factories, corporations, national trade unions, public health services. There are corrupt public officials and dishonest businessmen in all countries, but a social code which fosters a certain minimum of public and commercial morality is certainly one of the requisites for efficient operation of a modern economy.

One of the obstacles to economic development in Cuba, as pointed out to the mission of the International Bank for Reconstruction and Development by informed Cubans from many walks of life, was a prevailing "lack of confidence in others." This may be a significant factor in other Latin American countries and in some other cultural backgrounds as well. People do not expect integrity in public administration, private business enterprises, and labor organization. The effects of such a lack of faith are disastrous. The fact that investors are unwilling to be minority stockholders in corporations because they would expect to be cheated is said to be one of the main reasons that enterprise has to be confined largely to family firms. Lack of confidence in the integrity of government prevents it from performing the constructive role that is required in development. Mutual suspicions add to the difficulties encountered by those who seek to develop agricultural cooperatives and community projects of various kinds.

There is a notable absence in Latin American countries, and in fact in most underdeveloped countries, of the sense of community responsibility which many businessmen in the more advanced industrial countries have developed. This in turn is probably related, both as cause and consequence, to the hampering regulations imposed on business by governments. American private enterprises operating abroad can perform an important service if they will demonstrate and explain the concepts of community responsibility which have become a part of enlightened business thinking in this country in recent years.

We have been discussing the capacity to cooperate in terms of its importance for achieving a modern, productive economy. It also has an important bearing on the prospects that development will have a good political and social outcome. Lack of capacity for voluntary social cooperation makes dictatorships more likely. Individual freedom can be preserved in an industrialized society, where a high degree of coordinated effort is essential, only by means of a great amount of voluntary cooperation based on a keen sense of social responsibility and the necessity for teamwork.

BROADENING THE BASES OF POLITICAL POWER

A study focused on political implications of economic development must be particularly concerned with the distribution of political power. Power is the common currency of politics. Economic development always opens up new sources of power and makes some of the old sources relatively less important. In a country where land ownership has been the main source of large income and of political and social influence, commerce and manufacturing may offer new roads to the top. Where only a few have had enough leisure and education to exert an influence on public affairs, economic development may give such opportunities to entirely new groups of people. What individuals or social groups will wield the new types of power that come with development? For what ends? The answer will go far to determine in any given country whether the results of economic development are good or bad, as we have defined those terms.

When Germany and Japan became modern, industrial states the political influence of the old feudal aristocracy, with its warrior outlook, remained strong. The results were unfortunate for the world and for the people of these countries. In Russia, China, and other countries under Communist rule the old élite has been completely liquidated by revolution, but the new revolutionary élite is one bent on totalitarian despotism internally and aggression externally. In some underdeveloped countries, notably in parts of the Middle East, an old land-based élite has stayed in control and has either blocked development or limited it to forms which largely benefit its members. Thus they may have made stagnation permanent or, more likely, they have set the stage for violent upheaval out of which anything might come. Democratic political development accompanied economic development in the West, but modern history warns us that this is not inevitable.

A Guiding Principle

Are there any guiding principles which may help leaders of underdeveloped countries who prefer their countries to take the democratic path, and which ought also to be taken into account in international efforts to assist democratic development? One such principle is *broadening the bases of political power*. This will not give infallible answers to all questions that arise, but I suggest that it can give a direction to practical thinking which may avert potentially serious blunders and increase the prospect that economic development will be successful development.

The bases of political power are broadened when more people outside the hitherto privileged groups acquire the means of making their influence felt in government, in economic affairs, and in society generally. These means include education, energy (health), skills, money, experience in management or group leadership, self-confidence, initiative, and some degree of economic independence (in the sense of not being completely dependent for the opportunity to make a living on the will of a landowner, or the group in control of the government, or any particular employer). Economic independence is facilitated by wide distribution of land ownership, by existence of small or medium-sized enterprises, and by economic growth that creates a variety of opportunities for those who seek employment and for the self-employed, including the politically very important category of professional people. In other words, all who favor the democratic path to development should prefer, on political and social grounds, types of economic development that tend to diffuse skills, opportunities, wealth, initiative, self-confidence—and therefore political power—more widely. This is a necessary part of the process of building an economic and social base on which responsible, democratic citizenship can rest.

The same idea is often expressed by saying that it is necessary to develop a "middle class." This is true, and is really included in the general principle of broadening the bases and widening the distribution of political power. The make-up and other characteristics of a middle class must certainly differ rather widely, however, in such differing cultural environments as India and Chile, and in neither of these countries will a middle class resemble that of nineteenth-century England.

Broadening the bases of political power also means lowering the barriers of custom, caste, and prejudice and the barriers of educational and economic opportunity which prevent talented individuals from working their way upward into the élite, that is, into positions of leadership. There must also be *different,* though overlapping, élites in the major areas of social life—economic, political, educational, religious, artistic, and so on. Those who control the wealth should not also control the government and the educational system. Those who direct the police should not also direct the farms and factories and the artistic life of the country. Such a "separation of powers" distinguishes a healthy democratic society from that of some underdeveloped countries where privileges and power are concentrated in relatively few families. It also distinguishes democratic society from totalitarianisms of the left or right in which a party élite controls everything.

For these political and social reasons (aside from the question of efficiency in production) it is important to encourage a wide area of private initiative and enterprise. This is not the same as advocating that the government should, on laissez-faire grounds, leave economic development entirely to private enterprise or that it should avoid everything that might be labeled "socialistic." Many things which private enterprise does in the United States simply would not get done by private enterprise, at this stage, in many underdeveloped countries. The real problem is a positive one: how to build up private initiative and enterprise and encourage it to take hold and perform the many tasks for which it is well adapted. A positive program in the underdeveloped countries to encourage decentralized initiative and thus to enlist more talent in the details of economic progress is desirable on grounds of economic efficiency and because of the political basis it provides for active citizenship and self-government. More will be said on this in Chapter 11.

The Substance vs. the Forms of Democracy

We have deliberately put more emphasis on broadening the economic and social bases of political power than on changing the forms of democratic government, as by introducing parliaments and elections. Historically, in the West, the two grew up together and mutually reinforced each other. Over centuries the rise of trade and spread of wealth and education to new groups of people gradually led to more representative institutions and to a steady rise in the authority of representative bodies. The growth in power of representative bodies and acceptance of the principle of "one man—one vote" as the franchise was extended had a powerful influence in broadening the diffusion of wealth, political effectiveness, and social prestige. This came through such measures as universal tax-supported education, the graduated income tax, and social security. In underdeveloped countries today all these changes that took centuries in the West may be jammed into a few short decades with quite a different sequence, balance, and timing. It is easier and quicker to install the *forms* of democratic government than to achieve the *substance* of a broad diffusion of economic, political, and social competence without which the forms may be a snare and a delusion.

"The people," especially where they have had little opportunity for education or political experience, can sometimes be stampeded by skillful demagogues. They may be worked into an emotional frenzy by embattled reactionaries, perhaps in the name of religion, or they may be manipulated by astute Communist agitation and organization. Hence the

people are often more chauvinistic than responsible statesmen, less inclined to peaceful compromise, and prey to false
arguments for economic nationalism. These dangers are
most acute in the half-way stages of political advancement,
where the masses have learned to read and to understand
simple slogans but are still unfit for the heavy tasks of re-
sponsibile citizenship in a modern-type society. "A little
learning is a dangerous thing" is very true in the the transitional steps to a democratic society.

Can Dictatorship Promote Democracy?

Democratic forms in a country where most of the people
are illiterate, politically unsophisticated, fearful of those in
accustomed authority, and at the same time easy prey to
demagogues, may merely camouflage continued control by a
small segment of society. The Iranian Majlis has represented
mainly the great landowners, while the Shah, though a
hereditary ruler, has at times shown more interest than the
parliament in improving his country's economy, bettering
the lot of the people, and broadening the bases of political
power. In some situations a government that is dictatorial
in form may be a necessary means of breaking the strangle
hold of old ideas and old ruling groups. Ataturk comes to
mind—a dictatorial ruler who speeded up modernization in
Turkey. But by 1950 the country had passed sufficiently beyond the dictatorial stage so that an opposition party actually
came to power in a free election. The military dictatorship of
General Naguib in Egypt, with its land reforms and other
measures, may prove to be another example of "undemo-
cratic" methods promoting the substance of democracy and
making its forms eventually workable.

Such an admission that long-range democratic development may in certain circumstances be promoted by temporary dictatorship is, of course, a dangerous doctrine for those
who favor human freedom. Pushed too far, it leads into the
same pitfalls as the doctrines of Communism. Communist
theory holds that the dictatorship of the proletariat—really,
of the Party vanguard—is necessary in order to break the grip
of other classes and to prepare the way for a future classless
society in which the state can wither away, leaving demo-

cratic bliss. But the "temporary" dictatorship of Communist theory shows no signs of passing. How can anybody tell whether a temporary dictatorship, which might seem to be a better instrument for modernization than a corrupt and lethargic imitation of representative democracy, really will be temporary or will fasten itself upon the country and block democratic progress indefinitely?

Perhaps the best indication is the attitude which the dictator takes toward the means of broadening the bases of political power. Also, a willingness to contemplate at some stage a really free election, with freedom to express and organize opposition views and campaign for them, should rightly remain a touchstone of the sincerity of any government that claims to be ruling in the interests of the people. Our awareness that there has to be a substantial economic and social basis for democracy before democratic forms will work well need not blind us to the truly great utility of fundamental political inventions like civil rights and free elections in fostering social progress and safeguarding against tyranny.

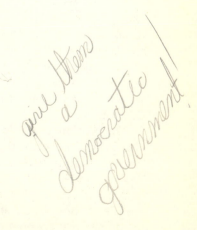

Chapter 11

HUMAN RESOURCES AND THE
ORGANIZING FACTORS

To achieve successful development, underdeveloped countries have to reshape some of their fundamental social institutions. They also have to establish and learn to operate many new institutions unfamiliar to them but essential for modern productivity and free society. This need for reshaping or building anew extends over the whole range of social institutions, from those with direct relation to modern production, like a banking system or land tenure systems, to the family institutions that make the difference between a large or small family pattern. Our purpose in this chapter and in the ones that follow on agrarian reform, capital formation, and population problems is to survey some of the more universal and critical areas of institutional change that are bound up with economic development. Our interest is in two points especially: (1) the relation of institutional changes to advances in economic productivity, without which there can be no successful development, and (2) their relation to the broader political and social outcome of development, especially to the distribution of political power, upon which we have put so much emphasis in our definition of successful development.

The notion that old social institutions can be kept unchanged while only the mechanical side of modern industrialism is imported—a delusion encountered in some of the Arab countries, for example—may lead to complete frustration, or it may lead to a social monstrosity dangerous to the people of the country and to their neighbors. It cannot bring solid, healthy economic and political development. On the other hand, the variety of ways in which the political, social, and economic organization for modern production can be set up and be made to give good results in terms of the tests we are using is fairly large—probably larger than most of us suspect.

Every underdeveloped country that makes a success of economic development will have to solve certain fundamental problems in institution-building, such as making educational opportunity widely available, achieving good public administration under a government responsive to the needs of the people, and stimulating individual and group initiative and harnessing it to the advancement of the general good. But in the *manner* of solving these problems there would seem to be room for almost infinite variation in detail. Today's highly developed countries have not all met them in the same ways. British institutions differ from Swiss or American or French, even though these countries share many traditions, techniques, and values. When we move outside the Western cultural background and think of these same fundamental problems in the setting of Egypt or Indonesia or Bolivia or central Africa, it is clear on reflection that the most appropriate institutional forms will be considerably different, even when the basic human aims are similar. I almost wrote "it is obvious" instead of "it is clear on reflection," but it is not obvious; the history of attempts to install the forms of parliamentary government, for example, in cultural settings where they did not fit, and the readiness of too many Americans to suppose that "free enterprise," if unhampered, would work in a quite different cultural setting, just as it does here, prove this.

It may seem inconsistent to stress cultural relativity and at the same time to say, as we have said, that the United States and the West ought to help underdeveloped countries to acquire democratic social technology. It is not really inconsistent. The hybrid corn that does well in Iowa is not suitable for Mexico; it was necessary to spend years breeding corn in Mexico appropriate to Mexican conditions. Yet the fundamental invention of corn-hybridization, the experience gained with it elsewhere, and the principles and methods that had been learned for developing a good strain were very valuable to Mexico—when applied with suitable local variation. It is the same with social institutions. The new institutions that underdeveloped countries will have to build in order to have successful, democratic development need not be, indeed cannot be, carbon copies of those in the United States or any other country. Yet there are fundamental principles, useful experiences, and social techniques that can be helpful—when applied with suitable local variation. In this and the following chapters we are looking for institutional factors that are likely to have a bearing on the success or failure of an underdeveloped country in seeking both economic advance and democracy. We are not prescribing for any country, but trying to uncover relevant principles.

The people of each underdeveloped country, exercising their own choice and suiting their own cultural conditions, will have to select among ideas from abroad and invent new combinations of those ideas with local customs. The assistance of Americans and other "outsiders" will be most effective, and of greatest benefit to all, if it helps the people of the underdeveloped country to make *their* choices and build *their* peculiar institutions. We must not be too shocked when many of them come up with systems that differ greatly from our own. Our strong interest is in fundamentals: whether development moves in directions that strengthen human dignity and freedom in the world.

DEVELOPING HUMAN RESOURCES

The basic resources of any country are the energy, skills, and character of its people. The building of institutions to develop these human resources is essential to economic advance. How effectively it is done and the *way* it is done also must have a great influence on the political outcome of development. For the kind of opportunities available in a country affects the distribution of political power and the capacity of a people to display the initiative and responsibility required in a free society.

Health

Poverty, sickness, and low productivity form a vicious circle. It has been persuasively argued by C.-E. A. Winslow, in a monograph for the World Health Organization, that the most economical way of breaking into this circle and starting an upward spiral of social development is by a public health program.[1] "Not infrequently," in the words of the authors of the United Nations *Preliminary Report on the World Social Situation,* "the removal of a disease is equivalent to the discovery of a new land or the extension of a frontier." In the Uttar Pradesh state of India a fertile tract of over two thousand square miles went to jungle a thousand years ago because malaria killed or drove out the cultivators. Now, with modern malaria control, thousands of fertile farms are becoming available. This results from a broad program, for "it is not merely a matter of providing DDT and bulldozers; it means tube wells to yield clean water; roads; public utilities (such as electricity); houses; hospitals and public health services; schools; new industries, not only to provide goods but to draw off surplus labour from farms which are being increasingly mechanized; co-operatives and social institutions. Here is an example in which the vicious circle has been broken." [2]

The attack on disease also means an effective increase in the human energy that can go into production. Good health is one of the preconditions for widespread initiative, active participation in community affairs, and growth of the "will to develop." Measures that bring better health to the whole population likewise lay a basis for a broader distribution of political power, for where only a privileged élite are reasonably healthy and vigorous and most of the people lethargic from repeated sickness power tends to remain concentrated.

A lasting improvement in health requires more than an intensive campaign spearheaded by foreign specialists. The key problem is building an effective health service, a permanent institution. How well this can be done also depends on other institutional factors, such as competence and honesty in administration, and ability and willingness of citizens to pay taxes.

[1] C.-E. A. Winslow, *The Cost of Sickness and the Price of Health* (Geneva: World Health Organization, Monograph Series No. 7, 1951), p. 9.
[2] United Nations, *Preliminary Report on the World Social Situation,* cited, p. 35.

Education

Alfred Marshall, the great English economist, wrote in his *Principles of Economics:* "There is no extravagance more prejudicial to the growth of national wealth than that wasteful negligence which allows genius that happens to be born of lowly parentage to expend itself in lowly work. No change would conduce so much to a rapid increase of material wealth as an improvement in our schools . . ." [3] Public policy in progressive industrial countries has long recognized the fundamental importance of a good system of public education, both for its stimulation of material productivity and for the competence and initiative of citizens on which democracy depends.

In underdeveloped countries, bettering the system of public education is one of the most important levers of economic, social, and political advance. The mission to Turkey of the International Bank for Reconstruction and Development concluded that, "Probably no other type of investment, public or private, will produce a greater return per unit of outlay" than investment in health and education. "A generally literate, vigorous and skilled people are not so spectacular or tangible a symbol of progress as a hydroelectric plant or a steel mill, but their value is infinitely greater." [4] The Iraq mission stressed the relation of education to the political and social problems of the country. So long as almost 90 percent of the population lacks fundamental education, it said, the benefits of economic development are unlikely to be diffused widely enough to produce stable social and political conditions. "Nor can democratic institutions be expected to thrive unless people are educated," and not merely in the limited sense of being able to read and write. They must have an understanding of civic rights and duties

[3] Alfred Marshall, *Principles of Economics* (London: Macmillan, 8th ed., 1920), p. 212.

[4] *The Economy of Turkey: An Analysis and Recommendations for A Development Program,* Report of a Mission sponsored by the International Bank for Reconstruction and Development in collaboration with the Government of Turkey (Washington: International Bank for Reconstruction and Development, 1951), p. 169.

and be prepared for community life in the complex modern world.[5]

The creation of a system of education, able to serve as a foundation for modern productive efficiency and responsible democracy, requires a large capital investment; the running costs also are high—though both are thoroughly justified by the yield they bring in national productivity if the money is well spent. Even more crucial, drastic institutional changes are required, in educational organization and administration, and also in the social attitudes and political power relations that determine educational aims.

In underdeveloped countries, skill and experience are usually as scarce in the field of modern educational administration as in modern public administration and business management. Yet there is an immense administrative task in building up a system of elementary and secondary schools, universities, vocational, technical, and professional schools. Also, an adult education program is essential for those who have missed schooling and for special purposes like health education, agricultural improvement, and industrial training. There are few trained teachers and supervisors to start with, and little plant or equipment.

The *kind* of education has a direct bearing on the prospects for economic development and on the political course it will take. A mission of educational experts supplied to China by the League of Nations in 1932 pointed out that a few schools were maintained on standards far above those of the impoverished country, while the primary and vocational instruction most needed by the people was neglected. They found an abstract kind of instruction not connected with surrounding life and criticized the lack of social ideals within the schools. There was a great gulf between the masses of the Chinese people and the intelligentsia. "Such an educational system is highly injurious to the masses and dangerous, because a carefully educated social élite not closely connected with general needs may become transformed into an unpro-

[5] *The Economic Development of Iraq,* Report of a Mission organized by the International Bank for Reconstruction and Development at the request of the Government of Iraq (Baltimore: Johns Hopkins Press, 1952), pp. 385-386.

ductive clique enclosed within the narrow bounds of its own interests." [6] More recently, economic development reports on Turkey, Iraq, and Iran have all emphasized the need for changes in educational philosophy. The school systems of these and many other underdeveloped countries have tended to produce a distinguished intellectual élite rather than to educate the common people or to raise up leaders to deal with the practical problems of development. Common shortcomings which constitute obstacles to economic growth and to growth of democracy are: neglect of rural education (although most of the people are rural); an abstract type of instruction not linked to practical problems; lack of vocational, technical, and administrative-managerial training; too many law students in the universities, and too few in engineering, science, agriculture, business, and public administration; authoritarian methods of teaching; learning by rote; extreme centralization of administration.

PUBLIC ADMINISTRATION

". . . of all the characteristics of national underdevelopment, administrative inadequacy is the most prevalent, the most difficult to overcome, and the least likely to be recognized, or if recognized, to be admitted, by the governmental authorities concerned," writes Hugh L. Keenleyside, Director General of the United Nations Technical Assistance Administration.[7] Another observer who has also had contact with the practical development problems of many countries, Willard L. Thorp, formerly Assistant Secretary of State with supervision over the Point Four program, holds a similar view. "An underdeveloped country," he says, "often has an underdeveloped government. By this I mean that it lacks an effective civil service system for selecting and training personnel, it lacks an effective budgetary control, it lacks a sound fiscal policy, it lacks a governmental structure which clearly divides responsibility among the ministries." This handicaps the country in carrying out its plans for economic develop-

[6] C. H. Becker and others, *The Reorganisation of Education in China* (Paris: League of Nations' Institute of Intellectual Co-operation, 1932), pp. 21-22.

[7] "Administrative Problems of the Technical Assistance Administration," *Canadian Journal of Economics and Political Science*, August, 1952, pp. 345 ff.

ment. The Economic Cooperation Administration encountered such obstacles even in Western Europe. "In the less developed areas it is a problem of major magnitude." [8]

A country attempting to move rapidly from an archaic to a modern economic and social system has to compress into a few decades a complex, interrelated set of fundamental changes which took place gradually over several centuries in the countries of original industrialism. Health programs, education, land reform, agricultural extension work, roads, irrigation, market facilities, and many other things have to move forward together in a fairly well integrated program if any of the reforms are to be truly successful. This means that the governments of underdeveloped countries striving to get their economies off dead center need to undertake more coordinated planning and to do more stimulating and guiding in economic and social fields than is necessary in the more advanced countries where patterns are already set. We have drawn the analogy between economic development problems and the problems that arise when a nation has to convert its economy quickly from a peacetime to a wartime basis. Both require a degree of governmental guidance that might not be needed or tolerated in other circumstances. All this makes competent public administration even more crucial for the advancement of underdeveloped countries.

The *kind* of administration, especially the social attitudes that it expresses and fosters, has political implications of the greatest importance for the course of development. Japan's transformation was brought about under a strong, centralized government and in a social order which permitted a group of determined people, working both through government and through family combines, to push the economy into modern industrialism with spectacular speed. The Soviet Union and its satellites have demonstrated another way in which tight, autocratic control by a small clique can be organized so as to accomplish rapid modernization. Is there a necessary conflict between the two ideals of speedy economic reorganization and progress toward democratic government and society?

[8] Willard L. Thorp, "Practical Problems of Point Four," *The Annals of the American Academy of Political and Social Science*, July, 1950, p. 97.

Certainly there is a challenge here for democracy. If democratically-minded leaders in underdeveloped countries are to meet this challenge, they will need all the technical help and all the inspiration they can get in the modern social technology of democratic management. Considerable progress has been made in this field in the last quarter-century in the United States and other developed countries of democratic persuasion. Business organizations and business schools have contributed much to it, as well as public agencies and schools of public administration.

Some of the principles that characterize democratic, as contrasted with authoritarian, management have been stated by David E. Lilienthal and Gordon R. Clapp in describing the way the Tennessee Valley Authority has gone about its work. TVA "constantly searched for, defined, and refined a unifying purpose that could be understood by all participants and demonstrated by day-by-day leadership and practice." Also, it "sought constantly to decentralize decision-making and action into the smallest possible units of activity and human energies." These principles led the managers, after purposes had been agreed upon with a wide range of persons affected, to rely on persuasion and education, to decentralize within the organization, and to delegate or transfer part of its work to local communities, states, and other agencies by agreements, contracts, understandings, and informal leadership. Among leaders of underdeveloped countries TVA is one of the most admired American achievements. Foreign visitors say they are interested in the TVA "because it seems to combine planning with methods which enlarge the areas of freedom for the individual. . . . TVA's experience may suggest that private and public managements will find that efficient methods are, in the long run, those which encourage and foster individual freedom and strength, and draw upon the community for understanding and participation in the tasks of the enterprise." [9]

The need for good public administration in development is increasingly being recognized. More attention is being

[9] David E. Lilienthal and Gordon R. Clapp, "Progress in Regional Planning in the U.S.A.," *Papers and Proceedings* of the Eighth International Congress for Scientific Management, 1947, pp. 235-243.

given in international assistance programs to promoting the growth of administrative capacity. The United States government has cooperated with governments in Latin America, and later in other parts of the world, on projects in health, education, agriculture, and other fields through *servicios* or joint commissions. One of the virtues of this device is that it provides helpful training in administration. The United Nations Technical Assistance Administration makes public administration aid one of the major aspects of its work. It has had a handbook prepared by an international group of experts to serve as a guide for identifying the steps that can be taken by a newly-organized country in setting up its administration, and for determining ways in which an older country can make improvements.[10] The U.N. Administration is cooperating in regional training institutes in Turkey and Brazil and has made plans for training centers in Latin America, Asia and the Far East, the Near East, and the Caribbean, including provision for ninety fellowships; it is giving attention to requests for direct assistance in the improvement of national administrations from Afghanistan, Bolivia, Burma, Ceylon, Ecuador, Greece, Guatemala, Israel, Libya, Panama, Paraguay, Turkey, and other countries.[11]

While administrative management is a strategic point at which to break into the vicious circles that keep an underdeveloped country in poverty, we must stress that improvement in administration cannot go far or last long in the absence of parallel changes in the rest of a society. Hugh L. Keenleyside quotes Mencius of 300 B.C., "The administration of government is not difficult. It lies in not offending the great families." Where political power is concentrated, as is generally true in underdeveloped countries,[12] the self-interest of those who wield it is likely to clash sooner or

[10] United Nations, Technical Assistance Administration, *Standards and Techniques of Public Administration with Special Reference to Technical Assistance to Underdeveloped Countries* (New York: 1951.II.B.7).

[11] United Nations, Economic and Social Council, *Fourth Report of the Technical Assistance Board to the Technical Assistance Committee* (New York: 1952. E/2213), Vol. I, p. 98.

[12] There seems to be almost a direct relation between the concentration of political power and the immaturity of a nation's economy, observes H. L. Keenleyside in the article cited above. He adds that this generalization is "inaccurate, but less inaccurate than most."

later with administrative reforms based on the modern, democratic idea that the state should serve all the people. Hence, in the long run, good administration in the modern sense depends on deep-going social changes which broaden the bases of political power. We are back to that key problem.

PRIVATE INITIATIVE AND BUSINESS MANAGEMENT

Too often we argue about questions as though they were either-or when both-and is closer to reality. This has interfered with straight thinking on the respective roles of government and private initiative in development.

In some underdeveloped countries there are rather doctrinaire socialist trends of thought which hold private business to be necessarily exploitative. Those who take this view would charge the state with direct responsibility for establishing and running most types of production. In America, opinion is more likely to gravitate to the opposite extreme. Some of the pronouncements of ardent "free enterprisers" seem to suggest that private business, local and foreign, would develop all the underdeveloped countries, if just left to itself. This neglects the fact that the basic utilities and the political and social requisites which make private enterprise an effective force in America are lacking in underdeveloped countries; otherwise they would not be underdeveloped.

Contributions of Private Enterprise

By encouraging constructive private enterprise, underdeveloped countries can gain profoundly important economic and political benefits and increase their prospects for "successful" development as defined in Chapter 5, and this for two main reasons:

1. From the point of view of productivity, an underdeveloped economy needs the energy and drive which private business initiative can contribute. Governments have tremendous tasks in building a proper framework for development. Many of these tasks, like education, public health, and the over-all planning, coordination, and guidance of development, have to be undertaken by governments if they are to be attended to at all. To the extent that governments can "delegate" to private enterprise the filling in of this frame-

work and the day-to-day details of managing production they are wise to do so. Thus a large source of human talent, motivation, and capital formation is tapped, and government machinery is relieved of huge burdens. Safeguards are necessary against antisocial phases of private enterprise, but techniques in this field are now highly developed. It is not as though no progress had been made in methods of "domesticating" the business system since nineteenth-century days of unregulated child labor, no trade unions, and monopolistic trust-building.

2. From the political and social point of view, a vigorous growth of private business enterprise—provided it is widespread, and not concentrated in a few hands—broadens the bases of political power, helps to create an independent middle class, promotes decentralization of authority and leadership, and helps to separate economic power from political and other forms of power. These are among the fundamental requirements, stated earlier, for development of democratic, free societies.

Positive Measures Required

To be *for* private enterprise is not the same thing as to be *against* enterprising government. The desirable results private enterprise can bring in underdeveloped countries, if a proper social base is laid for it and if it is properly stimulated and encouraged, will not come about merely by removal of government "interference." There are plenty of unwise government attitudes and regulations which tend to smother constructive business initiative. But the real task is much more positive. It is a task of institution-building. Private enterprise fails to function effectively in most underdeveloped countries not so much because it is repressed or interfered with as because it does not yet exist in the modern sense in which Americans automatically think of it. The problem is not merely to "release" it but to cultivate it.

Just as underdeveloped countries have underdeveloped governments, they also have underdeveloped private business communities. There is a lack of real business enterprise, business know-how, and business integrity, and of a sense of social responsibility. For private enterprise to make the contribution it should in these countries, personnel must be developed by training and experience, organizations must be established, and philosophies must change. This last implies changes in other aspects of a country's social system.

Land reform may have to precede business growth in some countries, because in a social setting where large landholdings are the symbol of and means to wealth, power, and prestige, there is little· incentive for private enterprise in trade or manufacturing. People with money and education are likely to look down on such occupations. Religious traditions will have to change in some countries, as they did in Europe at the time of the Protestant Reformation, if private enterprise is to flourish. Obstacles of caste and traditions which associate trade almost entirely with a particular ethnic group —for example, the Chinese in Southeast Asia—have to decline in some areas. Everywhere, of course, education, health, and reasonably effective government administration have a bearing on the supply of business talent and the growth of private enterprise.

There is certainly need for more imagination and experimentation on how to draw the energies of private enterprise into national development efforts. This is a field in which comparative case studies of historical experience and particularly of what is being tried today in various corners of the world ought to increase our understanding of the problems and stimulate inventiveness. In Puerto Rico, there has been a vigorous effort to stimulate private industry, especially by attracting established firms from the United States mainland. In Turkey and a number of other countries development banks have been set up to try to encourage private enterprises. The time-honored measures of subsidy and tariff protection, the influence of various kinds of tax systems, the possible role of applied research institutes and business advisory services, and the ways in which foreign investments can bring business training and experience into a country, all deserve study and restudy. The key issue is what can be done in underdeveloped countries under twentieth-century conditions and in various cultural settings to stimulate private business initiative and thus make this great source of energy available for the tasks of development.

Training of Businessmen

The low level of management skills is one of the chief obstacles to economic progress in underdeveloped countries; hence, measures to increase the supply of these skills should be ranked high among the strategic factors for promoting a sustained economic advance.

Programs for improving the practice of public administration and for training public administrators have been mentioned above. Relatively little attention seems to have been given thus far to systematic training of business enterprisers and managers for underdeveloped countries. Schools of business management are conspicuous by their absence in nearly all these countries. If our analysis is correct as to the value of active and socially responsible private enterprise, then trained business personnel is no less important than trained government personnel. Failure to maintain a balance here would weight the scales unnecessarily in favor of detailed government management of the economy.

The mission to Turkey of the International Bank for Reconstruction and Development found that one of the greatest deficiencies in the Turkish economy was lack of managerial competence, both in the state-run industries and in private firms. "We mean by management, not only the top-level officials, but also all levels of supervisors, foremen and crew bosses. . . . Programs of managerial and supervisory training would help to remedy this weakness." [13]

The state banks in Turkey, which have much to do with the direction of investment, have wasted scarce resources in ill-conceived or poorly timed undertakings, not so much because of mistakes in mechanical engineering, but because they "emphasized the technological and production aspects of their work to the neglect of the managerial, financial and marketing aspects." An extensive program for training engineers was instituted at an early stage in Turkey's efforts at industrial expansion, but little attention was paid to the problem of training men for management. "Problems of management and administration are different from, and in many ways more difficult than, the technical problems of

[13] *The Economy of Turkey,* cited, p. 117.

production; and they have been growing at an accelerating rate. Turkish officials have had little experience in dealing with them and opportunities for training in this field have been almost nonexistent." [14]

This is typical of the tendency to see the need for modern mechanical technology while failing to see the need for modern social technology (in this case, the technology of management). The same error is reflected in the disproportionate numbers of students from underdeveloped countries who come to the United States to study engineering as compared with business management.

The main reason for low productivity in the cotton textile industry of Brazil and certain other Latin American countries, according to a recent survey, is not the lack of modern equipment, although that is important in some older mills, but the poor organization and administration of the factories.[15] In Cuba I was impressed by the evidence of bad management in many United States-owned as well as Cuban-owned firms (and by outstanding exceptions in both groups). This was particularly noticeable in personnel matters, and surely was a factor in the incredibly bad labor situation.

The analysis of Iran's economy by Overseas Consultants gave much emphasis to the need for greater efficiency in management. This was the principal reason advanced for a strong recommendation that the Iranian government adopt the policy of transferring its industrial enterprises and mines to private ownership. The recommendation may have been wise for other reasons, some of which have been mentioned above, but it is by no means sure that private ownership in a country like Iran means good management, or even better management than that of government. In this matter the judgment of American engineers and businessmen, formed in a social environment quite different from those of underdeveloped countries, may not be reliable. Good management, in private enterprise no less than in government, is a social product. Private management, on the whole, is as backward

14 Same, pp. 33, 35.
15 United Nations, Economic Commission for Latin America, *Labour Productivity of the Cotton Textile Industry in Five Latin-American Countries* (New York: 1951.II.G.2).

in most underdeveloped countries as public administration. In Iran, the following picture emerges from the Overseas Consultants' report, which also urged measures to improve private management:

In privately-owned industries, most, if not all, of the profits were paid out as dividends, working capital was depleted, and funds for rehabilitation of plants and purchase of parts were not accumulated. Accounting practices are primitive; charges for depreciation are virtually unknown and, where applied, are inadequate. There is little appreciation of the importance of accurate accounting and statistical information. . . . Various means were used to avoid income taxes and to reap additional profits for directors and others in authority. . . . Directors tended to vote themselves exorbitant salaries and to show little or no sense of personal responsibility for the sound management of the corporation.

Purchases of raw materials have seldom been scheduled in terms of estimated requirements, frequently have been made at the wrong seasons and sometimes have been effected speculatively through middle men working in conjunction with directors of the company.

There seems to be little or no knowledge of modern merchandising methods. No new designs have been introduced for cotton print cloth within the past ten years by either private or Government factories . . .[16]

Changes in the Private Enterprise System

Private enterprise as practiced in most underdeveloped countries is closer to the nineteenth-century capitalism that Marx and Engels denounced so scathingly than to the socially conscious capitalism which we know in mid-twentieth-century America. Indeed, the United States has developed a set of business practices and attitudes which have altered the original character of the private enterprise system. This constitutes one of the most important advances in social technology of this century. Because of the exaggerations of some of the propaganda booming "free enterprise" in this country, it is necessary to note that the change required more than *laissez faire*. It was achieved by a judicious combination of *laissez faire* with essential contributions from government

[16] Overseas Consultants. Inc., cited, Vol. I, p. 46, Vol. IV, pp. 136-137.

(public schools and universities, homestead acts, farm advisory services, public health, social security, marketing data, subsidies to railroads and airlines, highways). And there were definite social pressures, largely expressed through government and trade unions, which encouraged the American businessman to be inventive on the human as well as the material side of his operations and to become more conscious of the community responsibilities of business. The result is not perfect, and American businesses do not all apply the best attitudes and practices, any more than all farmers use the most modern agricultural techniques. But the advances have been very real.

In consequence, the outlook and methods of the more progressive American businesses might well repay study by leaders in underdeveloped countries. Though conditions in America differ in many ways from those they face in trying to make private enterprise a constructive force, some ideas would be relevant, such as the notion of professional training for management; the philosophy which accepts social responsibility toward employees, consumers, and the general public as well as toward stockholders; and the developmental, as contrasted with the exploitative, point of view, expressed in applied research, low margins with high turnover, and the idea that high productivity, high wages, high consumer purchasing power, and expanding markets fit together.[17]

TRADE UNIONS AND LABOR LEADERSHIP

Free trade unions, competently led and dedicated to a philosophy which gives them a developmental outlook, are an important part of the institutional basis for a dynamic, modern economy in a democratic society. They are needed to work in partnership with socially constructive private enterprise, to help keep it constructive and to represent the interests of workers. In default of healthy unions of this type, Communists or others with ulterior motives are likely to dominate the labor movement. Even if they do not succeed

---

[17] Peter Drucker, in "Frontier for this Century," *Harper's Magazine*, March, 1952, gives an interesting summary of business philosophy which he suggests American businessmen, in cooperation with the American and other governments, might help to spread to underdeveloped countries.

in using their control of the unions as a steppingstone to complete power, such a situation will surely put many obstacles in the way of democratic economic and political advance. The development of free and constructively led trade unionism is one of the very important problems of institution-building in underdeveloped countries.

It is encouraging that trade union leaders in the Western democracies have taken steps through the International Confederation of Free Trade Unions to foster the growth of democratic unions in such countries as India, Pakistan, Egypt, Syria, Lebanon, and Greece. Both the American Federation of Labor and the Congress of Industrial Organizations are cooperating in this effort. A recent move has been to establish an Asian labor college in Calcutta where leaders from Asian countries can be trained in organizing and running free and democratic trade unions. The political stakes are high, and the difficulties are immense.

The rank and file of labor in underdeveloped countries, having had little education, is likely to be easy prey to unscrupulous manipulators. Sometimes unsuccessful doctors, lawyers, and others who have had the advantage of some education go in for labor leadership and use the influence thus acquired to seek political preferment or personal profit. Far too frequently, the Communists provide the most active, industrious, and skillful organizers. The prevailing philosophy of rank and file and of leaders, when it is not completely opportunistic, is likely to be one of "class struggle." The relation between productivity and high wages is rarely understood. Both employers and trade unions in newly industrializing nations lack the traditions and the skills that make for successful collective bargaining.

One of the real problems of economic development nowadays, which did not exist in earlier times, is the temptation of underdeveloped countries to imitate the advanced social legislation of highly developed countries, or even to go them one better, without first imitating their productivity. It requires a high quality of leadership, both in the labor movement and in government, to select those items of modern social legislation which can be used to smooth the path of development and prevent abuses without stifling economic growth, and to reject those which cannot be supported until more growth has occurred. The United Nations mission to Bolivia reported that Bolivian labor legislation seemed advanced and generous on the surface, but many of the provisions were probably doing more harm than good because the impulses of the legislators had outrun the possibilities of practical application. "It may be doubted whether all this legislation has resulted in any real improvement in the workers' standard of living, whether it has contributed to the formation of an efficient and responsible labor force, and whether it has brought about any increase in the productivity of the country's industries." [18]

APPLIED RESEARCH

A modern development in social technology which underdeveloped countries can use to tremendous advantage is organized scientific research, systematically applied to find solutions to problems in agriculture, industry, and social organization. It is now familiar in the technologically advanced countries in the form of agricultural experiment stations, industrial research laboratories, and, more recently, in applied research institutes attached to universities or set up independently. This is an example of a technique not available to the early-comers. It is one of the reasons which gives ground for hope that development can be carried forward more rapidly nowadays than in the past, and perhaps with fewer blunders.

For the most part, businesses in underdeveloped countries now spend little or nothing on research. In Cuba, for example, where the great sugar industry has gross sales of well over 500 million dollars a year in good times, not much more than 50 thousand dollars a year has been spent for research, though the future of the industry is clouded with uncertainty and there is a great need to increase efficiency and develop by-products. This is only one one-hundreth of one percent of gross sales, compared with 1.5 to 2 percent of gross sales

[18] United Nations, Technical Assistance Administration, *Report of the United Nations Mission of Technical Assistance to Bolivia* (New York: 1951. II.B.5), p. 98.

spent by typical research-conscious firms in the United States.[19]

A few governments have shown awareness of the important role which applied research can play in building up an underdeveloped country. The government of India, with the active personal interest of Prime Minister Nehru, has taken the lead in setting up a chain of national laboratories in chemistry, physics, metallurgy, fuels, glass and ceramics, food, and drugs, with plans for units in leather, building construction, road research, and electro-chemical research. By means of this aid small industrial enterprisers learn how to make good products, and they develop uses for local raw materials. India has also looked to applied social science research for aid in meeting urgent problems in human relations, including the tensions manifested in mass conflict between Hindus and Moslems following partition.[20] The Bank of Mexico has sponsored an applied research institute which combines practical research with training and serves the needs of both government and industry. It was started with the cooperation of a United States research organization, and at the end of five years it had not only solved many important technical problems but had developed into a permanent national institution able to continue without foreign specialists.[21] The International Bank for Reconstruction and Development has been advising Ceylon and a number of other governments on the establishment of similar research institutions and has set up a special staff unit to assist member governments in this respect.

One might ask, Why should underdeveloped countries bother with research centers of their own? Would they not

[19] International Bank for Reconstruction and Development, *Report on Cuba*, cited, p. 76. See also Chapter 9, "Applied Research," in which the International Bank mission recommended a specific plan for the development of industrial research in Cuba.

[20] See Gardner Murphy, *In the Minds of Men* (New York: Basic Books, 1953), a study of human behavior and social tensions, conducted at the request of the government of India.

[21] The International Bank's mission to Ceylon described the Mexican experience in its report. See *The Economic Development of Ceylon*, Report of a Mission organized by the International Bank for Reconstruction and Development at the request of the Government of Ceylon (Baltimore: Johns Hopkins Press, 1953), p. 80.

do better to depend on borrowings from the stock of technological and scientific knowledge already available elsewhere,
at least for a few decades? The answer consists of three
points.

1. The borrowing process itself can be greatly aided by
on-the-spot research, since material and social technology
from abroad almost always needs adapting to local conditions. In agriculture, it is well recognized that a strain of
cotton perfect for California might fail in Egypt because of
differences in climate, pests, and market demands. Even as
between different regions of the United States, it is standard
practice for the experiment stations to test *locally* before
recommending new practices to farmers. Similar problems
arise with machines. A charcoal engine may be better at
present than a gasoline engine for pumping water on farms
in some parts of Asia, because the rural people are more
familiar with charcoal and because it is simpler and cheaper.
Factory equipment designed for United States conditions is
not necessarily well adapted to the climate and labor skills,
the size of the market, and the relative costs of labor and
capital in another country. Social technology is even less
transferable without adaptation. A system of civil service
examinations, a curriculum for elementary education, a
banking system, a method of representative government, or
a procedure in personnel administration that gives the desired results in the United States or Europe may have quite
different consequences in Latin America or Southeast Asia.
There is a big job of "translating" technology, both in putting it into the local language and in selecting what is relevant and adapting it to local conditions.

2. Underdeveloped countries have special problems which
might yield to research but which have not been attacked
forcefully enough because they are not so important in the
countries that have the necessary scientific personnel. For
example, many underdeveloped countries are in the tropics,
while all the highly developed countries are in temperate
zones. Research institutes in the tropics would probably be
more concerned themselves, and would stimulate more work
by scientists elsewhere, on problems like the use of solar

energy, products from the tropical rain forest,[22] and tropical housing needs and methods. Tropical medicine has already made great strides under the spur of the military necessities of World War II, and international technical assistance in health work has shown what can be done when the powerful tools of science are brought to bear. Again, underdeveloped countries need research and engineering directed toward saving scarce capital, while in the West, where capital is much more abundant relative to labor, the bulk of our applied research is automatically directed toward labor-saving devices. Inventive research on smaller-scale equipment and on simpler tools than those now in use in the more advanced countries would be valuable in underdeveloped areas.

3. The innovating spirit needs to be fostered in underdeveloped countries, and one way is to build local institutions and to train personnel whose job it is to apply the scientific outlook to practical problems. Applied research institutes should also help to combat the tradition still strong in many underdeveloped countries that the scholar and the intellectual remain aloof from practical affairs.

Let me emphasize, finally, that the need of underdeveloped countries for built-in institutions of inventive research applies to social as well as to material technology and to the sciences of human relations as well as to the natural sciences. In underdeveloped countries, for reasons brought out in Chapter 10, applied social research deserves an even higher relative importance than elsewhere. In fact, research insti-

[22] Marston Bates in a provocative book speculates on the possibilities that must be latent in the environment that creates the tropical rain forest. Man hacks away at the margin, cutting down and burning to make little plots on which to grow cotton or corn, and when this fails, he complains about the poverty of tropical soil. But can soils really be "poor" that support the most complex vegetative growth on the planet? The tropical forest, Bates claims, is the most efficient system so far found for using solar energy to convert air and water and minerals into cellulose, lignin, and hundreds of other chemicals on which industries might be based. Perhaps the trouble is that instead of working with the environment, we work against it, trying to apply in the Congo or Amazon basins methods that work in Kansas, blaming the soil and climate instead of the method of agriculture when we fail.

What might happen if some fraction of the scientific and technological effort that has been lavished on problems of the temperate zone in the last few centuries were applied to tropical problems? See Marston Bates, *Where Winter Never Comes: A Study of Man and Nature in the Tropics* (New York: Scribner, 1952), especially pp. 242-243.

tutes staffed solely by chemists and physicists, plant breeders and mining engineers could, in the absence of an equally vigorous and intelligent attack on social problems, have the effect of hastening a warped type of development that in the long run might prove worse than useless from the point of view of human well-being. Applied research staffs composed of social scientists, together with social technicians from business management, public administration, education, law, and the other fields of social technology are needed to bring the most modern methods to bear on such problems as capital formation, marketing, rural changes, labor-management relations, better government, and education.

* * *

We have surveyed very briefly in this chapter certain types of institutional change involved in building up human resources and improving the "organizing factors" on which effective use of resources depends. While these problems may be met in a variety of ways, necessarily differing from one cultural background to another, somehow they must be met if hopes for development are to be realized. The effectiveness with which they are met and the *ways* in which they are met will have much to do with the degree of advance in economic well-being and with the distribution of political power.

The next chapters examine other areas of institutional change that are important in the transition from old to new methods of production. The political as well as the economic outcome of the development process will be much influenced by what happens in connection with the problems of agrarian reform, capital formation, and population growth to which we now turn.

Chapter 12

AGRARIAN REFORM

The changes in rural institutions generally lumped together in the term "agrarian reform" are bound to play an
extremely significant role in determining the political and
economic course of underdeveloped countries: (1) because
of their relation to economic productivity; (2) because action
or lack of action on these problems has a direct bearing on
the distribution of political power, on the quality of the people, and on their ability to carry the burdens of democratic
citizenship; and (3) because unsolved agrarian problems are
one of the major sources of tensions which Communists
exploit.

Historically, great changes in the rights to land preceded
or accompanied the transition in the West from medieval to
modern economy. Many of the underdeveloped countries
are now in the throes of corresponding changes. The United
Nations *Economic Survey of Asia and the Far East* for 1950
reported that since World War II "over one-fourth of the
population of the region has been affected by land redistribution and even more by rent reduction and other related
measures." [1] It described a variety of programs in different
stages of execution in Burma, China, India, Japan, Korea,
Pakistan, and the Philippines. Land and agrarian problems
are to be ranked among the two or three topmost "burning
issues" throughout Asia and the Middle East and in some
parts of Latin America. Since the great majority of people in
underdeveloped countries—often three-fourths or four-fifths
of them—live in rural villages and get their living from the

[1] United Nations, Department of Economic Affairs, *Economic Survey of
Asia and the Far East, 1950* (New York: 1951.II.F.4), p. 182.

251

land, it is natural that the most explosive tensions between the old order and the new hopes should come to focus in "agrarian reform."

Local conditions vary so widely that no generalization can apply to all areas. The most common complaints are the following:

Excessive concentration of land ownership.

Fragmentation of small holdings, which discourages modern methods.

Rack-renting, combined with usurious moneylending and perpetual indebtedness.

Absentee landlordism.

Lack of clear titles to land or water or insecure terms of tenancy, which discourage improvements.

Combined with these evils, and necessarily involved in any successful attack on them, are such things as isolation from town markets for lack of roads, grasping and inefficient middlemen, inequitable taxation, poor rural education or none at all, lack of technical advice, ill health, and rural overpopulation.

Agrarian Reform and Productivity

"The land tenure system almost completely blocks the development of a progressive agriculture," says the report of the United Nations mission to Bolivia, speaking of the northern Altiplano.[2]

The International Bank's mission to Iraq, accounting for the low yield of agriculture, points out that there are almost no peasant proprietors. Cultivated land is largely owned by sheiks and urban proprietors who have neither the equipment nor the knowledge to increase production. As the land assigned to the cultivators generally changes from year to year, they have virtually no incentive to improve it. The system undoubtedly retards progress and thus "undermines the health and vigor of the rural population, limits the market for industrial products and may in the long run jeopardize the stability of the social order."[3] Expert judgments in

[2] Report of the United Nations Mission of Technical Assistance to Bolivia, cited, p. 53.

[3] The Economic Development of Iraq, cited, pp. 5-6.

the same vein could be adduced for country after country, all pointing to the necessity of changes in the institutional structure surrounding agriculture in order to release the energies of rural people and make increased production possible.

Because land redistribution has been so sloganized, especially by the Communists, it is necessary to point out that, essential as it is in many countries as part of a comprehensive program of rural improvement, it will not automatically, or by itself, raise production levels in most cases. Unless the new peasant proprietors, along with their land, get better education, advice on good farming practice, and market and credit facilities, they are likely to be as badly off as before, sometimes even worse. There are areas where the landlord performs a real economic function. The quasi-feudal village in some countries, however out of step with modern ideas, provides a type of social organization and security. Scrapping the old arrangements without building new and better ones to perform the same function may result in a period of economic breakdown and social chaos. This is just what the Communists want, so that they can seize power. But those of us who favor a democratic path to development have reason to beware of any approach which is more negative than positive or which offers a simple solution easily propagandized.

In agrarian reform, not only the productivity of agriculture but also the opportunity for urban industry to grow and flourish is at stake, as the quotation from the Iraq report above suggests. A major obstacle to development of efficient manufacturing in underdeveloped countries is the small size of the market, which is in turn a consequence of the low purchasing power of the bulk of the people, most of whom get their living from the land.

Furthermore, so long as great landed estates continue to be the main source of wealth, power, and prestige, this very fact is likely to prevent the spirit of enterprise from developing in new lines. Even profits from trade and manufacturing are often invested in land, because land ownership is the recognized symbol of success. Wilbert E. Moore in his *Economic Demography of Eastern and Southern Europe* notes that Italy, Portugal, and Spain were leaders in the so-called commercial revolution that preceded industrialization in

Europe, and that there had long been important trading centers in Greece, on the Danube, the Black Sea, and the Baltic. Why was commercial development in these areas not followed by industrial expansion, as in England, Holland, and the rest of Western Europe? The question, Moore says, is a hotly debated issue in economic history, but in his view a major part of the explanation is found in "the economic and social significance of land ownership," which in southern and eastern Europe tended to inhibit the growth of non-agricultural enterprises.[4]

Political Aspects

Time and again we have had occasion to refer to the obstacles to democratic development which exist in many underdeveloped countries because of the political and social power of large landowners. We have also taken note of the political dangers that can arise from grafting industrialism, with its great increase in military might, onto a social and political system that remains dominated by the traditions of a landholding aristocracy, especially where that aristocracy has a warrior mentality, like the *Junkers* in Germany and their counterparts in Japan. Whether the economic and social basis for this type of influence is eliminated by agrarian reforms when a country enters upon rapid modernization, or whether the old land and power system is left more or less intact, may be an important factor in shaping a country's political future. Agrarian reform affects the internal political development by broadening the bases of political power and building democratic participation. It may also have considerable influence on a country's external political course, affecting its propensity either to go in for militaristic expansionism or to cooperate peaceably. I do not believe we can draw any sure conclusion on the complex interrelations that link agrarian reforms, or lack of them, to international aggression, but at least the historical experience is strong enough to be a warning.

Successful development as we have defined it in this book can hardly be achieved unless the people who cultivate the

[4] Wilbert E. Moore, *Economic Demography of Eastern and Southern Europe* (Geneva: League of Nations, 1945.II.A.9).

soil—the great majority in all underdeveloped countries—
are able to become independent, self-reliant producers and
citizens. The quasi-feudal relations that have been part of
the old rural order tend to keep people of many countries
from responsible participation in modern democracy. The
raising of educational and health standards and improvement in conditions of rural living which are involved in
comprehensive agrarian reform are, of course, justified for
their own sake under democratic concepts of social justice
and the dignity of man.

The influence of the institutional structure in agriculture
on the quality of the people and their capacity for economic
and political advance is illustrated in Lebanon. According
to Charles Malik, there is a great difference between the
people of the mountains, who own individual farms, and
those of the plains, where semifeudal share-tenancy prevails.
"The mountaineer who won his title to the land scarcely
a hundred years ago has transformed the barren and rocky
mountain terrain into fruit orchards and vegetable gardens.
He is literate, healthy, clean and progressive. His counter-
part on the plains has done nothing to increase the productivity of the soil and remains in a state of poverty and degradation." [5] "Latifundia" have had a pernicious effect on
the quality of people and citizenship in more states than
ancient Rome.

Lessening Vulnerability to Communism

As noted in Part II, agrarian discontent provided a large
part of the fuel for the Communist drive to power in China.
Earlier, "land to the peasants" had been one of the potent
slogans of Lenin in Russia. All across the underdeveloped
world today, from Guatemala to Iran and the Philippines,
agrarian issues, largely in the form of demands for land redistribution and attacks on landlords and rural moneylenders, are second only to "anti-imperialism" in Communist
agitation.

Rural institution-building which provides a constructive,
democratic alternative to the Communist formulas would

[5] Charles Malik, "The Near East: The Search for Truth," *Foreign Affairs*,
January, 1952, p. 249.

seem to be essential if the vulnerability of these areas to Communism is to be lessened.

The United States Seizes the Initiative

The American government, from 1950, has taken a strong, affirmative stand on agrarian reform. By making our position clear and backing positive programs we have seized the initiative and rather successfully undercut the Communists on this world-wide issue. At least this has been accomplished in the better informed international circles that are aware of what happens in the United Nations, the specialized agencies, and in governmental and private efforts under the Point Four program. The example is important, because it shows how an affirmative approach can spike Communist propaganda and put the Communists on the defensive.

After some fumbling, American occupation authorities pushed through substantial land reforms in Japan and South Korea. Our representatives have since been able to point to this program with considerable effect, especially after the truth began to get through about Communist land reforms in North Korea and elsewhere. In September, 1950, Secretary of State Dean Acheson appeared before the General Assembly of the United Nations and, citing the American-sponsored programs of land reform in Japan and Korea, continued:

These examples I have cited are not slogans or phrases. They suggest what can be done on a cooperative, democratic basis, by processes of peaceful change, which respect the dignity of the individual and his right to self-reliance and a decent livelihood. The result has not been what has been called land-reform in certain other parts of the world—to collectivize the farmer and to place him under the complete control of the government instead of the land-owner.

Equally important is the problem of the better use of land. Control of soil erosion, better seeds, better tools, and better fertilizers are needed in almost every country, but especially in parts of Asia, Africa, parts of the Middle East and Latin America, where people suffer greatly from the inefficient use of land.

The major responsibility in these fields rests, of course, with governments, but the United Nations should make special efforts to advise and assist governments in improving land use and productivity. A considerable portion of the funds pledged for the technical assistance programme is already available, to enable us to push ahead with an attack on such problems as these, as well as problems of health, education, industrialization, and public administration.[6]

Secretary Acheson's speech signaled the start of a vigorous campaign in favor of comprehensive agrarian reform, carried on by American delegations in the Economic and Social Council, the General Assembly, the Food and Agriculture Organization, the various regional economic commissions, and other international bodies. No uniform prescription was put forward, as it was recognized that circumstances are different in different countries and that each country has to reach its own decisions.

During the next two years at least five important resolutions on agrarian reform were debated in international assemblies as a result of American initiative. Technical studies and comparative reports on what is being done in different member nations were stimulated. As one follows the debates it is easy to see how the scope of the discussion and of the emerging resolutions has broadened, reflecting a process of education. What started as a rather sloganized interest in narrow "land reform," so far as most United Nations members were concerned, has become "agrarian reform," with longer and longer lists of subtopics covering almost every phase of practical measures that governments might consider for rural betterment. The prevailing view is now the positive and comprehensive one stated by Clarence J. McCormick, U. S. Representative to the 1951 session of the Food and Agriculture Organization:

We in the United States regard land reform in the broad terms of the improvement of all economic and social institutions surrounding farm life.[7]

Cynics may say that nothing is accomplished by inducing delegates, many of them from governments strongly influenced by landowners, to pay lip service to agrarian reform and to vote for resolutions on the subject in international

[6] United Nations, General Assembly, *Official Records*, Fifth Session, 279th Plenary Meeting, p. 26.
[7] U. S. Department of Agriculture, *Press Release*, June 11, 1951.

bodies. What counts for most is practical measures in the home countries. Something may be accomplished through a world climate of opinion, however, and in some border-line cases a governing class may even be persuaded that its best interest is to fall in line and concern itself more with the welfare of the people. At any rate, there is something gained by cutting the ground from under the fraudulent claim of the Soviet bloc in international gatherings that it represents the forces of "progress."

United Nations recommendations are not mandatory on governments, and the United States has always underlined that the assistance and advice of international agencies and also of our own Point Four program are available if wanted, but that it is up to the governments of underdeveloped countries themselves to initiate any reforms. American Point Four technicians are cooperating in the agrarian reform measures undertaken by the Shah of Iran and are assisting in broad programs of village improvement in India and elsewhere. Apparently, discreet pressure has sometimes been brought to persuade governments reluctant to offend powerful vested interests that some agrarian reform measures are necessary. Perhaps the pressure has not always been discreet; official quarters in the Philippines on at least one occasion have publicly resented American urging on this subject. The United States has also stimulated private discussions of agrarian problems, as in the Conference on World Land Tenure Problems assembled with official aid at the University of Wisconsin in 1951.

The United States is in a good position to offer help on agrarian problems, for in our own history we have worked out one of the best examples in all the world of land reform, desirable land use patterns, and general rural progress. True, our large land resources made the problem easy as compared with that of many countries. But we did have to make choices —as in the long controversy that preceded the Homestead Act of 1862, by which it was determined that the American West would have family farms rather than great plantations. Our choices were also expressed in rural education, agricultural colleges, experiment stations, and the extension service. South America also had it easy with respect to land resources, but the choices were different there, with results less happy both from the point of view of production and the point of view of political and social democracy.[8]

[8] This point was made by Theodore W. Schultz in an address to the Institute on the Economic Development of Underdeveloped Countries held February 4, 1952, by the Conference Group of U. S. National Organizations on the United Nations (mimeographed summary report, New York, 1952).

Chapter 13

CAPITAL FORMATION

In Asia, according to estimates made by the secretariat of the United Nations Economic Commission for Asia and the Far East, annual net investment is about 5 percent of national income. In dynamic economies in Western Europe and North America annual net investment usually runs about 15 percent of national incomes or more, and such rates of capital formation are associated with growth rates which allow consumption per person to rise by 1½ to 2 percent a year. The annual rate of capital investment in the Soviet Union and the Communist states of Eastern Europe is much greater than in Western Europe, and the rise in production is also more rapid, though this rise is not necessarily reflected in the consumption level of the people, because of Communist policies we have noted earlier. It seems safe to conclude, as does the ECAFE secretariat, that "in countries where population is increasing by 1½ percent per annum or more, an annual net investment of 5 percent or less of national income is not enough to raise the standard of living and may not even be enough to prevent the standard of living from falling . . ." At such a low rate of capital formation, the gap between the standard of living in Asia and in the West must continue to widen year by year, and "the relative difference cannot even be maintained unless capital formation in Asia approximates 15 percent per annum net, or more." [1]

[1] United Nations, ECAFE Secretariat, "Some Financial Aspects of Development Programmes in Asian Countries," *Economic Bulletin for Asia and the Far East,* Vol. III, Nos. 1-2, January-June, 1952, pp. 1-2.

Local Capital Formation Essential

It is important to distinguish *capital formation* from the *supply of capital*. Capital can be supplied, within limits, from outside a country. In underdeveloped countries, where national income is low, amounts of capital which are small in terms of the much larger national incomes of the highly developed countries can make a great difference in the local capital supply. For example, the gross national income of all the countries in the region covered by ECAFE, excluding China and Japan (but including India, Pakistan, Burma, Indonesia, the Philippines, etc.), was probably about 50 billion dollars in 1950.[2] Foreign investment of 1 billion dollars would be 2 percent of this, almost half the current capital formation of these countries. Sums of the magnitude which the United States provided for Western European recovery under the Marshall Plan would considerably more than double the present rate of additions to capital in the region.

Capital *formation*, on the other hand, is a social process. It must take place *internally* in much larger volume than before if a static, underdeveloped economy is to change into a progressive, developing economy. Capital from abroad can, in the right circumstances, be a powerful catalytic agent to stimulate the processes of domestic capital formation. Unless it does so, the foreign capital will be largely wasted from the developmental point of view, though it may succeed in extracting raw materials and transporting them abroad to meet the needs of more progressive economies, thus perpetuating rather than removing the gap between underdeveloped and developed countries.

It would probably be true to say that in every major case of really substantial, continuous development the great bulk of the capital has been supplied internally by the domestic processes of capital formation. Imports of capital, where present, have been mainly important as catalytic agents— often because they also brought technical knowledge. Perhaps this statement does not apply to some of the early cases where British and other foreign investors helped to install

[2] Same, p. 3.

in frontier communities railways and communications systems, improvements which are heavy consumers of capital. British capital helped substantially in outfitting European countries and also America in the nineteenth century; what proportion the capital brought in from abroad bore to capital accumulated within the country at various stages is an interesting question to which I do not know the answer. Britain, of course, as the firstcomer had to finance her own economic growth. Students of Japan's development seem agreed that Japan used relatively little foreign capital, but that this foreign capital had important catalytic effects. The Soviet Union industrialized with very little foreign capital beyond what had been invested in Tsarist days; its borrowings were technical knowledge and equipment which were imported and paid for. The Communist countries of Eastern Europe are industrializing without new capital from the West and apparently with a net outflow of payments to the Soviet Union.

Canada and Cuba come to mind as instances where foreign capital has bulked large, but it is instructive to note the differences between countries where internal processes of capital formation have taken hold and those where they have not. The progressive, continued development of Canada has been associated with active capital formation. But in Cuba internal social conditions have been relatively unfavorable to this process, and since the era of sugar-mill construction in the twenties the economy has not progressed very much.

The point is that, for development to "take," social institutions have to be built up and new social habits have to be formed which will achieve and maintain a higher level of internal capital formation. These institutions must handle two problems, because capital formation is a double-sided process: (1) The population must be induced or forced to consume less than the whole annual output, that is, to save—directly or indirectly; (2) the margin between total output and total consumption must be directed into productive investment which will increase the country's capacity to produce in subsequent years.

Potential Capital in Low-Income Countries

There is a widespread view that the problem of domestic capital formation in countries on very low income levels is almost hopeless because the margin between current output and absolute subsistence needs is so thin. This view neglects three sources of new capital potentially available in the great majority of underdeveloped countries. Whether these can be tapped or not depends on social attitudes and organization, including the presence or absence of an enterprising spirit among private owners and such political factors as who controls the government and for what purposes, political stability or instability, and the government's capacity to plan and administer. The three potential sources are:

1. *Existing surpluses now captured by a very small social group and not used for constructive investment.* Considerable sums go into luxurious living at home or abroad. Were these surpluses somehow channeled into developmental investment, they would in many countries substantially increase capital formation without reducing the consumption of the mass of the population. In Nicaragua, according to a mission of the International Bank for Reconstruction and Development, if only 10 percent of the income of the upper 1 percent of income receivers were to be invested productively, the current rate of productive investment in the country would increase by 50 percent.[3] One student of Philippine economic problems estimates that as much as one-fifth of the national income could be extracted annually for use in the development program if a serious effort were made to do so. But drastic changes in the economic and social structure of the country would be required, as well as new economic techniques, all of which would arouse opposition from powerful groups.[4] Frank W. Fetter has observed:

In a number of industrially backward countries the principal obstacle to domestic investment is not the absence of local funds

[3] *The Economic Development of Nicaragua,* Report of a Mission organized by the International Bank for Reconstruction and Development at the request of the Government of Nicaragua (Baltimore: Johns Hopkins Press, 1953), p. 99.

[4] Thomas R. McHale, "Problems of Economic Development in the Philippines," *Pacific Affairs,* June, 1952, p. 165.

that might be invested but a scale of social values, combined with political instability, which causes the wealthy groups within the country to spend their incomes on foreign travel or on foreign and domestic luxuries. In more than one Latin American country that is reputedly "short of capital," the sums that have been spent in Paris in the last half century by wealthy natives would have endowed the country with a modern transportation system and a well-equipped industrial plant. The same situation is found in some of the countries of the Orient.[5]

2. *Technological slack.* The most underdeveloped areas are just the ones where the injection of techniques already well known abroad, some of them fairly simple and inexpensive, can bring a rapid, immediate increase in output. In rural India, pilot projects in community development have brought increases in farm output of more than 40 percent in three years, mainly from such innovations as better seeds, fertilizers, and pest control. At the same time, health has improved and the people have been inspired to work together on community betterments. The new techniques make it possible, even while increasing current consumption somewhat, to divert labor time and other resources to the construction of roads, irrigation ditches, school buildings, workshops, and other items of capital equipment. Warren Wilhelm, in his analysis of developments in Soviet Central Asia during the decade 1928–1937, lays particular emphasis on "technological slack." Increased production resulting from better techniques seems to have been the main source of capital in this area. In this respect, he says, the most underdeveloped areas are the easiest to bring into rapid development.[6] This assumes, of course, that the *organizational* problem can be solved, which is one more reason for stressing the crucial role of social technology and political factors in development.

[5] Frank W. Fetter, "The Need for Postwar Foreign Lending," *Papers and Proceedings*, Fifty-Fifth Annual Meeting of the American Economic Association, March, 1943, p. 343.

[6] His argument for re-examining the assumption that a poverty-stricken area cannot save much capital and therefore cannot finance rapid development is well worth reading. See "Soviet Central Asia: Development of a Backward Area," cited.

3. *Labor slack*. In many underdeveloped countries, especially the most densely populated ones, there is a true "surplus population" on the land in the sense that even under present methods of cultivation a sizable fraction of the manpower could be removed without significantly reducing food output. Informed estimates of this margin in particular areas have not infrequently run as high as one-third of the labor force. Even where the population is fully employed at the busiest season, there is a tremendous amount of seasonal slack time in traditional agricultural methods. Properly organized rural industries should be able to tap some of it, thus increasing output and potential capital formation. We have already noted that a considerable amount of enforced idleness due to sickness may be remedied by not very costly public health measures. The great problems in tapping all this potential for capital formation are social, political, and administrative. A recent United Nations report on Libya calls attention to conditions in that country which might make appropriate a program of "Community Development Employment for the Utilization of Idle Manpower" like that already introduced in Greece and Ecuador by United Nations technical assistance missions. This program "encourages the voluntary use of idle manpower in economic development at the local level in work invested in projects of the people's own choice. The workers are offered a small incentive pay, and receive technical guidance from special experts provided by the Technical Assistance Administration. According to an authoritative and independent evaluation this programme has already brought 'surprisingly high yields from a low investment in primitive areas where manpower is abundant and capital equipment, material and administrative capacity are available only to a limited degree.' The encouragement of local initiative is important also in the educational sense, creating the attitudes and habits of self-reliance amongst the people without which a democratic development is unlikely to occur." [7]

[7] United Nations, Technical Assistance Administration, *A General Economic Appraisal of Libya*, prepared by John Lindberg (New York: 1952. II.H.2), p. 38.

Methods of Assembling Capital

For successful development as we have defined it, it is obviously necessary to increase domestic capital formation, but it makes a great difference how the increase is brought about.

In Britain and the other pioneer countries of early capitalism, capital was mobilized mainly by the growth of profits in the hands of private businessmen who then reinvested their wealth in productive enterprises. Nowadays, for better or worse, the old system based on unlimited profits and unequal income distribution is in nearly all countries both less workable and less acceptable than formerly. It still works in a modified fashion, but the welfare state and new ideas on economic justice have made it a less powerful engine of capital accumulation than it once was.

The Communists, in areas they control, have developed new methods of forced saving and investment which require an authoritarian government and society. They order labor about, apply the labor of millions of political prisoners to canals and other projects, take grain from the peasants by compulsory requisition, and channel production and distribution through state organizations, using the turnover or sales tax to siphon off the part of the national product the state wants for its purposes. Campaigns for sale of state bonds in a totalitarian setting make their purchase practically compulsory. Only officially sanctioned amounts of material and labor are allowed to go into production of consumer goods.

A country which chooses the democratic path to economic development must devise new and effective methods of capital formation which at the same time are democratic in spirit. Some of the political implications of the various possibilities are suggested in comments that follow on: (1) Private savings and investments; (2) Government taxation, borrowing, and earnings; (3) Inflation; (4) Investment in kind.

Private Savings and Investments

In this method of capital formation, some individuals and private firms must receive substantially more income than they consume, and they must use the surplus to launch or expand constructive enterprises themselves, or lend it to others who do so. This process requires:

1. An unequal distribution of income, for in low income countries only persons with considerably higher incomes than the average can save, and savings have to be fairly substantial and concentrated in order to be effective.

2. A saving and enterprising spirit on the part of recipients of the higher incomes.

3. Financial and business institutions for mobilizing private savings and putting them to productive use.

Many underdeveloped countries have the first requirement—that is, unequal distribution of income—and often in a more marked degree than the economically developed countries. What they lack are the second and third requirements.

England a century or two ago had a level of real income probably no higher than that of many underdeveloped countries now, yet it financed its own industrial development, mainly by private capital formation. One of the most important reasons seems to have been the prevailing "Puritan spirit." Idleness and waste were wrong; riches ought to be put to work making still more riches. By contrast, the typical picture in many underdeveloped countries today— for example, those of Spanish culture and those of the Middle East—is of recipients of large incomes spending them on luxury goods (and there are many more available than in the days of early capitalism). Or they invest in more land and urban real estate, or perhaps in a few types of commercial enterprise, or in a one-crop or a one-industry development that is probably already overexpanded. A considerable amount of money goes abroad for safekeeping or is simply hoarded at home.

For private capital formation to play a role in development there has to be a shift in the attitudes and habits of substantial income receivers, and also a corresponding growth in organizations which mobilize savings and channel them into constructive activity: commercial and savings banks, agricultural and industrial banks, insurance companies, credit unions, and securities markets. The more efficient and widespread such institutions become, the less necessary is it to have highly unequal income distribution in order to have private capital formation. These institutions can concentrate the savings of relatively small savers. The political and social desirability of building such institutions, which make it possible to benefit from private capital formation otherwise than by having ownership concentrated in the hands of a small number of very rich people, is obvious in the light of all that we have said earlier about broadening the bases of political power.

Government Taxation, Borrowing, and Earnings—How Governments Mobilize Capital Funds

Government can mobilize capital funds for use in development by taxing, borrowing, by reinvesting the earnings of government enterprises, and by obtaining royalties or agreed shares in the earnings of companies extracting oil or other minerals. For such sources of government income to be fruitful in capital formation there must be:

1. Wealth-producing activities within the country which generate enough income to be taxed, borrowed against, or otherwise collected.

2. Enough efficiency and integrity in the finance ministry, the central bank, and other government financial institutions to permit the government to collect and use funds effectively.

3. An economic development program, and government organizations of efficiency and integrity to administer it, so that a substantial share of government income goes into nation-building activities and not merely into current expenses and "monumental public works."

Good public administration, the crucial importance of which we have already discussed, is obviously the key to this type of capital formation. It is also important in encouraging private capital formation. Large public investments in such social capital as going systems of health and education, roads, irrigation works, and other basic utilities are necessary if private enterprise is to be able to do its part. This puts a heavy burden on governmental machinery, especially on systems of tax collection that may not be up to it. One of the most urgent problems of institution-building in most underdeveloped countries is a revision of the tax system so as to obtain more adequate tax revenues. This involves rethinking the kinds of taxes and changing the attitude of the public toward tax payment, which raises many difficult political problems.

If, in addition to tasks which only the state can perform, the government of an underdeveloped country proposes to build and operate new industries itself, its problems of administration and of finding managerial talent will increase enormously. It will have to collect a larger portion of the country's annual income to finance the necessary investments. One estimate is that modern welfare governments already need for current purposes some 15 percent of gross national income, and that a socialist development policy would require the raising of an additional 20 percent or so for gross capital formation. This would make it necessary for the government to collect in taxes about 35 percent of gross national income. In 1950 government revenues in the Philippines were 6 percent of gross national income; in India, 8 percent; Malaya, 11 percent; Burma, 15 percent; and Ceylon, 19 percent.[8] The political implications of having to collect in taxes any such sizable fraction of the national income, under the economic and administrative conditions of underdeveloped countries, would seem to be strongly authoritarian.

Inflation

The financing of economic development by creation of money and credit is an enticing possibility for governments of underdeveloped countries. This is especially true when (as is usually the case) the rate of domestic capital formation by other means is not rapid enough to support the pace of economic advance demanded by public opinion, and when capital from abroad is also not available in needed amounts. Since underdeveloped countries generally have unemployed or underemployed manpower, at first sight it might seem that the Keynesian argument would apply: increase aggregate demand by various means, including deficit financ-

[8] United Nations, ECAFE Secretariat, "Some Financial Aspects . . . ," cited, p. 3.

ing, in order to bring idle resources into productive use. But the problems of expanding output in underdeveloped countries are very different from those faced by economically advanced countries in a depression. The trouble in under-developed countries is more fundamental than insufficient monetary demand. Supply has to be built up, and the ob-stacles here are lack of going organization, lack of equip-ment, lack of skills—none of which can be remedied quickly by merely stimulating demand. "The old-fashioned prescrip-tion of 'work harder and save more' still seems to hold good as the medicine for economic progress, at any rate as far as the under-developed countries are concerned." [9]

One can think of circumstances in which deficit financing of carefully selected projects, limited in size and so chosen as to bring a quick increase in the supply of consumer goods, might not be inflationary, or not seriously so. Perhaps agri-cultural extension programs of proved effectiveness in bring-ing a rapid increase of food production can meet this test, and perhaps similar programs for aiding small industries to adopt better techniques. But the financing of large invest-ments in projects that pay off in consumer goods only after a long time, like large-scale industries, great dams and power systems, and roads, by the use of funds that do not repre-sent real savings will probably lead to a serious rise in prices. Such inflation has the effect of increasing the incomes of some people at the expense of others. In certain respects it may favor private capital formation, by increasing the profits of business enterprisers and by giving them a prospect of further substantial profits, thus inducing them to invest further. This is less likely to be true in underdeveloped countries, however, than in countries which have a large class of merchants and industrialists with traditions of con-structive investment. Inflationary profits that fall into the hands of inactive landowners or of peasants who convert them into gold or jewelry, or of persons with a speculative outlook, do not add to capital formation. The political con-sequences of inflation are likely to be further concentration of income and power, serious difficulties for the government

[9] V. K. R. V. Rao, "Investment, Income and the Multiplier in an Under-Developed Economy," *Indian Economic Review*, February, 1952, p. 67.

in keeping its revenues abreast of rising costs and in maintaining the loyalty of civil servants, and international difficulties because of pressure on the balance of payments and the currency.[10]

Investment in Kind

Finance is only one technique, though a very powerful one, for bringing resources together and organizing them for production of capital goods. When a country needs roads, irrigation canals, small buildings for village schools and dispensaries, wells and sanitary facilities, and when there is either a general surplus of manpower or seasonal slack in the traditional agriculture that occupies most people, it should be possible to form capital in important amounts without going through the mechanism of money savings and money investment.

Improvements which individual farmers may be stimulated to make on their farms with their own labor, involving comparatively small expenditures for materials, add to a country's capital. Much capital formation in the United States has been of this sort; think of the labor of the homesteaders. One of the great merits of community development schemes like those now being expanded in India is that they foster individual and collective efforts which create real capital out of resources that otherwise would go unused. The latest revision of India's five-year development plan proposes to carry the nonfinancial approach as far as possible. As reported by the *Eastern Economist*, "Finance has been dethroned, in the sense that the Planning Commission deliberately prefers voluntary work not rated in financial terms, which will by-pass entirely the problem of first creating money incomes and then matching them with goods . . ."[11]

[10] Two worth-while discussions are E. M. Bernstein and I. G. Patel, "Inflation in Relation to Economic Development," International Monetary Fund, *Staff Papers*, Vol. II, No. 3, November, 1952, pp. 363-398, and United Nations, ECAFE Secretariat, "Some Financial Aspects . . .," cited. The first takes the more uncompromising anti-inflationary position, while the second insists that "We must know why the inflation is occurring and what effect it is having on real output" before judging whether it is good or bad for development. It suggests that "the political dangers of allowing an economy to stagnate may in some cases be greater than the political dangers of inflation."

[11] "Economic Progress in the Plan," *Eastern Economist*, December 12, 1952, p. 947.

For larger public works and for the more complex and technical requirements of industry the regular financial methods will always be required, and some financing is necessary even for voluntary community projects. They generally need technical direction and a few key items of material and equipment not locally produced. But with the right type of organization and leadership, the method of direct capital formation by investment of labor and locally available materials would seem to offer substantial possibilities. Well-conceived programs of education, health, agricultural extension services, promotion of small-scale industries for villages and towns, and general community improvement can stimulate considerable capital formation in the aggregate of many small items. Also, such programs have decided advantages in encouraging a democratic spirit of community cooperation and spreading the benefits of development rapidly and broadly. All this depends, of course, on creating a truly voluntary spirit of cooperation. The slave labor that built the pyramids and the modern slave labor of the work gangs managed by the secret police in Communist areas are in a different and nondemocratic tradition of capital formation.

Chapter 14

POPULATION PROBLEMS

In some underdeveloped areas the prospects for really substantial gains in the living standards of the average man
seem dim indeed when one takes a realistic look at the number of people in relation to resources and at the way population growth tends to respond to improved conditions. Will
these countries be able to expand their production faster
than population expands? If not, the result of economic development efforts will be a greater *quantity* of people with
little or no gains in the *quality* of living conditions. This
would mean the frustration of eager hopes for economic
betterment. The political implications, internal and external,
would probably be disastrous.

The essence of the problem is this: Experience shows that
modern health methods and economic improvement quickly
bring a drop in the high death rates characteristic of underdeveloped countries. Their high birth rates, however, tend
to remain for a longer time near the levels formerly necessary
for the survival of the society. Birth rates depend on social
factors that, in the past at any rate, have always proved more
resistant to change. The resulting lag between the fall in the
death rate and the fall in the birth rate means a period of
rapid population growth. In past cases this lag has extended
over generations. If the underdeveloped country is already
overcrowded, as is unfortunately true in quite a number of
cases, and if there is little opportunity for large-scale migration, which is also true today, such a burst of population
growth may defeat the best laid plans for economic development.

Our analysis will show that there are some new elements

in today's situation which might make it possible, in countries now embarking on modernization, for their high birth rates to fall much more speedily than they have fallen in past cases. This prospect gives grounds for hope. A rapid fall in the birth rate is an essential condition for real economic gains in such important countries as India and Egypt. It is essential also if they are to have a reasonable chance of a democratic and peaceful political future. Yet the outlook is highly uncertain, for the social institutions which would have to be reshaped, and reshaped with unprecedented rapidity, are among the most conservative of all, touching as they do on family life, religious ideas, and most of the basic human values.

Population Growth in Underdeveloped Countries

Underdeveloped countries can be divided into two groups as respects population growth:

1. *Those growing rapidly now.* They have high fertility (birth rates) and moderate or low mortality (death rates). The Latin American countries are the main members of this group, but a few parts of Asia and Africa belong in it also, such as Ceylon and Egypt.

2. *Those growing at a moderate rate now, but with high growth potential.* They have high fertility, held in check by high mortality. If and when modernization checks the death rate, they will move into the first group. Most of the underdeveloped countries of Asia and Africa are in this category.

Latin America's population is growing faster than that of any other region. Because of high fertility (crude birth rates averaging 40) and moderate mortality (crude death rates averaging 17), the rate of natural increase is about 23 per thousand persons per year.[1] This means population growth of 2.3 percent annually, which, cumulating like compound interest, gives 30 percent more people in ten years. In Latin America as a whole the output of goods and services has to grow 30 percent a decade merely not to lose ground in the

[1] Unless otherwise noted, statistical data are from the United Nations, *Preliminary Report on the World Social Situation,* cited, Chapter II, "Background Facts on World Population and Population Trends," or from the United Nations, Department of Economic Affairs, *Statistical Yearbook 1951* (New York: 1951.XVII.5).

sense that really matters for economic well-being, namely, output per person. As the Red Queen said in *Alice Through the Looking Glass*, "Now here you see it takes all the running you can do to keep in the same place. If you want to get somewhere else, you must run at least twice as fast as that."

A rate of increase in gross output averaging 3 to 4 percent a year (a trend which means doubling in 20 to 25 years) is considered good in progressive economies like the United States and Sweden where the people are well educated, where institutions for capital formation are well established, and where traditionally there is a strong urge to work hard and get ahead. Countries that can count as real progress only the increase *beyond* 2.3 percent a year suffer a substantial handicap. Where population growth is rapid, much scarce capital must go into more (rather than better) houses, tools, schools, etc. On the other hand, population growth in some circumstances may stimulate more production than it absorbs. This would seem to apply to economies already quite dynamic, in countries not too densely settled.

The United Nations estimates annual birth rates in Asia and Africa at 40 to 45. Death rates are put at 25 to 30 in Africa and 28 to 32 in Asia. Because mortality is still very high, population growth generally does not exceed 1 percent to 1.5 percent a year. India's population is thought to be growing at something over 1 percent a year.

Infant mortality rates in these countries are especially high. If, as has already happened in countries of the first group, public health measures and increases in food production lengthen life-expectancy, particularly by reducing infant deaths, population growth rates may be expected to zoom upward. In that case the absolute growth in such countries as India will be tremendous, because of the huge base from which it starts. Even at the present moderate rate of increase, India faces the necessity of finding food, clothing, shelter, educational facilities, and so on for nearly 50 million *additional* people in 10 years. That is almost one-third of the total population of the United States.

In each of the two groups of countries, some are sparsely settled, some densely. Venezuela has 5 people per square kilometer, Chile 8, Colombia 10, Cuba 47, Iran 12, Turkey 27, Burma 27, the Philippines 65. These countries have more chance to absorb a rapid population growth during a transition period than such countries as Puerto Rico with 249 people per square kilometer, Ceylon with 115, India with 113, and Egypt (settled area only) with 538. Indonesia has an average density of 49, but the main island, Java, holds nearly 400 per square kilometer. If the United States, which has 20 people per square kilometer, were as densely populated as India, 900 million would have to make a living in this country instead of 160 million. At Puerto Rico's density we would have almost 2,000 million.

These densely populated underdeveloped countries live mainly from agriculture, yet some of them are as thickly settled as centers of trade and manufacture like Belgium (283 people per square kilometer) and the United Kingdom (207). This not only means a very low living level for their people today but also poses serious problems with respect to absorbing the surge of population growth that has usually accompanied economic development.

The Vital Revolution in Industrial Societies

In the West the rise of modern industrial society has been accompanied by a revolution in population balance. A preindustrial combination of high mortality and high fertility has changed to a modern combination of low mortality and low or medium fertility. The experience of England is fairly typical. Two centuries ago (1740) the death rate was in the neighborhood of 30 to 35 and the birth rate probably around 35 to 37. Recently the death rate has been less than 12 and the birth rate around 16.

One of the most striking achievements of industrial society has been this transition from a vital pattern wasteful of human life, in which there were many births with many early deaths, to the new pattern in which fewer children are born but more grow up and live longer.

The key fact, however, is that in this "vital revolution" which has accompanied the industrial revolution the birth rate has always responded more slowly than the death rate. England's death rate declined from 30 to 35 in the 1740's to 27 by 1800, to 22 by 1860 and continued to fall until it was 12 by the 1930's. The birth rate, however, remained near its old high level, about 35, until as late as 1880, more than a century after the death rate had started downward. Then it dropped rapidly to 30 in 1900, 25 in 1920, 15 by the 1930's and has since fluctuated between 14 and 20.[2] The lag between the effective action of forces influencing the death rate and those influencing the birth rate produces the surge of population growth characteristic not only of England but of all countries which up to now have entered upon modern economic development. Europe's population multiplied fivefold in the last three centuries, and throughout the world the population of European extraction increased probably more than sevenfold.[3]

Japan's experience does not differ in essentials from that of Europe. The death rate declined ahead of the birth rate, so that Japan's population increased during its period of modernization from about 30 to more than 84 million. Birth rates are now on the way down, but the transition to a new balance is by no means complete. "By the time it is complete the period of modernization will have lasted from a century to a century and a half and have resulted in a three- to fourfold multiplication of numbers."[4]

Death rates decline because of improvements in public order, better food, clothing, housing, and (especially nowadays) better facilities for the prevention and cure of disease. All of these are made possible by the more efficient transportation and communication, the new methods of agriculture and industry, and the general advance in science, technology, and wealth which are part of economic development.

The factors which bring an eventual fall in the birth rate are not so well understood, but it is clear that they involve

[2] For the earlier years, see A. M. Carr-Saunders, *World Population: Past Growth and Present Trends* (Oxford: Clarendon Press, 1936), pp. 61, 72.

[3] Dudley Kirk, *Europe's Population in the Interwar Years* (Princeton: League of Nations, 1946.II.A.8), p. 17.

[4] Frank W. Notestein, "Economic Problems of Population Change," paper read at Eighth International Conference of Agricultural Economists, August 15-22, 1952. See *Approaches to Problems of High Fertility in Agrarian Societies* (New York: Milbank Memorial Fund, 1952) and Marshall C. Balfour, et al., *Public Health and Demography in the Far East* (New York: The Rockefeller Foundation, 1950).

more complex, indirect, and slower changes. Urban life, which is characteristic of modern economy, makes it less convenient to rear large families. As living standards rise, individual ambitions and the desire to get ahead become more important. Where each infant born has a greater chance of living to maturity, parents have less reason to want a large number of births and prefer to give each child a better start in life, including a longer and more expensive education. The emancipation of women means that women have alternatives to early marriage and child-bearing as means of livelihood and prestige; they have new interests and diversions outside the family. Longer periods of education and training make for later marriage. The growth of a rational and secular point of view breaks down some of the customs that in a traditional· society tend to produce high birth rates. Many complex cultural factors seem to play a part in establishing the small-family pattern which distinguishes the more mature industrial societies from preindustrial or only partly modernized societies.

Dangers of Partial Modernization

One of the worst heritages of Western colonial rule in parts of Asia (quite unintentional, even motivated in part by humanitarian intentions) was a *partial modernization* which brought enough of modern ideas to keep more people alive but not enough to alter social institutions so that not so many would be born. It was considered good to build irrigation works and otherwise increase the food supply, to fight famines and epidemics, and of course the interests of the rulers required public order. But there was a feeling that native social customs and religions should be disturbed as little as possible, and only very late was there much of a shift from the traditional view that colonies should produce agricultural commodities and raw materials and not go in for industrial development. In consequence, the population of Java, which was 4½ million in 1815, is more than 50 million today. The Indian subcontinent had perhaps 150 or 200 million people in 1850, but today the population of India and Pakistan together is about 440 million. And there has been no tendency for the birth rate to fall in either place. This heritage of partial, unbalanced modernization means that these countries face the problem of transforming their economies and social structures from a starting position where population is already as dense as in highly industrialized regions. Consequently they have little "slack" to absorb the population upsurge that has always accompanied modern economic development.

The dangers of partial modernization are even more acute today because of the spectacular triumphs of medical science and public health techniques. By sanitation, DDT, antibiotics, and the rest it is now possible for a relatively few modern-trained people to push the death rate precipitately downward without much change in traditional ways of living and even without much education, except in a few specific health techniques. And this might occur with little accompanying change in the social factors which affect birth rates. In Ceylon the death rate fell almost 40 percent in three years as a result of the virtual elimination of malaria and in 1950 it stood at 12.6. The birth rate remained at 40. In Puerto Rico the death rate has fallen almost 50 percent since the 1930's and in 1950–51 it stood at 9.9. The birth rate had started to decline but was still 37.8. These lands have the death rates of "advanced" countries and the birth rates of "backward" countries.

Such a combination of modern death rates with archaic birth rates is likely to be a drag on the improvement of economic well-being even in countries with moderate population density. In countries already densely settled it must be disastrous if continued for long. It means more and more people to feed per acre of land. It means that painfully accumulated capital must be used, both in industry and in social services like education and health, not so much to improve output per worker or to raise individual opportunities as to take care of greater numbers of people. The steady pressure of more people on the land and of more people wanting jobs, where both land and industrial capital are scarce, keeps labor cheap. This discourages the mechanization and other labor-saving innovations which are needed to raise a country's productivity. The age composition of a population where the birth rate is high makes fewer productive workers support more nonproducers than in countries with lower birth rates. For example, 100 people of the most productive age group support themselves and about 56 children and old people in the United States and Canada, whereas in the underdeveloped areas on the average they support themselves and about 82 others.[5] Also, where there is both high fertility and high mortality, a very large percentage of children die without reaching an economically productive age and thus never repay to their families or the community the "investment" made in them. Quite aside from the human disappointments and sufferings involved, this is a great economic loss. It takes almost three times as many births in India as in the United States to provide a given number of productive, adult years.[6]

Europe's Experience Cannot Be Repeated

Europe's population cycle extended over a period of centuries. There was a long lag between the first downward movement of death rates and the later decline of birth rates. Europe was able to improve its living conditions remarkably while population was increasing. Today's underdeveloped countries face quite a different situation in three respects:

1. There are no outlets for mass migration today at all comparable to the outlets which North and South America

[5] According to the United Nations' *Preliminary Report on the World Social Situation*, cited, the estimated percentage of the population of northern America in the most productive age group, 15 through 59, is 64. About 25 percent consists of children under 15 and about 11 percent of people over 60. The estimates for Latin America, Asia, and Africa, all about the same in this respect, put the percentage in the most productive age group at 55, with 40 percent children under 15 and 5 percent people over 60.

[6] A very rough calculation (the statistics are not exact) illustrates the burden the Indian people carry because of a wasteful pattern of births and deaths: Of 100 babies born alive in the United States, there are on the average 95 still living at age 15. In India, only about 55 are still living at that age. The average life expectancy for persons who have come to the age of 15 in the United States is about 54 years. Let us deduct 2 years to allow for disabilities and say the "productive" life expectancy is 52 years. In India the corresponding productive life expectancy of those who reach age 15 is about 31 years. Multiplying the number who reach age 15 in each country by the productive life expectancy, we get the total number of productive years for each 100 live births, which is approximately 4,750 in the United States and 1,650 in India. Each birth in the United States results in almost three times as many productive, adult years as in India. (I am grateful to Howard Tolley for suggesting this calculation.)

provided for the growing population of Europe in the nineteenth and early twentieth centuries. Even if we had another North and South America, the size of the population in underdeveloped countries today is many times greater than the population with which Europe began its modern development. The entire intercontinental migration throughout the world in more than a century between 1800 and 1924 was hardly as much as the increase in the population of India and Pakistan in one decade at *present* growth rates.[7] But it is not inconceivable that these rates may double, as has been the experience in other countries where economic improvement and health measures have cut death rates.

2. The density of population in some underdeveloped areas today is already very high, many times that of Europe in preindustrial times.

3. Modern techniques make possible a much more rapid drop in the death rate than occurred in Europe.

Political Implications

Deliberate, organized steps are being taken in underdeveloped countries, some of them very densely populated, to reduce the death rate. But the birth rate is being left largely to automatic, indirect influences that operate only slowly. The resulting upset in the balance of births and deaths can produce, in fact has already produced, grave economic, social, and political consequences. If no new factor enters this situation, the economic development efforts and hopes of millions of newly aroused people will be frustrated by population expansion. The political implications, both internal and international, would be dire.

Where the birth rate remains high, the death rate must either remain high or, if it drops, it must sooner or later be forced up again, since no population can go on forever increasing at a compound interest rate. In the long run, the only way to have low death rates, with all this implies for economic and social well-being, is to have low birth rates.

[7] "Intercontinental migration . . . between 1800 and 1924 totaled approximately 60,000,000, of which 36,000,000 went to the United States between 1820 and 1924; about 10,000,000 of the latter subsequently returned to Europe." Imre Ferenczi, "Migrations," *Encyclopaedia of the Social Sciences,* 1933, Vol. 10, p. 436.

In the absence of a decline in births, one or more of the famous "positive checks" of Malthus must come into play: famine, pestilence, and war. We have vastly improved our ability to cope with famine and pestilence in modern times. As a result, the danger that political pressures will build up from unchecked population growth may be even greater. As Frank W. Notestein points out, "The very efficiency of modern medical techniques enchances this risk. It is now quite possible to keep people alive in spite of appalling living conditions. There is much less danger than there used to be that the failure to enhance production will lead to the curtailment of population growth by epidemic and starvation. . . . It is not at all unlikely that political explosion, and the economic disorganization which accompanies it, will provide the major check to population increase in the future." [8]

Prospects for Balancing Births and Deaths

The only hope of successful development for those underdeveloped countries which start with a very dense population would seem to be for them to balance deliberate modernization in the spheres of economics and health with equally deliberate and organized efforts to lower the birth rate nearly as fast as the death rate. No one knows whether or not such a policy can be adopted and effectively implemented. It would be something new in population history. Technical advances in birth control and in the social technology of spreading new ideas may help to make it feasible. The success or failure of development efforts in a number of extremely important countries depends on their finding ways to bring the birth rates into better balance with their death rates.

India affords an encouraging sign that the countries confronted with difficult population problems may see the need to grapple with them as directly as with other problems of development. Both the government's Planning Commission and Prime Minister Nehru strongly support "family planning" as a necessary part of the country's program for economic and social advance. The government has obtained ex-

[8] "Economic Problems of Population Change," cited.

pert assistance from the World Health Organization. Newspapers are strongly supporting the spread of birth control, and the government is taking steps to reach people in the villages who cannot read. Preliminary samplings are said to reveal a much more favorable reception at all economic and educational levels than had been expected. It appears that there is no positive bar to birth control either in the Hindu or in the Moslem religion. The Family Planning Association of India, with the leadership of some of India's most distinguished women, cooperated in the establishment at a meeting held in Bombay in November, 1952, of the International Planned Parenthood Association. The international organization will urge inclusion of family planning institutes in the national health programs of all countries, with the aim in each country of imparting birth control information to 80 percent of its women in the next ten years. It will also help to establish family planning associations in all countries that do not now have them, and will promote clinics and research.[9]

The United States and other Western countries will have to treat these problems cautiously. There is some danger that too much leadership on our part will be misinterpreted as a desire to keep other countries from growing bigger and stronger, allegedly to preserve national or racial supremacy. We have noted the Communist propaganda attacks aimed at American birth control advocates (page 150). The political influence of opponents of birth control in the United States and other Western countries is also a restraining factor. A Norwegian proposal in the World Health Organization in 1952 that this United Nations agency study the health aspects of the world population problem, including birth control, brought warnings from the delegates of several strongly Roman Catholic countries that action in this field would endanger the existence of the organization. After a two-day debate, a Belgian counterproposal forbidding action in this field appeared to have a majority, but the whole matter was dropped "in the interests of harmony." [10]

[9] *New York Times*, November 28 and November 30, 1952, dispatches from Bombay by Robert Trumbull.
[10] *New York Times*, May 20, 1952.

Research and invention in the social and biological aspects of the population problem seem very likely to produce important new techniques in the near future, and perhaps these may help considerably. Twenty "leads" out of which might come a new method or methods for controlling conception were listed in a recent survey of physiological research bearing on the problem.[11] Something like the often-rumored "pill" that would positively, safely, and cheaply prevent conception would make the population problems of India, Egypt, Java, Puerto Rico, and other areas seem less insoluble. On the social side, the factors which influence the will of people to plan their families so as to have fewer and better reared children, and the development of techniques to get the necessary practices known and adopted in rural areas without awaiting the long process of industrialization and urbanization, are crucial.[12] This would seem to be preeminently a field for the research establishments of underdeveloped countries that face the handicap of overpopulation.

Can birth rates be reduced within a peasant society, as a means of facilitating its transformation into an industrial society, instead of waiting for birth rates to fall as a delayed consequence of such a transformation? Unless ways are found to answer this question in the affirmative, some densely populated countries may fail in their efforts to achieve the development they now ardently desire, with incalculable consequences for themselves and the rest of the world.

The population problem gives added weight to one of the major themes of this book, namely, that the type of economic development and the way it is achieved may be quite as important as the additional output it yields. Concretely, if deliberate diffusion of new industry through the small towns and rural areas of India, accompanied by special efforts in rural health, education, and community develop-

[11] Paul S. Henshaw, "Physiologic Control of Fertility," *Science*, May 29, 1953, pp. 572-582.

[12] For an interesting suggestion by a sociologist, see W. F. Ogburn, "A Design for Some Experiments in the Limitation of Population Growth in India," *Economic Development and Cultural Change*, February, 1953, pp. 376-389.

ment, could be shown to change family patterns of more people more rapidly than a concentrated industrial development centering in the great cities, then the former might bring a more substantial economic advance than the latter. This might be true even if the urban type of development raised total output more quickly and at less cost. In the present state of our knowledge, a judgment of this sort would be quite uncertain. Nevertheless, this is the kind of problem that needs more attention. Also, because of the need to change old customs that sustain high birth rates, programs of economic development which attempt to get ahead with a minimum of social readjustment, perhaps in the interest of immediate efficiency, may well miss their mark.

Finally, in view of misunderstandings and propagandistic distortions, it can hardly be stated too often and too emphatically that reduction of birth rates in overcrowded countries is *not* put forward as a substitute for economic development, but rather as an essential condition for its success.

Chapter 15

RAW MATERIALS AND INDUSTRIALIZATION

The purpose of this chapter is to explore the political implications of the various ways by which production may expand in underdeveloped countries. Does it make a difference in the prospects for successful development if a few industries producing raw materials for export get far ahead of other sectors of the economy? Is there political as well as economic significance in the balance between agriculture and industry that emerges, or that development authorities seek to promote? How may a country's political and social development be affected by the relative emphasis on capital goods or consumer goods industries, centralized or diffused industrial development, large-scale or small-scale establishments?

RAW MATERIALS AND ROUNDED DEVELOPMENT

The United States and other economically advanced countries of the free world will need to import much larger amounts of raw materials in the future, according to the report of the Paley Commission.[1] The most promising sources are in underdeveloped countries of South Asia, the Middle East, Africa, and Latin America. If, impelled by these needs, American business and government try hard to boost raw materials production in such areas, what may this do to the outlook for economic development, and especially for development that meets the tests of success laid down in Chapter 5?

A certain stigma seems to have become attached to the

[1] President's Materials Policy Commission, cited.

idea of being a "raw materials country." It is associated with "colonial economy" and therefore with an inferior status. But peoples of underdeveloped countries, having new aspirations and national feelings, want passionately an equal status. Just as they object to political colonialism they object to any economic relation which seems like "domination" by foreign interests.

The demand for raw materials is notoriously unstable, and this is another reason why many underdeveloped countries want to make their economies less dependent on materials export. Eighteen important primary commodities, representing the major exports of selected underdeveloped countries, fluctuated in price by an average of 14 percent each year during the fifty years 1901–50. The exports of these commodities fluctuated even more in volume—an average of nearly 19 percent from one year to the next. The export earnings from these commodities fluctuated an average of 23 percent a year.[2]

It will be argued below that most of the political and economic drawbacks ascribed to raw materials production are the outcome of *overspecialization*. If the United States recognizes the need for helping countries that are suppliers of raw materials, while expanding output of these commodities, to develop also a balanced internal economy, and if the underdeveloped countries that possess the great advantage of readily marketable materials treat this as a means for supporting a general economic advance, then the political and other drawbacks will be much less. There would then be a basis for great mutual advantage in international investment and trade in raw materials.

Dual Economies

In the past, outside capital and technology have often set up modern, highly productive operations for extracting raw materials to be exported to the industrial countries, while age-old practices have continued almost unchanged in every other segment of an underdeveloped economy. The result, in the extreme case, is an alien enclave; a foreign island or

[2] United Nations, Department of Economic Affairs, *Instability in Export Markets of Under-developed Countries* (New York: 1952.II.A.1).

oasis of modern industrialism is established within a preindustrial country.

The Anglo-Iranian Oil Company in Iran, with its oil wells and its huge modern refinery at Abadan, the largest in the world, created such a foreign oasis. Its years of operation in Iran had little impact on the day-to-day economic life of the great bulk of the Iranian people, who continued to eke out a scanty subsistence by primitive agriculture under a system of near-serfdom. The Arabian American Oil Company in Saudi Arabia is another instance. This company, however, is following an unusually farsighted policy, trying to aid Saudi Arabia in general economic and cultural progress. Whether in the long run this can counteract the political hazards of the position remains to be seen.

In Indonesia during its colonial period, and in other parts of Southeast Asia, a situation developed for which "dual economy" became the standard descriptive term. Side by side, but moving on different planes, there existed on the one hand the traditional subsistence farming and small handicrafts of the villages and on the other the estates and mines producing rubber, oil, tin, and other materials for the world market.

Other cases, some extreme, some less extreme, in which development in the raw materials export sector has far outdistanced that in the economy as a whole are associated with the production of the nitrates and copper in Chile, tin in Bolivia, a variety of minerals in the Belgian Congo, sugar in Cuba, and bananas in Costa Rica and Guatemala.

Given enough time, economic and cultural forces set in motion by the raw materials development may in some cases, and without any deliberate program, lead to modernization of the rest of the economy. Training in new skills, injection of purchasing power through wage and other payments, establishment of transport and communication lines, and other consequences of raw materials extraction may stimulate general economic growth. But experience shows convincingly that "automatic" processes do not always take hold and become self-generating. The expansion of raw materials production has been a substantial factor in stimulating general development in some countries, but not in others.

In any case, the automatic processes are not by themselves rapid enough to meet today's necessities. They need deliberate reinforcement and supplementation.

The reason is that modern raw materials production is carried on by great concerns, highly organized, well-financed, in a thoroughly planned development. They move in with trained and experienced managers, a whole corps of engineers, and all the latest technical devices. They are backed by research laboratories and experience gained all over the world. It is not to be expected that other sectors of the economy, relying on a laissez-faire policy, will advance at anywhere near as rapid a pace. Hence, in the absence of a vigorous, well-planned, and well-financed effort to build them up, a distinctly unbalanced or lopsided development is likely to result.

Political Aspects of Lopsided Development

Lopsided development, in which the production of one or a few raw materials for export advances far out of step with the country's general economic development, is not likely to be "successful," as we have defined that term in Chapter 5. Also, it is almost sure in these days (the situation was quite different in the nineteenth century or even the early twentieth century) to lead to political troubles which will adversely affect both the interests of the local people and the security of foreign investments.

In the first place, lopsided development tends to sharpen existing inequalities in the distribution of privileges and means to power—wealth, education, opportunities, organizing experience, and so on. A relatively few people benefit enormously. Perhaps they are part owners, or influential politicians or even—where the operating company gives its employees perquisites not available to others in the community—the lucky, select group of employees. The masses of people go on as before, except for one important thing. Nowadays, the ease of communication guarantees that the community will soon be infiltrated with modern ideas and brought in touch with mass political movements, leading to nationalistic self-assertion and to demands for economic and social justice. Fifty or a hundred years ago it was quite possible for mines or plantations to be run from abroad on modern lines while all around life went on much as it had for centuries, relatively uncontaminated by new ideas. This is no longer true.

Secondly, lopsided raw materials development usually means foreign ownership and foreign management. Foreigners who are visibly engaged in shipping away the "riches" of the country for the use of industrialized countries abroad are a natural target for nationalistic agitation. The target is a convenient one, both for revolutionaries and for defenders of the *status quo*. The latter are glad to divert attention from evils in local political, social, or economic affairs by blaming them on foreign interests. Other irritations arise. Local people often find that they have little chance of rising to top positions. They envy foreigners working at their level but receiving much higher salaries. All these irritations are made to order for Communists with their stock-in-trade of "anti-imperialism."

Third, the creation of an industrial society *in part,* in the form of mines or plantations producing for export, brings together a group of workers who may form the basis of a class-conscious "proletariat." But the balancing or moderating "middle-class" group that is also a feature of a *complete* modern industrial society is lacking. The middle-class people who are occupied directly or indirectly with the raw materials produced in the lopsided economy may live in America, or Europe, or wherever the business operations are planned and financed, the machinery designed, and the product further processed. When the proletarian group is built up in one country and the middle-class group in another, class cleavages are added to national cleavages, again fertile soil for political agitators.

Fourth, a country where there has been little development, except in a few raw materials for export, is vulnerable to the instability of raw materials demand, to depressions originating in industrial countries, and to technological changes such as the introduction of substitute materials and synthetics. These economic hazards greatly increase the political risks. When economic disaster strikes, blame falls on the foreign firms and the nation they represent.

Finally, lopsided development does not create a good economic base for stable, democratic government. It provides no large group of self-reliant, independent merchants, or progressive and prosperous farmers, or skilled workmen and managers—people who feel that they have a good chance to get ahead, who have a stake in orderly progress, and who also have the education and social skills to be effective politically in other ways than as members of a shouting mob. At the same time, because of the huge government revenues that may be derived from the export of raw materials, there are likely to be high prizes for those able to attain political power. Obviously, this is a poor atmosphere in which to make progress toward the type of development that is in the interests of the people of the country, nor does it augur well for "successful" development as viewed from the United States and the world community.

The Case of Chile

These points may be illustrated by a concrete case. In a study of the Communist Party of Chile, S. Cole Blasier says that from 1937 to 1946 the Communists achieved more formal political power and prestige in that country than anywhere else in the Americas.[3] Although the situation has changed since then, his analysis of the factors that aided the Communists is pertinent:

Until the twentieth century, Chile was almost exclusively an agricultural country. . . . At the turn of the century, however, mining ventures, promoted and owned by foreign capital, began to attract labor from the large estates. In the northern deserts, rich in copper and nitrate deposits, rapidly growing mining settlements transformed peasants into industrial workers, the *rotos,* thus producing a new social class. To this day the core of Chile's industrial proletariat is in the mining regions. (p. 355.)

These workers had lost the security they enjoyed as peasants, when at least they had something to eat and a place to stay, and were completely dependent upon their wages. Often unemployed and discontented, many of them sought desperately for some way to better their lot. Resentment against

[3] "Chile: A Communist Battleground," *Political Science Quarterly,* September, 1950, pp. 353-375.

a social order in which they had little opportunity for political expression was channeled into strikes and riots and
into the formation of the Chilean Communist Party.

Furthermore, ". . . a comparatively small group retains
control of the Chilean economy, and extremes of wealth
and poverty still meet face to face." The moderating influence of a large middle group has been lacking both in economics and politics. "There is still no strong united party
of social reform in Chile."

The foreign ownership of the major industries, nitrate
and copper, made them convenient targets for Communist
propaganda. When the mines were forced to restrict production, as in the depression of the 1930's, a large segment of
the population was without employment. "Even more important, because these industries provide such a large part
of the national income, especially with respect to foreign
exchange, their breakdown brings prostration to the entire
economy." (The total value of Chilean exports fell from a
high of 276 million dollars in 1929 to 35 million dollars in
1932.) "Rightly or wrongly, many Chileans blame the foreign
owners for economic dislocations. Since many patriotic Chileans would prefer to see these basic industries owned and
administered by Chileans, the Communist campaign against
'foreign imperialists' readily finds a sympathetic audience." [4]

Hazardous Investment

The political consequences of lopsided development are
particularly hazardous for the investors, especially foreign
investors, who may have undertaken to expand production of
raw materials on a long-range basis. They are in the most
exposed position to become targets of passions aroused by
extremes of wealth and power, to be blamed for economic
depressions, and to suffer from the excesses of nationalism
or Communist agitation or both. In a nation with rounded
development, like Canada, there are many people experienced in business and many more who have at least some understanding of what is involved in productive enterprise,
why it is useful, and why stockholders have to have some return. They know that there are reasonable ways of recon-

[4] Same, pp. 375, 357.

ciling the public interest with private incentives. This is not the case where the investment in raw materials stands out as almost the only example of modern technology and modern business—as in Iran. The events of the last few years in that country illustrate the dangers we are talking about.

In Bolivia a revolutionary government recently national-ized the tin mines. Only a year or two earlier the United Nations Mission of Technical Assistance to Bolivia had de-scribed in its Report the very backward state of the rest of the Bolivian economy, the poverty, ignorance, and ill-health of most of the people, and the instability of government. Some delicately phrased lines on the indifference to Bolivia's general development of the tin mining companies, owned partly by wealthy Bolivians and partly by foreign investors, can now be read almost as an epitaph:

> . . . it must be recognized that in their policies relating to labour and public relations the mining companies have been slow in realizing and accepting their social responsibilities. . . . The mine owners should recognize more fully than has hereto-fore been generally the case their inescapable responsibilities in relation to the future economic development of the country that has been the source of their income. This recognition should be demonstrated particularly by a more positive attitude towards Bolivia as a field for the reinvestment of mining profits.[5]

What we have been saying bears on public relations and social responsibility, but it also goes deeper. Because of these political repercussions, twentieth-century investors in raw materials development have a very great interest (whether they realize it or not) in the economic and social structure of countries where they operate. A situation in which there is no middle group of moderate-income, enter-prising, socially responsible citizens, but only a top group of privileged people and a mass of underprivileged, is full of risk for the investors. Investments are more likely to be secure where there is rounded, balanced development and a healthy middle class. In most cases such development will

[5] *Report of the United Nations Mission of Technical Assistance to Bolivia,* cited, pp. 49-50.

not automatically occur, or not quickly enough, merely from the stimulus provided by greater production of raw materials.

Both or Neither

The President's Materials Policy Commission declared that "the habit of regarding diversified economic growth for the underdeveloped countries as an alternative to materials development is erroneous." It pointed out that economic development, to the people of these areas, means "a balanced growth of agriculture, manufacturing, and other industries directed toward maximizing real income and improving standards of living." The Commission took the enlightened view that an essential element in any American program for expanding raw materials production is "technical and financial assistance to the underdeveloped areas for a balanced growth of their economies . . ." It also urged that underdeveloped countries give consideration, from their point of view, to the ways in which materials production for world markets can help to support and advance their general development.[6]

Rightly handled, general development can promote materials development, and materials development can promote general development. There is much more complementarity than conflict between the growing American need to get more raw materials from abroad and the interest of the underdeveloped countries in developing their industry and agriculture and achieving a rounded economic growth. That is, the mutuality of interest exists if the decision-makers on both sides take a reasonably intelligent and long-range view. But to work out arrangements which will lead to mutual advantage will require careful thought. The problems will not be solved by market forces alone or by lecturing underdeveloped countries on the advantages of free enterprise.

From the standpoint of the United States, it would indeed be a grave mistake to assume that a program for helping underdeveloped countries to attain diversified economic growth (including industrialization) and a program for helping them to expand their raw materials production are

[6] President's Materials Policy Commission, cited, Vol. I, p. 73.

really *alternatives*. It would be closer to the truth in many parts of the world to say that, for political reasons, it is a case of *both* or *neither*. Investments for raw materials production in underdeveloped countries where general development is not going on at the same time are bound to be very insecure. If we want the raw materials, we had better encourage the general development (and, of course, there are many other reasons why it is in our interest to do so—see Chapter 2). On the economic level conflict may arise at times between the allocation of capital, managerial and labor skills, and other scarce resources for broad development of a country's economy and for specific raw materials expansion. Even here, I think, the relation will prove more often complementary than conflicting.

We must not forget that development is a dynamic process. It increases the amount of resources available. Though it uses capital, it creates new sources of capital and new habits of constructive investment. Though it draws on skilled labor and management, it trains more. Though it consumes natural resources, it leads to more thorough exploration of resources, improved accessibility, and more efficient extraction or use. To reason as though diversified development must compete with raw materials development for scarce factors of production is to think in short-run terms. From the longer-range point of view, it leads to a fallacy on the supply side analogous to the well-known fallacy on the demand side which implicitly assumes that total demand is fixed and that therefore industrial growth in a country must mean that it will buy fewer industrial goods from outside. In both cases the contrary is more nearly true.

As a concrete case, consider Canada. It is one of the most important sources of raw materials for the United States and at the same time a highly diversified industrial economy. Surely the consumer of Canadian materials is not worse off, price-wise or in other ways, in consequence of Canada's many other industrial and commercial activities. Some costs may be higher in a country like Canada, where both the extraction of raw materials and other industries are developed, than in a country like Bolivia or Iran, where everything is neglected except certain raw materials. But in Canada other costs related to efficiency and risk are lower. And there is no question as to where American capital and technicians would prefer to operate or where the flow of vital supplies is more secure against internal disorder.

Benefits from Expanded Output of Materials

The ways in which expansion of raw materials output can help an underdeveloped country's general economic development include the following:

1. Production and export of raw materials can provide a source of foreign exchange and government revenue to pay for imports of equipment and other items needed in promoting balanced development.

2. Materials development generally requires the building of such facilities as ports, railroads, roads, and power stations. With proper planning, many such facilities can be so located and designed as also to serve general development.

3. Modern methods of producing and processing raw materials require the development of mechanical skills and skills in business and organization among local employees, and also among local suppliers. Providing the raw materials developers take an enlightened attitude toward the training of local people, give them responsibilities, and follow a policy of carrying on as many ancillary operations as they can locally, the experience so generated is likely to be transferred to other local activities and thus facilitate general economic growth.

4. The wage payments, local purchases of supplies, and local payments of royalties, taxes, or dividends from raw materials operations provide a flow of purchasing power which, under proper conditions, will stimulate local developments in manufacturing, agriculture, and commerce.

5. Many of the great companies engaged in international raw materials development have adopted a long-range, enlightened view of their own self-interest and of their responsibilities not only toward employees but also toward the communities in which they operate. In consequence, it is not at all uncommon in underdeveloped countries to find that the schools, the houses, public health, and community recreation opportunities are better in vicinities where such

firms are established than elsewhere. Where this is the case, raw materials operations contribute to building up the human and social resources so fundamental to general economic advancement.

In the view of experts who have analyzed the raw materials situation with care, countries in a position to produce basic commodities for the world market are likely to find it more rewarding to do so in the decades immediately ahead. The outlook may not be bright for the producers of every raw material; some will encounter synthetic substitutes and other checks, and there will be ups and downs of demand. But the raw materials needs of the free world are expanding at a rapid rate, and the general view of experts seems to be that the trend will continue strongly upward. The underdeveloped countries, however, are rightly concerned about the *stability* of this demand. Though changes in attitudes and new techniques for controlling booms and depressions make unlikely another such collapse of demand as that which occurred in the 1930's, there are bound to be business fluctuations. These will have magnified effects on the volume of raw materials purchases and on raw materials prices. A good case can be made for international stabilization agreements using buffer stocks and other devices to smooth out some of the worst ups and downs of raw materials demand.

What Governments of Underdeveloped Countries Can Do

Governments of underdeveloped countries can take steps to see that their raw materials resources are developed in ways which contribute to diversification. Above all, they would be wise to make sure that revenues obtained from export of exhaustable assets like petroleum or other minerals are largely plowed back into a rounded program of general development. Also, countries possessing important raw materials sources can make good use of the bargaining power this gives them to obtain technical assistance and capital from abroad to develop the *non-raw-materials side* of their economies and to improve their basic human and other resources.

In Venezuela successive governments since 1945 have followed a policy they call "sowing the oil." Oil has provided some 60 percent of government revenues in recent years, and approximately 40 percent of all government expenditures have been devoted to improving the country's productivity—investment in transport and communications, agricultural and industrial development, sanitary works, buildings and homes. In addition, there have been large increases in the sums spent on education, health, and social welfare. What the permanent effect on the living level of the ordinary Venezuelan will be, and whether economic gains will be accompanied by gains in political democracy and stability, remains to be seen. But certainly the policy of using raw materials resources to aid diversified development is a wise one; it should bring good results if effectively administered. The essence of it is:

1. Cooperation with foreign investors, so as to attract the capital, technology, and management which cannot be provided within the country and which are necessary for efficient exploitation of the raw materials. A working partnership has developed between the government and the American and other foreign oil companies.

2. Taking a substantial share of profits by taxation or special agreement, without going so far as to "kill the goose that lays the golden eggs." Since 1948 the so-called "50–50" formula has been in force. The government's total receipts from oil are each year equal to the net profits of the companies. In addition, of course, the country's economy benefits from the wage payments and other local expenditures, the improvements in transport and power facilities, and the training and business experience provided by the companies' operations.

3. Plowing back the revenues so obtained into the economic and social development of the country.

This policy is made possible by realization on the part of both government and foreign investors that there is more to be gained by cooperation than antagonism. Experience under it has impressed inquirers from other countries. The director of the Iranian government's department of petroleum has said that there would have been no need for nationalization of the Iranian oil industry if relations with the

Anglo-Iranian Oil Company had been half as amicable as those which Venezuela maintains with its foreign oil companies.

The "50–50" formula has been adopted in Iraq and Saudi Arabia. Iraq is now embarking on a large program of general development, drawn up with the aid of a mission from the International Bank for Reconstruction and Development. Some 70 percent of the oil revenues have been earmarked for this purpose.

What Investors Can Do

How can private companies engaged in materials development in underdeveloped countries promote diversified growth outside their own sector without incurring the charge of interfering in local affairs? Within this limitation, they might well consider such actions as these:

1. When installing facilities such as roads, railroads, and power, try, in consultation with local authorities, to make them as useful as possible in stimulating new local industries and the general growth of the local economy. Some extra expense may well be justified, in the firm's own long-term interest, for these broader ends. The dredging of the Orinoco River, being carried out by the U. S. Steel Corporation in connection with iron ore development, may have even greater significance for the economic future of Venezuela's vast interior than the value of the ore itself.

2. Look for ways to help initiate other industries and commercial enterprises. United States firms in some Latin American countries have encouraged the establishment of local cement plants, agreeing to buy their product. A far-sighted oil or copper concern might well give friendly assistance to a local group interested in starting a shoe factory, by helping them to get in touch with good sources of technical, managerial, and financial aid. One American corporation, keenly aware of some of the points stressed in this chapter, has set up a staff committee on industrial development at the scene of an important foreign operation and provided it with technical personnel. The purpose is *not* to seek additional lines of venture for the company's own capital. On the contrary, the company feels that its own operations al-

ready bulk too large in relation to the rest of the economy; by helping other kinds of enterprises to get started it wants to achieve a smaller share of responsibility for the economic stability of the country. The committee is to make studies of industrial possibilities and to become acquainted with the industrial and investing community in the country and abroad, so as to know to whom to suggest favorable possibilities for action. The objective, to give the local economy a broader base and greater stability, is entirely in line with local desires and interests.

3. Develop training programs with the idea of helping to stimulate the country's general economic advance as well as with the company's immediate needs in mind. Many firms now offer scholarships to promising youngsters for education and training at home and abroad. Local schools or institutes for training in business management might well be given special aid. The company itself can be made a training ground for business initiative. Maximum use can be made of local talent, with advancement as rapid as the individual's capabilities justify. The firm can look with pride and approval on employees it has trained who decide to set up pioneer business ventures of their own.

4. Join with local business and governmental agencies to encourage laboratories or institutes of applied research and development, and contribute to their support. These would be concerned not so much with problems of the raw materials industry itself as with the problems that need to be solved in order to advance *other* sectors of the country's economy.

5. Demonstrate in company practices and encourage in employees a lively sense of community responsibility and civic obligation.

INDUSTRIALIZATION

"Industrialization" is a term often used loosely. In the narrow sense it may mean the rise of manufactures. In the broad sense it may mean use of power tools, large capital investment, sophisticated technology and organization, all implying an extended division of labor and exchange of goods in a money economy. In this broad sense we can even speak of the industrialization of agriculture. Modern manufactures never have a large growth except as part of a more comprehensive development. They require transportation, communication, wholesale and retail trade, finance, public administration, teaching, and health services. For this reason it is misleading to think of industrialization as growth of manufacturing alone. Agriculture itself becomes more efficient as part of the industrialization process, so that its output may increase at the same time that there is a relative if not absolute decrease in its labor force.

The Shift from Agriculture to Industry and Services

Most people in underdeveloped countries live on the land in rural villages and get their living by subsistence agriculture. Modern economic development has always been accompanied by a shift out of agriculture and a corresponding shift into practically all other types of economic activity. There is a high statistical correlation between the proportion of the occupied population engaged in nonagricultural production and the height of per capita real income. This holds both for historical comparisons (the same country at different dates) and for intercountry comparisons. It has also been demonstrated in interstate comparisons in the United States. Although there is probably some bias against agriculture in the methods of constructing the statistics, the relationship nevertheless seems to be a real one.

In this matter as in others, however, it is a mistake to think in terms of one-way cause and effect relations. There is an *association* between industrialization and the high productivity which makes high average incomes. The two are parts of an interlinked process; one does not proceed very far without the other. It is equally true to say (1) that high productivity produces industrialization and (2) that industrialization produces high productivity. Three things explain the observed correlation.

In the first place, higher productivity (which may start in more efficient agriculture, as well as in newly-established trade or manufacturing) means higher incomes. When people have more income to spend they generally increase their expenditures on nonfood items more than they do on food. In consequence, manufacturing, trades, and services expand more than basic food production. The result is an occupational shift out of agriculture.

Secondly, the improvements in agricultural efficiency which accompany industrialization decrease the number of farm workers required to produce a given output. The increased "roundaboutness" of agricultural production in industrialized societies has the same effect. In a preindustrial society all the men working at food production work directly on the land. In an industrial society many of them work in fertilizer and implement factories, trading firms, experiment stations, editorial offices of agricultural magazines, and so on. All this tends to decrease the proportion of the working population engaged directly in agriculture as productivity rises.

Thirdly, we have been living in an epoch when the changing nature of production and demand has moved workers out of agriculture into factories and services. The price system stimulates such shifts by offering larger rewards in the occupations where expansion is needed. Hence, wages and productivity per worker (measured in value of output) have tended to be higher in nonagricultural occupations. It is not a law of nature, however, that industry is inherently more productive than agriculture. The relation may change again at some future time, with further shifts to industry and with extension of modern education and new techniques to rural areas.

Interdependence of Agricultural and Industrial Development

It is unwarranted to conclude from the observed correlation of high income with a high proportion of nonagricultural working force that the way to make a country richer is to establish manufactures at almost any cost, by high tariff protection or other forms of subsidy. But it is equally unwarranted to hold (save in exceptional cases) that a large and sustained rise in a country's level of real income is likely to come about *without* a considerable shift out of agriculture into other occupations—that is, without a substantial degree of industrialization.

Modern agriculture, as practiced in the more developed countries, yields immensely more value per worker than either the agriculture or the industry of technologically less advanced areas. The practical point for those who would promote economic progress is that a rise in average income is most effectively brought about by improving productivity all along the line, in agriculture *and* in industry. The result will inevitably (with some qualifications for effects of foreign trade) be the shift in occupational structure already described—that is, a shift out of agriculture. But if that shift is brought about "artificially," faster than it is justified by real increases in productivity, the result may well be a loss rather than a gain. Argentina and other countries have recently illustrated how the national economy may suffer from policies which neglect and even burden agriculture (by foreign trade controls, taxes, and in other ways) for the sake of a subsidized expansion of manufacturing.

Denmark, New Zealand, and Iowa can be cited as outstanding examples of high income "agricultural" areas. Their average incomes are among the highest in the world. In a real sense their prosperity is based on modernized, highly efficient agriculture, yet in terms of occupational structure all three are examples of *industrialization* rather than of straight agricultural development.

The percentage of the economically active population engaged directly in agriculture is only 29 in Denmark (1948), 21 in New Zealand (1950), and 28.5 in Iowa (1950). These are no longer "agricultural" countries in the sense in which underdeveloped countries are agricultural, for, in the latter, 50 to 85 percent of the working population gets its living directly from the land. In Denmark 28 percent of the economically active population is engaged in manufacturing; in New Zealand, about 32 percent in manufacturing and construction; in Iowa, 15 percent in manufacturing and another 5.5 in construction. In all three areas there are more people occupied in trades, utilities, professions, and services outside of both agriculture and manufacturing than are occupied in either of these fields alone.

The conclusion is that it is unreal to think of "agricultural development" and "industrialization" as separate or conflicting in a long-term program. Industrialization is inseparable from substantial, sustained economic advance, because it is both a *consequence* of higher incomes (people spending relatively more on manufactured goods and services, relatively less on food) and a *means* to higher productivity (enabling agricultural efficiency to rise by shifting some people out of agriculture, especially where there is rural overpopulation, stimulating innovations, and in other ways). Improvement in the productivity of agriculture is one of the most solid means of promoting industrialization; in fact, unless agriculture does modernize substantially, industrial expansion in most underdeveloped countries is likely to be cut short by lack of markets, for the great majority of the population will not have the necessary purchasing power. Conversely, agricultural improvements cannot go very far unless there is industrial development to take up the released manpower and to provide a solid technical base for the equipment and services essential to modernized agriculture.

General statements such as these apply, of course, in different measure to different underdeveloped countries. They must also be qualified to accord with the possible role of international trade in modifying each country's market situation and supply situation. Just where the most effective measures might initially be taken to start a self-generating process of economic growth—whether in a broad attack on agricultural backwardness, or in promoting new crops, or new industries, or in improving basic utilities like transportation and power, or general and vocational education, or, more likely, a judicious combination of these and other attacks—can only be determined after careful study. Better than any general dogma which views industry as inherently more productive than agriculture or vice versa, and which favors expansion of one at the expense of the other, is a project-by-project approach. Such an approach avoids these big abstractions and considers in each case the concrete advantages and disadvantages to be had from specific types of development—this particular type of agricultural project, that specific industrial development, and so on.

Types of Industrial Effort—Political Implications

The types of industry most appropriate for a country's economic development, and the choice of those to be developed first, depend on the nature of resources (including managerial and labor skills) actually and potentially available, on potential markets, internal and external, on the relative costs of producing different items domestically as compared with importing them, on the situation as to under-employment and population pressure, and on many other factors which will differ from country to country.

Are there any *political* implications in one sequence of industrial development as compared to another which should be weighed in decision-making?

Should more emphasis be placed on heavy industries (production goods) or on those which turn out consumer goods? Communist industrialization policy everywhere stresses the former, rapidly building up the economic base for military power while the ordinary people have to wait a long time for tangible gains in their level of living, despite their efforts and sacrifices. Underdeveloped countries that hope to take the democratic route to economic development probably cannot afford, in the political sense, to impose such large or long-continued sacrifices on their citizens as can coercive, totalitarian governments. For them a policy of encouraging first those industries which offer the most promise of fairly immediate advances in living levels seems more suitable. In some cases resources and market conditions may favor considerable growth of the heavier industries, including chemicals for fertilizers, transport equipment, etc. But sound policy will also encourage, rather than restrain, the multitude of consumer goods industries, often small and unspectacular, which directly cater to the needs of an economically advancing population. This is also the result which will naturally follow if private initiative and freedom of enterprise are encouraged to supplement the direct undertakings of governments.

Another issue is centralized, large-scale, urban industry vs. decentralized, smaller-scale, rural and town industry. Again, this is not a question of exclusively the one or exclusively the other, and the best course will obviously depend on a great number of conditions that vary considerably from one underdeveloped country to another. On political and social grounds, however, and even in many cases on economic grounds, there are strong arguments for deliberately favoring the decentralized type of industrial development. It is more likely to broaden the bases of political power and to build more quickly a responsible, self-reliant citizenry. Probably—though on all these matters the experience on which to base conclusive judgments is lacking—it will carry the modern outlook more quickly into rural regions and bring a more rapid fall in the birth rate than could be had by waiting for a large part of the rural population to move to the cities.

On such grounds as these, one could justify diffusing manufacturing activity instead of concentrating it in the big urban centers, even if this involved some cost in technical and economic efficiency. There is good reason for thinking, however, that in many situations decentralization and diffusion of industry may also be justified on strict grounds of economic efficiency, when account is taken of the social overhead costs of moving people to central cities, housing them, and providing utilities. Some of the most recent trends in technology help to make smaller, diffused manufacturing operations more viable—for example, cheap electric power, automotive transport, improved communications. The social technology of the agricultural extension service and similar educational aids might also be applied to small industrial operations.

It is important to make a distinction between "cottage industries," in which the work is done in homes, and small-scale industries located in rural areas or towns but designed to take maximum advantage of modern techniques and equipment. The first may be appropriate in some circumstances as a transitory or emergency device; but there is danger in saddling a group of people with fundamentally inefficient methods of production that will not be able to stand up under competition. It is modernized, small-scale industry that we are talking about. The advantages of carrying industrial techniques to the places where the people are, or close to them—and in underdeveloped countries this means the rural regions, the provincial towns and villages—rather than concentrating industries exclusively in large cities and attracting people to them are so great as to deserve the most intensive effort. Technological inventiveness and careful experimentation need to be brought to bear on the problem of making small-scale, diffused industries efficient and viable.

Leaders of underdeveloped countries concerned with promoting industrial growth would be well advised to study Switzerland. This highly industrialized country has one of the highest living levels in the world. But its industries are decentralized to a remarkable degree. There are no big industrial agglomerations, as in Britain and Germany; the large cities are commercial rather than industrial. There are hardly any slums. About every tenth factory worker owns and cultivates a small farm. There is a very even distribution of wealth. The country has no important sources of coal and iron or other raw materials sometimes thought to be essential in an industrial country. It has no basic heavy industry, not even a single blast furnace. Its manufacturing is diversified and is carried on mainly in small plants.[7] The political power structure promoted by the Swiss type of industrialization seems especially favorable to democratic development.

The United States and Industrial Development

There is a myth, widely believed in underdeveloped countries, that the United States does not want them to develop industries for fear of competition, and because we want to keep them as "semicolonial" suppliers of raw materials. This view is not confined to Communists, but they work in and out of season to spread it (see Chapter 7).

In fact, neither the policies of the United States government nor those of American business have reflected any such animus against industrialization. There will always be segments of opinion in any democratic country that take a shortsighted view, but the true national interest of the United States, as we noted in Chapter 2, is strongly in favor of raising the productivity of underdeveloped countries, and this generally means industrialization. Also, for a number of good reasons, there is a much greater disposition in the United States than in most industrially advanced countries to take the view that industrial advancement elsewhere makes better

[7] Kurt B. Mayer, *The Population of Switzerland* (New York: Columbia University Press, 1952), especially pp. 254-258.

customers and suppliers and that this overbalances the factor of new competition. (See Chapter 2.)

Then how has the myth arisen? One explanation is that American capital has hitherto been attracted to underdeveloped countries mainly for exploitation of raw materials resources, such as petroleum. This reflects no desire to prevent manufacturing from developing. Rather, it results from the fact that manufacturing is more hampered, on the whole, by the insecure conditions under which capital and business enterprise, especially if they are foreign, operate in most of these countries. Equally important is the lack of broad enough internal markets to make manufacturing investment attractive. Modern manufacturing is dependent on a public with purchasing power. Where security and a market for manufactures exist, there is as much readiness on the part of American capital to go abroad into manufacturing as into raw materials production. This is true in Canada. United States business investments in Canada are 48 percent in manufacturing industry and only 29 percent in mining, smelting, and petroleum projects combined.

Increasingly of late, American capital has been going into manufacturing abroad. There may be a major trend in the making if the "climate" in enough less developed countries turns favorable. Also, leading American firms have shown considerable willingness to lend their technical know-how and managerial experience for the purpose of starting new industries in underdeveloped countries.

For example, the Singer Sewing Machine Company has agreed to supply to local owners in Ceylon the necessary techniques for setting up a shirt factory. Its experts are advising on factory buildings, layouts, and flow charts. It is helping to train the employees of the new factory.

Sears Roebuck and Company began its overseas operations with a store in Havana in 1941. Today it operates twenty stores in Latin America—in Mexico, Cuba, Venezuela, and Brazil—and a new one is to open in Colombia. When Sears started its store in Mexico City in 1947, 90 percent of the merchandise it sold was made in the United States. Shortly afterwards the company contracted with a Mexican manufacturer of refrigerators to produce the company's standard model. This process has been repeated in Mexico and elsewhere, Sears enabling local manufacturers to expand or to set up new businesses by helping them with technical advice and capital.[8] Today, 60 percent of the goods sold in Sears stores in Latin America are made in Latin America. In Brazil the ratio is 90 percent. Of the five thousand Sears employees in Latin America, less than 2 percent are United States citizens.

The Grace Company at Paramonga, Peru, acquired a run-down sugar mill and surrounding cane fields. It modernized the factory, rehabilitated the fields, developed new crops and processes, established a paper industry (based on a new process for using bagasse) and a chemical industry. As a result, Paramonga is now a thriving town of ten thousand people, with their own markets, library, schools, swimming pool, theater, and hospital. Of the 4,200 workers employed, only four are United States citizens in permanent residence. Training is provided in various branches of engineering, and Peru, which formerly imported almost all its paper, now exports paper.[9]

In Brazil and Chile steel mills have been erected with the aid of U. S. technicians and financed in part by the U. S. Export-Import Bank. At Huachipato, Chile, when operations began in 1950 there were 140 Americans in top technical posts teaching Chileans how to run the plant. In April, 1953, there were 70, and by mid-1954 there will be only 15. "Americans here compete for the honor of working themselves out of a job as quickly as possible," a journalist reported, adding that 20 percent of those who signed up for three years left at the end of two, their jobs completed by training Chilean replacements faster than scheduled.[10]

In Japan, "One hundred and sixty-one of America's leading industrial enterprises, taking advantage of the best investment climate in Asia, have built in Japan a private

[8] See on the growth and results of this policy in Mexico: Richardson Wood and Virginia Keyser, *Sears, Roebuck de Mexico, S. A.* (Washington: National Planning Association, 1953), the first case study in a series on "United States Business Performance Abroad."

[9] From a speech by Isador Lubin, U. S. representative to the Economic and Financial Committee. United Nations, General Assembly, Second Committee, *Official Records*, Sixth Session, 198th Meeting, October 30, 1952, p. 27.

[10] *Christian Science Monitor*, April 15, 1953, dispatch by Irving Kalin.

technical-assistance program that is reaching impressive dimensions. . . . While Japan is in no sense an underdeveloped country, the war and occupation set it back ten years behind the West in industrial techniques. . . . There is hardly a field, from steel and electric power to hats, hosiery, and antibiotics, in which the Japanese have not obtained patents, technical assistance, specialized machinery and equipment, and even the privilege of sending their engineers into U. S. factories for months of training." [11]

Another reason for the myth that the United States wants to keep underdeveloped countries from industrializing is the way in which the trade barrier problem has become confused with the industrialization problem. United States representatives, since the initiation of the Trade Agreements Program in 1934, have argued against high tariffs and other forms of trade restriction. But the first thought of most leaders of underdeveloped countries desiring to promote industrialization has been to foster local industries by shutting out foreign competition. The historic arguments of Alexander Hamilton and Friedrich List find many modern echoes. Even the staunchest advocates of freer world trade have had to admit, with John Stuart Mill, an element of validity in the "infant industry" argument for protection. The indiscriminate application of that argument, however, is self-defeating for the interests of the country concerned, as well as harmful to the world trading system as a whole. It might help to clarify the United States position if our representatives were to put more stress on *positive* methods of encouraging industrial growth—methods which increase the basic productivity of a country and which foster well selected industrial projects not likely to need indefinite tariff protection.

Another factor in the misinterpretation of United States attitudes on industrialization is that representatives of underdeveloped countries have at times asked American aid for ill-planned, grandiose, even grotesque proposals for installing some highly complex industrial operation quite unsuited to the markets and resources of the country at its current stage of development. To encourage such proposals would be to

---

[11] Jerome B. Cohen, "Private Point Four in Japan," *Fortune*, April, 1953, pp. 148 ff.

burden the economy of the underdeveloped country with a costly failure rather than to advance it. At times it has seemed that every country, no matter how small, wants a steel mill. United States representatives have had to resist requests for aid on badly conceived proposals, endeavoring to point out the greater benefits to be had from less ambitious but more useful beginnings. Again, one of the best ways to make the United States attitude less subject to misinterpretation would be to accentuate the positive, by focusing attention on a quest for the best ways to start and to build up truly viable and productive industries in countries that begin at a low level of general development.

Toward a Positive American Policy

It is important for the United States to counteract the opinions, suspicions, and Communist propaganda referred to above. To the extent that there is any basis in fact for the anti-industrialization myth, our attitudes and policy should be revised, while the large element of misunderstanding and misrepresentation in it should be counteracted by all the public relations means at our disposal. The American national interest requires a strongly positive attitude on our part toward development of new manufacturing industry, as of other types of production, wherever conditions in an underdeveloped country warrant it.

More study is needed of the relation of industrialization to the whole process of economic growth, and of methods for selecting and fostering suitable types of industrial expansion best adapted to a balanced development. Therefore, it may be suggested that the United States would do well to repeat in the field of industrialization the approach that since 1950 has given such good results in connection with another set of thorny economic, political, and propaganda problems— namely, agrarian reform. If the United States were to seize the initiative on the industrialization issue as it did on the agrarian reform issue, it could probably raise the international discussion of this topic in the United Nations and other forums to a new, higher level of positiveness combined with realism.

Chapter 16

THE WORLD ENVIRONMENT

Economic modernization of an underdeveloped country always changes power relations, internal and external.

Internally, some groups gain in influence, others lose, as the changes necessarily associated with economic development affect the distribution of education, wealth, prestige, experience in administration, and the other ingredients of power. From the standpoint of the aims by which we have defined successful development, it makes a great difference whether these internal changes result in concentrating power in the hands of a few authoritarian rulers, such as the successors of a feudal aristocracy or a new Communist Party élite, or whether they diffuse power more widely so that the people of the country cease to be servile subjects and grow to the stature of upstanding, self-respecting citizens in a self-governing community.

Externally, the economic advance of a formerly underdeveloped country presents its neighbors and the world with a new political force. What had been a negligible factor or even a political vacuum attracting conquest from outside now has to be reckoned with, because of increased military and economic potential and increased capacities for self-assertion, negotiation, and leadership in dealings with other countries. From the standpoint of the objectives accepted in this study it makes a great difference whether this enhanced international power is used for military threats and aggressive expansion or for peaceful and cooperative pursuit of reasonable national interests in a developing world community.

The way that a developing country's new political power will be shared and used, internally and externally, will depend not only on its cultural heritage and on the relative emphasis it gives to different kinds of development projects but also on the world political and economic setting in which development goes forward. Particularly important in the world setting are: (1) the extent to which collective security and peaceful settlement of international disputes can be relied upon; (2) the relative prestige of democracy and totalitarianism; (3) the degree of progress in turning passionate new nationalisms into constructive channels (the manner of the transition from what remains of colonialism is one factor); (4) international trade opportunities for developing countries; (5) the revival of international investment; and (6) the type and size of external aid programs by which underdeveloped countries may be assisted. These are topics to be explored further below.

This analysis of the impact of the world setting should suggest some things which the United States in its own interest might do to shape the course of development in underdeveloped countries, without intervening obnoxiously in their affairs. For our political and economic position gives us considerable influence on the world setting—not the ability to make it just what we would like, but more influence than that of any other power, unless it be the Soviet Union. When we have an affirmative program our influence is second to none.

Millions of people in this country and abroad have heard of "Point Four," but few will recall points one, two, and three of the same speech. When the President of the United States declared, "we must embark on a bold new program for making the benefits of our scientific advances and industrial progress available for the improvement and growth of underdeveloped areas," he had just laid down three other objectives for American foreign policy: first, strengthen the United Nations; second, aid world economic recovery and increase world trade; third, strengthen freedom-loving nations against aggression.[1] A thesis of this chapter is that points one, two, and three are essential if Point Four is to have a reasonable chance of success.

[1] Inaugural address of President Harry S. Truman, January 20, 1949.

COLLECTIVE SECURITY AND PEACEFUL SETTLEMENT

Japan's development was warped from the first by the over-riding aim of military strength. This aim will warp the development of underdeveloped countries in the future unless a collective security system can be built up which is reliable enough to safeguard the peacefully inclined nations and to discourage those with ideas of aggression. There are two aspects to this problem. One is the strengthening of the military capacity of the free world and the willingness of its members to act together to resist any military attacks by the Communist bloc. The question is whether the free world can and will protect those that throw in their lot with it.

The other aspect, quite aside from the general rift between the Communist and the non-Communist blocs, has to do with curbing aggressive ambitions of any country directed against its neighbors and promoting peaceful settlement of disputes which are bound to arise. Disputes like those between Israel and the neighboring Arab states and between India and Pakistan over Kashmir arouse much bitterness. If the settlement, as in the past, depends mainly on which nation can display or use the greater military power, and if nations feel that their chief protection against ambitious neighbors or against being pushed around by great powers is their own preparedness to fight, then their development policies will be influenced in a bad direction—from the point of view of the objectives we have set forth. The development of military goods industries will be pushed at the expense of consumer goods industries. Authoritarianism, supported by the need for quick national strength and by super-patriotic emotions, will prevail over popular rights and popular participation in government.

The kind of world order which the peoples of the world are striving, with imperfect success, to establish through the United Nations is profoundly important as a political setting for truly successful economic development.

THE PRESTIGE OF DEMOCRACY

There are fashions in political systems as in other aspects of human affairs. In the nineteenth century free institutions and parliamentary government seemed destined to spread over the whole world. After World War I there was a resurgence of tyranny in the modernized form of Fascist, Nazi, and Communist totalitarianisms, all of which challenged ideas of individual freedom and responsible government that had hitherto seemed to accompany modern economic growth. Today it is a real question for the awakening peoples in underdeveloped countries whether the "wave of the future" and the way forward for them is some form of liberal democracy adapted to their needs or some form of totalitarianism or dictatorship—the Communist variety, or perhaps some home-grown variety like that of Franco or Peron. But if the democratic idea seems to be on the upgrade in the world, then political trends in newly developing countries will be influenced in the democratic direction.

This supposes, of course, that people in the developing countries are able to learn with reasonable accuracy what is going on. Better two-way communication between the less developed and the more developed countries of the free world is of fundamental importance for the whole political outlook, and we shall allude to it again. Assuming that truth can flow without too much distortion, the degree to which we in the United States and other free countries make democracy work well and live up to the precepts of democratic ideals will have a considerable influence on political trends in the developing countries.

How well democracy works will be judged by the peoples of underdeveloped countries largely by what they think it means for themselves. For example, the overwhelming majority in the underdeveloped world is nonwhite. What they read, or experience when they travel, about racial discrimination in the United States is likely to affect them more deeply than comparative data on standards of living. The fact that there is now a very decided improvement under way in the United States in this matter, in contrast to our past bad record, strengthens the prestige of the American type of democracy and makes it less vulnerable to Communist and other attacks. Also, we must remember that the people of most underdeveloped countries, including those that have won national independence, tend to identify themselves emotionally with the people of colonial areas. Hence, the way democracy works in the treatment of colonial peoples and in the fostering of their political, economic, and social progress is likely to have an even greater bearing on its prestige in the underdeveloped world than the way it works in Europe and America.

Some underdeveloped countries—India is a notable example—are now engaged in a great effort to achieve economic and social advancement rapidly and by democratic methods. In such countries the prestige of democracy is definitely at stake. Practical progress in health, nutrition, the handling of land problems, the growth of industrial and agricultural production will all be noted by leaders in other countries and will be compared with similar results in Communist-ruled areas, such as China. We in the United States thus have a great stake in the success or failure of democratic efforts at development in India and elsewhere, for the outcome will go far toward shaping the political climate of the world that we and our children will live in.

NATIONALISM AND SELF-ESTEEM

One Western idea which has caught on throughout nearly all the underdeveloped world is nationalism. It has attracted to itself most intense emotions, not only for reasons similar to those which have made nationalism the most powerful social force in the West over the last few centuries, but also for a special reason. Nationalism in the East serves as an outlet for long accumulated feelings of humiliation and resentment because of the inferiority in which the peoples of most underdeveloped countries have found themselves in their political, economic, and social contacts with the technologically more advanced West. Manifestations are the mobs shouting antiforeign slogans in the streets of Teheran, the success of the Communists' anti-imperialist propaganda, and the extreme suspicion with which the activities of foreign investors and official proposals for economic cooperation are viewed in many underdeveloped countries.

The emotional element in this new and often flamboyant and touchy nationalism has to be emphasized. It may lead to responses which in the coldly rational view, especially the view that looks primarily to economic advancement, may be foolish and harmful. To understand the politics of economic development in the underdeveloped world today we must keep reminding ourselves that men seek not merely material well-being but also the well-being denoted by such social-psychological terms as respect, status, and self-esteem. These intangibles, now bound up with sentiments of nationality, have often led men to sacrifice material advantages and even risk life itself.

In general, the people and the policy-making officials of the United States (especially in Congress) lack a sufficient appreciation of the psychological factor. The striving of men in underdeveloped countries to re-establish their self-esteem, after being in an inferior position toward the West, is certainly one of the most important political aspects of the world environment in which development goes forward today. It is at this point that inadequate evaluation of the forces at work is most likely to lead to blunders and disastrous failures of policy by Western governments and Western business.

A crucial task of statesmanship for political and economic leaders is to find ways to channel the powerful impulses of nationalism toward constructive goals. Sound programs of economic development are, of course, basic in such statesmanship. Economic development is needed, not only for the material benefits it can bring, but also to impart a feeling of hope and progress and to build a solid foundation for a restored self-esteem. If the teachings of modern psychology are right, this is one of the best ways to head off the more extreme, pathological forms of nationalism. We must hasten to add, however, that economic development in itself is by no means a guarantee against perverted nationalism.

Nationalism has important constructive functions to perform in the process of modernization by building a wider sense of community, breaking down traditional barriers of caste and class and parochialism, and inspiring individuals with a sense of civic obligation. It also carries two great dangers.

First, the extremes of nationalism rampant in the world today (and not only in the underdeveloped countries) imperil the international cooperation which is necessary in a world grown as interdependent as ours. Examples are aggressive efforts to expand national boundaries, inability to compromise disputes with other nations, and the raising of barriers to trade and investment which deprive all concerned of the potential benefits of international exchange.

Second, extremes of nationalism stifle the growth of individual freedom. Hitler's storm troopers sang, "We spit on freedom, *das Volk* [the nation] must be free." It seems that people will rally more strongly to an emotional and somewhat mystical will for "collective freedom" than to desires for individual freedom.[2] A patriotic wish to be free of real or fancied foreign domination and resentment stemming from a national feeling of inferiority can ruin prospects for the growth of internal freedom. We have noted how the Japanese were more eager to get the unequal treaties revised than to obtain the popular rights advocated by liberals. The propaganda by which Communists try to entice the people of underdeveloped countries into their totalitarian police systems plays on these same motives: nationalism and a burning desire to restore injured self-esteem.

This is why it is so important to satisfy legitimate aspirations for "collective freedom" in self-rule, for equal status and respect, and for economic advancement. Otherwise it will hardly be possible to hold in check the more pathological manifestations of nationalism which would sacrifice individual freedom and international peace.

THE TRANSITION FROM COLONIALISM

Whether the remainder of the colonial system will be liquidated over the next few decades in a constructive or destructive manner is one of the topmost questions bearing on the world political environment, in so far as the underdeveloped areas are concerned. Its significance (and not only in present colonial areas) can hardly be overrated. The reasons are:

1. Colonial issues have become a symbol among the peo-

---

[2] Cf. P. A. Reynolds, *War in the 20th Century*, an inaugural lecture delivered at the University College of Wales, Aberystwith, November 8, 1950 (Cardiff: University of Wales Press, 1951).

ple and leaders of underdeveloped countries generally. This is most true in important areas of Asia and the Middle East that have only recently acquired their own independence. As we have said, these people identify themselves emotionally with the people of the colonies and identify colonial issues with the social humiliations which they have suffered in past relations with Westerners. In many of these countries there still is a widespread feeling—which I believe to be mistaken, but we are talking about *their* attitudes—that their freedom is no more endangered by Communism than by Western "imperialism." Whether these people will be suspicious and hostile toward the West, toward its attempts to build a strong security system for the free world, and toward Western democratic ideas, will depend in great degree on how the West handles the colonial problems that face it in Africa and a few other places. To them, this is a crucial test of the West's sincerity in its talk about freedom.

2. Large territories containing important economic resources are still in colonial status, principally in Africa. The outcome of the development process now under way in these areas is going to be very important, politically and economically, not only for the people that live there but also for the rest of us. There is still a chance for constructive action to prevent Africa from being set against the West, as Asia was, but the opportunity will not be for long.

3. The greatest political liability of the West in the world struggle with Communism, at least in the underdeveloped countries where the struggle is most in doubt, is the association with "imperialism." Of course, no matter what the West does, Communists will make false charges. But as long as certain Western countries continue to rule colonies without clearly acknowledged goals of liberation the Communists will be able to make true charges, also. The present situation seems to offer proof of the whole "anti-imperialist" line. It lets the Communists pose falsely as friends of "national liberation" and guarantees that any Western attempt to arouse a crusading enthusiasm in underdeveloped countries in the name of freedom will fall flat. Actually, the West is much less imperialistic, both in spirit and in practice, than it used to be, while the great recent expansion of imperialism has been

in the growth of a new-style colonial empire under the Soviets. We and our friends in underdeveloped countries ought to be acquainting people with that fact. Recent progress toward self-rule in Western colonies and former colonies, coupled with the news that filters through from some of the Soviet-ruled areas, has already started to modify attitudes in underdeveloped countries. The prestige of Western democracy and of the democratic path to development will rise with each definite step which demonstrates that the remaining Western colonies are not to be ruled indefinitely but are being prepared for planned liberation. The new Soviet imperialism will then stand out more clearly by contrast.

On the other hand, a series of conflicts and wars between Western colonial powers and local nationalist movements (with Communists grasping leadership wherever they can) would be disastrous to the West's political position throughout the underdeveloped world. Enormous political damage has already been done to the cause of the West by the failure to give enough recognition, soon enough, to national aspirations in Indo-China. Similiar situations may be building up in North Africa and in other parts of Africa. Such political fumbling has the effect of letting the Communists harness the most potent force in the underdeveloped world—nationalism—to their bid for power. This is what the Communist leader, Ho Chi Minh, was able to do in Indo-China. Not only that, he has been able to attract widespread sympathy among other peoples in Asia who are themselves anti-Communist, because they are even more anticolonial. An astute journalist writes from Singapore of opinion in the Indian community there:

These Indians are opposed to communism. They are opposed to colonialism. Of the two, they would rather see the former operated anywhere in Asia by Asians than the latter operated anywhere in Asia by non-Asians.[3]

Planned Development Toward Liberation

In 1939 there were about 700 million people living under one variety or another of colonial rule established by Western powers. This was a reflection of the great technological

[3] *Christian Science Monitor*, April 28, 1953, dispatch by Ronald Stead.

superiority of the West in recent centuries and of the developments in transportation, communication, and industry which had made it feasible for Western power to be exerted over long distances, using the resources of distant places in the Western system of production. But already by 1939 changes were under way. New acquistions had come to an end. The principles of trusteeship and responsibility for the welfare of inhabitants were being asserted and had crystallized in the League of Nations mandate system. Some former colonies had acquired self-government or independence and others were well on the way.

The most rapid changes have come in the last decade. In that period territories inhabited by nearly 600 million people have acquired a new status either of complete independence or of self-government with voluntary "commonwealth" ties: the Philippines, India, Pakistan, Ceylon, Indonesia, Burma, Korea, Syria, Lebanon, Jordan, Israel, Libya, and Puerto Rico. Less than 200 million people remain under Western colonial rule.[4] Of these nearly 150 million are in the African territories of Britain, France, Belgium, and Portugal. Under the United Nations system, some colonies are held on terms of trusteeship which provide for international supervision, but the administering powers have agreed also to submit information reports on *all* nonself-governing areas, and this is leading to a gradual increase of international accountability.

It is as clear as anything can be in politics that powerful new forces are at work which will insure the continuation of the trend toward liquidation of colonialism until all the old relationships are completely readjusted. This will take some time, but all indications are that the time will be short, not more than a few decades at most. The inhabitants of some of the remaining colonial areas obviously need a further period of tutelage before they are able to "stand by themselves under the strenuous conditions of the modern world," as the League of Nations Covenant put it. An abrupt plunge into independence, without adequate internal preparations and without adequate external arrangements for

[4] I am aware that 600 from 700 does not leave 200. The discrepancy is due to growth of population since 1939 and to rounding.

security and for assistance, would not be good for them or for the world. One of the many dangers of a policy of drift is that revolts will force independence without adequate preparation. What is needed is a *planned development toward liberation.* "Liberation" in this context means either (1) self-government combined with *voluntary* maintenance of a tie with the former ruling power, or (2) complete independence, or (3) a period of assisted independence in which the United Nations provides an especially large amount of technical and administrative aid (a pattern partially established in Libya).

The time-honored test of a colony's readiness to pass from dependent status to independence has been trial by battle. If it was able to stage a revolt and defeat the forces that the metropolitan power was able to send against it, or to make enough of a nuisance of itself, particularly by choosing a time when the metropolitan power was weak or heavily engaged elsewhere, then the colony became a sovereign state. That there are better ways of handling the transition to free nationhood than this has already been demonstrated in a number of modern instances. The importance to the cause of the West and to the prospects for successful economic development throughout the world of facing and solving this problem in a forehanded way can hardly be exaggerated.[5]

[5] I commend to the reader's attention the interesting "open letter to the President" by the editor of the *Pacific Spectator,* Robert C. North, in the Winter, 1953, issue of that review. He urges a "Dulles Plan" under which the United States would join with other countries, "those that have colonies, those that were colonies, and those that still are colonies," in a joint program "not to contain this explosive nationalism, but, by gradually and systematically granting a scheduled independence, to guide it into constructive channels." As envisaged by Mr. North, the plan would consist of "a series of transitional programs for the step-by-step transformation of Indo-China, Tunisia, Morocco, and similar areas from colonies or semi-colonies into independent republics. Each program will have its own specifications according to the material resources of the colony and the political sophistication of its people; and each, of course, must have its own timetable. Some, like the already accomplished British plan for India and the United Nations action in Libya, will move rapidly; others will proceed much more slowly. But in either case, there will be two important elements: the achievement of independence by a fixed date will be guaranteed through multilateral agreement; and the integrity of the area, both during the transitional period and after the granting of independence, will be protected by international military force—the preponderance of manpower being recruited locally."

European Colonial Policies

The British have already rather definitely committed themselves to a path which means planned liberation for their colonies. The boldest experiment in African home-rule is in the Gold Coast, where a policy of "creative abdication" since 1951 has brought a democratic constitution and a cabinet mainly African under Prime Minister Kwame Nkrumah. Though formerly an "anti-imperialist" firebrand much interested in Communist technique, he now says, "I am a friend of Britain. I desire for the Gold Coast the status of a Dominion within the Commonwealth . . ." [6] In recent official pronouncements on British colonial policy the goal, as the veteran colonial statesman, Lord Hailey, says, "is invariably described as 'self-government within the Commonwealth.' But this qualifying condition is nothing more nor less than a pious hope. . . . The fundamental basis of self-government is the withdrawal of all external control, save only in such measure and for so long as it is voluntarily accepted by the colony concerned." [7] In practice, Burma was set free and did not stay in the Commonwealth. India, Pakistan, and Ceylon decided to maintain Commonwealth ties, but without compulsion to do so. From all reports, the feeling toward Britain in the Indian subcontinent is now markedly friendly, proving that the attitude expressed by Lord Hailey pays off politically. It contrasts sharply with what happened in Indonesia. There the Dutch, though their administration was in some respects very good, tried to maintain alien control for too long. Withdrawing ungracefully in the face of colonial revolt, they left a legacy of hatred which for a long time will hamper their business and personal as well as political contacts.

The French, Belgians, and Portuguese in their administra-

The recommended program would also provide technical advice and economic aid, public health assistance, sound training in law and administration, also education and inspiration, "not just for the upper classes, but for all the people, as in any strong and well-functioning democracy." (pp. 3, 5-6.)

[6] See *Time*, February 9, 1953, p. 25.

[7] Lord Hailey, "A Turning Point in Colonial Rule," *International Affairs*, April, 1952, p. 183.

tion of African territories have shown a relative absence of racial intolerance and discrimination. But they have given very little indication of forehanded willingness to plan for and encourage a process of political development which would ultimately allow their colonies to enter the family of nations as independent states, choosing whether or not to retain ties with the mother country. The French have tried to avoid the issue by setting up the theory that their dependencies are like French provinces, that the inhabitants are Frenchmen with a different skin color, and that they will gradually advance in status within the French Union. But as Lord Hailey comments, "You do not produce the kind of change of which we are now thinking, merely by insisting that a colony is an integral part of the metropolitan country, if in reality it continues to be governed as a political dependency and is made to realize the fact." [8] French leaders do not seem to have learned the paradox that as dependent areas, like children, grow up, the family connection is more likely to continue if there is genuine progress toward self-rule and if the hope for future association is built on voluntary preference rather than constraint.

American Policies

The United States can point to a good record in political relations with its former colonies. We promised independence to the Philippines and kept the promise. Though we can fairly be criticized for some of the economic stipulations imposed at the instance of American pressure groups, and perhaps for not having given enough attention to economic and social preparations for freedom, most Filipinos are glad to stand up and testify against the charges of "imperialism" hurled at America. Cuba was not annexed, as it easily could have been. Puerto Rico has recently attained a favorable type of commonwealth status which is approved by its people. Hawaii and Alaska are nearing the goal of statehood. We report periodically to the United Nations on the administration of the former Japanese mandated islands taken over after World War II. The future of Okinawa and some other areas of military occupation is still to be settled. The Virgin

8 Same, p. 181.

Islands and the Panama Canal Zone are the only other areas now ruled from Washington as dependencies.

In general, however, the tendency in underdeveloped countries is to associate the United States with the colonial powers of Europe rather than to look at our own record. Behind the scenes, the United States has on occasion urged more liberal policies on the Dutch (in the Indonesian issue) and the French (over North Africa and Indo-China) to a degree which has aroused their resentment, but it has refrained from any clear and politically valuable statement that American policy will work consistently toward the goal of an orderly, planned liberation.[9] In the Trusteeship Council and other United Nations bodies the United States has tried to take a moderate position, but it has often voted with the colonial powers against the demands for more rapid changes put forward by members of the Asian-Arab bloc. Also, in the execution of the Marshall Plan for European recovery our government's economic cooperation with European governments has extended to projects for the expansion of output in their colonies, and this has appeared to align the United States further with their outlook on colonial issues.

Collective Security and the Colonial Issue

Neither the European colonial powers nor the free world as a whole would be strengthened by a series of colonial wars—a practically certain result of a policy of drift—nor by the ill will and reaction against democratic ideas which such unnecessary conflicts would arouse in the rest of the underdeveloped countries.

At the same time, precipitate and unprepared withdrawal would be no service to freedom in the long run. At a time when the Communist bloc has built up great military strength it would be foolhardy and irresponsible to advance

[9] Since this was written, Assistant Secretary of State Henry A. Byroade has spoken on "The World's Colonies and Ex-Colonies: A Challenge to America" at the conference on "Twentieth Century Colonialism" held by the World Affairs Council of Northern California. This speech, delivered October 31, 1953, represents definite progress in defining America's position and making it clear to the world. See the reprint of the address in *Department of State Bulletin*, November 16, 1953, pp. 655-660.

self-government or independence in some areas prematurely and thereby allow strategically important resources to be seized by the other side, or be made unavailable to the free world by chaotic or hostile internal politics. It would also be reckless to neglect the effect of any colonial readjustments and their timing upon the defense capacity of European nations in the face of Soviet military power.

These are points that need to be given careful thought by some of the Asian-Arab nations. They press in the United Nations for rapid revision of existing colonial ties, but at the same time want to maintain a neutralist attitude when it comes to organizing collective resistance in a clear case of aggression, as in Korea. The feasibility of a constructive program of planned liberation depends in part on the breadth of support which can be rallied behind a system of collective security.

Economic Development and the Prospect of Self-Rule

There is a reciprocal relation between political development, progress toward self-rule, and economic development. The latter is necessary as a basis for democratic self-government, but the *kind* of economic development is also important. Some kinds, exemplified in French North Africa, create strong vested interests in colonial status and raise difficult issues when the demand for self-government becomes inexorable. But economic development that produces an indigenous middle class and a wide distribution of economic and political power is a preparation for political freedom. For this reason exclusive concentration on the extraction of local mineral and other resources for sale abroad is not politically sound. Such operations need supplementing by deliberate measures to develop the internal economy so as to build up a self-reliant, middle-income group of skilled workers, farmers, managers, independent businessmen, and professional people, capable of responsible citizenship when the time comes for the colony to take over its own affairs.

On the other hand, self-government or the prospect of it is an important stimulant to rounded economic development. Where there is alien rule and no announced program for progress toward planned liberation two things happen. First, economic growth is likely to consist of an overlay of foreign-managed plantations, mines, and industries on a native pattern of subsistence agriculture—in other words, the dual economy characteristic of many colonial areas. This type of development is not likely to become self-generating or to bring a progressive economic, social, and political advancement of the local people. A government primarily responsive to local needs is necessary to give the kind of leadership required for a grass roots development that lifts the level of all the people. Of course, a benevolent government from outside may do a more effective job of responding to local needs than an incompetent, exploitative government which a local minority might impose on an independent but politically immature people. This is the justification for tutelage at a primitive stage of advancement. But the type of development program fostered by a government responsive to local needs (either a self-government or an outside authority committed to planned liberation) will differ in important respects from those of most colonial regimes in the past.

Second, the motivation for economic progress is low. The energies and the scarce leadership talent of the dependent country are likely to be diverted into a bitter struggle for independence. Nationalistic agitation absorbs the effort which ought to go into grappling with urgent local economic and social problems. Not least important, the alien rulers serve as scapegoats on whom all the evils of the subject country can be blamed, not only those for which they are responsible but also those which can be remedied only by diligent action of the local people themselves. The recent history of India illustrates these points. Since becoming independent India has shown a remarkable release of energy and a no less remarkable new willingness of local leadership to face up to tough problems (for example, the population problem) which could be by-passed so long as British rule offered an easy explanation for the country's troubles. In Syria, according to Charles Malik, a consequence of former colonial rule is that "A whole generation has been schooled in the negative—if necessary—discipline of resistance, and it must take some time before the more positive virtues of responsibility, planning, statesmanship and strong government can perfect themselves." [10]

Political independence, however, does not automatically ensure economic development. China, Thailand, Tibet, Afghanistan, Liberia, Bolivia, and Haiti have been ruled by their own independent governments in recent times without making striking progress in economic modernization. Some areas under colonial administration made more. It would be wrong to imply that independence is always a positive factor and colonial rule always a negative factor in economic development. The more enlightened modern colonial administrations have been performing functions necessary to development, such as provision of public order, administrative competence and integrity, technical skills, and basic equipment in transportation, communication, and sanitation. It is vital to the well-being and advancement of dependent peoples that these functions, which they are not yet able to perform for themselves, continue to be performed. Tutelage of some sort must be provided for some time in large segments of Africa and some other places.

The problem which statesmen must face is how to reconcile the need for tutelage with liquidation of the old concepts of irresponsible and indefinitely continued rule of one people by another, now political anachronisms. In the modern idea of administration over dependent peoples as a trust, in planned economic and social development as a preparation for increasing political responsibility and ultimate self-rule, and in the new international institutions for United Nations supervision and aid, we already have the needed elements for solving this problem. Progress in this field is one of the most vital contributions that can be made toward improving the outlook for successful economic development, not only in the remaining dependent areas but throughout the underdeveloped world.

OPPORTUNITIES FOR FOREIGN TRADE

The kind of economic environment that prevails in the world during the years ahead will have much to do with the

[10] Charles Malik, "The Near East: The Search for Truth," cited, p. 238.

political as well as the economic outcome of the drive for development in underdeveloped countries. Opportunities for international trade and the revival of international investment are likely to be as important as any other factors in influencing (1) the speed with which economic advance can take place within the underdeveloped countries of the non-Communist world, (2) their choice between a Communist or a democratic path, and (3) the internal political pressures which, even given an orientation toward the free world, might bring an authoritarian and militaristic development rather than a liberal one.

If underdeveloped countries find stable and expanding markets in the free world for their present export products and for new products that should appear as development progresses, then they will be able to earn substantial amounts of dollars and other currencies with which to pay for the equipment, supplies, and expert assistance that they need in their development programs. They will also be able to pay interest and dividends necessary to attract outside capital. Lacking such markets, the pace of development will be slower, the ability to form capital locally and to attract capital from abroad will be less, the need for intergovernmental financing by the United States will be greater, and more of whatever aid we provide will have to take the form of gifts.

A United Nations study has shown clearly how crucial to the ability of underdeveloped countries to get the machinery and other development goods they need from abroad is the market for their exports. Between World Wars I and II foreign exchange receipts of underdeveloped countries from capital inflow were generally small as compared to export proceeds and much less stable, while in the period 1946–1950 capital inflow was "even less significant . . . both in absolute terms and in relation to export proceeds. . . . Countries where long-term investment capital amounted to more than 10 per cent of export proceeds were the exception, and such an inflow was chiefly occasioned by the development of resources particularly suited for exports, such as oil in Iraq." [11] Even a very large increase in the international flow of capital

[11] United Nations, Department of Economic Affairs, *Instability in Export Markets of Under-Developed Countries,* cited, p. 67.

would not substantially change the dependence on exports. If the capital flow is to take the form of sound investment rather than gifts and defaults, export possibilities must expand sooner or later so that debts can be serviced and earnings transferred.

From the political standpoint, a stable and expanding market in the free world will encourage underdeveloped countries to choose the democratic path toward development, with international cooperation through trade and investment (and in other ways) an integral part of their development policies. Lack of markets would encourage autarky, promote the use of newly-developed political and military power for empire-building, and make the Communist world system seem more attractive.

The countries of the Communist bloc boast that under their state-controlled economic systems they have no trouble from depressions or unemployment, or from the pressures of private producers whose sales or prices might be harmed by imports from abroad, and that they are therefore in a position to offer a guaranteed market of great stability and expanding size to countries that join with them. There is enough truth in this boast so that we have to take account of it. Unless the economic environment in the free world is at least reasonably attractive, offering stable and expanding markets to the underdeveloped countries, they may be swayed in the direction of Communist totalitarianism.

Decisive Influence of the American Market

In determining the economic setting for development the influence of the United States, because of its sheer economic weight, can come close to being decisive. Though the United States has only 6 percent of the world's population and about the same fraction of its land area, it produces 40 percent of the aggregate of national incomes in the world and nearly half of the world's industrial output. The rise and fall of American demand for raw materials are crucial for the export earnings of many underdeveloped countries and hence for their ability to finance equipment imports. The American economy represents by far the largest source of savings which could be channeled into international loans and investments and by far the largest capacity to make grants-in-aid. A decision in America about price and production policy for synthetic rubber has immediate repercussions on the ability of natural rubber areas like Malaya and Indonesia to finance development programs and may significantly affect their vulnerability to Communist agitation. A triumph of political logrolling which puts up our tariff or quota barriers so that some tiny segment of American industry or agriculture does not have to meet the competition of imports may seriously unbalance the international accounts of a small friendly country and perhaps throw it into depression. As an American official ruefully remarked, "We are so big that every time we turn over in bed we pull the covers off somebody."

A pause in American economic growth which we experience as a mild recession has a greatly amplified impact on some of the countries that are suppliers of materials to our industries. In 1949 we had such a recession. Our gross national product was down only 1 percent as compared with the year before; the index of industrial production was down 8 percent, and nonagricultural employment 2 percent. But the United States imported 17 percent less from the sterling area (from all areas, 6 percent). Another recession year was 1938. The gross national product was 6 percent below 1937, industrial production 21 percent, and nonagricultural employment 6 percent. But the value of United States imports from all areas was down 35 percent and from the sterling area 47 percent.[12]

Political Wisdom of Larger and Steadier Imports

If Americans want to encourage sound economic and political development in underdeveloped countries, one of the most effective ways would be to put buying power into their hands by large and steady American imports, which means stabilizing our economy at a high level and lessening our import restrictions.

Stabilization is particularly important in our economic impact on the world environment in which development will

[12] James R. Nelson and Donald K. Palmer, *United States Foreign Economic Policy and the Sterling Area,* Center of International Studies, Princeton University, March 9, 1953, p. 23.

take place. In case of a threat of business recession in the United States, such as might come with a leveling off of armament expenditures or from other causes, it would be wise to take special measures to step up both the flow of American private investment capital abroad and public outlays for loans and grants-in-aid to underdeveloped countries. Such increased export of capital would assist domestic stabilization measures, though only to a modest degree. More important would be the effects on the rest of the free world. By helping to offset the loss of dollar buying power caused by a fall in our imports, the outflow of American capital would promote rapid and steady development and a sense of confidence in the free world system.

An international group of experts appointed by the United Nations has recommended that lending countries should fix annual targets for long-term investments and agree to make up the difference between the target levels and actual capital flow by government deposits with the International Bank for Reconstruction and Development. Lending countries should offset in the same manner any increases in their own monetary reserves induced by a fall in effective demand for imports. In signing this report a distinguished American economist, J. M. Clark, wrote:

> We are probably taking some chances if we try to do too much with fiscal policy. But we are also taking chances if we do too little to stabilize income and employment at a high level. In terms of fluctuations, the United States might be inclined to accept a moderate amount of irregularity, and rely on its social security system to provide for the resulting unemployment. But the impact of our fluctuations on other countries will not allow us, as good citizens of an interdependent world, to decide the question in the same terms that might govern us if we were isolated. I recognize that the world situation, analysed in this report, imposes an obligation on countries that rank as industrial leaders, and makes it to their interest to demand a higher performance from themselves than they might be inclined to do on domestic considerations alone. To put it in what may be a more pertinent light, this world situation warns us to take very seriously—more so than we otherwise might—the risks of doing too little, as against the risks of using imperfectly tested fiscal devices.

In view of the world situation, I am prepared to take considerable risks of the latter sort . . .[13]

The indirect effects of lowering American trade barriers would probably be more important for the development of underdeveloped countries than the direct effects, at least for the near future. By and large, our trade barriers do not greatly restrict imports of raw materials from the underdeveloped countries, though there are exceptions (sugar, for example). By taking more manufactured and semimanufactured goods, however, from Europe, from Japan, and from other industrialized and partly industrialized countries the United States would start a chain reaction which would create better markets in these countries for the raw materials of underdeveloped areas. And, eventually, as the underdeveloped areas themselves begin to be able to export certain types of manufactured and semimanufactured goods at a low enough cost to meet competition, easier access to world markets would encourage further and more rapid development and greater loyalty to the democratic, free world system.

Some American producers would be hurt by lowering trade barriers against foreign competition. The injury would be minor in most lines and would be more than offset so far as the total welfare of the country is concerned by (1) the growth in foreign demand for other types of American goods, resulting from successful economic development, (2) savings to taxpayers in a lessened necessity for foreign aid, and (3) the savings in military costs and the general political benefits reasonably to be expected from the improvement in the world economic environment and the growth of free world strength. The gains to the whole nation from tariff reduction would be so substantial that it would be a good investment to pay compensation where necessary to those relatively few groups who would be harmed.

REVIVAL OF INTERNATIONAL PRIVATE INVESTMENT

Revival of international private investment on a large scale, with wide geographical distribution of investments and wide

[13] United Nations, Department of Economic Affairs, *National and International Measures for Full Employment;* a separate and concurring statement by J. M. Clark (New York: 1949.II.A.3), pp. 103-104.

distribution among different branches of industry and commerce, would constitute a most helpful change in the world economic environment for development. It would help to speed development and make it more likely to go along the democratic path.

Private investment is capable of bringing to a developing country not merely capital but also important techniques which are best taught by practice and example. This is particularly true of direct investment—that is, investment carrying some degree of management responsibility. By association with local business, and by example, private investment from abroad often helps to stimulate local capital formation.

The Flow of American Private Capital

The United States is obviously the greatest potential source of capital for international investment today, and at the moment the only large source. However, American private capital and enterprise have not been playing nearly as significant a role in the development of underdeveloped areas as they might. The outflow of American private capital for long-term investment abroad, according to Department of Commerce estimates, in the last few years has been at the rate of 1 to 1½ billion dollars annually, plus reinvested earnings to the amount of another half or three-quarters of a billion dollars. Much of this has gone to comparatively well developed countries like Canada, and much of the rest into petroleum. Recently more American capital has been going abroad into manufacturing, distribution, mining, and smelting enterprises, but there has been no large flow into the diversified types of production in underdeveloped countries that would most benefit them economically and politically. Eric Johnston, Chairman of the President's International Development Advisory Board, suggested as a possible yardstick that "Great Britain, at the height of her world economic power, sent as much as 2½ percent of her national income into foreign investment. Two percent of our own national income today would exceed 5 billion dollars . . ." [14]

From the standpoint of the political problems that are the

[14] "Breaking the Barriers to Capital Investment Abroad," *Department of State Bulletin*, October 6, 1952, p. 540.

focus of this book, we must also note that the attraction to private capital has been least in some of the areas where the *political* benefits from active development would be greatest. This will no doubt continue to be true, since these are likely to be the areas of greatest risk. The risk factor imposes definite limitations on the role that private international investment can play in the earliest stages of development in the politically crucial areas. It means that the important lending activities of the International Bank for Reconstruction and Development and direct loans or grants by United States government agencies cannot be entirely replaced in the visible future by any feasible flow of private capital. This warns us to beware of the slogan: "Get public capital out of international development and leave it to private enterprise." Both public and private capital will be necessary if we are going to succeed in establishing an environment that favors the democratic path to development.

With the economic recovery of Western Europe, perhaps there may be a gradual resumption of foreign investment from that area. Some other countries, such as Canada and Japan, may also supply a certain amount of capital to underdeveloped areas. It is quite possible, of course, for a country to be a net importer of capital and yet to have some of its industrial and trading firms engaging in investment abroad. But all these sources are bound to be minor for some time, as compared with the possibilities of capital export from the United States.

How Encourage International Investment?

There is much current discussion of means by which private investment might be encouraged to flow in larger amounts to the underdeveloped areas. Therefore, this is a topic which we need not treat in detail. The obstacles that dissuade businessmen and potential investors are well known: the risk of confiscation or expropriation, currency controls which prevent return of profits or withdrawal of capital, unreasonable labor and social legislation, discriminatory enforcement of laws and tax discrimination, unstable governments, and the counterattraction of investment opportunities in the prosperous and better known American market.

The International Development Advisory Board, in a report during the chairmanship of Nelson Rockefeller, gave particular attention to the problem of private investment, holding that the flow of capital from the United States to the underdeveloped areas should be at least doubled and perhaps tripled. "Such an increase, joined with a smaller public investment through national and international agencies and the more effective mobilization of local capital, could give a revolutionary lift to the economies of the underdeveloped areas." The Board recommended a combination of measures:

1. Tax incentive. Income from business establishments located abroad should be taxed only in the country where the income is earned.

2. Bilateral tax and commercial treaties recognizing principles of fair and reasonable treatment of investors.

3. Underwriting, for a fee, the transfer risk on foreign dollar obligations through the Export-Import Bank.

4. A new affiliate of the International Bank, an "International Finance Corporation," to help private investors obtain supplementary capital in local currencies and to act as a catalytic agent in local capital formation.

5. An assistant administrator in the proposed Overseas Economic Administration charged with no duties other than to encourage the maximum and most effective use of private enterprise.[15]

National Diplomatic Protection

The hard core of those obstacles to international private investment which are summed up in the phrase, "a bad investment climate," consists in large part of mutually reinforcing fears. Underdeveloped countries fear that private capital from abroad will serve as an instrument of "penetration" and result in political or military intervention, or economic domination of the country by foreigners. In combination with emotional feelings of inferiority, and the drive for equal status, respect, and esteem in many of these countries, this fear produces behavior which discourages and alarms investors. On the other hand, businessmen who might make

15 International Development Advisory Board, *Partners in Progress*, cited, pp. 78-79.

constructive investments in such countries fear that their capital will be seized, or their enterprises discriminated against by nationalistic laws and decrees, or their earnings frozen. Unfortunately, past experience offers considerable justification for both sets of fears. Only if means can be found to remove some of the grounds for them and to build an attitude of confidence on both sides will it be possible for private international investment to make the contribution that it should to the economic progress of underdeveloped countries. This is an area in which the impasse is unlikely to be broken without new methods, social inventiveness.

A political and legal factor not usually given the attention it deserves is the inadequacy of the time-honored system called "national diplomatic protection of citizens abroad" either to protect investors or to reassure underdeveloped countries. It may be that over the long pull the radical idea of building up international protection instead of national protection for boundary-crossing investments and gradually denationalizing such investments has something to offer toward establishing the conditions in which more productive capital flows could occur.[16]

National protection of the investments of citizens abroad has worked with singular ineptness. The investor often gets either much more or much less protection than he deserves. In the first case, weaker countries become more fearful of the power of foreign-owned enterprises and add new restrictions and discriminations. In the second case, the lack of confidence on the part of investors is intensified.

The investor gets more protection than he deserves when the protecting government has a political ax to grind and wants a pretext for strong action. This was often true a half-century or even a quarter-century ago. The memory of this type of intervention and the fear of its happening again help to explain the suspicious hostility with which some weak countries continue to regard foreign capital.

More often nowadays the shoe is on the other foot. The

[16] On the failure of national diplomatic protection to provide an effective framework for modern international investment I have written at length elsewhere. See Eugene Staley, *War and the Private Investor: A Study in the Relations of International Politics and International Private Investment* (Garden City: Doubleday, 1935), especially Chapter 16.

protecting power, for political reasons, may be unable or unwilling to give the investors (their nationals) vigorous protection of their full legal rights as against arbitrary breaches of contract, confiscation, and discriminatory treatment. Strong international *mores* have been built up against intervention. The larger powers often do not want to imperil much greater national interests, such as the political friendship of a regional bloc or access to a strategic military position or supply source, by using on behalf of investors pressures which surely would be misrepresented. Iran can repudiate a contract with the Anglo-Iranian Oil Company. Bolivia can nationalize tin mines partly owned by investors in a number of foreign countries and bargain later about compensation. Guatemala can push around the United Fruit Company. The point here is not the rights or wrongs of any of these actions, but the fact that national diplomatic protection provides little real security against arbitrary treatment of investment interests. At the same time, the suspicion that diplomatic protection may be attempted combines with nationalistic passions to produce "defensive" measures against foreign capital. Often such measures are ill-advised; in some cases they practically prevent foreign capital from doing constructive work. It can be argued that private investors are more harmed than helped by the backing of their national governments in some parts of today's world.

Serious thought might well be given to ways of building up *international* supervision and protection of boundary-crossing investments. This might begin with the working out of a multilateral code of fair treatment and the establishment of a continuing commission for supervision and conciliation. Such a commission might gradually acquire some sanctions for its decisions. Other ideas suggested by this approach are an international commercial court, a United Nations consular service to gather and publish impartial commercial and investment information for the encouragement of trade and investment, and provision in certain circumstances for international incorporation so that it would be possible to "denationalize" some kinds of international capital movements while preserving their private business character. These are obviously suggestions of a more venturesome type than any under current discussion, and they cannot be looked to for immediate results. Success in working them out would itself be a sign of a considerable change in the world economic and political environment.

CONCLUSIONS

In this chapter we have sought to identify some of the factors in the world environment that will interact most potently with local conditions to determine the course of future economic development. One such factor is the system of collective security and peaceful settlement which the nations of the world have been seeking to build, mainly through the United Nations but also in other ways. Whether this system works well or badly, whether it can or cannot be relied upon to stem aggressions and compose disputes, will influence underdeveloped countries wavering between the Communist world order and the free world order, or between militaristic, authoritarian, aggressive tendencies in their own society and more liberal influences.

Another important factor in the world environment is the prestige of democracy. Underdeveloped countries will observe democracy's successes and failures in America and other countries of the West. Also, they will compare the progress of countries under Communist leadership, like China, with that of countries trying to follow a democratic path to development, like India.

Everywhere is the powerful force of nationalism, which the West introduced into the world and which now has taken hold in the underdeveloped countries with a passion that inflames all other issues. The prospects for individual freedom may be smothered by angry struggles for "collective freedom" unless the world environment gives greater satisfaction to the needs for respect and self-esteem among peoples emerging from former positions of economic, political, and social inferiority. The nature of the transitions still to be made from colonialism will have a profound effect on the political atmosphere in which even those underdeveloped countries that are no longer colonies make their choices, for colonialism has become a symbol and, in their eyes, a test of the West's sincerity in its devotion to claimed ideals of human freedom and dignity.

Finally, the world economic setting will have much to do with determining whether underdeveloped countries achieve a healthy economic growth and take a political course that favors democracy and strengthens the free world. Will the setting be one that encourages developing countries to put their trust in a steady advance of international trade and lets them harvest the benefits of wide international specialization? Or will it impel them to turn in upon themselves in pursuit of an illusory self-sufficiency, or to seek access to needed markets and supplies by conquest, or by gravitating into the Communist bloc? Will it be an environment in which the investment climate is sufficiently favorable so that private capital and the technical and managerial experience attached to it can play a constructive role and thereby hasten the economic advance of underdeveloped countries? Or will these resources continue to be only meagerly available to underdeveloped countries because of mutual lack of confidence and fear of unfavorable political and economic events? These questions are second to none in their bearing on the prospects for "successful" development as defined in Chapter 5.

Chapter 17

PROBLEMS OF EXTERNAL AID

Many of the underdeveloped countries will promote the growth of their economies in one way or another no matter whether they receive substantial outside aid in the process or not. The *character* of that development, however, is likely to be strongly influenced by the types and amounts of aid available. The outcome is much more likely to be favorable, from the standpoint of the objectives for successful development set up in Chapter 5, if there is substantial international aid than if there is not.

By substantial aid I mean not only large amounts of technical assistance but also of capital. Initially, the capacity of an underdeveloped country to use capital productively may be surprisingly small—limited by lack of organization, trained personnel, and all the social obstacles we have stressed. At this stage technical assistance is its main need from outside, with comparatively small amounts of capital, much of which may have to be in the form of grants for nonself-liquidating projects in education, health, access roads to rural areas, and the like. If these efforts succeed and development begins to roll, the capacity to organize and manage improves, more and more personnel with basic training for modern production appears, the market begins to broaden, and in consequence the capacity to use capital in productive projects may go rapidly upward. At this stage the limits on the speed of internal capital formation in a country still close to the subsistence level are likely to become a real limiting factor on the speed with which production can increase. India, for example, seems to have reached this stage.

If, at this stage, substantial capital is available from outside to supplement what can be formed internally (and to stimulate internal capital formation, for it does that too) the rate of economic growth can be considerably increased, and the strains and frustrations and political risks of the development process are likely to be considerably less.

Self-Financing—The Political Risks

It is possible for underdeveloped economies to modernize themselves with very little capital from outside. Japan's imports of capital were small, though some of it came at crucial times. The contribution of foreign direct investments to the advancement of technical know-how, also, was greater than would be indicated merely by the size of the investment. The Soviet Union industrialized its economy with practically no aid from foreign investment capital except for the foreign-owned installations confiscated after the revolution, though it imported machinery in the early days on short-term or intermediate-term credits and hired services of foreign experts.

That it is possible for development to go forward with a minimum of outside capital does not, however, lead to the conclusion that this is the most desirable way. We are interested in the *results* of economic development, including the political results, and not merely in economic development at any political and social cost, toward whatever goal.

Both Japan and Russia achieved their development in an authoritarian political and social framework. The outcome in both cases, from the standpoint of the peace of the world and democratic ideals, was highly unfavorable. Perhaps it takes authoritarian methods to carry through rapid development without external financial aid in countries that start from a low level and have no windfall income from readily exportable resources. If so, and in view of the universal pressure for rapid development, the free world has a tremendous stake in seeing to it that international capital aid as well as technical aid is available in really substantial amounts to countries that would like to follow a democratic path.

A country starting from the extreme poverty level of, say, India is bound to have a long, hard pull at best to educate and train personnel, accumulate capital, and install and operate productive facilities on a scale which will bring marked improvement in living conditions. In the absence of outside aid, the only way to accumulate capital is to increase production without taking much of the benefit in more consumption, or even while pushing consumption standards down. Where the people are already near the subsistence level this may mean extreme hardship. Somehow the people must be motivated to change their accustomed ways quickly, to work hard, and to forego present consumption so that capital investments can be made. The totalitarian methods of motivating people include a monopoly of information and propaganda and the terrors of the police state, so applied as to whip up an artificial enthusiasm for the projects of the state planners, to break opposition, and to enforce cooperation or at any rate conformity. Antiforeign propaganda and fear and hate campaigns are standard techniques. If motivations more compatible with democratic and peaceful objectives are to be used successfully, the *voluntary* enthusiasm, cooperation, and initiative of the people have to be aroused. *It seems likely that the motivations of democracy require for their sustenance more in the way of tangible benefits now, or soon, than a totalitarian regime needs to provide.*

Outside Aid May Be Decisive

Outside help through grants, loans, and investments which assist in providing technical services, equipment, and supplies can greatly lessen, though they can never remove, the strains and hardships of the crucial early years of development. Aid at key spots in the program, correctly timed and in adequate amounts, may make it possible for tangible results benefiting ordinary people to appear more quickly. The need to hold down the level of consumption in order to accumulate capital for further development would then be somewhat less urgent. People could begin to enjoy more to eat and wear, and to afford better education and health services, earlier than if the rigorous necessity of going it alone forced their government to skim off nearly all the increased output for the support of further development or even to depress an already narrow margin of subsistence. Under the psychological and economic conditions of a "go-it-alone" situation, the chances of successful development as we have defined it would appear to be slight in some of the very countries whose course will be most important in shaping the kind of world we and our children will live in.

The issue has been stated clearly and fairly with respect to India by one of that country's leading economists, V. K. R. V. Rao. In analyzing the first Five-Year Development Plan of the Indian Planning Commission he pointed to the modest aims of the plan. Under the circumstances facing India, little more could be attempted than to construct the base for subsequent development. Because the program does not hold out large hopes, there is danger that it may not supply the psychological lift so essential for the success of a great and dynamic social experiment. India, says Dr. Rao, is trying to pursue its planned development while retaining Western liberal values. The fate of this "great and perhaps unique experiment" may turn on the results accomplished during the next five years. If this first Plan succeeds, it "may well pave the way for social transformation free from class violence. If any one person can make it succeed, it is Prime Minister Nehru; and if any one thing can, under the limitations imposed by the existing political and social situation in India, concretely and effectively aid him in achieving its success, it is vision, imagination and understanding on the part of those economically developed nations of the world that are in a position to give assistance in finance, technique and equipment. If the most powerful nations of the world will only realise that economic development of the underdeveloped areas constitutes at least as effective insurance against war as armaments do, not only will world peace be much nearer attainment but also India's first Five-Year Plan will be much more certain of achievement, and possibly also of expansion and enlargement. Whether such wisdom will dawn on these nations, and in time, is a question to which no wise man would venture an answer." [1]

Trade and Aid

The "trade not aid" slogan is much less applicable to the underdeveloped countries than to Europe. Now that the

[1] V. K. R. V. Rao, "India's First Five-Year Plan—A Descriptive Analysis," *Pacific Affairs*, March, 1952, pp. 22-23.

European countries, with the aid of the Marshall Plan, have recovered their war-damaged productive capacities they are in a position to pay for their own import needs, if only they can find receptive markets in which to sell their export goods. Europe has a large installed capacity of modern factories and farms, with the skills, organization, transportation and communication equipment, educational and health services, and the other facilities needed to operate them. In the underdeveloped countries all these things have to be created. Their problem is not merely to market the output of existing productive capacity and to achieve a gradual expansion. It is rather to increase that productive capacity radically. This requires the social transformations we have discussed and also capital investments that, by comparison with the lower outputs of their economies, are huge—though not huge by our standards.

The more realistic slogan to apply to most underdeveloped countries is "trade *and* aid." Some, like Iraq, Saudi Arabia, and Venezuela, have no need for straight financial aid so long as trade conditions will permit them to market their lucrative raw materials resources at a good price. Others, like India and Pakistan, need much more substantial financial aid than they have been getting; they need grants as well as loans and direct investments if their gallant efforts, against terrific difficulties, to pursue a democratic course of development are to have a reasonably good chance for success. Most countries will fall somewhere in between, in terms of the outside capital aid needed to make successful development possible. All the underdeveloped countries need technical aid in production and in establishing the social and administrative framework for successful development. In each case, of course, the better the trading opportunities for marketing a country's export products the less its need for outside financing in order to accomplish given results in development.

Both Public and Private Capital Needed

We have already stressed the tremendous improvement which a large-scale revival of international private investment would make in the world environment for development. But no amount of private investment that is at all likely can obviate the need for governmental technical and financial aid on a considerable scale in the years just ahead, especially in the underdeveloped countries where the political stakes are greatest.

This is true for two reasons:

1. The "climate" which private capital needs in order to function effectively includes such basic utilities as education, public health, reasonably good administration, roads, irrigation, and agricultural extension services. These needs must usually be met through public administration and by public investment. If they are inadequately met, because of lack of resources or for other reasons, neither local nor foreign private enterprise will be able to take hold effectively in other segments of the economy. In such situations international public aid, technical and financial, may be the best way to remove the blocks to private investment. It may pay tremendous "dividends" by starting a process which opens the way to private initiative and becomes self-generating. This is one of the arguments, and a strong one in my judgment, for a special international fund able to make loans at low interest rates or outright grants for essential projects of economic development that cannot be financed by private investment or on regular banking principles.

2. The risk to private investors is greatest exactly in those areas where the political reasons for developmental assistance are most convincing. Governmental aid must take the initiative in these areas. To the extent that its efforts are successful, the risks which discourage investors will gradually decline and private capital can begin to carry a larger share of the load.

A flexible combination, adaptable to the circumstances of each case, is essential if outside aid is to have the best chance of producing good results. There is need for both public and private technical aid, private investment and public investment, equity investment, loans, and grants-in-aid. The extent of the need for grants will be less if development can go forward in a world trading environment where there are stable, expanding markets for the exports by which developing countries can earn the means to pay for imports of development goods and to pay returns on borrowed capital.

Voluntary Contributions—Norway and India

Norway, India, and the United Nations signed an interesting agreement in 1952 which combines bilateral with multilateral development aid and governmental with private, voluntary contributions.

Norway undertook to assist the government of India in a program of development projects, and for this purpose provided an initial 10 million kroner ($1,400,000) of government funds to a newly-established Norwegian Foundation for Assistance to Underdeveloped Countries. This Foundation would seek additional funds by direct contributions from the Norwegian public. The government of India, in accepting the offer of Norway, agreed to make available local finance in rupees for mutually agreed projects. The United Nations undertook to provide, at the request of the two governments, assistance in planning and carrying out the projects. It was anticipated that Norway would send doctors, engineers, fishery experts, and other technical personnel to India. Indians would also be invited to Norway for technical training.

There is much in this novel pattern which might usefully be considered, and in some respects imitated, in other countries, including the United States. American philanthropic foundations have performed great services over the years in their sphere of international development aid. Their activities and experience were some of the main roots of the whole Point Four program, and their pioneering activities are continuing today—for example, in the Ford Foundation's assistance to the government of India for building up its rural community development work. Churches and educational institutions, labor organizations, farm organizations, business firms, and many other private groups have made voluntary contributions in one way or another that add to the flow of international development aid. Until now, however, there has never been any general public appeal of the type to be carried on by Norway's Foundation for Assistance to Underdeveloped Countries, nor any large-scale effort to coordinate and increase the many voluntary efforts already being made in this field.

The public and the many private organizations that would be interested might be expected to respond favorably to a well-planned campaign for expanding the direct people-to-people contribution in development aid. This would necessarily involve an educational effort to acquaint many more Americans with the needs and problems of economic development. Besides adding to the resources available for aid, such a campaign through voluntary organizations might result in a better informed public and hence in wiser formulation of governmental and business policies on development abroad.

GOVERNMENTAL AID—BILATERAL AND MULTILATERAL

International public aid to the development programs of underdeveloped countries is being carried on today (1) bilaterally, as in the Point Four program and the Export-Import Bank loans of the United States, where our government deals directly with the government of an underdeveloped country; (2) multilaterally, by the Technical Assistance Administration of the United Nations and by specialized agencies affiliated with the United Nations (the International Bank for Reconstruction and Development, the International Labor Organization, the Food and Agriculture Organization, the United Nations Educational, Scientific and Cultural Organization, the World Health Organization, and the International Civil Aviation Organization); and (3) by methods which are partly bilateral and partly multilateral, as in the Colombo Plan for Southeast Asia which functions as a clearing house to facilitate direct arrangements between the donor governments and the recipient governments in the Plan.

Advantages of Multilateral Aid

From the standpoint of the political implications of development, there are very significant advantages in *multilateral* aid:

1. Political suspicions about the purpose of aid programs are less intense when the aid comes through the United Nations or other multilateral agency than when it comes from a single great power; this helps in getting the job done.

Many underdeveloped countries have only recently achieved independence; all are aware of present weakness. All are extremely sensitive about anything that might appear to be, even when it is not in fact, foreign political or economic "domination" or interference in their internal affairs. There have been cases in which governments of underdeveloped countries have refused technical and economic aid, though needing it badly, because they feared it might bind them to a foreign power. United Nations missions are less vulnerable to popular denunciation as agents of foreign "imperialists" and "monopolists," and to charges that they are the thin end of the wedge, and that the country is being taken over. For this reason, they are in a better position to help member governments carry out needed reforms and to give advice in such sensitive fields as public administration. The International Bank can impose conditions on loans which, if made by a single power, might arouse political furor.

2. The fact that the underdeveloped countries themselves are members of the United Nations and of the specialized agencies maintains self-respect and gives that "sense of participation" which helps to develop responsibility. When aid comes directly from the United States, or some other single power, it is bound to carry more of an odor of paternalism and perhaps encouragement of the handout or Santa Claus psychology. Experience with the Organization for European Economic Cooperation in the European Recovery Program suggests that when many claimant countries are represented in a joint organization they will to some extent act as a check on each other's extravagant claims. It is also arguable, without much experience as yet to test the conclusion, that governments are likely to be somewhat less hasty about unilateral denunciation or violation of contract agreements with multinational agencies than with single governments. The single creditor government may have political reasons for not insisting too vigorously on the fulfillment of pledges, and it can more readily be portrayed as a rich exploiter than can a group of nations which include other underdeveloped countries.[2]

[2] See the discussion of multilateral vs. bilateral aid by Jacob Viner in Bert F. Hoselitz, cited, pp. 200-202.

3. Multinational agencies can draw on a greater variety of experience and technical personnel than can any single country. Norway and Japan are good sources for advice on fisheries. Denmark has much to contribute on rural education and agricultural cooperatives. India, though receiving aid itself, can supply able experts on malaria. Under the United Nations program, experts have been recruited from more than sixty countries. The conditions in underdeveloped areas are so diverse, and usually so different from American conditions, that American methods in industry, agriculture, and in the organization of social, economic, and political affairs may not be the most suitable for imitation. A country receiving aid through the United Nations and its specialized agencies may pick and choose and thus avoid the danger of adopting institutions, organizations, and techniques unsuited to its circumstances.

4. For all the foregoing reasons, a United Nations agency can usually get more development results for a dollar's expenditure, in most underdeveloped areas, than can the United States operating singly. This is the conviction of many persons who have been in close touch with development work under both types of programs. It assumes, of course, that the advantages of the United Nations approach will not be dissipated by the cumbersomeness of multinational organization or by lax standards of administrative efficiency and competence. National programs are also subject to the dangers of waste and inefficiency, but there are some additional difficulties in international undertakings, and the very soundness of the multinational principle makes it all the more imperative to set high standards of efficiency in execution.

5. The multinational approach enlists more countries in the role of donor. While other countries in the near future will not be in a position to contribute on anything like the scale of the United States, every little bit helps, and over the long pull multinational aid should enable more adequate programs to be financed by a wider sharing of the burden. Even now in the field of technical assistance some countries that are recipients of aid are able to help others in special fields, and this kind of interchange should grow.

6. Technical and economic assistance through United Nations agencies is one of the best means of building up the prestige of the United Nations and the loyalty of the peoples of the world to it, thus strengthening the institution on which our best hope for future peace and security depends.

Bilateral Aid Also Essential at Present

On the other hand there are some advantages in *bilateral* programs of development aid, and a number of circumstances which make it necessary for the United States, in particular, to continue to administer its own program in addition to contributing to United Nations programs. The main reasons are:

1. It is undesirable for any one country to contribute too large a share toward a United Nations program. The United States share of the subscribed capital of the International Bank is 35 percent. The United States has contributed about 60 percent of the funds used in the first few years of the "expanded program" of United Nations technical assistance. The 12 million dollars provided by the United States in 1952 for this program and the somewhat smaller amount contributed in 1953 are but small fractions of the amounts the United States has been spending directly in its bilateral Point Four program. If the whole American program were to be channeled through the United Nations, the cry of American domination of the organization would be loud, and many of the peculiar advantages of the United Nations aid might be sacrificed. On the other hand, to cut down the total of American aid in the development of underdeveloped countries while waiting for others to be able to match our contributions would, at this juncture in world history and in view of the tremendous issues involved, be most unfortunate. It would harm the American national interest, the interests of the peoples of the underdeveloped countries and of the world community. The conclusion seems inescapable that until other countries are able to increase their financial contributions to United Nations development programs, or until the United Nations develops some independent revenue of its own, the United States must continue

to supplement aid through United Nations channels by considerable amounts of its own direct aid to underdeveloped countries.

2. This is a time of political tension when the peace and freedom of all peoples are threatened by the powerful, expansion-minded Communist bloc. Strategic and military factors vital to the defense of the free world must therefore influence the allocation of part of the international development aid provided by the United States and other countries. Since the United Nations includes countries that are a likely source of aggression against the free world, and also countries of a "neutralist" persuasion, aspects of development aid most directly related to defense must be handled through other channels.

3. The total of international development aid is likely to be greater with bilateral arrangements than without them. Historic associations and the influence of special ties of friendship or interest will often stimulate one country to aid a particular country more generously than it will aid the average participant in a general fund.

The Bolivian Experiment

Some of the advantages of multilateral aid for underdeveloped countries, especially where the real need is internal reform, are highlighted by a unique experiment undertaken in Bolivia. Previous chapters have repeatedly brought out a fact well known to those experienced in the problems of underdeveloped countries: The main obstacle to economic progress in many cases is not lack of knowledge, or of technical know-how in the narrow sense, or lack of capital, but rather the unwillingness or incompetence of governments to do what is needed. In Bolivia, a plan for United Nations assistance has been undertaken which for the first time faces up to this fact. Whether this experiment succeeds or not is less important than the pathbreaking nature of the venture. It may lead to some acceptable alternative between a colonial type of alien rule on the one hand and the stagnant futility of some independent countries on the other, where standards of education, of politics, and of administration are still too low for the effective management of constructive development plans.[3]

In 1950 a United Nations mission to Bolivia headed by Dr. Hugh L. Keenleyside, a Canadian who has subsequently become Director-General of the Technical Assistance Administration of the United Nations, surveyed Bolivia's economy and found a paradox. ". . . Bolivia has within its boundaries all the resources necessary to provide a sound economic foundation for a national life distinguished by a wide diffusion of culture, by progress and prosperity. But these results have not been achieved." [4] Also, it found that studies and recommendations on Bolivia's needs going back forty years were piled in government archives. All recommended more or less the same things, and little or nothing had ever been done about any of them. This is a fairly common experience of advisory missions in underdeveloped countries.

The explanation, the mission decided, lay in the governmental and administrative instability that has consistently marked the history of Bolivia. There had been eight revolutions in the last ten years. The mission took the view that there would be no hope of success for a program of economic development until some remedy or partial remedy had been found for constantly fluctuating official policy and erratic administration.

All this was fully discussed with Bolivians, including responsible government officials. It is significant that this mission brought the Bolivian officials into its own conferences from the start, instead of holding private discussions and coming out with a completed report in the manner of most such missions.

With the concurrence of the Bolivian government, a proposal was evolved by which the United Nations would assist Bolivia to obtain the services of a number of experienced and competent Administrative Assistants of unquestioned integrity drawn from a variety of countries. The Bolivian government would appoint these men on a temporary basis

[3] See the illuminating dispatch by Michael L. Hoffman from Geneva, *New York Times,* October 20, 1950.
[4] *Report of the United Nations Mission of Technical Assistance to Bolivia,* cited, pp. 2-4, 9-10.

to positions of influence and authority as integral members
of the Bolivian civil service, with rank corresponding to that
of an Assistant Secretary in the United States. Salaries and
allowances would be paid by the Bolivian government, with
the United Nations providing financial assistance for this
purpose. The outside experts would perform regular duties
in the Bolivian civil service and would also direct and assist
in the training of Bolivian personnel so as to develop a Bolivian civil service of experience, competence, and integrity
as rapidly as possible.

"This proposal," said the mission's report, "constitutes
a new development in the methods by which the United
Nations endeavours to extend friendly, and unselfish but
mutually beneficial assistance to one of its members. Because
the aid is offered by the United Nations as a whole, and because the personnel involved—as in the case of the present
Mission itself—will be drawn from a variety of national
sources, there can be no question of any single external
authority gaining undue influence in Bolivia." [5]

An agreement was drawn up and approved in which the
Bolivian government indicated its acceptance of the main
recommendations of the mission's report. The United Nations, in addition to providing the salary supplement which
was needed in order to recruit the high type of man required, also made available an annual sum for office equipment and other necessities unobtainable in Bolivia. The
United Nations also agreed to provide forty fellowships to
Bolivians for use outside of Bolivia and to make available
technical assistance in various fields. Some of the specialized
agencies also undertook to provide technical assistance.

Shortly after the plan went into effect a new revolution
(1952) brought a regime to power which was committed
to social and political policies profoundly different from
those of the former government. (It was this regime that
nationalized the tin mines.) When in opposition, it had been
critical of the arrangement with the United Nations; on coming to power it declared that the agreement must be modified, but indicated that it wanted United Nations technical
assistance to continue. After a year of "on the job" adjust-

[5] Same, pp. 2-4.

ments, understandings which had come about in side-by-side work of U.N. experts and Bolivian officials were crystallized in a revised agreement of May 2, 1953. This made unmistakably clear in words what had always been clear in fact, that the program would be carried on "always in accordance with the principles of sovereignty" of Bolivia. Some of the experts, called technical consultants, would continue to form part of the Bolivian civil service. They were at work in the Ministry of Finance, the Central Bank, the Controller General's office, and in agriculture, labor, and social security. Important new duties were also assigned to members of the U.N. mission, such as aiding in the work of a National Planning Commission which the government had decided to create. Additional technical experts were requested in mining, development of a sugar industry, agricultural climatology, and public administration. All told, the program at the middle of 1953 called for 7 technical consultants and 17 experts, and recruitment was in progress to fill 10 places. The U.N. team already in the country came from 11 different countries.[6]

In view of national sensitiveness and fear of foreign domination, it is unlikely that cooperation of this sort could have been accepted by Bolivia from a single foreign government; it is rather remarkable that such an arrangement was entered into even with the United Nations. There were some charges at first of "Yankee imperialism," but these faded in face of the multinational background of the men sent by the U.N. Of the six technical consultants on the job early in 1953, one was Italian, one French, one Swiss, one Belgian, one British, and one stateless (Hungarian origin, awaiting U. S. citizenship). There was an understanding that consultants were not to come from countries contiguous to Bolivia and that the number from any of the major powers would be kept to a minimum.

It is important to recognize the limitations as well as the possibilities of this social invention pioneered by the United Nations and Bolivia. Aid in administration cannot elim-

---

[6] Carter Goodrich (U.N. Technical Assistance Board Representative in Bolivia), "U.N. Aid in Bolivia Weathers Changes," *United Nations Reporter*, American Association for the United Nations, June 10, 1953.

inate obstacles to economic development which come from public disorders and uprisings, nor can it provide leadership at the *political* level. The United Nations has not undertaken to police Bolivia, nor can it do much directly to modify the attitudes and cleavages in Bolivian society which have kept people from working together and have inhibited development. Possibly, given a chance to work over a period of time, United Nations aid in public administration might have a considerable effect in facilitating such deeper changes. But, as we have emphasized before, the cultural heritage which people bring to the tasks of modernization is at least as important as the outside influences that impinge on them in shaping the course of their development, and what people are able and willing to do for themselves will always be the biggest factor in their progress, regardless of external aid.

EXTERNAL AID AND REFORM

Drastic changes in economic, political, and social institutions are necessary in any underdeveloped country if economic development is to "take" and become self-sustaining. Furthermore, since our tests of success are broader than mere increase in economic efficiency, successful development requires changes that lay the groundwork for democratic participation. All this has been emphasized in previous chapters.

Let us use the term "reform" as a shorthand expression for all the changes in organization and conduct of government, business, and social affairs which are necessary in a "successful" process of modernization. Reform therefore means, in the discussion that follows, the building of new institutions for public health and education, more efficient public administration, political leadership more responsive to the needs of all the people, changes in land tenure systems, rural credit arrangements, and other agrarian relationships required for improvement in the output and well-being of farmers and for solid growth of democracy, modernized business methods and better management, new customs and institutions to encourage capital formation, free and responsible trade unions, and, where population growth threatens to defeat development, changes in traditional ideas on the size of the family.

A Dilemma

All such reforms are bound to be resisted by some groups in the population, sometimes by very powerful groups. Reform is always more or less controversial. This is true even for changes that, from our point of view as outsiders, might seem to require no argument, such as the widest possible spread of education.[7] Tradition, habit, religious beliefs, ignorance, and misunderstanding of the true nature of a proposed change all support established ways. The result may be opposition to reforms even among those who stand to benefit most from them. This is in addition to opposition from some groups that fear to lose positions or privileges.

All this poses a dilemma for any outside nation that, like the United States, has a political, economic, and humanitarian interest in promoting the sort of development of underdeveloped areas which will be successful in the broadest sense. If we concentrate on a narrow range of direct production problems to help these countries raise their economic efficiency, without doing anything to stimulate "reform," our efforts may be wasted, or worse. On the other hand, if the United States does show an interest in internal reforms it runs against the principle of noninterference in the domestic affairs of sovereign nations. Furthermore, on practical grounds we have to be careful lest espousal by a foreign government of internal reforms should boomerang by antagonizing not only the conservatives but also supersensitive nationalists. Our support might in some circumstances defeat the very reforms we should like to aid. There is much to be said for the principle that it is better for people to

---

[7] A colleague who participated in the 1930's in a rural education experiment in one of the problem areas of the southern United States told me this story:

On an inspection tour he asked a county administrator whether he was having any trouble with the program.

"Well," was the reply, "only with some of the controversial subjects, like arithmetic."

"Arithmetic! Is arithmetic controversial?"

"It sure is. When some of these sharecroppers learn how to add up their own accounts there's going to be the Devil to pay."

manage their own affairs, even when they manage them badly.

The dilemma may be put another way. If we assist "reactionary" governments to suppress popular discontent, while privileged social groups prevent changes in land customs, business methods, educational systems, and the rest, a political explosion may result which will give the Communists just the kind of opportunity they are most adept at exploiting. If, on the other hand, we declare ourselves in favor of "revolution" against outmoded regimes and actively encourage dissident elements, the old ruling group may be repudiated before any democratically-minded group is strong enough to take over. The power vacuum thus created would provide opportunities for a well-organized Communist minority to seize power.

These are some of the headaches that come with world power and world responsibility. Robert C. North has put the matter very well:

If the West gives aid, it will be feared for its imperialism; if it withholds aid, it will be denounced for its indifference. If it establishes garrisons, it will be attacked as expansionist; if it keeps its troops at home, it will be written off as impotent and unable to keep its commitments. If it expresses no political preferences (or relies solely on military might), it will be accused of siding with reaction and the status quo; if it supports progressive forces, it will be condemned for intervention.

In other words, we are damned if we do and damned if we don't.[8]

Aid through Nongovernmental Channels

The dilemma we have described provides one good reason for our government to encourage maximum activity by private, voluntary associations and businesses along lines that serve our Point Four aims.

Demonstrations of new social ideas can be carried out by American private groups and foundations in ways that avoid much of the stigma that attaches to intervention by a foreign government. The Near East Foundation, for example, has

[8] Robert C. North, "Asian Violence in a Cold-War World," *Pacific Spectator*, Winter, 1951, p. 12.

done excellent work in rural improvement, development of cooperative organizations and the like, without any question of imposing unwanted ways on local people. In the same part of the world American privately supported educational establishments, such as Robert College in Istanbul, the American University at Beirut, and the American University in Cairo, have had a quiet but profound influence. Their graduates have done much to raise standards of public administration, for instance.

American business firms in underdeveloped countries demonstrate modern methods of business organization and practice. Sears Roebuck has worked a revolution in the retail trade of some Latin American countries by popularizing the system of single, clearly marked prices, and by the concept of volume distribution with low markups and rapid turnover. Our better managed firms can foster, by example and by training of local personnel, that sense of civic obligation and community responsibility which is now widely accepted in American business circles but which is often conspicuously lacking in underdeveloped countries. American trade unions are now making a very important contribution, in cooperation with some of the European unions, toward training competent labor leadership for free trade unions in underdeveloped countries. This is a field of crucial importance which has too often been pre-empted by the Communists.

Exchange of students and teachers is a long-standing device for encouraging the two-way flow of ideas between countries. We need a flow to us as well as from us if America's influence is to be wise and helpful in the sensitive fields of institutions and values which we are now discussing.

The impact of American news, movies, books and magazines and foreign travel by Americans and by citizens of underdeveloped countries are powerful factors making for social change in these countries. From the standpoint of encouraging the "successful" development which is the American interest, the influences are sometimes fortunate, sometimes unfortunate. In a democracy we neither can nor should undertake to regiment these multifarious, private, and haphazard contacts so as to support some central foreign-policy purpose. Democracy must rely on the intelligence, good will, and sense of responsibility of private individuals and organizations. In the field we are discussing, the better our purveyors of news and entertainment as well as our business people, educators, and representatives of all sorts of voluntary groups understand the need for development abroad and the true nature of the American interest in it, the more effectively will that interest be advanced.

Ours is a plural society, not totalitarian or government-centered. American private groups and individuals, working with private groups and individuals in underdeveloped countries who want to make the kind of progress that we want to encourage, represent the true genius of democracy.

Multinational Channels

The dilemma posed by the universal need for reforms to prepare the way for successful development, and the equally universal objection to foreigners mixing in domestic affairs, is somewhat less acute when underdeveloped countries are aided through multinational organizations of which they are themselves members. This is part of the strong case for channeling as large a proportion of development aid as feasible through the United Nations, the International Bank, and the other specialized agencies of the United Nations.

It would have been most impolitic for the United States government to point out to the Bolivian government that the major obstacle to economic development in Bolivia was the administrative incapacity of the government and to offer a team of administrators to assist at the deputy minister level. Yet, as we have seen, a United Nations mission headed by a Canadian was able to do exactly this, and personnel coming from a variety of different countries can assist Bolivia without arousing suspicion of ulterior motives. The need for tax reform and for changes in the laws under which foreign firms do business stands in the way of constructive investment in some underdeveloped countries and thus helps to block development. If an agency of the United States government urges such reforms, it will be regarded as a screen covering the self-serving interests of American firms, or even preparing the way for American "domination." But the International Bank can make similar recommendations to a member country with more chance that its advice will be considered on its merits.

In the fields of education, reform of land tenure systems, population policy, labor and social legislation, and many others, multinational organizations in which the underdeveloped countries themselves participate can ordinarily exert more influence of the wise and tactful sort that counts for most than can an agency of the United States. In the words of the report on United States foreign economic policy made under the chairmanship of Gordon Gray:

. . . It is frequently not possible for any one country unilaterally to give effective guidance on internal operations without creating fears or suspicions of interventionist motives, which would defeat major purposes of the program. Such programs, therefore, will frequently be most effective if operated through international organizations, staffed in part by nationals of countries in which the particular underdeveloped country has confidence.[9]

Reinforcing Desirable Trends

U. S. aid programs in underdeveloped countries are unlikely to produce the kind of results we want, and may even produce bad results in the sense defined earlier, if "reforms" are not simultaneously carried through in the countries concerned. At the same time, American officials have to move slowly in deciding to try to encourage particular reforms, for reasons already explained.

In general, it is probably wise to limit any direct American suggestions on matters of internal reform to proposals for which there is already substantial support by competent and responsible persons in the country itself, and even then to play down American initiative in getting such questions considered. There may, however, be occasions where public knowledge of American support for particular changes will help rather than hinder our broad purposes. For instance, the clear position that the United States government has taken in encouraging agrarian reform measures in the last few years, though it may have irked conservative landowning

[9] *Report to the President on Foreign Economic Policies* (Washington: U. S. Government Printing Office, November, 1950), p. 98.

groups and governments dominated by them in some countries, on the whole has strengthened our political position in the underdeveloped world—especially with groups that are on the way up in power and influence, if not yet in control of government. Even on an issue which commands this high degree of popular support, however, it is one thing for the United States to make its views generally known and to offer to aid in suitable rural development programs and quite another, much more risky, to seem to press our views on a foreign government in regard to a particular reform.

The American government can do many things to encourage the sprouting of reform impulses in underdeveloped countries, and when those impulses lead to request for help in launching a good program it can quickly reinforce a desirable trend. Indirect means of sowing the seeds of reform include stimulation of the nongovernmental activities mentioned above. Conferences, like the World Land Tenure Conference at Madison, Wisconsin in 1951, are another. That conference, organized by the University of Wisconsin with the support of the United States Mutual Security Agency and the Technical Cooperation Administration of the Department of State, brought together 71 persons from 38 nations outside the United States; its discussions of problems and ways of meeting them undoubtedly planted new thoughts on rural reform. "Whispering in the ear" of the governments of underdeveloped countries, without official or public action, is another technique well known to diplomacy.

When a government asks for help in constructive reform measures, either spontaneously or because seeds broadcast or deliberately planted have begun to sprout, then our government has an opportunity to reinforce a favorable trend. This is the most important type of opportunity open to us. Aid at this stage not only helps the particular country to move forward when conditions are right but also encourages reform elements in other countries to gain influence with their governments.

If we do not give vigorous support to governments that are trying to move in progressive, democratic directions when they need it and want it, we are likely to be forced into the position later of having to back a government that is bad by our standards for the sole reason that it is the only available alternative to a Communist regime. Once things come to that pass, under present world conditions we have to choose the non-Communist alternative because (1) each addition to Communist strategic resources and strategic position adds to the peril of the whole free world, and (2) it is practically impossible for a people to shake off a Communist regime, but there is a chance of improving a bad non-Communist government. For the United States, however, this is a terrible dilemma. When in order to prevent a Communist seizure we have to back a corrupt or unpopular or foreign-dominated government, we do immense political harm to our world position. The best way to prevent such situations is to "accentuate the positive" by giving all possible aid to hard-pressed non-Communist governments that are prepared to carry out democratic reform measures.

How long will it take us to learn that when a progressive reform government happens to be in power in an under-developed country we should go all out in aiding it to grapple with its economic and political problems? The American Congress, not merely the Executive, must learn this lesson, for the tendency is to demand the showing of an emergency to justify appropriations for foreign aid. By the time the emergency is visible we are likely to be faced with the unpleasant choice mentioned above. In that case, also, the appropriations are likely to go mainly for military rather than economic aid. In the end, we find ourselves spending for emergency military measures, with bad political repercussions, much more than might have been required to get better results by forehanded economic aid.

The Case of Iran

Iran had a reform government from June, 1950, when Ali Razmara became Premier, until his assassination in March, 1951. The United States had been saying that there would be no aid until there was a reform government. But when such a government appeared we failed to give it immediate and substantial aid. At the same time the British were inflexible about concessions in the pending revisions of the Anglo-Iranian oil agreement. Both the United States and

Britain allowed an opportunity to slip by. Subsequent events brought a fanatical antagonism against the West, acute danger of a Communist coup, and a loss in the oil national-ization controversy immeasurably greater both in money and prestige than the concessions and the economic aid that might possibly have set Iran on a different course.

Possibly it was already too late in 1950 for the United States and Britain to have done anything that would have altered this chain of events. Perhaps things had gone too far already by the time of Razmara. Also, the Iranian gov-ernment as well as the United States government was re-sponsible for some of the difficulties that kept them from getting together on an adequate aid program. These situa-tions are never black and white. The point is that the United States and Britain did not give serious enough attention and try hard enough to deal positively with these great issues in a highly strategic part of the world. The bad results could have been foreseen, and the proof is that they were foreseen.

On September 5, 1950, the *New York Times* published the following dispatch from its Teheran correspondent, Al-bion Ross:

Washington had made it plain during the ambassadorship of John C. Wiley that United States aid would not be forthcoming here until there was a reform Government in Iran. There is now a reformist Cabinet in Teheran. Responsible Iranians had made it equally clear that once there was a reform government an economic shot in the arm would be needed. American advisers here and Ambassador Wiley agreed and advised Washington that a program of swift economic aid, estimated at $100,000,000 to $200,000,000, would be needed to get Iran's seven-year plan and the nation's economy generally off dead center . . .

A reform Cabinet, headed by Gen. Ali Razmara, was formed almost simultaneously with Dr. Grady's appointment. Virtually everyone in Teheran who could read a newspaper knew that the Americans were prepared to regard the Razmara Government as a reform regime.

But there is no economic aid. The Export-Import Bank in Washington is now discussing a loan of $20,000,000 to $30,000,-000 to be extended in limited grants over a period of four to five years.

. . . there is evidence, documented by certain American experts, that Iran should be able to finance her own economic rehabilitation. It is necessary, however, to be in Teheran to understand why the American diplomatic representatives insisted that refusal of a substantial program of immediate economic aid would be politically catastrophic.

A visitor to Teheran hears everywhere he goes that the absence of United States economic aid is seriously weakening the reform movement and the Cabinet's capacity to drive through a reform program . . .

The prevailing opinion here is that Washington's failure to deliver economic aid will benefit Russia primarily. More important, it will weaken the Cabinet and benefit the strongly entrenched opponents of reform.

Henry F. Grady, former American Ambassador to Iran, has testified to the same effect. In 1952 he said:

The joint failure of the British and ourselves to do what was properly expected of us has played directly into the hands of Soviet propaganda and Tudeh (Communist) activity. Both are well organized and extremely effective. The formula we have successfully used elsewhere to meet the Communist threat has not been used in Iran though the mission I headed in June 1950 went there for precisely that purpose.

The net amount of our economic aid during the last year and a half has been less than two million dollars whereas during my two years in Greece we gave aid to the extent of over a million dollars a day . . .[10]

[10] Henry F. Grady, "Tensions in the Middle East with Particular Reference to Iran," *Proceedings of the Academy of Political Science*, January, 1952, pp. 116-118. Ambassador Grady also criticized the British for their unwillingness to be more flexible about the Anglo-Iranian oil agreement; a few additional nonmonetary concessions might have strengthened Razmara's hand considerably.

The drift of events in Iran was summed up as follows by Richard P. Stebbins in *The United States in World Affairs, 1950* (New York: Council on Foreign Relations, 1951), pp. 313-314:

A $25 million developmental credit for Iran was announced by the Export-Import Bank on October 10, and $500,000 in technical assistance funds was set aside to support the work of an Iranian-United States Joint Commission for Rural Improvement. But release of the credit was delayed by technical obstacles, and the technical cooperation project would make slow headway at best against the massive poverty of Iranian village life. Meanwhile the hopes initially aroused by Iran's own seven-year development plan were being dissipated, as funds and personnel were drained off for current operations and quarreling broke out between Iranian bureaucrats

The return to power of the reform-minded Shah, on August 22, 1953, suggests that the West may get a new chance in Iran—perhaps one more than it deserves. If so, it will be interesting to see whether experience has yet taught us that in the struggle over the path to be taken by underdeveloped countries "a stitch in time saves nine."

Opportunities in India, Egypt, and Elsewhere

India offers the greatest current test of our perspicacity in these matters. Prime Minister Nehru and his government are laboring mightily to set India's vast inertia moving along the path of democratic progress, and by democratic methods. They are applying a program of land reform; they have made the franchise effective nation-wide; they are finding methods to carry improved agricultural practices, health, education, and community self-help programs to the villages; they are facing up to the problem of population policy; and they are endeavoring with limited resources to advance the transportation, communication, and industry of the country. Now is the time when substantial external aid might make all the difference between success and failure in what is bound to be a nip-and-tuck race between progress achieved by moderate, democratic methods and the hopelessness and discontent which could throw this key country into the hands of its eager Communist movement.

In Egypt the regime established by General Naguib may prove to be a reform government in the sense in which we have been using that term. While it is in form a military dictatorship, it appears to have launched a major effort to deal with land reform, political corruption, and other problems which have blocked Egypt's development under the old system, and to do it in ways which promise to broaden the bases of political power and eventually prepare for more democratic participation. Perhaps the pattern in Turkey, where a military dictatorship broke

and American engineers retained to direct the project. New tensions were building up over the status of the Anglo-Iranian Oil Company, and the precarious tenure of Premier Ali Razmara symbolized the uphill character of the Shah's fight for reform against the regime of privilege and vested interest with which his parliament was identified.

the country out of old ruts and put it on the road to modern democracy, may be repeated. Technical and economic assistance from outside may well determine whether this course can be followed or not, for Egypt faces tremendous difficulties, especially in view of its overpopulation.

These and other situations like them show that America does have opportunities to use its influence toward shaping the kind of world we would like to live in, without pushing people around as the Communists do, and without unwelcome interference in the internal affairs of other nations. The results, of course, can never be guaranteed. The flow of history is too complex for that. Some countries, no matter what we do, will evolve in ways that scandalize us. Also, there are bound to be cases where the people of a country do not appear to want the economic advancement, freedom, and human dignity which we think they ought to want, at least not enough to work hard and to change old ways. Or they may continue to tolerate a government or a social system that blocks the path of progress. There is not much we can or should do in such cases except wait, remembering that the ferment of ideas dissolves the most solid-appearing pillars of the old order rather quickly these days.

The main point we have been making above is that many countries in the world today are trying desperately to move in the direction of economic, political, and social advancement in which it is strongly in our interest that they should move. We have opportunities to reinforce their efforts, and we have the economic and other means with which to do it. If we fail to seize such opportunities when they arise because we are not alert to them, then America will be lacking in astute political leadership. If we pass up the opportunities for reasons of "economy," it will be one of the falsest economies ever perpetrated.

Chapter 18

GUIDELINES FOR UNITED STATES POLICY

In a democracy like ours, the policy-makers are not only the elected and appointed officials but likewise the citizens. Their understanding or misunderstanding of problems sets limits within which officials can act. Also, American policy is made not only by our government but also by all who make international decisions in business, industry, news organizations, and so on, and by the great variety of private groups and individuals whose activities form part of the impact of the United States of America on world affairs.

How can American government, business, and private associations and individuals improve the prospects that economic development in the underdeveloped areas will be successful, in the broad sense in which we defined a successful outcome in Chapter 5? It is not the purpose of this study to lay down an action program. Yet our analysis has been policy-oriented, and it may be useful in this final chapter to bring it specifically to bear on some questions connected with the American foreign aid program. Having done so, we shall then turn to still broader problems of American thought and action with respect to underdeveloped areas and endeavor, in the last part of the chapter, to pull the many threads of our analysis together by stating the guidelines for American policy which they suggest.

AMERICAN AID

First of all, can we make our influence really count? The International Development Advisory Board faced the economics of this question in a report to the President in 1951.

The task of helping a billion people to better their lot may seem a hopeless one, it said, but in terms of the relative size of their economies and ours the picture is different. "According to United Nations estimates, the total annual income for the billion inhabitants of these areas [*i.e.,* underdeveloped areas not under Communist control] would run about 80 billion dollars. The current United States national income alone is well over 250 billion dollars annually, while that of the countries of Western Europe totals between 140 and 150 billion dollars. . . . Taken alone, the economy of the United States has more than three times the productive output of all the economies of the underdeveloped areas together. Combined, the economies of Western Europe and the United States have five times the economic weight of the underdeveloped regions. It is in those terms that the job to be done should be measured, not in population numbers but in economic output." [1]

Types and Amounts of Aid

It was concluded in the preceding chapter that American interests can best be served by a combination of many types of aid, including both technical and financial help, provided by government, business, and private associations of all kinds. Some of the financial help will have to be on a grant basis, but much can be done by repayable loans and direct investments if measures to improve the "climate" for a flow of private capital can be made effective. It is in the interest of the United States to channel an increasing proportion of governmental aid through multinational organizations, though at present a large program administered directly through our national agencies is also necessary. It was also concluded in the preceding chapter that internal "reform" is essential to the success of any aid program in underdeveloped countries. Nongovernmental groups can, without incurring the stigma of foreign intervention, do more to stimulate the will to undertake necessary changes than can our government directly, and so can multinational organizations. The American government, however, can encourage

[1] International Development Advisory Board, *Partners in Progress,* cited, p. 12.

the sprouting of reform impulses by indirect means and, most important of all, can use its foreign aid program to quickly and strongly reinforce such impulses when governments of underdeveloped countries experience them and want external aid in applying them.

At best, it will be a long, slow job to get solid results from our technical and economic aid. Because the job is so important and so full of difficulties and uncertainties, it is essential to insist on high standards of administration. Praiseworthy aims are not a substitute for effective execution.

"How much is it going to cost?" "How much ought we to be willing to spend from public funds on development aid?" Answers to these questions should tell the American people some plain truths: The development problem that faces the free world is a big one; our stake as a nation in successful development of underdeveloped countries is enormous; our economy is the only one capable of supplying outside capital for development in amounts large enough to have a substantial impact; yet up to the present our governmental aid to underdeveloped countries and our private investments in underdeveloped countries have hardly begun to meet the urgent needs for development—the great bulk of our foreign aid program having gone either to Europe or for military aid. It would be pleasant to believe that technical assistance alone can do the job, or that private investment will supply all the developmental capital that is justified in the national interest, or that we can accomplish our essential aims without costing the taxpayers anything in grants-in-aid. But such beliefs would not be sound in terms of the vital interests of the American people and what it takes to safeguard them.

No global computation will be attempted here of the amount of external aid which the underdeveloped countries need, in addition to locally available capital, to produce some desired rate of progress. The amount of direct or indirect financial aid which it will be wise, in the American interest, to make available to a given country for development purposes will have to be determined in the light of specific situations and specific projects. Where American public funds are sought, the purposes and amounts should be carefully tested, project by project, in terms of the contributions that would be made by the projects toward the broad objectives which we seek. In some countries there will be little or no need for outside financing (for example, in those having large oil revenues), but technical and organizational help may be very much needed. In other countries the whole developmental effort may collapse, or not even get started, unless there is a period of considerable financial help.

In general, there are three reasons for thinking that a realistic evaluation of American interests will require both an increased flow of private capital and larger governmental outlays for loans and grants to underdeveloped countries in the years immediately ahead.

1. In the very first stages of a development program the capacity to use capital effectively is quite small. Surveys have to be made, specific projects have to be laid out, and key administrative and technical personnel have to be assembled or trained. But soon more and more countries will be reaching the position where the bottleneck to development is not lack of sound projects and personnel capable of undertaking them but lack of capital.

2. As rearmament expenditures level off in the United States, assuming that no new military crisis develops, it will be sound policy to use more funds to promote the nonmilitary aspects of our world interests. At the same time, a higher rate of capital export to underdeveloped areas will be desirable from the standpoint of economic stability, in the United States and abroad, in case there should be a tendency toward a post-rearmament slump.

3. If Communist tactics turn to an era of less open hostility toward the non-Communist world, as may happen, the importance of rapid economic and social advance in the underdeveloped countries outside the Iron Curtain will be even greater. For it would be fatal to assume that Communist leaders have lost their long-range hope for world revolution. A peaceful interval would very likely give local Communist parties a still better chance to come to power by playing on economic frustrations and national aspirations. It is essential that India and other non-Communist countries

should not lag conspicuously behind China and other Communist-controlled areas in their rates of development. If Communist-controlled countries should be relieved of some of the concentration on heavy industry and armaments imposed by their present policies, they might set a fast pace in economic development.

Alan Valentine has well said of United States government expenditure on aid to underdeveloped countries, "Paradoxically, the more successful the program the sooner it will cost more, and then the sooner it will begin to cost us less. For initial success will open the doors for further enterprise and investment, and later, greater success will bring the area's economy to the point where its own capital and know-how can replace the need for further United Nations or United States help, which can then begin to diminish." [2]

Meanwhile, there is practically no danger that the United States government will spend more than our national interest requires on economic aid to underdeveloped countries. The danger is all the other way. Underdeveloped countries are not represented in Congress where the appropriation logs are rolled, and the compelling American interest in the advancement of the underdeveloped parts of the free world is less easy for statesmen to explain than for narrowmindedness and shortsightedness to obscure. There will probably always be a bias toward underevaluation of the true national interests in international development.

Military Aid and Economic Aid

One aspect of the current American aid program which needs restudy is the relation between military and economic aid in underdeveloped countries. In the light of the situations we face, is the present combination the best for our over-all objectives? A survey on this point might well be made under government auspices with participation of the National Security Council and the International Development Advisory Board, or might be made outside government by some private group. It should weigh questions like these:

[2] Alan Valentine, "Variant Concepts of Point Four," *The Annals of the American Academy of Political and Social Science,* July, 1950, p. 60.

In how many countries, how far from a potential firing line, does our contingent of military aid personnel exceed our personnel engaged in technical aid to education, health, agriculture, and other facets of economic and social development?

How much are we spending in each underdeveloped region on military aid and how much on development of the civilian economy?

To what extent are military aid and economic aid interrelated so that one helps the other (*e.g.*, road construction)?

In the light of changes brought about by recent apparent shifts in Soviet policy, by the progress of free-world rearmament, and by other factors, does the make-up of our aid to these countries need any shift in emphasis?

Two considerations would need especially careful thought in connection with the last question: (1) the nature of the Soviet Communist threat; and (2) the effect of our aid on the social structure in underdeveloped countries.

It is a wrong diagnosis which sees the Communist menace as mainly a military threat, though Communism certainly wields a tremendous military force which has to be held in check by our own preparedness and that of friendly countries. In most underdeveloped countries the politico-economic threat is the major one. This will be even more true if Communist leaders decide that the rearmament of the free world makes it desirable to play down military action and to play up politico-economic penetration and internal revolution, perhaps under cover of a "peace offensive." Security against such a Communist policy requires us (1) to keep our military guard up; (2) to meet the Communist hope of economic depressions and international quarrels among the developed countries of the free world by disappointing it; and (3) to strengthen the politico-economic resistance of the underdeveloped areas against Communist subversion by helping them to establish a genuine trend of progress in economic growth, growth of freedoms, and growth of social capacity to use the new freedoms wisely. In such a situation we would get more American security, dollar for dollar and man-hour for man-hour, from putting relatively more into politico-economic strengthening of underdeveloped areas and relatively less into arming them.

The effect of the amount and kinds of military and economic aid on the social structure in each underdeveloped country ought also to be carefully weighed from the standpoint of long-range American interests. Are we helping some of these countries to create more military officers than businessmen, to have more modernized know-how in military staff planning than in marketing, educational administration, industrial relations, and farm cooperatives? The role of modernized military forces in countries where other things are much less modernized is problematical. Is it wise for us to cooperate in such countries in the creation of military forces substantially beyond the needs of domestic order? More thought should be given to ways of coordinating our military assistance with our politico-economic aims.

The Spirit of American Aid

How successful American development aid may be in serving the broad objectives of our world policy will depend as much on the spirit in which the aid is given as on the amount and kinds of aid.

Fundamental is the spirit of helping people to help themselves. Our interests will best be served when our aid stimulates initiative, self-reliance, and responsibility. Continued dependence on us would be a failure. We should be clear that the American interest is to build upstanding partners, not to train people to depend on a rich uncle nor to create satellites.

We should not even be much concerned about gratitude. Gratitude is pleasant as a spontaneous by-product of a mutually satisfactory relationship, but it certainly should not be one of our primary objectives. We hope that our aid programs will generate friendship for the United States, and they will if they are conducted in the right spirit; but we certainly must not set out with the notion that we can buy friendship. We are after something much bigger and more vital to our national interests than gratitude or temporary political friendship. We are out to get results in terms of the kind of world we should like to live in. We want to influence the course of social evolution, the capabilities of men to produce and consume, the attitudes and the skills and the social structures which make it possible for men to govern themselves and to cooperate in peace with other nations.

Unlike the Communists, who also want to influence the course of social evolution, we have no predetermined formula. Democracy is more an attitude than a formula. It is founded on respect for the worth of each individual human being, and its aims run in terms of those things which are necessary for the dignity of man. The democratic path to development is not one path but many paths, the only requirement being that each should lead toward a greater human dignity for the people concerned, in accordance with their own preferences, so long as these are consistent with the rights of others. In this spirit, the purpose of democratic development is to release the potentialities of people so that they may shape their own future, not have it shaped for them by somebody else.

Our interests are not well served by doing things *for* the people of the underdeveloped countries. Hence, American aid ought to be much less concerned with physical structures than with what happens in the attitudes and capabilities of local people. When aid ends, it should leave going institutions. In the words of Gordon R. Clapp, who has had experience in development problems both as Chairman of the Board of the Tennessee Valley Authority and as chief of a United Nations Economic Survey for the Middle East, "How we do the job is really more important than the material results our money pays for. . . . In our impatience to get things done, in our desire to get on with the job that history has more or less thrust upon us we may be sorely tempted to take hazardous shortcuts. We may be tempted to push slow and unstable governments aside, brush away less competent local people, and rush in shock troops of unsensitive technocrats to do the job for them. If we succumb to these temptations, we may dam the undeveloped rivers more quickly, but we would damn the world in the process." [3]

The spirit of our aid is most definitely shown in the tech-

[3] "Aid to Under-Developed Areas," Address by Gordon R. Clapp, Institute of Public Affairs, University of Virginia, Charlottesville, July 10, 1951.

nical personnel and other representatives that the American government and private business and voluntary groups send abroad. To the people with whom they come in contact they *are* American policy. The selection of representatives with suitable personality and a proper training and briefing on attitudes conducive to good human relations, as well as on the cultural background of the areas in which they work, is most important. For development service abroad, a man should be a good teacher as well as a good construction engineer or economist, and this also means he must be willing to learn. We need men like Chaucer's student: "Gladly wolde he lerne, and gladly teche."

We must realize, too, that our aid cannot be effective in a truly developmental sense, and will not serve our long-range purposes, unless it is merely marginal to the efforts that the people and government of an underdeveloped country put forth themselves in order to accomplish *their* purposes. American aid can act as a catalyst, and in some circumstances it is likely to turn the balance between success and failure. But, as George F. Kennan has said, we cannot make up for efforts that are perfunctory or inefficient or fainthearted. "Above all, our will cannot replace their will." In a situation where people seem to say, in effect, "Unless you aid us we will not aid ourselves," our aid would probably be misdirected. "Unlike our Communist adversaries, we have no desire to infuse into others a foreign will to the exclusion of their own. . . . Being free men ourselves, it is in the company of free men that we would wish to move." [4]

Finally, the spirit of our aid ought to be marked by a real humility. The temptation to play God is strong for any nation as big and as far ahead in many fields of endeavor as ours. But we do not have all the answers. Even if we did, our way of doing things would not be the best for other peoples, and least of all should we try to impose it on them. George Bernard Shaw once quipped, "The Golden Rule is really: 'Don't do unto others as you would have them do unto you—their tastes may be different.' " An anthropologist, Clyde Kluckhohn, quotes Shaw's witticism and adds that

[4] George F. Kennan, "Foreign Aid in the Framework of National Policy," *Proceedings of the Academy of Political Science,* January, 1950, pp. 109-112.

the important thing in successful intercultural relations is that whatever is done "shall bear some meaningful relation to the cultural values and expectations of both sides." [5] Respect for the values of other cultures does not mean we should give up our own, or fail to insist that what is done with our help should be in line with the democratic and peaceful objectives on which we base our world policy. The touchstone is *mutual* respect, cooperation toward *jointly* agreed ends.

GUIDELINES

We may now review the analysis of this study, endeavoring to draw from it useful principles on which to build an evolving American policy toward the underdeveloped areas of the world.

Know Our Interests

In our dealings with underdeveloped countries it is well to have thought through the interests of the American people and to be frank about basing our policy on them. None of these interests is dishonorable or basically incompatible with the legitimate interests of people in other countries. An honest statement of interests will furnish the most fruitful basis for cooperation and will arouse the least suspicion.

Our interests are not merely the interests of the political state but of the American people. The best brief summary of our concern for the development of underdeveloped areas is this: To build the kind of world we and our children would like to live in. This means a world of peace and security, of personal freedom and human dignity, of economic well-being—for ourselves and others.

The specific interests of the American government, American business, and American private associations and individuals in development of underdeveloped areas cover practically the whole range of American interests in world affairs. It is important to know that our aims are plural. No single aim is *the* motive for American interest in economic development. The relative importance among motives depends upon

5 Clyde Kluckhohn, *Mirror for Man: The Relation of Anthropology to Modern Life* (New York: Whittlesey, 1949), p. 189.

what groups in our citizenship we are talking about, whether we are thinking of immediate or long-range problems, and whether the world situation is that of 1949 or 1954 or 1965. These multiple interests and motives can be classified as follows:

1. Permanent political interests. America will be more secure and our own pursuit of happiness more effective in a world where other people are making progress toward better living conditions and where the democratic way of life is gaining. Political and economic trends are contagious in a world as small as that of the twentieth century. We are therefore interested in economic advancement and in broader distribution of political power, educational advantages, and other aspects of social progress in underdeveloped countries.

2. Special political interests. America and the whole non-Communist world face the threat of an aggressive Communist totalitarianism which already has a sizable fraction of the world's people and resources under its control. It seeks to expand its system by a ruthless combination of internal subversion that plays on all kinds of discontents and military force where feasible. So long as this menace continues (and experience warns us to regard gestures of conciliation from such a regime as tactical maneuvers), we have a vital interest in lessening the politico-economic vulnerability of underdeveloped countries to Communist subversion and in building up the military strength of the free world. The strategic position and the strategic raw materials resources of many underdeveloped countries, and the fact that Communism now aims its principal thrust at them, make it highly important that we obtain their cooperation in free world defense, and vital that they not be forced by internal pressures to switch to the Communist side.

3. Economic interests. Our own prosperity, the continuing advance of American living standards, and a sound economic basis for defense are better assured in an expanding world economy. The dynamic industrial growth of America depends to an increasing degree on imported raw materials, and most of the best potential sources are in countries now underdeveloped. The efficiency of our production and therefore our incomes will be higher because of specialization and exchange made possible by expanding trade with underdeveloped areas and by mutually advantageous investments in them.

4. Humanitarian interests. A fellow feeling for other peoples as human beings makes it an interest of ours that they should have less hunger and sickness, better opportunities for education and self-advancement. This is best brought about by helping them to produce more, which means helping them to learn modern techniques and to achieve economic progress.

A true appreciation of American interests will force us to recognize that our objectives must be *multi-valued,* not single-valued. That is, if we pursue any segment of national interest too single-mindedly the result is likely to be detrimental to other aspects of our interest and may even react adversely on the first, because all are interrelated.

The Scripps-Howard press, under the caption "No Hand-Outs for Neutrals," editorially challenged the idea of Point Four aid for India. Why, asked the editorial, should we "finance ambitious 'do-good' programs for nations which refuse to stand up to be counted?" [6] The error here is to treat a valid part of the American interest—namely, building a defensive military alliance against Soviet aggression—as though it were the whole of our interest. Indian neutralists are mistaken, in my judgment, much as American neutralists were mistaken in the 1920's and 1930's, but that should not lead us to neglect either the tremendous political and economic advantage to America if India can successfully carry through its internal program of development along the democratic path it has set for itself, or our humanitarian interest in the Indians as people. Furthermore, the writer's neglect of these other interests would increase the risk of India's being thrown completely into the Communist camp, which would be a disaster even by his narrow interpretation of our interest.

Similarly, too narrow a concentration on the humanitarian segment of our interest, valid though it is, could imperil other interests and even be self-defeating. To aid in the eco-

[6] Quoted by Richard L. Strout, *Christian Science Monitor,* January 16, 1952.

nomic development of Iron Curtain countries, on the humanitarian ground that we ought to help people no matter what their political system, would in present circumstances unquestionably be to strengthen the military power of the Kremlin and make it more likely that more people would be subjected to a most unhumanitarian oppression.

American interest in economic development for the sake of obtaining more raw materials, valid and important as it is, could react detrimentally on other important interests if pursued to the exclusion of our interest in diversified economic growth and the growth of the capacity for solid citizenship and self-government in underdeveloped countries. Such single-mindedness would also be self-defeating even from the narrow viewpoint of getting raw materials, for, as we saw in Chapter 14, the political risks in neglecting a rounded, diversified development are enormous these days.

A continuing problem for Americans will be to know the full range of our interests relating to the underdeveloped areas and to weigh those interests with due regard for their interactions.

Recognize the Interests of Underdeveloped Countries

To find the best ground for mutual cooperation we also need to understand the interests of others.

A ferment at work in all the underdeveloped countries has produced nearly everywhere an increasing pressure for economic advancement. This revolution of rising expectations is rooted in the improved communications of the twentieth century, which have brought knowledge of other countries and the realization that poverty is not inevitable.

Even more important for Americans to realize is the strength of the psychological drive in underdeveloped countries for improved status, respect, and self-esteem. This takes the form of demands for political and economic independence, "anticolonialism," and "anti-imperialism." It supports flaming nationalisms that are extremely assertive and sensitive and sometimes emotional to the point of irrationality. It is also part of the reason, though not all, for the stress put on industrialization as a goal of development in many less developed countries, for industry has become a symbol of advanced status, while agriculture and raw materials extraction still carry a "colonial" stigma in the minds of many.

Closely associated with national desires for firm independence and higher prestige is interest in building up military potential. In a number of historical cases (we have cited Japan and Turkey), psychological-political-military interests have had a stronger influence on actual policy decisions than demands for improved living conditions. The situation is somewhat different now, because the popular demand for economic well-being has grown. Still, where situations arise that seem to impinge on national freedom, status, and dignity, psychological, political, and military interests are likely to override the interest in material advancement.

For American policy to be effective it is as important to assist in the building of legitimate self-esteem in these countries as in the building of physical production; in fact, the two are in many ways interdependent. Also, we have to work with, rather than against, the nationalist spirit, helping to channel it in constructive directions. Hence, it is essential that the whole spirit of our aid should be to cooperate with people in ways that make them more self-reliant, helping them to help themselves. J. J. Singh, President of the India League of America, reported after a recent visit to South and Southeast Asia that he "was once more made aware that one of the main causes of the resentment against the Western powers is their arrogant assumption that the 'white fathers' know what is good for the backward Asian peoples. . . . A little friendly gesture, a little consideration, a little less of 'see what I am doing for your country,' a little respect for the aspirations and hopes of the Asian peoples will go a long way." [7]

Awareness of these interests and attitudes will affect American policy and practices at many points. For example, in the choice of personnel for government programs and for business representation abroad, what has been called the "Sahib mentality" has to be avoided at all costs. There is a strong case for organizing business operations as joint ventures with local interests, for rapid training and promotion of local

[7] J. J. Singh, "How to Win Friends in Asia," *New York Times* magazine, September 28, 1952.

personnel, and for more attention to good public relations than used to be thought necessary in underdeveloped areas. Governmental aid in development will usually best serve our interests when it emphasizes the joint approach and the multinational approach.

The political impact of America's policy toward underdeveloped countries depends very much on the degree of understanding in America of the way these various peoples think and feel. We make blunders and injure our own cause because of our own lack of knowledge.

The peoples of underdeveloped countries, on their side, need to know and understand more about America. Most of them are consciously or unconsciously influenced by the stereotype of "capitalism," which Marx and Engels drew in nineteenth-century Europe, and by the clichés of Lenin and his followers. What they have known personally of capitalism has generally been associated with colonialism, which gives it a bad odor. It is important for them to learn something about the modernized, socially responsible, "mixed system" —capitalism modified by political and social controls—which is the present-day reality in America. Also, they need to know the truth about the encouraging *trends* in American race relations, the democratic way in which we are meeting this and other hard problems, the deep concern of the American people for a better world, the lack of any desire on our part to rule other people, and the determination of Americans to stand with others against anyone who would impose his system, be it Nazism, Communism, or something else.

Most of the conflicts and suspicions which arise between the United States and underdeveloped countries are rooted in failures of communication. They think we mean things we do not mean, and vice versa. Where the real interests and wants of each side are understood, instead of clichés and propaganda slogans, generally it is possible to find mutually advantageous solutions to problems, or at least workable compromises. There is a tremendously responsible job to be done, therefore, by press and radio, movie-makers, scholars, travelers, businesses that have contacts abroad, trade unions, church groups, voluntary associations and individuals in the arts and professions, and all others concerned with channels of information. Our development policy can be made or ruined by the effectiveness or ineffectiveness of two-way communication.

Understand the Communist Appeal

The main thrust of the Communist attack today is directed at the underdeveloped countries. The struggle now going on to determine whether most of these countries take the Communist or the democratic path to development is likely to decide our own future security or insecurity, along with the fate on this planet of the ideals of freedom which have grown up in Western civilization.

The Communist attack is most dangerous in underdeveloped areas, for experience has shown that, contrary to the belief of early Marxists, it is not societies with a mature industrial capitalism that are most susceptible to the Communist brand of revolutionary dictatorship. Rather, it is those which have begun to stir out of centuries-old poverty and ignorance but have not yet attained living conditions tolerable by modern standards, or a broad distribution of political power and civic skills. None of the early-comers to modern industry in the West succumbed to Communist revolution, though the prospect looked good to Marx and his followers. They escaped because of a rapid rise in economic productivity and because of far-reaching economic, social, and political changes carried out by the *evolutionary* processes of democracy. The greatest issue confronting this generation of mankind is whether today's underdeveloped countries can move forward by a similar process and whether they can do so rapidly enough.

We cannot afford to underestimate either the military or the politico-economic side of Communist methods for seizing power in underdeveloped areas. In practice, we are most likely to underestimate the politico-economic. Congress votes large programs for military supplies and economizes on information and economic aid in regions where the basic struggle concerns the ideas and beliefs that determine in which direction the weapons will be pointed.

Bad economic conditions provide good breeding grounds for the Communist virus, although the *level* of material welfare is probably less important than the *trend and prospects* in determining susceptibility to Communism. The main Communist appeal, however, is not to the material wants of man. It is to the human desire for status, equality, freedom from domination or oppression, especially domination by foreigners. Fraudulent as such an appeal is in view of Communist practices where they have control, it is their most effective weapon in the struggle to gain power. Their key slogans in underdeveloped countries employ words like "imperialism," "imperialists," "colonial," "semicolonial." Even local target groups are characteristically denounced as tools ("lackeys" and "running-dogs") of foreign imperialists. The significance of this fact for the policy of the United States and the free world is very great, but the conclusions it leads to have not yet been adequately translated into practice.

Modern Communism is a highly developed technique for seizing and holding power. It uses mass movements, and since the masses in underdeveloped countries are mostly peasants it has learned how to build mass movements on peasant discontent, using slogans of agrarian reform and nationalism. These are *manipulated* mass movements. Mass discontent does not spontaneously take the highly specific political form of Communism. The key to Communist success is its leadership group—the devoted, trained Party leaders and "cadres." The recruits for this active nucleus of Communism in underdeveloped countries come, not from the proletariat or the peasants, not from the abjectly miserable, but from the relatively well-off "intelligentsia"—lawyers, journalists, teachers, students. These are the people most touched by the emotions connected with personal and national humiliation and with the quest for status, respect, and self-esteem. They are likely to be frustrated; because of their education they have become misfits in their traditional society. This group, more than any other, is aware of the misery of the masses, more resentful of real or imagined oppression; it has an awakening social conscience. The intellectuals need explanations, ideas, programs. Communism provides them. It provides both a grand ideology to explain present evils in emotionally satisfying terms and a formula for action that gives an especially large role to the intelligentsia.

Communism's most strategic export to underdeveloped countries is ideas. The Communists are running a "technical assistance" program concentrated on a certain kind of social technology. That is, Communism supplies an ideology and techniques for manipulating and organizing human relations, allegedly to the end of correcting injustices and promoting economic and social progress. This is its source of strength. A most important guideline for American policy, in order to counteract Communism in underdeveloped areas, is to give greater attention to ideas, and to helping people who want to practice democracy to learn the necessary social technology.

The Need for an Affirmative American Policy

It is important to know in our own minds, and to let the peoples of underdeveloped countries know more clearly by our words and deeds, what we are *for* as well as what we are *against*.

The type of program symbolized by Point Four is by all odds the most affirmative concept that has been introduced into American foreign policy in this generation. If it is adequately supported—by public funds, by the growth of private investment and trade, and by related actions that demonstrate America's sincere interest in the progress of all peoples toward self-government and toward cooperation based on mutual respect—then it will also prove the most effective defense against the Communist threat.

It is essential to combat Communism, but policies organized too exclusively around that negative idea leave the initiative with the Communists. If we try to build the solidarity of the free world on *mere* resistance to the menace of Communism, then the Communist tacticians can throw us off balance by "zigging" the zigzag Party line so that Communist movements all over the world adopt a studied attitude of sweet reasonableness. Having weakened the anti-Communist solidarity, they can then renew their pressure. Affirmative policies cannot be undermined in that way.

A "positive" foreign policy is often advocated in this country in terms which suggest that "positive" really means more active anti-Communism. Proposals to stir up resistance behind the Iron Curtain, to land Chiang Kai-shek's Nationalist forces in Communist China, or to create wider and more effective military alliances may or may not be good ideas, but they are negative ideas. They are directed to the weakening of the enemy's power and the frustration of *his designs*. This is important. But it is also important to use whatever opportunities we have—and we have many—to work with our friends in creating and carrying out *designs of our own* in that major part of the world that is still accessible to us.

The curiously negative interpretation of "positive" comes from a preoccupation with military concepts in our thinking about foreign policy and an underemphasis on politico-economic concepts. That is understandable in view of the immense threat we are under, but it is not wise. Affirmative policies—affirmative is better than "positive" because of the confusion just mentioned—are open to us most of all in the realm of the economic, social, and political advancement of the free world. We should not be hesitant about presenting our own ideals and the "ideology" of democracy, without forcing them on others. We should continue to affirm these ideals concretely in programs of international public and private cooperation directed toward more efficient production and wider distribution of the benefits of production and coupled with better health, more educational opportunity, personal and national freedoms, and human dignity.

Persistence and Flexibility

Economic development and the social and political progress that we want to see along with it are not to be had by a wave of a magic wand. Economic development is a long-range job. It cannot take place in countries like India or Egypt or Bolivia without deep-going cultural changes that affect almost all the habits and accepted ways of life. This means disturbance, readjustment, relearning, together with education and technical training for millions. Not all the first results will be happy ones, and some of the most important good results will be a long time in showing up. We should recognize, also, that it will not be possible, as it was possible in the Marshall Plan for European recovery, to fix a term when economic development undertakings are to end.

Where governmental action and public funds are required, will the American people, and the Congress, be in so much of a hurry for immediate results that they will not support sound, long-range programs? Will they lack patience and persistence? Will they scrap the whole effort when one or two experiments go sour? These are questions that will test our capacity to wear the mantle of leadership of the free world which, whether we like it or not, has fallen on our shoulders.

One of the lessons that is most clear from the experience of private business firms, foundations, and governmental Point Four operations is that economic development takes time to get rolling; it cannot be effectively promoted on a year-to-year basis. The President's International Development Advisory Board, in recommending a consolidated administration for our foreign economic operations, urged that "Whatever the name, it should avoid the implication that economic development is a short-run, emergency policy." [8]

We need persistence, and we also need flexibility. There is a tremendous variation in the concrete problems of economic development from country to country. Therefore no rigid formula will work.

One such rigid formula, and the one most likely to endanger the sound formulation and execution of American policy toward underdeveloped areas, is the "leave it to private enterprise" formula. It is one thing to urge, as I have in this book, that everything possible be done to encourage a greater participation of private capital and private trade in the economic upbuilding of underdeveloped countries. But it is quite another thing to argue that private enterprise *alone* can do what is necessary to develop the economies of underdeveloped countries.

Responsible committees that have given careful study to development problems have not made this mistake. The 1951 report of the International Development Advisory Board laid particular stress on enlarging the role of private enterprise. Partly for this very reason it recommended the creation of an International Development Authority to finance a portion of the cost of public works, essential to economic advance in the underdeveloped countries, which cannot be financed on

[8] *Partners in Progress,* cited, p. 21.

an ordinary loan basis. It also recommended an International Finance Corporation to act as a catalytic agent in encouraging local and international capital to go into constructive undertakings in underdeveloped countries.[9] This realistic view recognizes that the "climate" which makes modern private enterprise feasible includes adequate public investment. In a truly underdeveloped country development may not be a self-starting operation; an initial push of considerable dimensions may be required before private enterprise can take hold effectively.

The view in some circles that "Our Government should make it clear that it regards foreign economic development as the function of private enterprise . . ."[10] would be self-defeating, should it prevail. The convention which adopted this statement expressed "strong disapproval" of the proposal for creation of an International Finance Corporation. It "strongly opposed" participation by the United States in any agency designed to supply governmental funds for economic development purposes abroad on a grant basis or at nominal rates of interest. It held that "the provision of equity capital for industrial undertakings abroad is the function of private enterprise," and that "provision of public funds for economic development purposes abroad" may deter private capital formation.[11] This statement holds too rigidly to a fixed formula. Its unqualified condemnation of methods of action that are absolutely essential in the economic and political circumstances of some areas, if development is to progress in a free world setting, would weaken the prospects for the growth of private enterprise in these countries. Should such advice be taken literally, it would be most detrimental to the broad national interests of the United States.

Development Means Change in Social Institutions

Economic development is a massive problem in human education and social readjustment. We are least likely to go wrong when we think of it in these terms rather than as a

[9] Same, Chapters 7 and 8.
[10] *Final Declaration of the Thirty-Ninth Foreign Trade Convention* (New York: National Foreign Trade Council, 1952), p. xiv.
[11] Same, pp. xxiv-xxv.

problem in mechanical equipment and mechanical skills, important as these are. The most important obstacles to economic development in underdeveloped countries are social obstacles. For modern methods to work productively, far-reaching changes in the way of life have to take place. Even if our sole concern were the increase of material output, these considerations would be relevant. They are doubly so when we are also concerned with the political and social concomitants of economic development, as we assuredly must be in a wise formulation of American policy.

A properly balanced American policy toward underdeveloped areas must concern itself, not merely with material technology and physical capital, but even more with social technology and with the intangible capital represented by the building of social institutions and the development of human skills and democratic methods of organization and management. Sometimes there is a willingness to invest men and money in "hardware" or earth-moving projects while neglecting the real key to the success of such investments from the point of view of the broader aims of our national policy, namely, the encouragement of appropriate social changes and improvements in social technology.

In technical assistance programs more emphasis should be put on the social side of technology—public administration, business management, labor leadership, educational leadership, leadership in the communications media, cooperative movements, democratic political organization, and the countless civic activities carried on by voluntary citizens' groups in democratic countries. These are the keys to successful development. It would be foolish, of course, to suppose that our social technology can or should be transferred from our culture to a vastly different culture without substantial modification. Also, it is essential not to lose sight in these matters of the principle stated by President Eisenhower in his inaugural address in January, 1953: "Honoring the identity and the special heritage of each nation in the world, we shall never use our strength to try to impress upon another people our own cherished political and economic institutions." Nevertheless, with these cautions, there is as much need in underdeveloped countries for aid in acquiring the know-how of modern social organization as for aid in acquiring the know-how of machine operation.

Values and the Will to Develop

Beyond the problems of technology, material and social, lies the still more difficult question of the *will* to develop. That involves the values of the people of a given culture—their preferences, what they want out of life. Also, it involves the question of whose values are to be controlling, those of the existing élite or of some broader or different group? Can and should the United States influence these things? Once we see the key role of changes in institutions and values in the process of economic development, we are up against knotty problems of internal reform—shifts in the political power of various groups, changes in land tenure, educational policy and other fundamental social relationships. Unless changes occur in these matters in underdeveloped countries, their economic development programs are likely to stagnate or to produce a demonic result rather than the success we would like to see. But outside interest in these matters runs into the sovereign independence and the national feelings of underdeveloped countries. We have discussed the resulting dilemma and possible ways around it in Chapter 17.

Without imposing our value preferences on other peoples, we can help to make their choices clear. Nations, like individuals, often want incompatible things. For example, they may want active industries and higher incomes but not real competition among businessmen or lower profits per unit of sales. Property owners may prefer traditional landholding to financing new enterprises. Underdeveloped countries may want fine highways and public buildings and a cradle-to-the-grave social security system, but not an honest tax system or a nonpolitical civil service or labor laws designed to encourage productivity and honest effort as well as to protect labor's rights. They may want good health, plenty of food, and a low death rate, but not a changed family system and a low birth rate. Outsiders can help them to help themselves by pointing to the connections between these things. The choices remain theirs.

The main pressures on the peoples of underdeveloped countries to change accustomed ways and make new choices among life's values are not intentional pressures, whether from the United States or any other source. Rather, they are impersonal pressures impinging from all sides out of a changing world environment. These the peoples of underdeveloped countries cannot escape. Their real choice is not whether to change, but how, how fast, and in what directions.

However much we have to be aware of cultural differences, there are also many common values—common strivings for freedom and human dignity and for better material conditions of life. Even where there are striking differences of emphasis, similar human aspirations provide much solid ground on which to rest joint efforts.

The Importance of the World Setting

Whether economic development turns out well or badly in political and human terms will depend in part on the world setting in which it takes place. A country as large and powerful as the United States cannot help influencing this setting. We cannot shape political and economic conditions, even in the free world, just as we would want them, but when we have an affirmative policy American leadership can affect trends.

The United States can use its immense weight to build up the United Nations system of collective security and peaceful settlement, and to strengthen the military defenses of the free world against the continuing threat of Communist aggression. There are pitfalls in overemphasis on military aid, but without a strong system of mutual security economic development will have little chance of taking peaceful and democratic lines in today's world. The working of democracy in our own country, especially in the area of race relations, is of special interest to underdeveloped countries. Conversely, economic and social progress in key underdeveloped countries of the free world, as compared with the Communist world, will gain or lose prestige for democracy everywhere. So will the manner in which Western countries handle the remaining transition from colonialism. Colonial questions are chiefly important as symbols of still deeper problems that reach into every part of the underdeveloped world. The fiery nationalism of underdeveloped countries expresses the urgent need of peoples who feel inferior (economically, politically, socially) to acquire status, respect, and self-esteem. Whether these needs can be met constructively depends both on them and on America and other great countries. Again, our actions and attitudes cannot be controlling, but they will influence this vital aspect of the world setting.

The economic environment in the free world will have much to do with determining the comparative attractiveness of the democratic path and the Communist path to development. It will also help to determine whether the underdeveloped countries choose a free type of economy and society or an authoritarian, militaristic type combined with attempts to conquer outside "living space." The stability or instability of the American economy is among the major factors that will determine this economic environment. So are our policies on tariffs and trade. So is the degree to which we are successful, in cooperation with others, in reviving a healthy flow of international private capital and getting it to take part in constructive projects in underdeveloped countries.

Economic Development—A Means, Not an End

Growth of economic output is wanted for the benefits it can bring to human beings in the underdeveloped countries and in the rest of the world, including ourselves. But what it actually does bring depends on the way economic growth comes about, the directions it takes, what groups control it, and the political, social, and economic framework (domestic and international) in which it goes forward. It would be a great mistake to let the mere increase of physical production be elevated to the lofty status of an end in itself. A guideline for American policy is to see economic development as a *means* and to think often about the ends that we and others want it to serve.

Economic development is not a cure-all. Growth of production in underdeveloped countries is a *necessary* but not a *sufficient* condition for their evolution in a manner that promotes peace, freedom, and prosperity. Modernizing production methods creates opportunities for a better life, and also dangers for the people directly concerned and for us.

We and they need to consider the question: Production for what? Is production to support aggressive armaments? To fasten more firmly the rule of a narrow, privileged class, local or alien? To strengthen a new élite in the form of a self-appointed "vanguard" seeking to extend a modernized tyranny over the world? This would represent the pathology, not the health, of economic development. But the modern history of Germany, Japan, and Russia reminds us that economic development can go wrong and be put to bad uses.

We return, then, to the thoughts that began this study. For people in the underdeveloped countries, who constitute the great majority of mankind, economic development is essential to progress in human dignity. We in the West who pioneered the modern means of material and social progress are concerned with more than sharing the know-how that, for us, has unlocked such great benefits and troubles. We are concerned with survival. The insulation of distance has broken down; the underdeveloped countries are in ferment; extreme contrasts between the modernized West and the rest of the world in food, clothing, housing, health, education, personal freedom, and political participation cannot continue indefinitely. Under the world conditions of today, either the human benefits that we like to think of as characteristic of Western civilization will also become available to the rest of the world, or they will be lost even to the West.

While it is essential to the well-being of the West and of underdeveloped countries alike that economic modernization take place, the process is bound to bring great changes in political and social structures, and such changes rarely occur smoothly and easily. There will be excesses and disappointments as peoples that have had very little political power in modern times acquire more of it. We can expect no simple, direct relation between economic development and effective democracy or peaceful international attitudes. We in the United States—having a vital interest in the future of underdeveloped areas—can help them somewhat by endeavoring to make world conditions favorable for democratic development, and by bilateral and multilateral aid programs. On occasion our help might turn the scales, but only where the great weights in the pan are put there by the efforts, initiative, and sacrifices of the local people. For underdeveloped countries to achieve a rapid rise in economic productivity is a tough task; to do it by ways which make men free rather than slaves is in some ways even tougher. If the outcome were certain it would not be part of the human adventure.

PART IV

DEVELOPMENT IN THE SIXTIES

It is now (1961) eight years since completion of the manuscript for the first edition of this book, from which the preceding three parts are reprinted. Part IV is new and brings the analysis down to date. Its three chapters deal first with noteworthy trends of the middle and late 1950's related to the world problem of development, then with trends in United States policy and opinion, and finally with the necessity for rethinking and reorienting United States policy.

Chapter 19

TRENDS OF RECENT YEARS
RELATED TO DEVELOPMENT

Far from slackening, the revolution of rising expectations among the less privileged peoples of the world continued to gather intensity throughout the 1950's. It spread to new areas, changing the course of society even in countries hitherto isolated by massive mountain barriers, as in Nepal and Bhutan.

Its most notable advance was in Africa, where even five years ago very few observers would have predicted such a quick and irresistible sweep of the independence movement and of the modernizing trends associated with it.

The profoundly significant changes of attitude referred to as the revolution of rising expectations include both new economic aspirations, based on the realization that better food, clothing, health, and educational opportunities are attainable by use of modern technology, and new political aspirations, reflecting the desires of formerly subject peoples for respect, status, and self-rule. The economic aspirations are by no means the dominant ones; in fact, political aspirations for self-rule, improved status, and respect seem to be more highly valued by most peoples. But the two sets of aspirations are generally tied together, and progress toward one is oftentimes—though not always—both an incentive and a means for progress toward the other.

For example, we have the report of a responsible French observer who revisited parts of the African continent in 1960, particularly former French colonies. He was struck by "the veritable revolution that is transforming economic and social life." The new African governments "have set to work with admirable determination and common sense and are making nationwide efforts to raise the standard of living. Young people have been mobilized, in one way or another, and they all share the same faith—almost a 'mystique' of progress. . . . When you compare this with the apathy of the past, you begin to wonder whether that wasn't partly due to a kind of 'irresponsibility complex' which has disappeared now that these people feel that they are working on their own account." [1]

The winds of change blowing through Africa, as also through Asia, the Middle East, and Latin America, are transforming economic, social, and political life. It seems inevitable that modernization will soon penetrate even the remaining tribal societies. Whether this is a good thing or not, whether the people will really be better off or happier, is hardly the question any more. The real problems are how the transformations are going to proceed, under what kinds of leadership, with what guidance and external assistance, and how the benefits may be maximized and the dangers and drawbacks minimized—both from the standpoint of the peoples directly involved and from the standpoint of world peace and prosperity.

Liquidation of Colonialism

The pace of political as well as technological change is very rapid these days. The original edition of this book advocated planned development to prepare for liberation of colonies, arguing that powerful new forces would continue the liquidation of colonial interests until all the old relationships were completely readjusted. "This will take some time, but all indications are that the time will be short, not more than a few decades at most." (Page 321.) Less than one decade later the passing of traditional colonialism is almost complete! As of early 1961 there were only about 120 million people remaining under colonial rule of the old type. (It is debatable whether the new type of Communist rule over other peoples should or should not be called colonial.) More than 825

---

[1] Robert Lemaignen, a member of the Commission of the European Economic Community, as quoted in *Bulletin from the European Community*, July 1960.

million people, nearly three-tenths of the population of the world, live in countries that have acquired national independence in the last fifteen years. Seventeen new national states with 84 million people came into being in Africa in the year 1960 alone. Of the remaining colonial territories, several are heading toward early independence. We have seen the end of an epoch and the beginning of a new one fraught with new hopes, problems, and opportunities.

Events in the former Belgian Congo following attainment of independence in mid-1960 dramatize not only the internal troubles of politically inexperienced societies confronted with the responsibilities of self-government, especially where the colonial power has not prepared them, but also ways in which the weaknesses of these new regimes can result in showering sparks on the international powder keg. This experience demonstrates the urgent need to build up the capabilities of the United Nations to provide, on behalf of the world community, a wide range of assistance to the newly independent and newly developing countries. The *need* for strong world community institutions to meet these situations continues to grow by leaps and bounds. Whether the *feasibility* of such institutions—which means changes in the thinking and in the emotional loyalties of peoples and leaders—can be made to evolve with similar rapidity is the world's basic problem.

Income Levels and Disparities in Income

One of the minor revolutions of our time is the revolution in world statistics. During the 1950's national income accounting has extended its conquest to nearly every country. The United Nations now publishes a *Yearbook of National Accounts Statistics*. Using these data and supplementing them where necessary by other estimates, Everett E. Hagen and Mikoto Usui of the Center for International Studies, M.I.T., have compiled a world table of average income per capita by countries as of 1957. They have converted gross national products from local currencies into dollars by the use of foreign exchange rates, in some cases with adjustments which seemed necessary and reasonable. The map at the beginning of this

book is based on their results. The relative positions of countries do not differ greatly from those shown in the first edition
(pp. 16–17). The low-income countries on the map (below
$300 of GNP per capita in 1957) may be taken as roughly
corresponding to the "underdeveloped" group, the middle-
income countries (GNP per capita of $300–$600 in 1957) to
the "intermediate" group, and the high-income countries
(GNP per capita of $600 and up in 1957) to the "highly
developed" group.

As Hagen points out, translation of national product figures
into a common unit by use of foreign exchange rates permits
a reasonably accurate *ranking* of countries according to per
capita income, but it is not a reliable method for measuring
the true *disparity* of income between high- and low-income
countries. "Typically, goods and services produced and used
within a low-income country are cheaper, relative to the
same goods and services in say the United States, than those
that enter into foreign trade, so that conversion of the country's national income to dollars by use of the foreign exchange
rate understates the true income. Further, the degree of
distortion apparently increases, the lower the income of the
country concerned." [2] Accordingly, to obtain a more accurate
indication of relative real incomes, Hagen has multiplied the
per capita GNPs below $100 by three, those between $100
and $300 by two and a half, those between $300 and $600
by two, those between $600 and $1,200 by one and a half,
and those above $1,200 by one. Using these adjusted income
figures, he arrives at a comparison of the proportions of world
population and of world income found in countries of different income groups. (See Table 1.)

This world distribution of income based on country averages is not comparable with figures showing distribution
among individuals or families within single countries. Were
the poorest individuals or families in the world, from whatever country, classed together in one group and the richest
in another, the indicated income disparities would, of course,
be very much greater. In other words, if we discard our habit

[2] Everett E. Hagen, "Some Facts about Income Levels and Economic
Growth," *Review of Economics and Statistics,* February 1960, p. 63.

TABLE 1

RELATIVE SHARES OF WORLD POPULATION AND OF WORLD INCOME

	Percent of World Population	Percent of (Adjusted) World Income
Countries of lowest income group	49.7	16
Countries of next to lowest income group	17.2	13
Countries of middle income group	18.0	26
Countries of next to highest income group	7.5	17
Countries of highest income group	7.7	28

Source: Everett E. Hagen, "Some Facts about Income Levels and Economic Growth," *Review of Economics and Statistics,* February 1960, p. 64.

of looking at the world through national averages and look instead directly at *people* (as citizens of the world), the world social problem of income disparity is considerably more acute than shown here.

Economic Growth Slowly Gathering Momentum

During the 1950's, economic growth came to be accepted as an important objective of policy in developed and under-developed countries alike. In United Nations debates it was put forward as an aim of the world community. Among the underdeveloped countries, the actual progress achieved varied greatly from country to country. On the whole, there was forward movement. Some forged ahead rather rapidly. Others achieved some of the prerequisites for later advance. A United Nations survey, viewing the record of the 1950's in historical perspective, reports: "In much of the world's under-developed regions, though average levels of living still remain danger-ously low, a serious beginning towards self-sustaining growth has been recorded." There has been "a marked rise in the volume of investment within the under-developed areas as a whole. For many of the countries in these areas, the higher rate of investment attained in the last decade marks a significant break with the stagnant economic conditions of the past and it has already borne fruit in an acceleration of economic growth." This inception of a new and more vigorous phase "has been particularly true of the African and Asian regions where governments of numerous countries, in the years since the attainment of national independence, have for the first time embarked upon large-scale programmes of economic development." [3]

Table 2 shows economic growth rates in the 1950's for a number of underdeveloped countries and also for certain countries in the highly developed or intermediate groups. These countries, for which data happen to be available, are not necessarily representative of their respective groups. Also, the range of performance within each group is wide, and this should warn us not to forget that there are great differences concealed within any general averages such as those on which the following statements are based. With this caution, it is nevertheless interesting to note that United Nations statisticians, using data for 1950–1957 from 42 countries and territories in underdeveloped regions and 19 countries in industrialized regions, find the gross national products of the former growing at just under 4 percent and the latter at just over 4 percent. But the populations of the former are expanding much more rapidly than the populations of the latter. Hence, *per capita* product in the less developed, poorer countries is growing more slowly than in the relatively developed, richer countries—2⅓ percent annually as against 2⅔ percent. "By absolute standards the material situation of the less developed countries as a whole has been gradually getting better, by comparative standards it has been getting worse." [4]

The Managing Director of the United Nations Special

[3] *World Economic Survey 1959*, 60.II.C.1 (New York: United Nations, Department of Economic and Social Affairs, 1960), pp. 5, 63.

[4] *Five-Year Perspective, 1960-64, Consolidated report on the appraisals of the scope, trend, and costs of the programmes of the United Nations . . . in the economic, social and human rights fields*, prepared by the Committee on Programme Appraisals, 60.IV.14 (New York: United Nations, Department of Economic and Social Affairs, 1960), pp. 10-11.

TABLE 2

RATES OF GROWTH IN OUTPUT, SELECTED COUNTRIES, 1950–1958

Some Underdeveloped Countries	Average Annual Rate (percent)
Iraq	11.1
Turkey	7.8
Rhodesia and Nyasaland	7.0
Greece	6.9
Philippines	6.7
Burma	5.6
Mexico	5.5
Colombia	5.2
Ecuador	5.1
Thailand	5.0
Guatemala	4.9
Brazil	4.8
Peru	4.3
Portugal	3.9
Ghana	3.8
UAR (Egypt)	3.3
India	3.3
Ceylon	2.8

Some Intermediate or Highly Developed Countries	
Japan	7.9
Germany (Federal Republic)	7.4
Italy	5.5
Netherlands	4.5
France	4.3
Canada	4.0
United States	3.3
Norway	3.0
Belgium	2.9
Sweden	2.9
Chile	2.4
Denmark	2.3
United Kingdom	2.2
Cuba	2.2
Argentina	1.7

Source: United Nations, *World Economic Survey 1959*, 60.II.C.I. (New York: Author, 1960), Tables 2–9 and 1–2, pp. 73 and 23. Based on gross domestic products in constant prices. See the source for certain variations in the period covered and in concepts.

Fund, Paul G. Hoffman, has put the matter well: "Estimated income per person in the 100 [underdeveloped] countries and territories associated with the United Nations averaged approximately $90 in the year 1950. It probably reached slightly over $100 per person in 1959. National income grew at the rate of 3 percent a year, but, because there were two hundred million more mouths to feed in these countries in 1959 than there were in 1950, the net increase in income per person was only about 1 percent, that is, about $1 a year. Over this same decade, income per person in the Netherlands increased by more than $300, in the United Kingdom, Western Germany and Switzerland by more than $400, and in the United States and Canada by more than $500. Now we all know that statistics about the less developed countries can hardly be more than educated guesses, and notably that dollar estimates of income are understated when compared with those of the advanced countries. But clearly, in both relative and absolute terms, the rate of increase in the poorer countries was too slow—dangerously too slow." [5]

Communist and Non-Communist Economic Growth

Table 3 shows growth rates in eight centrally planned economies under Communist rule, as reported by the United Nations on the basis of official sources and as estimated by the United States government's Central Intelligence Agency. Statistical pitfalls, such as different ways of defining and pricing production, stand in the way of direct comparison between figures from these countries and the ones given earlier for other countries. It is probably correct to say, however, that the Communist countries have generally higher rates of economic growth, though in most cases—even without allowing for exaggeration built into the statistics—their growth rates are not as high as Japan's in some of its periods of most rapid growth and no higher than those of some of the most rapidly growing non-Communist countries. The most remarkable growth rate is that claimed by mainland China. It is necessary to treat Chinese figures with some skepticism,

[5] Address of Paul G. Hoffman to the New York State Bankers Association, Lake Placid, June 17, 1960.

in view of Peking's own revisions of previous overstatements, particularly in agricultural output, and in view of serious food shortages that have appeared. Even so, it may well be that mainland China has increased its output in the last decade more rapidly than any other major country, and perhaps more rapidly than Japan or the Soviet Union at comparable stages in their histories.

TABLE 3

RATES OF GROWTH IN OUTPUT,
COMMUNIST COUNTRIES
(average annual percentage increase)

	Based on published official data of these countries [a] 1949–1958	Estimate by C.I.A. of U.S. Government [b] 1950–1959
China (mainland)	12.3 [c]	9.0
U.S.S.R.	11.5	7.0
European satellites		6.5
Bulgaria	10.3	
Poland	9.4	
Rumania	9.3	
Czechoslovakia	8.0	
Eastern Germany	8.0 [c]	

[a] Source: United Nations, *World Economic Survey 1959*, 60.II.C.1 (New York: Author, 1960), Table 3–1, p. 112.

[b] Source: *Comparisons of the United States and Soviet Economies, Supplemental Statement . . .*, prepared by the Central Intelligence Agency in cooperation with the Department of State and the Department of Defense, for the Joint Economic Committee, 86th Cong., 2d sess. (Washington: GPO, 1960), Table 1, p. 48.

[c] 1950–1958.

A particularly inviting comparison involves two pairs of Communist and non-Communist countries: East Germany with West Germany, and mainland China with India.[6] The

[6] For this comparison and references to more detailed studies, see Wilfred Malenbaum and Wolfgang Stolper, "Political Ideology and Economic Progress," *World Politics*, April 1960, pp. 413-421.

economic growth record favors non-Communist West Germany in the first case, Communist China in the second. However, the two Germanys are economically developed, while China and India are underdeveloped countries. Therefore, the latter comparison is bound to be much more impressive to other underdeveloped countries. And, subject to qualification when more becomes known about the true trends in Chinese agriculture, it appears that Communist-ruled China has been expanding its output at a rate several times that of democratic India.[7]

Rates of economic growth by themselves fail to tell us many things we should like to know about effects on the lives of people. How much of the new production, for example, is

[7] Wilfred Malenbaum has well summarized the comparative economic performance of the two countries during the 1950's (article cited above, pp. 414-415):

"In 1950 both India and China had per capita incomes of about $50—lower than in any other large nation. The two countries initiated their development operations at about the same time and from the same type of economic structure. In both, at least 80 percent of the working force was in agriculture and small-scale enterprise. If anything, India gave promise of greater progress in view of its advantages in basic resources per man, in transport facilities and modern industry, and in training and leadership attributes. . . .

"Yet by 1959 per capita gross national product in India was only some 12-15 percent above its 1950 level, while in China it had expanded to about double the earlier figure. . . .

"With an initial gross investment ratio just below 10 percent, absolute real investment in China had increased by 1958 to five times the 1950 level; in India it about doubled. Foreign aid did not explain this difference: indeed, China's investment was more nearly financed from its current output than was India's. . . .

"The Chinese put more effort into expanding physical output as against services; a larger proportion of new capital was allocated to agriculture and small industry; the degree of utilization of resources, and especially of labor, was increased significantly. Over the whole period, government played a much larger role in economic life in China than in India. And of course, compared with India's, China's producers and consumers had limited freedom of choice—in techniques of production, in final goods for consumption. Greater regimentation in China was accompanied by considerable flexibility on the part of government. In response to actual developments in the economy, relative emphasis was shifted away from the initial concentration on heavy industry, for example. By and large, China's economic progress has been steady. In India, government adheres to models of growth which are permissive; comparatively few restraints are imposed on individuals whose usual ways of life did not in the past generate economic expansion. There have been impressive spurts of industrial output in India's essentially private modern industry sector, as well as some record crops in years with favorable monsoons. The total performance has been less even. . . ."

making itself felt in more to eat and wear, better education and health? Comparisons of output omit, of course, the human costs of Communist China's forced pace, including the sacrifice of freedoms for which men have oftentimes been willing to lay down their lives. Leaders of other underdeveloped countries are not unaware of these costs, though the Communist propaganda control over information from mainland China minimizes knowledge of them and plays up the achievements.

The spectacular production revolution carried out under Communist auspices in mainland China will have a continuing and probably increasing effect on political and economic thinking in the less developed countries of Asia and Africa. The demonstration of speedy growth is itself the most important form of influence. In addition, the government of the People's Republic of China is already using some of its resources for economic assistance to countries outside the Communist bloc, clearly with political motives. Grants, interest-free loans or lines of credit, technical cooperation agreements, and trade and payments agreements have brought Communist China into relation with countries near and far, among them: Cambodia, Ceylon, Nepal, Egypt, Guinea, Indonesia, Yemen, Burma, and Cuba.

Soviet Development Aid

Soviet development aid must be considered in two parts: aid to other members of the Soviet-Communist bloc, and aid to non-Communist countries. Soviet policy on development aid to non-Communist countries has undergone a drastic shift in recent years—one of the most notable happenings in the development field during the 1950's.

a. Soviet Aid to Communist Bloc Members

The Soviet Union has long fostered economic development of associated countries within the Communist bloc. In mainland China, judging from the evidence that filters through the blockades on reporting imposed both by the Communists and ourselves, rather massive Soviet aid has taken the form of (1) advice and assistance in the preparation of industrialization plans; (2) technical aid and managerial advice in the execution of these plans; (3) machinery and equipment, often including complete plants, financed by loans at a low rate of interest or repaid directly by Chinese deliveries of agricultural and mineral products; and (4) large-scale assistance in the training of technical and managerial personnel, both in the Soviet Union and by Soviet experts on the job in China.[8] An agreement in 1953 provided for Soviet financial and technical aid to build or rebuild 141 industrial plants. The loan element in Soviet aid to China has been relatively small and the gift element even smaller; in fact, the Chinese have largely paid in goods for Soviet aid. Estimates of the number of Soviet technicians in China have varied from 10,000 to 50,000. Even the lower figure exceeds the number of technicians provided by the United States under its aid programs in all countries (just over 7,000 in 1960). There were press reports in 1960 that large numbers of Soviet technical aids were being expelled or withdrawn from China, coincident with the controversies over ideology and policy between the Communist parties of the two countries.

It appears that Soviet aid in the industrialization of other Communist countries is now dispensed largely within the framework of the twenty-year development plan laid down in 1960 by the bloc's Council for Mutual Economic Aid (Comecon). Such aid includes cooperation in research and designing, exchange of scientific and technical information, instruction and refresher courses to train a pool of skilled manpower, and industrial construction. A total of 814 industrial projects being constructed with Soviet help was reported in a Soviet journal[9] early in 1961 (see table on p. 409).

b. Soviet Aid to Non-Communist Countries

As for development aid to underdeveloped countries outside the Communist bloc, Soviet policy has executed a major

[8] Based mainly on T. J. Hughes and D. E. T. Luard, *The Economic Development of Communist China, 1949–1958* (London: Oxford University Press, for the Royal Institute of International Affairs, 1959), especially pp. 72-73, 75, 200.

[9] *Kommunist*, no. 2, January 1961, p. 17. Slightly different figures were given in an earlier article in *Ekonomicheskaya Gazeta*, no. 121, October 19, 1960, which was summarized in the *New York Times* of October 22, 1960.

	Major Enterprises	Workshops, etc.
China	291	59
Poland	68	8
Czechoslovakia	8	8
Hungary	27	4
Rumania	60	23
Bulgaria	45	25
Albania	58	23
North Korea	30	15
Outer Mongolia	21	10
North Vietnam	16	15

strategic shift since the death of Stalin in 1953—indeed, starting in a small way before his death. When the United States launched its "Point Four" program and also encouraged the United Nations to undertake the Expanded Program of Technical Assistance, the Soviet Union at first stood on the sidelines and scoffed. It warned the recipients of aid that this was an imperialist trick to exploit and enslave them by new means (see pp. 144–152 of this book). The Soviet bloc contributed nothing to the United Nations program during the early years and gave no important aid to non-Communist countries directly. In a way, it is a tribute to the effectiveness of the United States aid program that this Soviet policy a few years later underwent a radical change.

The Soviet Union, the European satellites, and Communist China have increasingly provided development aid to non-Communist countries, first in South Asia and the Middle East, more recently in Africa and Latin America.[10] Assistance

[10] On this aid and its significance I have benefited from the opportunity to read in manuscript parts of Henry G. Aubrey, *Coexistence: Economic Challenge and Response* (Washington, 1961). Also see case studies in the National Planning Association's series on *The Economics of Competitive Coexistence;* the paper by Aubrey on "Sino-Soviet Economic Activities in Less Developed Countries," in U. S. Congress, Joint Economic Committee, *Comparisons of the United States and Soviet Economies,* 86th Cong., 1st sess. (Washington: GPO, 1959), Part II, and subsequent testimony by Aubrey and others published in the Hearings of the Committee; Joseph S. Berliner, *Soviet Economic Aid* (New York, 1958); Thomas C. Mann, "Agricultural and Assistance Programs of the Sino-Soviet Bloc," a lecture published in *The International Age in Agriculture,* U. S. Department of Agriculture Graduate School, 1960.

takes many forms: loans, grants, technical assistance, training, and complete construction projects. An example of the latter is the Soviet Union's construction and equipment of a steel mill in India and training of workers to run it. Soviet assistance is not usually provided free, but against credits at low rates of interest (2 or 2½ percent) to be repaid in export commodities of the assisted country. However, grants and interest-free loans have also been made (especially by Communist China), and there is great flexibility in aid terms and methods. It should be noted that a considerable part of Communist bloc "aid" is really bilateral trade bargains, the Communist country supplying machines, materials, construction and technical services, even complete factories, against repayment by the newly developing country in commodities.

U. S. government sources estimate that from 1954 to the middle of 1960 Communist bloc credits and grants to non-bloc countries for economic purposes totaled $3.2 billion, though only a small part of this was disbursed during the period. So far the amount is considerably less than that provided by the United States. It is still smaller, comparatively, if all Western aid is counted or if private international investment is included.[11] However, Communist bloc aid has been more concentrated in politically sensitive areas, and in some of these areas matches or overmatches Western aid.

What motivations and strategy lie behind the decisions of the Soviet Union and its allies in turning from Stalin's policy of economic isolation to a very active policy of technical and economic assistance to non-Communist countries? We can be sure that they hope to hasten the inevitable (as they see it) world spread of the Communist economic and political system. But how?

In considering the significance of Communist bloc aid, and

[11] A comprehensive study by the Organization for European Economic Cooperation, published in April 1961, estimated the flow of capital funds, governmental and private, to underdeveloped countries for the years 1956–1959. The total from North America and Europe, counting all types of nonmilitary grants, loans, and investments except credits of less than one year, was $27,300,000,000, of which about half came from the United States. The amount supplied by the Sino-Soviet bloc during the same period was, in terms of disbursements, just under $600,000,000, but commitments (mostly for funds not disbursed during the period) totaled $2,300,000,000. *The Flow of Financial Resources to Countries in Course of Economic Development, 1956–1959* (Paris: Author, 1961), pp. 9, 12.

also of our own aid, it is useful to distinguish two kinds of effects. One is the relatively slow but fundamental change in the economic, social, and political situation of a country which comes from modernizing its methods of production and its social organization. The other is the more immediate but less lasting impression aid makes on the minds of government leaders and people in recipient countries. American aid, with its stress on productive projects which may not even be known as outside aid to many of the people affected, is aimed principally for the first, longer-range effect. Our major interest is, and should be, to help develop healthy, resistant societies, able to advance human well-being and to maintain their independence against external pressure and internal subversion. Whether we get thanks and political credit for the help is, and should be, secondary. The Soviet Union, in so far as it holds to the Communist aim of ultimate take-over of power in the developing country, no doubt has a negative interest in long-continued success of development programs under a non-Communist government.[12] Its major concern in development aid, therefore, is probably the second type of effect: to reap psychological and political credit for its help, to demonstrate the high level of Soviet science and technology, to strengthen the prestige and political influence of the Communist bloc, thereby aiding its world policies in general and preparing to take advantage of any opportunities in the underdeveloped countries for further Communist expansion.

Soviet propaganda associated with development aid incorporates the regular themes earlier addressed to underdeveloped countries (see pages 145–147) and some new emphases:

1. The Soviet peoples are friends and brothers of the new and poor nations in the struggle against "imperialism" and share their aspirations for economic as well as political independence.

2. The countries of the Soviet bloc have recently raised themselves from backwardness and have achieved remarkable

---

[12] Some have speculated that Soviet political strategists render developmental aid in the belief that development under a non-Communist system is bound to fail; it will go far enough to produce false hopes, then frustrations, paving the way for internal take-over by standard Communist tactics. Also, the beginnings of modern development will create a working class and trade unions within which Communist leadership can be exerted.

rates of economic growth; they have demonstrated a new and better system for attaining economic emancipation, rapid development, and international status.

3. The Soviet Union and the other countries in the "Socialist camp" offer disinterested assistance, while the capitalist-imperialist powers, especially the United States, are motivated by profit-seeking and by the desire to use less developed countries as pawns in the cold war. These allegations are unfortunately reinforced not only by deep anticolonial and nationalistic sentiments in the new countries but also by aspects of our own behavior. As Henry G. Aubrey says, "a nagging insistence on linking assistance to private business tends to support the Communists' taunts that Western aid is a pretext for profits." And aid justifications which state our purposes in negative, anti-Communist terms instead of in terms of a positive world program help to intensify suspicion that we look at underdeveloped countries as pawns in a power struggle.

The following excerpts from Indian press reports of Mr. Khrushchev's visit to India in February 1960 illustrate several of the Soviet propaganda themes:

Mr. Khrushchev said [in a Calcutta speech] . . . that the main object underlying Soviet aid to India was that the Soviet people, who had built up their economy on Socialist lines, were interested in developing India's economy. He contrasted Soviet economic assistance to India with that of the Western countries and said it was incredible that capitalist countries could give disinterested aid as Russia was giving. . . . Why were capitalist countries giving aid to India? He did not know the terms and conditions of credit, but one thing was definite, that the capitalist countries would not invest their capital anywhere unless it yielded good profits. . . . If an underdeveloped country came up economically, the profits of capitalist countries would diminish and their markets shrink, he said. He added that capitalist countries were trying to help India to keep her in what they called "the free world" and what the Russians called "capitalist slavery." [13]

Speaking to the Indian Parliament: "The Soviet people sincerely rejoice in the achievements and the radiant prospects of the independent national development of Asian and African

[13] *Hindustan Times,* February 15, 1960.

states. . . . The Soviet Union has always rendered and is willing to render in future friendly disinterested assistance and support to all countries in their struggle for freedom and independence, in their struggle against the age-old economic backwardness. . . . It is through the repression and plundering of colonial peoples that the economic welfare and high living standards were attained by a number of highly developed countries. . . . Things go differently with the Soviet Union. Our wealth, our industry have been created in the historically shortest period at the price of the strenuous work of all our people. While we have no surplus capital, we, nevertheless, render ever-increasing assistance to the States in need of it. . . . We are guided by the sincere desire to help in every possible way the peoples of former colonial countries to reach in the shortest time the genuine economic independence and to raise substantially their living standards. . . . The Soviet people have created their own first class industry, scored big successes in the development of agriculture and achieved great progress in science and culture. . . . We believe that the supreme right of man that secures him freedom is the right to work, to secure existence today and tomorrow, his liberation from a dreadful threat of unemployment and poverty. . . . To work for your own self and for society, but not for the exploiters—in this we see the genuine social justice. . . . In the Soviet Union, every citizen has the real right to work, to rest, to social security in old age and in case of disablement, and the right to education. Our people have no fear of unemployment, everyone is afforded ample opportunities for revealing his creative forces and abilities." [14]

The Soviet bloc still contributes only scantily to United Nations development programs. For 1960 the United States pledged $40 million to the UN Expanded Program of Technical Assistance and the UN Special Fund, subject to the condition that its contribution would not exceed 40 percent of the total contributions to each of the two programs. The U.S.S.R. for the same year pledged $2 million to these programs, the Ukrainian S.S.R. $250,000, and the Byelorussian S.S.R. $100,000.[15] India, Canada, Sweden, and several others

[14] *Times of India,* February 12, 1960.

[15] United Nations, General Assembly, *Statement of Contributions Pledged for 1960 to the Expanded Programme of Technical Assistance and to the Special Fund,* A/CONF.18/1, June 28, 1960. The Soviet Union's 1961 pledge was $3 million, the Ukraine's $375,000, and Byelorussia's $150,000.

each pledged more than the Soviet Union. Also, in the past there have been difficulties about the use of Soviet funds contributed in rubles which are expendable only for Soviet goods or services.[16]

The Soviet insistence upon rendering its aid bilaterally and its refusal to make more use of the channels of the United Nations and the specialized agencies naturally raise suspicions about the true disinterestedness of Soviet motives.[17] This is a major political and propaganda weakness in the Soviet position on assistance to less developed countries, and one which the United States should exploit to the full, by putting more and more emphasis on the United Nations in its own aid policies and by challenging the Soviet Union to do likewise.

The Rising Role of Recovered Europe and Japan

Europe has changed in the last decade from a source of weakness to a source of strength in the Western world, from an area requiring external economic aid to an area able to render aid. The dynamism of an economically advancing and politically vigorous Europe on the road to unification will now be a major force in world development. Europe's progress has significance for the future of underdeveloped countries in several ways.

First, the success of Marshall Plan aid, both in assisting European recovery and encouraging European unity, provides the advocates of other aid programs with an important precedent. Probably never has the American taxpayer made a better investment, in terms of added security and other bene-

---

[16] See R. L. Allen, "United Nations Technical Assistance: Soviet and East European Participation," *International Organization,* Fall 1957, pp. 615-634.

[17] Mr. Khrushchev found it necessary to defend the Soviet position during the India visit referred to above. He did so in a manner that must have been unconvincing to his hosts:

"The Soviet Prime Minister did not favour the idea of pooling the resources of all the nations to assist underdeveloped countries. He said often such a proposal was made by the Great Powers. . . . 'We not only favour such aid, but we render that aid also. But we do not understand this talk of a common pool.' Aid could only be effective if it helped to develop the economy of a country. It was different from doles. 'This position we adhere to and will continue to do so.' Sometimes aid distributed through the U.N. could be likened to a drop of medicine prescribed by a doctor which did not have much effect on the patient." (*The Statesman,* New Delhi, February 17, 1960.)

fits per dollar. Admittedly the development problem in underdeveloped countries is larger and more difficult than was the recovery problem in an already developed Europe. It can be misleading, perhaps even dangerous through arousing false expectations, to think of the new task in terms of the old. Still, the good results of a creative approach to the one do encourage a creative approach to the other.

Second, some of the techniques which proved useful in the European Recovery Program are suggestive in relation to development problems elsewhere. The principle of mutual participation by aid-receiving nations and donor nations in working out plans and allocating and supervising the use of external aid is an especially notable aspect of Marshall Plan experience which should not be forgotten in aid policies toward newly developing countries.

Third, Europe's example gives impetus to movements toward international economic institutions, common markets, and regional federations or confederations in other parts of the world, particularly where the urge to industrialize is impeded by the limited markets of small nation states.

Fourth, Europe is now in a position to carry a larger share of international developmental assistance and is beginning to do so. The establishment of the Organization for Economic Cooperation and Development (OECD) to replace the Organization for European Economic Cooperation (OEEC), which played the main role in coordinating European recovery efforts, symbolizes a new orientation toward world problems. In OECD the eighteen members of the former organization are joined by the United States and Canada, and one of its principal concerns will be aid to underdeveloped countries.

While it is good that the capacity of Europe to provide developmental aid has risen so markedly and that the corresponding responsibility is being recognized, there are certain cautions we should bear in mind when assessing the significance of these facts for United States policy. It would be a sad mistake for the United States to take the view that since Europe can now carry more of the burden we can therefore decrease our total of grants, loans, investments, and technical aid for underdeveloped countries. The development problem is so large and so important that the United States should be expanding its efforts, at the same time urging other countries to do likewise. Furthermore, desirable as it is for the United States and European nations to consult and to coordinate policies and efforts, it would be most unfortunate to build up either the reality or the appearance of a Western "donors' club" or cartel as an alternative to broader efforts through the United Nations and regional agencies in which the newly developing nations play an active part.

The United States should be especially careful to avoid any exclusive association with European countries with respect to regions where the emotions carried over from recent colonialism are still strong. This applies, of course, most strongly to Africa. A continuing friendly interest by European governments and peoples in African development is an asset of considerable importance to Africa and the world. So is the intimate acquaintance of many Europeans, as a result of colonial service, with African conditions and problems. However, not all of the ideas learned in colonial times—for example, ideas on how to treat Africans—are applicable, now that Africans have the responsibility of ruling themselves. The newly independent Africans, on their side, will for a long time be quick to detect and to resent even the slightest appearance of an attempt to reimpose colonial conditions under some new guise. Especially in those territories where the colonial parting was bitter, there will be suspicion and hostility toward Europeans and white men. The best hope for assisting progress under these conditions undoubtedly will be on a world community rather than a European or European-American base, working through African organizations. Administrative, technical, and educational talent must be drawn from diverse races and nationalities, under auspices which carry no hint of threat to the independence of the new countries.[18]

Outside Europe, other nations have also moved toward a higher capacity and willingness to assist in the development of less developed countries. Canada, Australia, and New

[18] For a suggestive exploration of these problems, see Guy Benveniste and William E. Moran, Jr., *African Development: A Test for International Cooperation* (Menlo Park, Calif.: International Industrial Development Center, Stanford Research Institute, 1960).

Zealand have been contributing for some time through the Colombo Plan in South and Southeast Asia. Japan, where the economy in the 1950's made a vigorous recovery from World War II and is now growing impressively, has provided reparations of developmental type in the Philippines, Indonesia, Burma, and Vietnam, and in the last few years has undertaken a number of projects in technical assistance and provision of equipment, while also encouraging Japanese investment activities in developing countries. Israel, which has a high level of technical talent, is engaged in technical cooperation with countries such as Burma and Ghana.

Growth in Developmental Experience and Institutions

A trend of no mean importance which will make the development situation in the 1960's considerably different from that of the 1950's is the steady accumulation of practical experience in promoting development and the maturing of developmental institutions, national and international.

By now, the great majority of the underdeveloped countries have more or less systematic plans for fostering development. Generally, there is a special government agency responsible for making plans and appraising results. Special development financing institutions, such as development banks and agricultural or industrial banks, have been established in many countries. Numbers of educational and training institutions have come into existence, though not nearly enough to meet the developmental needs. Agricultural extension services, community development organizations, industrial advisory services, modernized business enterprises, research institutions, and many other parts of the institutional framework needed for moving a country ahead have been established in less developed parts of the world in recent years. The initial mistakes and flounderings to be expected in such radical new departures have already been lived through in some countries, though probably not yet in most. However, the first-hand experience with developmental concepts, problems, and institutions and the practical familiarity with the workings of the new developmental agencies are very much more widespread than they were even five years ago.

The United States development aid program has added some institutional innovations, two of the most significant being the Development Loan Fund and the increasing use of food surpluses for development purposes under Public Law 480 and the Mutual Security legislation. The experience with technical and economic assistance in the 1950's and critical appraisals of it inside and outside the government prepared the way for the reorganization and the new approaches to policy which the Kennedy administration is establishing in 1961.

Among the international institutions for aiding development, the World Bank has grown to a membership of sixty-eight nations. Its commitments exceed $5,000 million in fifty-four different countries. Asia and the Middle East, taken together, are now receiving the largest share of the loans. Whereas ten years ago, even five years ago, the Bank drew its funds largely from the United States and Canada, today its securities have been established in half a dozen other money markets and are held by investors in forty different countries.

Two new institutions affiliated with the World Bank have added to the scope and flexibility of its operations. The International Finance Corporation, set up in 1956, furthers economic development by investment in productive private enterprises in association with private capital and management, without government guarantees. The International Development Association, established in 1960, is designed to provide capital assistance to less developed countries through loans on more flexible terms than the World Bank.

The United Nations Expanded Program of Technical Assistance, initiated in 1950 at the suggestion of the United States following President Truman's "Point Four" speech, had established a firm place for itself by the end of the decade. Rightly characterized by a committee of appraisal as "the outstanding development in international economic and social action since the formation of the United Nations," this Expanded Program has made available more than 8,000 experts, technicians, and training personnel to the less developed countries since 1950, and more than 14,000 fellowships, mostly for study and training abroad. The United States contribution, which at the outset was 60 percent of an annual budget of about $20 million, is currently 40 percent of an annual budget of about $32 million. The main problem is shortage of funds. It has not been possible to keep pace with the mounting number of well-conceived and high-priority requests for technical assistance from member countries.

On January 1, 1959, the United Nations Special Fund came into existence, with Paul G. Hoffman, who had administered the Marshall Plan, as its first Managing Director. The Fund concentrates on "pre-investment" work, especially by supporting surveys and feasibility studies to reveal wealth-producing potentialities, applied research to find new uses for local materials and products, and manpower training and technical education to develop the human resources of underdeveloped countries. By December 1960 it had allocated $96 million in Special Fund resources for 115 projects in more than 50 countries and territories. The total value of these projects, including funds of the governments being assisted, amounted to $227 million.[19] The Special Fund itself does not usually engage in field operations, but subcontracts the execution of projects to the United Nations and certain of its specialized agencies. It is also empowered to contract for the services of other agencies, private firms, or individual experts. If the Special Fund attracts more support, it could prove to be the most important institutional innovation of recent years in the development field. Not the least of its merits may be the leverage it offers for achieving much-needed coordination in the development assistance activities of the United Nations and its family of specialized agencies.

Regionally, the economic commissions of the United Nations established in Latin America, Asia and the Far East, Europe, and most recently in Africa are performing increasingly important roles as centers for studies and reports, coordination, and exchange of experience with respect to development problems common to countries in their parts of the world. The Colombo Plan has made a useful place for itself as a loose arrangement for partial regional coordination of bilateral development aid in South and Southeast Asia. The Arab States in 1959 established the Arab Development

---

[19] *United Nations Review*, February 1961, p. 53.

Bank. Inter-American regional development cooperation may be entering a new and more active phase, built around the Organization of American States, the Inter-American Development Bank which began operations in 1960, the proposed common market groupings, and the new social and economic programs for which the United States is indicating that it will offer increased leadership and funds.

Advances in the Art and Science of Development

Along with the growth of experience and institutions, the social technology of development—meaning techniques of planning economic and social advance, of stimulating and guiding economic and social change, and of supplying and using outside assistance—progressed steadily in the fifties. For example, planners learned to be considerably more realistic in setting targets and in relating policies to the targets. Current development plans are less likely to be mere exercises on paper and more likely to be serious action programs. Practical experience has accumulated and understanding has grown with respect to the delicate problems of fostering dynamic balance between rates of change of output in different sectors of economic activity—agriculture and industry, consumer goods and capital goods, exports and imports. There has been a rapid spread of statistical measurement in relation to various aspects of development, facilitated by sampling techniques which represent an important economy of effort. While statistical information in the less developed countries still leaves much to be desired, their policy-makers and international assistance personnel are able to appraise current trends and diagnose favorable and unfavorable developments considerably more quickly and accurately than before.

The well-known techniques of agricultural extension have continued to be adapted and improved for use in new situations, and have been broadened into a significant new approach to rural modernization known as community development. In turn, experiments are now under way in the adaptation of these rural community development techniques to cope with urban community problems as people flock to the cities in the newly developing countries. Extension techniques have also been adapted to the problem of modernizing small-scale industry. In India, the government has pioneered since 1954, with aid from the Ford Foundation, in a nationwide network of Small Industries Service Institutes and Industrial Extension Centers to provide small industrial entrepreneurs, or would-be entrepreneurs, with technical advice, economic information, marketing aids, help in obtaining financing, and suitable factory premises in industrial estates.

Researchers in the social sciences have turned their attention increasingly to the problems of newly developing countries. One evidence is the rapid rise in the number of relevant doctoral dissertations, especially in economics, but also in cultural anthropology, sociology, social psychology, and political science. The understanding of economic growth processes and of related social and political processes is certainly on a more solid scientific basis today than it was a decade ago. Yet, having said this, it must be recognized that we are still abysmally ignorant by comparison with what we need to know in order to guide development more successfully and by comparison with the better factual and theoretical knowledge that we could reasonably expect to achieve were research to be supported in this field with just a little of the sense of urgency that nations devote to research for better bombs and missiles.

On the broad theory and practice of economic development, a number of useful treatises have appeared, also many textbooks.[20] The collection and analysis of solid quantitative data about historical instances of economic growth and cross-sectional comparisons of economies at different levels of development are providing a better foundation for scientific understanding.[21] A fruitful new analytical concept of the last few years is the notion of "take-off" into self-sustained growth; associated with it is analysis of the pre-conditions of self-sustained growth and a suggestive analytical framework for

[20] Among the treatises, one of the earliest and still one of the best, combining as it does acute scientific analysis with practical sagacity and good writing, is W. Arthur Lewis, *The Theory of Economic Growth* (Homewood, Ill.: Irwin, 1955).

[21] See, for example, the notable studies by Simon Kuznets, published in several issues of *Economic Development and Cultural Change;* also his *Six Lectures on Economic Growth* (Glencoe, Ill., 1959).

viewing the several stages of growth.[22] Careful historical studies of development in particular countries have helped our general understanding of development processes and problems.[23] Fruitful new points of view have been thrown into the scientific discussion by many thinkers working actively to understand the development process and to draw policy implications.[24] The technical basis for development "programming"—that is, determining investment targets that are mutually consistent and optimize use of resources—is being advanced to new levels of sophistication.[25]

What may be the creative frontiers in the 1960's for scientific advance in understanding development processes? Surely one will be the cultural, motivational, and communications aspects of development, where much fruitful activity has recently been evident.[26] Also, political science, which until recently has been strongly culture-bound, is at last showing signs of producing concepts and tools of analysis that will enlarge our scientific understanding of the political systems and the problems of political change found in newly developing countries, including the systems of tribal and traditional societies.[27]

[22] See W. W. Rostow, "The Take-off into Self-sustained Growth," *Economic Journal*, March 1956, and *The Stages of Economic Growth* (Cambridge, 1960).

[23] Outstanding is William W. Lockwood, *The Economic Development of Japan* (Princeton: Princeton University Press, 1954).

[24] As examples, see Ragnar Nurkse, *Problems of Capital Formation in Underdeveloped Countries* (New York, 1953); Gunnar Myrdal, *Rich Lands and Poor* (New York, 1957); and Albert O. Hirschman, *The Strategy of Economic Development* (New Haven, 1958).

[25] Cf. the widespread use today of the input-output or interindustry techniques pioneered by W. Leontief of Harvard; the experiments of the UN Economic Commission for Latin America in development programming; the studies of Jan Tinbergen at the Netherlands Economic Institute, Hollis B. Chenery at Stanford, and others on investment criteria and quantitative methods for applying them.

[26] For example, Daniel Lerner with Lucile W. Pevsner, *The Passing of Traditional Society: Modernizing the Middle East* (Glencoe, Ill.: Free Press, 1958); the Center for International Studies, M.I.T., "The Transitional Process," Part I of *Economic, Social, and Political Change in the Underdeveloped Countries and Its Implications for United States Policy,* Study no. 12 for the Senate Committee on Foreign Relations, in *United States Foreign Policy,* 86th Cong., 2d sess. (Washington: GPO, 1960); David C. McClelland, *The Achieving Society* (Princeton: Van Nostrand, 1961).

[27] For an encouraging example of this new interest, see *The Politics of the Developing Areas,* edited by Gabriel Almond and James S. Coleman (Princeton: Princeton University Press, 1960).

A very important frontier for scientific study and also for social invention related to development will be—or at any rate ought to be—the overlapping areas between education and the processes of economic, social, and political development. One aspect which has begun to receive considerable attention is manpower planning and manpower development. Another is the criteria by which to make intelligent decisions on the allocation of funds and personnel among the different levels and types of educational activities, from primary schools to universities and adult education. Still another is the subject matter that should be learned and taught in different cultural environments at different stages of a country's development. Imaginative experimental research is greatly needed on educational organization and teaching techniques adapted to the needs and conditions of newly developing countries with very low incomes.

Population Growth

Trends in population growth have turned even more sharply upward since Chapter 14 (Population Problems) was written, and the importance of the points it makes have been underlined by new studies.

"Never in the history of mankind," says a 1958 analysis by the United Nations, "have numbers of the human species multiplied as rapidly as in the present century." From 1,000 million in 1850, world population attained 2,500 million in the hundred years to 1950, and projections (using medium assumptions) indicate growth in the following fifty years to more than 6,000 million by the year 2000.[28] Each quarter-century, each decade, is showing not only a larger increase but a higher *rate* of increase. The underdeveloped regions are experiencing the most rapid population growth. Their population is expected to triple in the last half of this century while the population of the technologically more developed regions grows by some 73 percent. Whereas the underdeveloped countries have today about two-thirds of the world's population, by the end of the century, on the most plausible

[28] United Nations, Department of Economic and Social Affairs, *The Future Growth of World Population* (New York: Author, 1958), p. 21.

assumptions about the future course of birth and death rates, these same countries will have more than three-fourths.

Population growth rates of two and even three percent annually are common now in Latin America, the Middle East, Africa, and Asia as the result of rapidly falling death rates while birth rates remain at or near the high levels formerly needed to maintain the societies. This makes the problem of raising real income per person considerably more difficult. A growth of four percent annually in national output represents only two percent gain in per capita output when population is growing at two percent, and only a one percent gain if the population increase is three percent. Finding the capital to equip present numbers of people with the modern tools and education that they need so as to increase their productivity and attain higher living standards is hard enough; the task becomes almost a labor of Sisyphus when large annual investments in houses, food production, textile factories, vehicles, power, schools, health centers, and other things are required merely to keep up with population growth. There is grave danger that much of economic growth will be absorbed in an increase in the *quantity* of people without substantial betterment in the *quality* of living.

The case of India was cited in the first edition of this book (p. 275). India's population was "thought to be growing at something over 1 percent a year," but the rate was likely to "zoom upward" with improvements in health measures and food production. Census data released in 1961 showed a population of 438 million, higher than anyone had predicted, indicating a growth rate in the 1950's of more than 2 percent a year. If growth continues at this rate (the rate will go higher still, unless unexpectedly effective countermeasures are taken) there will be a net increase during the 1960's of 100 million people. This means that within a decade India will have to feed, clothe, and outfit with tools and houses and schools more *additional* people than half the present population of the United States! India's development planners are seriously concerned. They are proposing to spend five times as much (about $52 million) on "family planning" in the Third Five Year Plan, beginning in 1961, as in previous plans. At least one Indian state (Maharashtra) is offering free sterilization operations and cash compensation for loss of working time.[29] Meanwhile, the successes in death control continue to out-distance those in birth control, partly because much greater efforts and funds are available. For example, the United States agreed in 1960 to give India $10 million more to help eradicate malaria, bringing such U.S. aid to India in the seven years of the antimalaria campaign to $94 million. "The campaign has slashed the annual malaria death toll in India from 800,000 to fewer than 10,000. About 4,000,000 cases of malaria were reported last year, compared with 75,000,000 in 1953." [30]

The explosive growth of population released by modern health measures and by economic improvement is a grave danger to success in development. But there are several factors on the hopeful side. One is the dramatic result of a program started by the Japanese in 1949 for lowering the birth rate in their country. From 33.7 births per 1,000 population in 1948, the rate had fallen to 18.0 by 1958. Another is continued progress toward radically improved techniques of birth con-trol, particularly an oral contraceptive. But even after the attainment of an ideal contraceptive—safe, harmless, easy to use, and cheap—the psychological, sociological, and communi-cations problems involved in educating millions of semiliter-ate people to planned parenthood will remain. These are, in fact, going to be the crucial problems.[31]

The bearing of population growth and population control on the outlook for economic development is better under-stood and more widely appreciated today than it was a few years ago.[32] It has been seriously suggested that in some densely populated, low-income countries threatened by a burst of population growth the yield on investment in social

[29] *New York Times,* November 4, 1960.

[30] *New York Times,* November 3, 1960.

[31] For a review of scientific research on new methods of contraception and for a discussion of the costs and social problems in bringing the results into use on a large scale, see Richard L. Meier, *Modern Science and the Human Fertility Problem* (New York: Wiley, 1959).

[32] A solid study which has contributed to this understanding is Ansley J. Coale and Edgar M. Hoover, *Population Growth and Economic Development in Low-Income Countries: A Case Study of India's Prospects* (Princeton: Princeton University Press, 1958).

measures designed to bring lower birth rates would be considerably higher, in terms of future advances in living levels, than could be had by an investment of corresponding amounts in traditional development projects such as irrigation, transportation, or industry.[33]

On problems of population control, most of the initiative should come from the countries directly concerned. Initiative by the United States and other Western countries would be too easily misinterpreted. But, in the words of the Draper Committee's recommendation to the President of the United States, our government should "(1) assist those countries with which it is cooperating in economic aid programs, on request, in the formulation of their plans designed to deal with the problem of rapid population growth, (2) increase its assistance to local programs relating to maternal and child welfare in recognition of the immediate problem created by rapid population growth, and (3) strongly support studies and appropriate research. . . ." [34]

Weapons and the Changed World Environment

Finally, to all these trends directly related to development we must add one very important change in the world environment. Every well-informed person knows about it, but few have thus far faced up to its implications.

This is the drastic increase in the range and destructive power of weapons, which has changed the nature of war. Henceforth the use of maximum force by modern nations against each other means mutual annihilation, or near to it. No nation, no matter how well armed, can any longer assure physical security for its own citizens by military means. The United States, the Soviet Union, and other nations can achieve security only through some world system which will protect all of them by preventing war. Such a world system implies a far more radical internationalism than most of us have ever before been willing to contemplate. It will surely

[33] Stephen Enke, "The Gains to India from Population Control: Some Money Measures and Incentive Schemes," *Review of Economics and Statistics,* May 1960, pp. 175-181.

[34] The President's Committee to Study the United States Military Assistance Program, *Composite Report* (Washington: GPO, 1959), Vol. I, pp. 96-97.

require, for example, some type of world policing to insure observance of arms controls and to forestall aggression.

This will be impossible unless there is a radical change in attitudes throughout most of the world. It will require recognition of the common interest in strengthening the world community and a rise in the sense of loyalty to the world community so sudden—if it is to be achieved before the delicate balance of terror collapses—that it will be a political miracle. Yet, in view of the alternatives, we have to strive to produce this political miracle.

Survival depends on how rapidly men can adjust their thinking and their loyalties to the new situation created by modern science. That we live in "one world" is now irrefutably a fact. But the recognition of this fact and the necessary adjustment of political attitudes, especially the transfer to the world community of a substantial portion of the emotional attachments which peoples now feel toward national communities, are still far from attainment. Here is where the idea of world cooperation in development may perhaps, if imaginatively pursued, make a great contribution to the security as well as the economic and social advancement of mankind. A world-wide struggle against poverty offers one potentially unifying objective. It is not only a good thing in itself, but it can and should be used as an occasion for building world loyalties, institutions, and habits of cooperation. The rising political influence of new nations, especially in the United Nations, will give this objective a continually more powerful appeal. It may be that a world program for aiding underdeveloped countries offers one of the few hopes for diverting civilization from its trend toward suicide.

Chapter 20

UNITED STATES POLICY PROBLEMS
AND PUBLIC OPINION

The "Point Four" program was launched in 1949, and its initial momentum carried over for several years into the 1950's. The rest of the decade witnessed a deterioration in the breadth of view, sense of purpose, and generosity of spirit of the official United States approach to the problems of under-developed countries. This in turn contributed to a loss of initiative. The positive values of international cooperation to bring the benefits of modern technology to peoples struggling to emerge from poverty continued to be affirmed by United States spokesmen. But these values were more and more over-laid and masked by domestic appeals based on short-range national security and anti-Communism.

Looking back, we can see that the Korean war marked a turning point. The Marshall Plan had concentrated on eco-nomic objectives, though the motives behind it were, of course, broadly political. Similarly, the "Point Four" idea and its early implementation focused on the need for develop-ment. Military assistance, where required, was at first pro-vided through other, special programs. Following the Com-munist attack in Korea, and as the cold war intensified and became chronic, development aid, military aid, and in-between types of economic aid justified as "defense support" were combined for presentation to Congress in a "Mutual Security" program. The dominant arguments employed to loosen Congressional purse strings for this mixed bag of mili-tary and developmental assistance became more concerned with resisting the military and political strength of Com-munism, less concerned with a "bold new program" for making the benefits of scientific and industrial progress available to the peoples of underdeveloped areas.

Compounding this tendency was a change in political outlook, especially on the relation of government to economic life and social welfare, which came with the change of administration in 1953. On the whole, the Republican party is more hesitant than the Democratic about government intervention in economic and social affairs and less inclined to tax the rich to aid the poor—though the difference between the two parties is no doubt less than the difference between progressives and conservatives within each party. From May 1955 to September 1957 the International Cooperation Administration was headed by a member of the conservative wing of the Republican party who obviously had little enthusiasm for the program he was officially running, believed that he should act in terms of a narrow type of national self-interest, and proclaimed rather rigid views, which were disturbing to independent leaders abroad, about the types of internal economic activity American aid should foster. One effect was a let-down in morale within the agency. This repelled imaginative and dedicated talent and thereby contributed to administrative deficiencies which weakened the standing of the program with Congress and the public.

Later there was considerable recovery from this low point, evidence of searching for good new approaches, and willingness to innovate. But for an idea like world development to catch fire, it is essential to have exceptionally strong Presidential leadership, and this was not forthcoming during the Eisenhower administration. At this writing, the Kennedy administration is formulating its approach to world development issues, and it remains to be seen how Congress and the public will respond.

Leading Issues of Development Policy

In the last few years much more discussion has taken place in the United States than ever before about the problems of underdeveloped countries and about policies and methods for assisting their development. This in itself constitutes an important trend. There is a ferment of new ideas, a searching for constructive new approaches. Some excellent raw materials that will help the shaping of policy have been produced in the form of official and unofficial studies and reports.[1] A reformulation of purposes, a re-evaluation of methods, and a new enunciation of American policy are due. Here are some of the issues that the Executive, the Congress, and the public will have to face:

A Positive Purpose for Development Aid? Experience in the 1950's suggests that to look upon development aid mainly from the defensive viewpoint of checking Communism and to present it in these terms is self-defeating. Necessary as it is to build bulwarks against Communist pressures, aggressions, and subversions, the situation requires, and the world has a right to expect of the most powerful country and the most advanced economy, a purpose more positive than this. Aside from reacting to Communist moves, what do *we* propose? Can we accentuate the positive, regain the initiative? Will our leaders be able to convince the American people (and the world) that we want to help less developed countries build up their productive powers, incomes, education, health, national freedoms, and individual freedoms because we feel that this kind of human progress is worth while in itself, and because in this interdependent age we can achieve the kind of world we want to live in only by cooperating with other peoples for the attainment of common aspirations?

Social Reform and Development? How far should we go in making our influence felt on the side of progressive reforms and "social justice" in countries receiving developmental aid? The issue is partly one of efficient use of aid, for some of the traditional patterns of economic, social, and political life may, if unchanged, bar a country from achieving self-sustaining economic growth. Inappropriate reforms, or improperly timed reforms, may also retard the development process. The issue involves, too, the reputation of the United States: Are we for the people or for the privileged groups? How, without

[1] Some especially interesting items (which are listed in the bibliography) are the book by Millikan and Rostow; the studies prepared under the direction of the Senate's Special Committee to Study the Foreign Aid Program (1957); the studies prepared for the Senate Foreign Relations Committee (1959 and 1960), particularly no. 12 by the Center for International Studies, M.I.T.; and the report on private investment by Ralph I. Straus.

intervening objectionably in domestic affairs, can we contrive
to make our influence felt on the side of popular aspirations?
We can let it be apparent that we quickly and gladly assist
regimes that are striving to correct social situations which produce a few rich and many poor, also that we are hesitant and
reluctant about assisting repressive regimes, even though they
claim anti-Communism and "stability" as a basis for our
favor. We can take a positive attitude, in appropriate situations, toward land reform and improvement of the status and
opportunities of less privileged rural groups, along with development of rural productivity; toward spread of education;
toward social gains like better housing for low-income groups;
toward progressive tax systems which divert income from
conspicuous consumption to national development; toward
recognition of trade unions and development of responsible
trade union leadership and collective bargaining as industry
rises; and, of course, toward all the standard measures to introduce modern science and technology and stimulate economic growth. The instinct of some of our conservatives may
be to side with those in other countries who stand on the
status quo. But the wise conservative in this era of rapid
change is the progressive conservative. Not social reform, but
the absence of it leads to revolutionary outbreaks. Reforms
which scandalized many conservatives of the day and still
annoy some—universal suffrage, free public education, progressive income tax, trade unions, social security—along with
the rapid increase in productivity based on new science and
technology and better management, were the effective anti-
dotes against revolutionary Marxism in the West during the
late nineteenth and early twentieth centuries. (See pp. 102–
109 of this book.)

Continuity and Scale of Aid? The world's underdeveloped
countries pose not a temporary problem but a long-term one.
Their development will be a vital issue at least for several
decades. This is increasingly being recognized by policy-
makers in the executive branch and in Congress, and ways are
being sought to plan United States aid in longer-term perspective and to assure more continuity of support than is provided by annual authorizations and appropriations. Furthermore, the dimensions of the world development problem are

huge, though not unmanageable in terms of the resources potentially available if the will is found to bring them to bear. Will our government (and the governments of other economically advanced countries) find it politically feasible to propose, and will the people support, the comparatively massive and long-continued effort that the world situation requires?

Development Aid Separate from Military Aid? Is it good policy to lump developmental and military assistance together as "foreign aid"? Would it not be wiser to distinguish the two rather carefully in thought and action? Of course, defense and development supplement each other. In countries under active Communist attack by guerrillas and subversion the two must be closely integrated. But it is important that in the nonaligned countries American interest in development be presented as an interest in the growth of strong, independent, prosperous, and free nations and that it not be associated with military alliance-building or pressures to take sides in the cold war.

Bilateral or Multilateral Emphasis? Should our developmental aid be primarily a United States program, or should we seek to internationalize it and to channel it so far as feasible through United Nations agencies? Reasons will be given below for moving toward the latter policy. However, bilateral as well as multilateral methods will continue to be necessary. But bilateral aid can and should increasingly be coordinated under a multilateral umbrella, through systematic consultation and reporting centered in United Nations and regional agencies.

International Investment—Public and/or Private? What of the respective roles of public, intergovernmental capital (grants and loans) on the one hand and of private international investment on the other in fostering development of underdeveloped countries? The well-informed view today is that both are needed, the desirable and feasible combination varying from case to case in accordance with a country's situation and its stage of development. Hopes were expressed by American officials some years ago that private investment could soon take over the job of supplying the international capital needs of underdeveloped countries. This is now seen to be illusory, especially as concerns the least developed countries. International private investment can effectively assist growth in economies that have reached or passed through the take-off; it is not very effective in bringing economies to this stage. Also, in many situations where the political reasons for assisting development are strong the investment climate is not attractive to private capital, except possibly in oil or other extractive export industries which can operate independently of local markets (and often without giving much impetus to the domestic economy). In the least developed and in politically unstable countries, therefore, reliance must be placed mainly on international public funds for the outside capital required to bring the country to the stage in which growing markets, better education and administration, and an improved general outlook for security and progress will enable private capital to function constructively. In countries that have reached this stage, much can and should be done by the local development authorities, and by the United States and other countries in cooperation with them, to encourage a more substantial inflow of private investment, particularly of types that help to introduce new techniques of production and management.

Attitude toward the Public and Private Sectors in Developing Economies? Should it be part of the purpose of United States aid to promote in newly developing countries a pattern of "private enterprise" much like our own? Should we oppose and try to discourage "socialist" tendencies? If so, we will find ourselves running head-on into widely and strongly held views in many newly developing countries where "socialism" is a term more or less equated with "social progress," including many ideas that we also believe in without calling them socialism (for example, educational opportunities for all). We had better steer around such semantic difficulties by talking positively about concrete economic and social advances that are clearly desirable, apart from ideology. The choice in a number of underdeveloped countries is not between free enterprise and socialism, but between a democratic type of socialism and the Communist variety. Furthermore, as informed opinion now recognizes, the role of the state in fostering the rapid transformation of stagnant, underdeveloped economies into growing ones is necessarily more active and comprehensive than the role we find appropriate in our own advanced economy. The pressure to produce quick results in newly developing countries creates situations analogous to those of wartime, in the sense that drastic shifts in production and a multitude of correlated changes have to be brought about in a short time. In wartime even the United States found it essential for the government to build plants and undertake direct economic controls. In a number of countries, state initiative exerted to get a stagnant, traditional economy off dead center, through a large-scale public investment program as well as in other ways, has proved to be more of a stimulant than a handicap to the private sector. Experience around the world demonstrates that systems of widely differing types with different degrees of public and private activity can produce economic growth. One of the strengths of democratic philosophy is that it can tolerate diversity, and we should not forgo this advantage.[2]

Attitude Regarding Forms of Government? Granted that it should be part of our policy to encourage the growth of genuine democracy by our aid to newly developing countries, how flexible should our thinking be in adjusting this broad aim to the specific situations of countries where the requisites for modern representative institutions—for example, universal education and an efficient communications network—do not yet exist? Experience suggests that the attempt to engraft the forms of representative democracy as known in the highly developed countries of the West may in some situations have the paradoxical effect of impeding democratic development. The result may be to create confusion and to strengthen privileged groups which can manipulate the system so as to block needed reforms. The problem of political development is as complex and difficult as that of economic

[2] "Nor does it make sense in terms of the security interests of the West to let it appear that competition with Communism means that the West, like the Communists, wants to use aid to impose some particular kind of economic or political system on the underdeveloped countries. The West should stress the *diversity* of its political and economic institutions for it is this diversity which, more than anything, sets Western ways apart from Communist." Eugene R. Black, *The Diplomacy of Economic Development,* William L. Clayton Lectures at the Fletcher School of Law and Diplomacy (Cambridge: Harvard University Press, 1960), p. 47.

development and deserves much more thoughtful attention than it has received thus far.

Export Markets—Will We Provide Earning Opportunities for Newly Developing Countries? Much of Communist bloc "aid," as noted earlier, is really trade bargains in which development goods and services are paid for by agreed shipments of commodities from the newly developing country. This form of assistance, though not a gift and not necessarily involving even a long-term loan, can none the less be very helpful. In effect, it offers opportunities for the newly developing country to earn its own way by producing export goods to pay for the imports it needs in development. This is good psychologically, and it helps meet employment problems that plague so many newly developing countries. The non-Communist world, with its "unplanned," free (or comparatively free) international market, offers in the aggregate much larger opportunities for exports of newly developing countries than the Communist countries. But these opportunities are uncertain, not very predictable in terms of quantities that will be taken or prices, and there is vigorous competition which new exporters, especially, find it hard to meet. Must we not find ways to assure newly developing countries that they can reasonably count on an expanding market for their exports, so that they have an incentive to work hard at exportable production and thus acquire ability to pay for most of their own development needs? Development loans will ultimately prove unsound unless the export possibilities of the assisted countries expand. It appears from recent studies [3] that the rise in world demand for the primary products of newly developing countries is not sufficiently rapid to enable them to earn the foreign exchange required for development merely by increased exports of such products. The United States and other advanced economies must face the issue of adjusting their internal production and foreign trade to accommodate new kinds of imports from the developing countries, including manufactured products, particularly labor-intensive types in which these countries will have a

[3] GATT, *International Trade 1959* (Geneva: Author, 1960), and earlier reports; United Nations, *World Economic Survey 1958,* 59.II.C.1 (New York: Author, 1959), Chapter 1, and same for 1959, Chapter 5.

comparative advantage. At the same time, we must face the issue of inventing and applying better methods to smooth out the more violent fluctuations in the export markets for the primary products of developing countries. It is in our interest and theirs that as soon as possible they should be in a position to earn rather than have to beg the development funds they need.

Public Opinion

It is apparent that policy issues facing the United States in the 1960's with respect to underdeveloped countries are going to make exceptional demands for farsightedness and generosity. Will public opinion rally to the kinds of action, including the contribution of funds, that would be dictated by wisdom and full knowledge of the facts?

When one reflects, it is no obvious and easy thing the American people have to be asked to do: to pay taxes to help develop far-off nations whose dominant ideas may depart widely from our own popular views on the best politico-economic arrangements, whose products may one day compete with ours, and whose leaders sometimes proclaim rather stridently their criticisms of our actions and their nonalignment in the power struggle which engages so much of our energies. It is remarkable, in fact, that our democracy has been capable of the degree of farsightedness it has shown, and friends in underdeveloped countries should not underrate this achievement.

Public opinion studies on attitudes in the United States toward aid programs reveal one fact of salient importance. Attitudes depend more on the level of understanding and information than on any other factor. Those voters with most understanding and information are most favorable to aid programs.[4] This is encouraging, for it suggests that the American people are likely to respond to leadership that helps them to acquire an accurate picture of the world situation.

A Roper opinion poll in 1958 asked a nationwide sample of voters: "In regard to the underdeveloped nations of Asia and Africa, which of these statements comes closest to ex-

[4] This conclusion was stated in the first edition of this book and remains valid, as do the other observations about public opinion on page 34.

pressing what you think our country should do at the present
time?" The results, by educational level, were: [5]

	Grade School or Less	High School (percent)	College
We need to expand our program of aid and loans to Asian and African countries	11	17	28
We should keep our aid and loans to Africa and Asia at about the present level	36	44	46
We should cut back our aid and loans to Asia and Africa	27	21	16
Express no opinion	26	18	10

Of those who had attended college, 74 percent were for continuing aid at the same level or increasing it, but this was
true of only 47 percent of persons with no more than a grade
school education. A Gallup poll in 1955 obtained similar results on this question: "Under the Marshall Plan, we sent
aid to the non-Communist countries of Europe. Do you now
think it would be a good idea or a poor idea to send such aid
to non-Communist countries in Asia?" [6]

	Grade School	High School (percent)	College
Good idea	48	58	67
Poor idea	30	26	22
No opinion	22	16	11

The margin of support among those who had attended college was 3 to 1, among those who had attended grade school
about 5 to 3. A 1957 Gallup poll on a related issue (Should
Congress appropriate about the same amount as in previous

[5] Elmo Roper and Associates, "The Public Pulse," National Newspaper
Syndicate release of April 19, 1958.

[6] George Gallup, Director, American Institute of Public Opinion, Press
Release of March 4, 1955.

years to aid other countries and help prevent their going Communistic?) showed closely similar results.[7]

In 1958 Dr. Gallup's pollsters asked respondents two information questions: whether they had heard or read about the foreign aid bill then being considered by Congress, and whether they could name approximately the amount the President had asked the Congress to appropriate. Using these simple tests of amount of information, they found that responses to the question, "In general, how do you feel about foreign aid?" broke down as follows: [8]

	Uninformed	Partially Informed (percent)	Well Informed
For foreign aid	46	56	62
Against foreign aid	31	34	32
No opinion	23	10	6

An interesting sidelight is provided by a laboratory test run by the American Institute of Public Opinion in 1957. A "selected group of voters" (size and representativeness not indicated) recorded their reactions to a television speech by President Eisenhower in which he took to the public the administration's case against threatened Congressional cuts in the foreign aid appropriation. An electronic device registered a minute-by-minute profile of the audience's level of approval. The test "revealed that the President made his most convincing bid for public support of his foreign aid program when he told listeners that helping poorer countries reflected 'our own national character' and that we must not lose our 'sense of kinship with all free men.' " [9]

Response to Leadership

Public opinion in a free society is mostly a *latent* force. It is not able by itself to conceive and carry through a course

[7] Release of January 11, 1957.

[8] Release of March 30, 1958.

[9] George Gallup, Director, American Institute of Public Opinion, "Estimated 34 Million Voters Reached by Ike in Foreign Aid Plea," Special Release, May, 1957.

of action. But it will crystallize behind a program that is carefully worked out and effectively presented. Time after time in recent decades, American opinion has responded remarkably to support bold leadership in plans of action that would have seemed unacceptable a little earlier.

The role of leadership was stressed by James Reston of the *New York Times* in a discussion of "National Purpose." He illustrated by the Marshall Plan. When the Marshall Plan was devised in Washington the sickness of the European economy was creating a crisis of great magnitude. The bare bones of a four-year program costing perhaps as much as $20 billion were worked out and approved by President Truman. Reston printed a story about it one Sunday in the *New York Times,* "and by 10 o'clock that morning, the late Senator Arthur H. Vandenberg of Michigan, then Chairman of the Foreign Relations Committee, called me at home and said: 'You must be out of your senses. No administration would dare to come to the Senate with a proposal like that.' Yet once the lead was taken and the need documented, Senator Vandenberg ended up as a key supporter of what almost everybody agrees was the most far-sighted piece of legislation since the war." [10]

Secretary of State George C. Marshall broached the idea that led to the Marshall Plan in a brief talk at the Harvard commencement in 1947. The subsequent development of opinion is so significant and so indicative of the role of the public, the Congress, and the Executive in rising to the challenge of a novel world situation that it is rewarding to consider it further. The following analysis is by H. Schuyler Foster, Chief of the Public Studies Division, U. S. Department of State: [11]

Secretary Marshall's proposal was immediately received with sympathy by a number of editors and columnists, who realized that some program of U. S. aid to our war-torn European allies

---

[10] "Our History Suggests a Remedy," in *The National Purpose* by John K. Jessup and others (New York: Holt, 1960), pp. 113-114.

[11] "American Public Opinion and U. S. Foreign Policy," address before the Middletown University Club at Middletown, Connecticut, in *Department of State Bulletin,* November 30, 1959, pp. 798-799; reprinted as Department of State Publication 6925, January 1960.

was essential; but the Marshall Plan did not immediately commend itself to a majority of the general public, according to nationwide public opinion polls. More Americans in the summer of 1947 were unsympathetic to the idea than applauded it. Certainly it is not surprising that this brand-new idea in the world—that our country should give (or lend) $4 billion or $5 billion a year to other countries—should not be instantly recognized by a majority of our people as in the best interest of the United States.

The Gallup poll threw further light on the public opinion situation of that time by pointing out that Marshall's proposal was regarded as a good idea by two out of three of those sampled who had attended college, but by only one out of three of those whose education stopped in grammar school. The other two-thirds of this less educated group were not all opposed to Secretary Marshall's idea—many of them gave no opinion; but the opponents were numerous enough to outweigh the approval from the college-educated in the nationwide poll.

What should a government leader do when a policy which he believes vitally important to the interests of this country is not approved by a majority of the American public? You remember what General Marshall did. With the backing of President Truman, he took the issue up in the normal manner under our system of democratic government. He laid his plan before the appropriate committees of Senate and House; he was followed, in further public hearings, by his aides, who explained in fuller detail the plan which was destined to produce a remarkably rapid European recovery.

The explanations and discussions before the committees were faithfully reported and discussed in the press, on the radio, and thus in local communities throughout the country. By the following spring, when Congress enacted the European Recovery Program, this plan had the support of the great majority of newspapers and commentators, of numerous outstanding national organizations, and also of a substantial majority of the general public—including a majority of those having only a grammar school education. What is more, this nationwide discussion of 11 years ago was so thorough and pervasive that it has provided a firm foundation for popular support of later large-scale programs of economic aid intended for other areas and justified for other purposes.

The fact that American opinion rallied to the Marshall Plan (and before that to Lend-Lease) does not guarantee, of course, that it will respond in the same way to the different circumstances and needs of today respecting underdeveloped countries. But similar principles would seem to apply. Political leadership must gauge the real necessities of the world situation, then bring clearly and forcefully to the attention of the American people a well-considered program of action. This program must be patiently explained and debated. The public must be given the information to understand it. Such a program, as the experience of the Marshall Plan shows, may go beyond the immediate willingness of the general public to accept. But when the situation is explained and the relevance of the proposed measures is persuasively shown, the American public is capable of intelligent and generous response. Behind the facade of the "big, obvious, clattering America of Hollywood and Madison Avenue and Washington," as James Reston says, there is a quieter, more genuine America where there is real concern for the outside world, interest in its problems, generosity, and resourcefulness.

Chapter 21

FUNDAMENTAL RETHINKING OF
UNITED STATES POLICY

The political leader, even when he seeks to lead rather than follow public opinion, must limit his proposals to what can be made politically acceptable within the very near future. The scholar or the writer on world affairs has somewhat more latitude. He can afford to go further beyond the immediately acceptable, and it is part of his job to do so—to help create the climate of opinion, the latent response to leadership, which the political leader can then crystallize into support of concrete measures.

For this reason, I have resolved not to be overly concerned with immediate feasibility in the pages that follow. The question, "Will Congress or the public agree to this at the present time?" will deliberately be subordinated to the question, "Is this the right thing, the wise course, the direction in which Congress and the public should be advised to turn their thinking?" Some of the positions advocated may be ahead not only of public opinion in general but even of the informed opinion of today. They may, however, have a chance of being acceptable in five years, if opinion leaders prepare the way. In these days when political realities are changing with unexpected rapidity (note the too-cautious forecast about the liquidation of colonialism mentioned earlier), what seems visionary at the moment may turn out soon to be realistically apparent to all.

Needed: A Big Idea

"I do not myself think it is wishful thinking," wrote Walter Lippmann in 1959, "to believe that Congress and the people, who are now bored with foreign aid . . . would respond much more readily if it were inspired by a big idea, rather than by small and calculating notions of how to score points in a contest." [1]

Any philosophy in which "stop Communism" is the central theme is too negative. Even if judged by the test of effectiveness in countering the inroads of Communism in the newly developing countries it is unlikely to be as successful as a policy that focuses on positive economic and social advance.

Lippmann himself suggests the principle "that rich nations in the world community, like rich individuals in their own community, have a duty to help the poor raise themselves out of poverty." But is this not too paternalistic for a statement of major purpose? It smacks a bit of the squire in the manor house.

The promotion of economic growth, more or less as an end in itself, is also inadequate to provide a sound core of philosophy for development aid. As this book is concerned to point out, economic growth is a *necessary* but not a *sufficient* condition for the results we really want. Economic growth can provide the means for internal oppression and external aggression, as well as for better living, larger freedom, and peaceful international cooperation. Much depends on how the growth comes about and on the world political environment in which it takes place. It follows that a philosophy of development aid ought to emphasize not only increase of economic output but also the political and social context, including the channels through which international aid is provided.

A philosophy of "free world" development is too limited.[2]

[1] *New York Herald Tribune,* January 29, 1959.

[2] In my view, we should drop the term "free world" and talk instead about *promoting freedom in the world*. When we mean the non-Communist world, or states allied with us, or the North Atlantic nations, or nations that practice representative democracy and civil liberties (these are not identical groups), let us use the accurate term.

It is unfortunately not true that the battle for all the major types of freedom has been successfully completed in all the non-Communist countries, or even in our own country. To imply that all non-Communist countries are "free" has undesirable effects on dissident groups struggling against dictators or against feudal or other conditions of unfreedom. Successful leaders of such

The major problem of our time is to prevent the schism in civilization between Communists and non-Communists from bringing down the whole of civilization. The only way for either side to "win" in the struggle called the cold war is some day to supersede it, to have it lapse. Granted, we face today the problem of strengthening the defenses of the non-Communist world against the demonstrated readiness of the Communist bloc to expand by any means, including military force and internal subversion. But our concern for immediate defense can and should be supplemented by a concern for longer-range construction, looking toward a more viable world order. Our policy job is to create the conditions under which there is a chance of moving from the hostile co-existence world of today to at least a peaceful coexistence world, and perhaps ultimately a cooperative world community, without exposing ourselves or others to conquest or annihilation in the transitional stages. This, it will be argued below, requires on our side a philosophy of cooperation in world development that is not exclusive to any bloc but is open-ended. We should stand ready to take development out of the cold war, to separate it from competitive power politics.

A New Philosophy of Cooperation for World Development

The philosophy of development aid to be expounded here focuses on the task of building a viable world community. This means aiding the less developed countries to increase

---

struggles may well react: "The oppressive regime that we have overthrown was classified by the United States as part of the 'free world'; so we had better get out of such a phony 'free world.'"

Furthermore, the strict dichotomy implied by "free world" tends to harden the division between the two "worlds," and this could work against freedom in a situation where the best hope may be gradual penetration of freedom into Communist societies rather than dramatic transfers from one world to another. We should candidly recognize that advances in some aspects of freedom have occurred under Communism—for example, more opportunities for education and health, and more freedom for women. There are variations within Communist countries in the degree of restriction on thought and expression. Some loosening has occurred in the Soviet Union since the days of Stalin. Is it not our cue to encourage such loosening, also to seek further growth of freedom in the non-Communist countries, not overlooking our own country where racial problems still demand attention? Such an attitude is better expressed by "promoting freedom in the world" than by the "free world" slogan.

their productive power, enhance their freedom, and advance their social well-being, *and doing so in ways that encourage a sense of world community and increase the effectiveness of world institutions.*

The events of the 1950's have immensely strengthened the case for a world community approach to the problems of the underdeveloped countries. My own views have shifted further toward this way of thinking, though I am glad to see on rereading Chapter 3 that eight years ago I was groping in the same direction.

Modern science and technology, including new social technology, have made it feasible to extend the benefits of civilization to all mankind, not just to a privileged elite in a few countries. At the same time, new techniques of mass destruction have rendered war suicidal for mankind. Yet where is the political basis for a world system capable of preventing war and fostering cooperation? Is it going to be possible to develop loyalties and emotions attached to the idea of the world community, without which notions of a peaceful world order are bound to remain in the realm of idle dreams and paper constitutions? We should bring to this problem of enlarging the range of human loyalties as much creative imagination and hard work as has gone into enlarging the range of missiles.

International cooperation in development is probably the most effective instrument available today for promoting the growth of the sense of world community. In view of the world-wide eagerness for development and the still largely untapped capabilities of the technologically and economically advanced countries for assisting this development, the world is faced with a magnificent opportunity and challenge. Development, conceived as a unifying project of the world community, not only could raise the living levels of those two-thirds of the world's inhabitants who have thus far benefited rather little from modern science and technology, but could do so in ways that increase our desperately low odds of avoiding mutual destruction. On the other hand, mere economic growth of the newly developing countries without strengthening the world community—as would be the case in an atmosphere of nationalistic measures and power-bloc assistance—would probably increase our dangers.

Such a philosophy of world development should, I suggest, at least supplement and preferably replace the narrower interpretations of national interest which we now employ in thinking about policy toward underdeveloped areas. Our problem as Americans, citizens of a leading state in a world menaced by disintegration, is in some respects like that of certain eminent Virginians, Pennsylvanians, and New Yorkers who saw the need for "a more perfect union" of our original thirteen states. The threat today is more dire and the problem more difficult, but one principle is the same: the principle that the interests of the whole of an interdependent community must be given priority over the sectional interests of its parts, otherwise even the sectional interests will be lost. Another chapter in American history is also instructive for us today; that is the controversy over "internal improvements." Was it right that, through the Union, resources should be drawn from the more highly developed states of the East to build roads and canals in the newly developing states of the West? Henry Clay argued that the Union possessed the power "to execute such internal improvements as are called for by the good of the whole. . . . a wise and considerate government should anticipate and prevent, rather than wait for, the operation of causes of discontent." We must learn to think of developments needed for the good of the whole world community, not as "foreign" aid, but as the "internal" improvements of an age when the world has become an interdependent, though divided and quarrelsome, community.

This philosophy of world community development implies a fundamental change in the foreign policy creed of our nation and of other nations. In the words of Eugene Rabinowitch, editor of the *Bulletin of the Atomic Scientists,* "This creed has always been . . . that the purpose of foreign policy of any nation is the *furthering of its national interests.* . . . Now, the American people have begun to recognize, albeit dimly, that in the atomic age, our most important national interests . . . are unattainable except in the context of an increasing world security, and of an economic progress for all mankind. The concept of national security based on national military power . . . has become obsolete; and that of national prosperity based on utilization of world-wide natural resources, without regard to the well-being of the rest of the world, is obsolescent. . . . *The only proper aim of foreign policy in the atomic age is the furthering of the interests of mankind.*" [3]

This may sound idealistic, visionary. Perhaps it is, in terms of acceptability at the moment. But it is stark realism in terms of the requirements of a world situation that all too few among our leaders of opinion correctly evaluate. It will be argued below, especially for the benefit of those who feel that realistic foreign policy thinking must revolve around the Communist threat, that this broader approach in terms of the interests of mankind and the building of a viable world community provides the best platform from which to deal with that threat.

Mutuality and Multilateralism

Our aims in cooperating for world development should be equally concerned with fostering the economic, social, and political advancement of the less developed countries and with doing so in ways that strengthen the sense of world community. The two aspects will not usually be inconsistent. Greater emphasis should be put on mutuality and multi-lateralism in development efforts, both because this is the best way to get the development job done and because doing the development job this way builds the sense of world community and lays the basis for the stronger world order without which economic and technological advancement could bring mankind to disaster rather than well-being.

The arguments for multilateralism in development aid have often been stated in the last few years and are well known. Most newly developing nations prefer aid through multilateral organizations (especially United Nations agencies) in which they participate and in which they have a voice in setting broad policy. This is more compatible with national dignity and self-respect than bilateral aid. It is less likely to arouse resentment against donor attitudes which

[3] *Bulletin of the Atomic Scientists,* September 1960, p. 259. Italics in original.

can readily be felt as patronizing. It inspires less fear that "strings" impairing a country's independence will be attached, or that aid will be used as a means of pressure on behalf of foreign political or economic interests. United Nations aid is not tied to the commercial advantage of any country or group of countries, does not come from any single race or creed, and does not carry pressures to line up with one side in the cold war.

From the standpoint of the United States and other countries that are suppliers of developmental aid, multilateral methods have important advantages. They enable the burden of contributions to be shared more widely. In view of the need to plan for a substantial increase in the total amount of international aid during the sixties, it is desirable to tap every source of support, while increasing our own support. Multilateral programs have a wider range of choice than bilateral programs in recruiting experts for technical assistance, also in training and other facilities. Experts and training facilities can even be provided by some of the underdeveloped countries, with advantages in some cases because they come from a background not so far removed from conditions in the countries being helped. Multilateral agencies, having no national diplomatic axes to grind, are in a better position to insist on adequate effort and performance by the aid-receiving countries as a condition of aid. The onus of saying "no" bilaterally can give pause to the diplomats of a donor country, particularly in a situation where there is competition among donors for the political influence thought to go with aid.

This is not to say that multilateral, United Nations aid programs have no drawbacks and problems. On the contrary, there are many. Among them are the logrolling that takes place in international supervisory bodies, the necessity for geographical spread in staffing that may put unsuitable persons in responsible positions, the jurisdictional jealousies that seem to develop at least as much among international as among national administrative agencies, and the inefficiencies and misunderstandings that can arise in a staff drawn from a variety of language, legal, cultural, and administrative backgrounds. On the whole, however, the advantages mentioned earlier outweigh the drawbacks, even now. Especially because of the nonpolitical nature of development aid through United Nations agencies, because agencies in which the recipients participate can take a tougher line and insist on higher standards of self-help than can bilateral donors, and because of the wider recruiting range, the average aid dollar spent through United Nations agencies probably buys more in developmental accomplishment than the average aid dollar spent through the United States bilateral program. Such a judgment, admittedly tenuous, is based not only on my own casual observation but also on discussion with an able administrator who has had an important role first in U. S. bilateral and then in United Nations aid activities. It must be one of our aims to develop and improve the capabilities of international organizations still further. This can be done only by giving them more responsibility and more adequate resources with which to do their tasks.

Mutuality—that is, responsible participation in the policy-making process both by countries receiving and by countries supplying aid—is an essential feature of true multilateralism. As the Secretary General of the United Nations, Mr. Dag Hammarskjöld, said on his return from a visit to Africa:

"For these countries, it is infinitely easier to receive financial assistance and technical assistance . . . through an international body than on a bilateral basis, and it is infinitely easier for them to receive it through an international body of which they are members. That is to say, internationalization of aid is not achieved by switching from the system of one country giving another country aid to a system where one group of countries gives the country aid. The bilateral character is then maintained. It is not until and unless the receiving country feels that this is an act of solidarity within an organization where they have equal rights with the donors that you really reach the optimum point not only psychologically, but politically and economically." [4]

Mutuality connotes a spirit of partnership and requires flexibility of mind, particularly tolerance of diversity in development patterns. Americans must not expect their own

[4] Quoted by C. V. Narasimhan, "A New Approach to International Cooperation," *International Development Review,* May 1960, p. 12.

preconceptions of the best ways of economic, social, and political advancement always to prevail, though in a climate of mutuality friendly advice will have a better chance of being accepted. The important thing is to achieve a world community system capable of maintaining a framework of stability within which each nation can pursue its own well-being according to its own preferences, so long as it does not threaten others.

Building United Nations Capabilities

For all these reasons, we should have a strong bias in favor of rendering assistance to newly developing nations through multilateral organizations in which they are represented. Wherever possible we should channel our aid through United Nations organizations. *For it is just as important to use development aid as an instrument for strengthening the institutions which are necessary for a viable world community as it is to achieve economic growth.*

At present, however, there are rather severe limitations on the extent to which it is feasible to channel aid through the United Nations.

First, it would be a mistake to damage the multinational character of the United Nations program by allowing too large a proportion of its support to come from one country. Whether the present 40 percent ratio of U. S. contributions might safely go somewhat higher is a matter of political judgment, but obviously contributions from the rest of the world must rise if the United States is to contribute substantially more.

Second, if bilateral programs were to be suspended entirely in favor of aid through the United Nations the effect would undoubtedly be to reduce the total amount of international assistance for underdeveloped countries, which is undesirable. Historical ties, regional traditions, political interests, and cultural affinities will often impel one country to aid another bilaterally or within the context of some special group (like the Colombo Plan, or the OECD, or the OAS, or the British or French ex-colonies, or the Communist bloc's Council for Mutual Economic Aid) to a greater extent than the country would be willing to contribute for similar purposes through a general United Nations program. However, ways should be sought to coordinate bilateral and special group aid with the United Nations effort, bringing such aid more and more within the multilateral framework and rendering it so far as possible multilateral in spirit, even though not in form.

Third, there is perhaps some danger of placing a heavier administrative and political load on United Nations agencies at a given moment than they can successfully carry; we do not want to court failures that would discredit the world system. But one of the important ways of building up United Nations capabilities is to provide more resources than the relatively meager ones now available to the United Nations.[5]

Development Goals

An adequate philosophy of development must include in its goals economic advancement toward higher living levels, social advancement toward modern concepts of social justice, and political advancement toward greater national freedom and personal freedom and responsible exercise of these freedoms.

On the economic side, what is required is not that the rich countries should agree to support the poor ones, but rather to assist them to build up their own wealth-producing capacities. The reasonable and necessary goal of a world

[5] Besides larger contributions from member states, ways must be sought to provide the United Nations with independent sources of revenue. One practical approach would be to give the United Nations exclusive authority to tax certain new sources of wealth which are being opened by advances in science and technology and which are not now within the jurisdiction of national states. Among these are ocean resources, polar resources, and space communications and traffic rights. It is highly probable that it will soon be feasible to drill for oil through the bottom of the ocean, on the high seas. Ways are likely to be found to recover the mineral-bearing nodules that litter extensive areas of the ocean bottom and to harvest ocean plankton or other potentially valuable constituents of the seas. Now that systematic exploration of polar regions is feasible, mineral resources may be found there. The use of orbiting satellites for relaying telephonic and TV signals and for other purposes will probably come to have considerable monetary value; these activities ought to be regulated and taxed by the United Nations. Such potential sources of wealth would yield little revenue at present, and national states would find it relatively painless to cede these tax possibilities to the United Nations. But over the decades ahead, the revenue from these sources could become quite important.

development program is to help as many countries as possible to attain within the next decade or so to the condition that economists describe as self-sustaining economic growth. A country having reached this stage is able to provide through its own efforts (including its capacity to borrow and trade in the international markets) for continued economic progress. In order that a poverty-stricken and undynamic economy may become self-propelling in this sense, internal changes are required in motivations, habits, and institutions, along with considerable investments in transportation, communications, schools, and other modernizing services. External capital and know-how to provide an "assisted take-off" can be extremely helpful at this stage. However, aid from the world community cannot be offered on a promise to *accomplish* the take-off, but only to assist the country's own efforts, for the most significant elements in achieving self-sustaining economic growth are internal leadership and the will to bring about the necessary changes.

The basic aims of development must include social advance as well as the growth of national income. In many of the underdeveloped countries land reforms will have to be carried out before modern ideas of democracy and social justice can become firmly rooted. Better opportunities for education, improved health, community development, improved working conditions, a more respected status for labor, and a rise in the status of women are among the many other social aspirations of modern-minded people in the emerging countries which will have importance in their development goals. There are many social problems that are likely to come with modernization, among them rapid growth of population as death rates decline while birth rates remain at traditional levels, rapid and largely unguided urbanization, and the problems associated with factory-type production and a proletarianized labor force. If the unhappy social aspects of early industrialism in the West are not to be repeated on a larger scale, steps must be taken in time to achieve a better integration of economic and social development.

As for political development, a minimum goal of a world community program must surely be to help newly independent countries to make their independence workable. The supply, on request, of temporary administrative and technical personnel, the training of local personnel for administration, and the facilitation of observation trips and study abroad to encourage the growth of the needed political leadership are practical measures which will be wanted and appreciated in many countries. Open discussion in world assemblies concerning the ideals of democratic government and personal freedom which are now under challenge from the Communist countries and from some other dictatorial regimes are desirable. Finally, a major political aim of a world development program should be to build a sense of common values and common loyalties in the world community, so as to help provide the underpinning for a world order that can prevent war.

It may be said that a world development program that looks beyond economic growth to stress social and political development as well represents unwarranted interference in the internal affairs of nations. There is, of course, a delicate line between outside help and unwarranted interference, whether in multilateral or bilateral relations. But is it not a sound position to be ready to supply the maximum effective help to those countries (considerable in number and importance) where the local leadership is such that they want and request help in achieving widely agreed social and political goals? Second, is it not wise to promote open discussions in world assemblies and in conferences, educational undertakings, and by other means of communication in order to explore for further areas of agreement on such goals?

World Community Development and U. S. National Interests

United States foreign policy must proceed, in the present world situation, at two levels simultaneously. One is the *defensive* level. We must build up power, jointly with our allies, to deter or resist attacks, threats, or pressures. Since it is the Communist bloc which threatens our safety today, policy at this defensive level is mainly anti-Communist. The military component of "foreign aid" functions entirely at this defensive level. Some of our economic assistance to other countries is also for the purpose of strengthening important defense positions (Korea, Taiwan).

All that a successful policy at the defensive level can do is give us time to try to accomplish something more positive. At the second or *constructive* level of American foreign policy our purpose must be to create a more viable world order—one in which we and other peoples can feel less menaced by war, and in which modern science and technology can be utilized for human well-being. International cooperation to assist world-wide economic, social, and political development is the most effective instrument available to the United States for practical pursuit of its long-range interests at this constructive level. Such developmental cooperation will be most effective in furthering our true interests, as argued above, when it is organized on a basis of mutuality and multilateralism, through United Nations agencies so far as feasible.

Laws and appropriations in support of world development programs have to be voted by national legislatures. The U. S. Congress, in considering the terms and amounts of United States contributions, will increasingly take into account, it is to be hoped, the broad reasons already sketched. But there will also be a demand, when spending the American taxpayer's dollar, for justifications couched in terms of "national interest." While the calculus of national interest, if narrowly applied, can lead us astray, a broad view of the national interest is consistent with the principle urged above that an approach to world development which looks first to the interests of all mankind is the wisest and most effective approach in the interest of the United States. The analysis presented in Chapter 2, "The Viewpoint of the United States," takes such a view of American national interest, and its arguments need not be repeated here. The United States continues to have, with respect to world development: (1) *general political interests*—"What kind of world do we want to live in?"; (2) *special political interests*—the most urgent being the need to keep before the peoples of the world workable alternatives to Communism; (3) *economic interests*—gains in productivity to be anticipated from wider trade, investment, and raw materials accessibility, and also from more rapid scientific and technological progress as latent human talent now smothered by lack of opportunity is given new scope in underdeveloped countries; [6] and (4) *humanitarian interests*—a concern for people.

World Community Development and Relations with the Communist Bloc

The challenge of Communism in the newly developing countries has two aspects.

First, and most important, is the danger that failure to make visible headway in the dynamic development demanded by new popular aspirations will lead to frustration, turmoil, and a desperate turn to the Communist system as a way of getting things done. This would mean the repetition in country after country of something like the experience of China in the decades before Communist take-over. Our policy problem in this connection is to do everything we can to foster successful development, and our principal means are the various forms of international development aid. From this standpoint, the fact that the Soviet Union is willing to build a steel mill in India and factories in Ghana can even be helpful—provided there are truly no political strings attached and the operations do not become screens for interference in internal affairs or pressures on foreign policy. It is, of course, very much in the interest of the newly developing countries themselves to avoid such traps, and most of them are extremely wary of infringements on their jealously guarded independence.

Second, there is the danger that Communist bloc members will successfully use inducements, pressures, and maneuvers—some of them linked with technical and economic assistance—to build up political influence and sympathy for the Communist cause and thus to infiltrate and subvert the underdeveloped countries. This is what is usually meant in discussions of the Communist bloc's "aid offensive." The threat is real, most particularly where there are also internal pressures associated with a failure to develop, and in new nations with leadership inexperienced in Communist tactics. But

[6] See pp. 60–61 on this "greatest untapped resource in the world."

here again, it is the interest of independence-loving nations to be vigilant on their own behalf, and the leaders of many of these nations are rather skillful at separating economic aid from political infiltration. Our cue is to *keep the alternatives open* so that these leaders, under the pressure of inexorable demands for development, are not forced to risk political interference for the sake of development aid.

Communist bloc assistance to non-Communist countries is likely to increase still further. The United States will have a choice of alternative policies. One policy would be to oppose such assistance by making competing offers of our own, by exerting various pressures to discourage acceptance of Communist bloc aid, and by seeking, so far as feasible, to align the newly developing countries with us and our allies. There would be serious difficulties in such a policy. It would impair our relationships with newly developing countries, jealous as they are of their freedom of action. The policy would probably prove ineffective, for many of these countries, in their eagerness to speed up economic growth, would surely continue to accept aid from the Communist side as well as our side. And a tendency to match Communist bloc offers of assistance with counteroffers would encourage ill-conceived projects and prove both expensive and wasteful.

A much more promising alternative is to oppose to Communist-oriented aid, not simply American-oriented aid or Western-oriented aid, but greatly stepped-up aid under United Nations and other multilateral auspices in which there is participation of recipient and donor countries. We would urge the Soviet Union and its allies to join with us in taking the struggle against world poverty out of cold war politics, by drastically shifting the flow both of Soviet and United States aid into multilateral channels related to the United Nations. If this were done, the nations receiving aid would be insulated from the power-politics pressures of either side. If the Soviet Union and its allies refused to cooperate in a world community system of development where the newly developing countries themselves have a strong voice in policy-making, they would be advertising to the world that they seek to impose their own system. In so doing, they would come into conflict not merely with the

United States or the West, but with most of the non-Communist world. They would be swimming against the powerful tide of Asian–African–Latin American aspirations.

In other words, the best way to meet the Communist threat is not to seek to line up the newly developing nations with us in a fight against Communism, but to ally ourselves with them in a world community struggle against poverty, disease, ignorance, and oppression wherever found. We should urge that the Soviet Union and its allies, along with ourselves and our allies, contribute more substantially to this struggle, through United Nations channels that would to some degree filter out self-seeking pressures from the contributing nations or power blocs.

In view of Soviet statements about the speed with which their production is overtaking United States production, we should mobilize pressure of world opinion behind an invitation to them to join in greatly increasing the development funds of the United Nations and related agencies. Why not propose to double our development contribution to the United Nations and urge them to match our contribution *in whatever proportion they estimate that their economy bears to ours?*

How about Communist China? Should a philosophy of world community development extend to this large, underdeveloped but rapidly developing segment of the Communist bloc? The answer, it seems to me, is conditional. If the Soviet Union and the other countries of the bloc which are in a position to be substantial donors of development aid make their full proportionate contribution to the United Nations, and if Communist China, on admission to the United Nations, accepts the obligations and standards of the Charter, then there would be every reason for providing it with United Nations developmental assistance on the same terms regarding proper use as apply to other members. Likewise, Chinese contributions should be sought for assistance through the United Nations to other countries. One of the major problems of the years ahead will be for the world community somehow to moderate the bellicose and despotic behavior of the regime in charge of this portion of the human race. Surely contact and communication and endeavors to find a few common grounds for cooperation are more likely to help in this than exclusion, though there will be enormous difficulties.

Turning again to the Soviet Union, one common interest of the United States and the U.S.S.R. is survival. Possibly there may also be common ground in cooperation to meet human need by aiding the less developed countries to make better use of modern science and technology. Both great powers have an urgent interest, if they can only perceive it, in using their present primacy, which will not last forever, to create a viable world community, so that the diffusion of technological, military, and political power to new countries can proceed peacefully, rather than with the traditional accompaniment of a series of wars.

Implementing a World Development Program

A world development program to meet the challenges of our time must deal with many problems. Among them, five deserve special comment.

1. Commitment to Long-term Purpose. The first problem is to bring the United States and other leading nations to accept a clear, continuing commitment to cooperation in world development. Realism requires that we recognize the need for continuity of effort over several decades.

For the decade of the sixties, the economic target suggested by Paul G. Hoffman, Managing Director of the United Nations Special Fund, is eminently suitable—high enough to require dedicated effort, but not so high as to be unattainable. The target he proposes, as mentioned earlier, is to double the average annual rate of growth of per capita income in underdeveloped countries, making it two percent during the 1960's.

Besides economic growth targets, other goals should be set in terms as concrete as possible for such fields as education, health, population control, the position of women and of underprivileged groups, rural and urban community development, effective planning of urban growth, and training of administrative and managerial personnel.

2. Better Coordination in World Development Aid. There

is no lack of institutions engaged in international development aid. At this stage what we need is not more agencies but larger resources, administrative improvement, and better coordination among agencies that exist.

Especially we need to strengthen the United Nations instrumentalities, greatly increase their funds, and move toward a situation in which a central United Nations institution would orchestrate the many varieties of international aid available to the developing countries. For this purpose it is desirable to create a World Development Authority within the United Nations system, perhaps by expanding the UN Special Fund. The World Development Authority would have four main functions:

(1) It would help governments, on request, to formulate development programs, or would help them to find needed technical assistance for this purpose.

(2) It would administer a fund to share with newly developing countries the cost of pre-investment projects such as resource surveys, training institutes, applied research, and the like, so as to prepare the way for productive inflow of capital. It might also administer a fund for grants and subsidized loans to help provide public facilities and services that would not, at least initially, produce recoverable revenues and therefore could not meet banking standards, but that are essential in order to bring an economy to the stage of self-sustaining growth (schools, communications facilities, agricultural and industrial extension services, urban improvements, irrigation, and the like). Or this type of developmental investment might be handled by a related agency, perhaps an outgrowth of the new World Bank affiliate, the International Development Association, but with a greatly increased capitalization.

(3) It would help newly developing countries to obtain capital and technical assistance from other sources, including governmental and intergovernmental agencies and private investors. It would advise, on request, how to attract private international investment on terms mutually beneficial to the developing economy and the investors.

(4) It would act as a clearinghouse for information, a reporting center, and a center for development studies and

guidance with respect to all forms of international development aid and the progress of newly developing countries.

In order that such a World Development Authority be
firmly and efficiently administered, it must have a strong
executive, responsible on broad policies but not on detailed
administration to a board on which donor and recipient
countries would be represented. It would be necessary to
develop an expanded international civil service of high
quality. Steps would have to be taken to coordinate the activities of United Nations specialized agencies and other de-
velopment-assisting agencies more fully.[7]

3. Adequate International Funds for Development. Two
kinds of international capital flow are needed in increased
amounts in order to speed the development of underdeveloped countries. One consists of grants or loans on terms that
represent substantially less than normal returns to capital
and therefore include a considerable element of subsidy. International aid of this kind is particularly necessary for economies in the pre-take-off stage. It is needed to provide more
education and training, to improve health, to explore resources, and to assist in the difficult initial steps toward a
modern production system.

The second consists of fully repayable loans and investments. Such capital may be supplied through public or private financial institutions or by direct investment of business
enterprises in newly developing countries. Capital flow of
this type supplements local savings and speeds up development in countries where the foundation for development has
been laid and directly remunerative opportunities are appearing faster than they can be met. The loans and investments
help to expand power and transportation facilities, to exploit
mineral and other resources, and to build industrial and commercial activity.

These two kinds of capital shade into each other, of course.
To achieve the impetus in world development that we want,
capital must flow internationally in a wide variety of forms,

[7] For an able discussion by a most experienced international administrator,
see Commander Sir Robert G. A. Jackson, *The Case for an International
Development Authority* (Syracuse: Syracuse University Press, 1959). A valuable
introduction by Harlan Cleveland deals with the history of the idea of an
international development authority.

from straight grants to commercial-type investments, suited in each case to the very diverse situations of less developed countries with different problems and at different stages.

Has not the time arrived to seek a United Nations agreement by which each economically advanced country would undertake to make available at least one percent of its national income each year for capital flow (grants, long-term loans, and investments) to underdeveloped countries? Poorer countries should be asked to obligate themselves to give and lend a smaller percentage of national income, ranging down to token contributions by the least developed countries. Each should contribute something, to establish the principle of a joint, world community effort. Half of the agreed quota should consist of nonrepayable contributions, either through United Nations development agencies or through other multilateral or bilateral channels, for use in *bona fide* development programs in underdeveloped countries, details to be reported to the United Nations. The other half could be made available as repayable long-term loans or investments. Credit would be taken for the net amount of new private investment made by the nationals of the assisting country in underdeveloped countries for purposes considered by the receiving country and by the United Nations to have a constructive, developmental character. The balance would be made up by loans of public funds, either through multilateral lending institutions like the World Bank or national agencies like the United States Export-Import Bank and the Development Loan Fund.

An annual flow of one percent of the national income of the economically advanced countries (say those with per capita national incomes above $600 a year) would amount to $8 billion or more. Under the arrangement suggested, half of this sum would be available for expenses of international technical assistance or as grants (perhaps in combination with loans) to assist countries in laying a basis for self-generating development. The other half would comprise loans and investments, for use in underdeveloped countries where there is shortage of capital but ability to repay.

4. Stimulation of International Private Investment and Trade. Private investment cannot do the initial job of get-

ting the least developed countries out of their rut of tradi-
tionalism and preparing the way for modern economic growth
—or at least it is unlikely to do so quickly enough. The political and economic uncertainties at this stage are too great,
and the essential investments in education, administrative
organizations, pre-investment surveys and the like are not of
the types directly remunerative to private capital. But private
investment from outside can be a powerful aid to the further
development of countries where the processes of economic
growth have started and the prerequisites are present. There
is a strong trend toward recognition of this fact in underdeveloped countries (outside the Communist sphere). In
India, Burma, and Ceylon, for example, the early post-inde-
pendence fears that outside capital might be a subtle means
of re-establishing foreign domination are less intense, and
positive efforts are being made to attract desirable types of
investment for the constructive help they can give in attaining the host country's development objectives.

The time would seem to be ripe for working out an international charter and code of behavior for private international investors and host governments, so as to stimulate more
effective utilization of international private capital and enterprise. Reference is made in this connection to the discussion
on pages 235–239 and especially to certain ideas mentioned
on page 238: the building up of a system of *international*
supervision and protection of boundary-crossing investments;
an international commercial court; a United Nations consular service to gather and publish impartial commercial and
investment information for the encouragement of trade and
investment; and provision for international incorporation of
business enterprises in certain circumstances, so that it would
be possible to denationalize some kinds of international capital movement while preserving their private business character.

United States leadership is needed also in opening world-
wide markets to the exports of newly developing countries,
so that they will be able to earn by their own efforts as much
as possible of the developmental capital they need, and so
that they will be able to pay interest and amortization on
borrowed capital. The United States and other highly de-

veloped countries should plan to import an increasing flow of the labor-intensive types of manufactured products from the newly industrializing countries. And we must be more cooperative and inventive than we have been in the past about finding ways to mitigate the more extreme impacts on the export earnings of newly developing countries from fluctuations in the markets for primary products.

5. *Peaceful Mobilization of Education and Research.* Knowledge is the most potent of all resources for improving the economic lot of mankind. It is a most peculiar resource, in that it can be added to one region without subtracting it from any other. Indeed, the more widespread knowledge becomes, the more rapidly it grows. For it increases by being applied under new circumstances and by the cross-fertilization of ideas passing back and forth among many minds.

Transfers of knowledge are involved, of course, in most types of technical assistance. But international cooperation for development has underemphasized in the past the two powerful tools of economic and social progress represented by education and research.

A massive program for building up or strengthening educational systems and training teachers should receive high priority in a world development effort. Each country should be encouraged to prepare a long-range development plan embodying not only a capital budget but also a manpower budget. The latter is usually neglected. However, balancing the requirements and the supply of trained manpower is no less important to successful development than the financial balance. International cooperation can appropriately be requested for expanding educational and training facilities to meet the most urgent skill deficits revealed by such planning.

Educational assistance is particularly needed by the new nations of Africa. Such assistance, whether in Africa or elsewhere, should preferably be rendered under arrangements supervised by regional or other agencies related to the United Nations, to prevent educational aid from becoming an instrument of power politics or of political or cultural domination.

Research, meaning fundamental quests for scientific knowledge and also applications of such knowledge in solving practical problems, is being more and more consciously used as a tool of progress in the highly developed countries. Huge sums are nowadays allocated for research designed to solve problems in military defense, industry, agriculture, public health, and other fields. It has recently been estimated that both the United States and the Soviet Union are spending something like two percent of their national incomes on research and related development of new products and processes.[8] Until now, however, relatively little research has been oriented toward the special problems of the newly developing countries. The great majority of the world's scientists and technologists are in the highly developed countries. Their work is oriented, more or less automatically, toward the kinds of knowledge and the kinds of solutions to problems that seem most important in their environment. For example, the research done on temperate zone agriculture is enormously out of proportion to that done on tropical agriculture, because the countries that have the research personnel and facilities are located in the temperate zones. The underdeveloped countries, however, are mostly in or near the tropics. Again, research designed to improve production techniques in the highly developed countries is especially concerned with labor saving. In the underdeveloped countries, by contrast, capital is the relatively scarce factor and a higher priority should go to research on capital-saving techniques.[9]

To be sure, underdeveloped countries can draw upon the world pool of scientific and technological knowledge. But very often effective tapping of this knowledge requires additional research, of an adaptive sort, to meet the peculiarities of soil or climate or consumer tastes or cultural traditions or habits in the newly developing country. Thus, the hybrid corn of Iowa was not suitable for Mexico, and Rockefeller

[8] *Increasing the Effectiveness of Western Science* (Brussels: Fondation Universitaire, 1960), report of an international study group convened as a result of discussions in the Science Committee of the North Atlantic Treaty Organization.

[9] See the discussion of research needs and a proposed program in Eugene Staley and David C. Fulton, *Scientific Research and Progress in Newly Developing Countries* (Menlo Park, Calif.: Stanford Research Institute, 1961).

Foundation specialists aided Mexico for years in local development of hybrids to meet Mexican conditions. Research on local materials, local industrial problems, local problems of social adjustment to technological change and to urban growth, local diseases or carriers of diseases affecting plants, animals, and man, and many other practical problems of economic and social development is needed in every newly developing country. Research should be expanded also on topics of importance to underdeveloped countries generally, chief among them, perhaps, the social processes involved in technological, economic, social, and political change and the methods best adapted to rational guidance of these processes.

There should be, therefore, as part of the world cooperative effort for development of underdeveloped countries, a greatly expanded program of scientific and technological research especially designed to meet the needs of these countries. Central in this program should be the establishment or strengthening in every underdeveloped region of research institutes concerned with development-oriented research. One could visualize a network of such establishments, and it would be a highly productive use of technical assistance funds to subsidize continuous interinstitutional cooperation between these research establishments in newly developing countries and appropriate institutions in the technologically advanced countries.

The Task of Leadership

There are two prime tasks of world affairs leadership today.

One is the stabilization of peace. The short-range aspect of this task is to prevent the tensions of our day from leading to a major war that would unleash cataclysmic weapons. The long-range problem is to build up the strength of the world community and world institutions so that nations can be freed from the constant menace of war and can turn science and technology instead to the betterment of man's life.

The other prime task is the central concern of this book: the economic, social, and political advancement of underdeveloped countries, representing two-thirds of mankind. This task is coequal in importance with the first, because of the human values directly involved, and because cooperation on this second task, if carried through with emphasis · on world community interests and with maximum use of United Nations agencies made stronger for the purpose, is one of the best ways to facilitate progress on the first task. It is a practical way to foster the sense of world community, the indispensable underpinning of political and emotional loyalty without which world institutions for stabilizing peace cannot be effective.

Can the political leadership of our time bring the people of our country and of other countries to perceive the true nature of the situation that confronts the human species, in such a way as to activate the best impulses and the intelligence of all of us? "Where there is no vision the people perish."

SELECTED BIBLIOGRAPHY

The following list contains a few of the many good studies of economic development that have been written in the last two decades; no attempt has been made to provide an exhaustive bibliography of the large and rapidly growing literature on this subject. The list is restricted to works in English and, for the most part, covers nonofficial and nonstatistical publications. Valuable surveys by the World Bank and the various economic commissions of the United Nations, for example, have been omitted, as have most of the publications of U. S. and foreign government agencies. References to these may be found in official indexes and in the source materials published quarterly in *Foreign Affairs*. For additional reading on economic development and related matters, see the bibliographies included in many of the works cited here or the bibliographies cited at the end of this list.

ADAMS, RICHARD N., and others. *Social Change in Latin America Today: Its Implications for United States Policy.* New York: Harper, for the Council on Foreign Relations, 1960. 353 p.

ALLEN, ROBERT L. *Soviet Economic Warfare.* Washington: Public Affairs Press, 1960. 293 p.

AMERICAN ASSEMBLY. *International Stability and Progress: United States Interests and Instruments.* New York: Graduate School of Business, Columbia University, 1957. "Competitive Coexistence and Economic Development in Asia," by Edward S. Mason, pp. 59–97; "American Aid and Economic Development: Some Critical Issues," by Thomas C. Schelling, pp. 121–169.

AMERICAN ECONOMIC ASSOCIATION. *Papers and Proceedings* of the Seventy-first Annual Meeting. May 1959. "The Role and Character of Foreign Aid," three papers by Harlan Cleveland, John H. Davis, and C. Tyler Wood. Pp. 203–241.

AUBREY, HENRY G. *Coexistence: Economic Challenge and Response.* Washington: National Planning Association, 1961. 340 p.

BENVENISTE, GUY, and WILLIAM E. MORAN, JR. *African Development: A Test for International Cooperation.* Menlo Park, Calif.: Stanford Research Institute, 1960. 170 p.

BERLINER, JOSEPH S. *Soviet Economic Aid.* New York: Praeger, for the Council on Foreign Relations, 1958. 232 p.

BLACK, EUGENE R. *The Diplomacy of Economic Development.* Cambridge: Harvard University Press, 1960. 74 p.

BOSKEY, SHIRLEY. *Problems and Practices of Development Banks,* published for the International Bank for Reconstruction and Development. Baltimore: Johns Hopkins Press, 1959. 201 p.

CLEVELAND, HARLAN. *See* American Economic Association.

——, GERARD J. MANGONE, and JOHN C. ADAMS. *The Overseas Americans.* New York: McGraw-Hill, 1960. 316 p.

COMMITTEE FOR A NATIONAL TRADE POLICY. *Industrial Development Abroad—Threat or Opportunity?* Washington: Author, 1959. 19 p.

COMMITTEE FOR ECONOMIC DEVELOPMENT. *Economic Development Abroad and the Role of American Foreign Investment.* New York: Author, 1956. 37 p.

DAVIS, JOHN H. *See* American Economic Association.

ELLIS, HOWARD S., ed. *Economic Development for Latin America.* New York: St. Martin's Press, 1961. 479 p.

GALENSON, WALTER, ed. *Labor and Economic Development.* New York: Wiley, 1959. 304 p.

GRAY, GORDON. *See* U. S. President.

HABERLER, GOTTFRIED. *International Trade and Economic Development.* Cairo: National Bank of Egypt, 1959. 36 p.

——, ROBERTO DE O. CAMPOS, JAMES MEADE, and JAN TINBERGEN. *Trends in International Trade.* Geneva: General Agreement on Tariffs and Trade, 1958. 138 p.

HANCE, WILLIAM A. *African Economic Development.* New York: Harper, for the Council on Foreign Relations, 1958. 307 p.

HIGGINS, BENJAMIN. *Economic Development: Principles, Problems, and Policies.* New York: Norton, 1959. 803 p.

HILGERDT, FOLKE. *Industrialization and Foreign Trade.* 1945. II.A.10. Princeton: League of Nations, 1945. 171 p.

HIRSCHMAN, ALBERT O. *The Strategy of Economic Development.* New Haven: Yale University Press, 1958. 217 p.

HOSELITZ, BERT F. *Sociological Aspects of Economic Growth.* Glencoe, Ill.: Free Press, 1960. 250 p.

——, ed. *The Progress of Underdeveloped Areas.* University of Chicago Press, 1952.

——, ed. *Theories of Economic Growth.* Glencoe, Ill.: Free Press, 1960. 344 p.

JACKSON, SIR ROBERT G. A. *The Case for an International Development Authority.* Syracuse University Press, 1959. 70 p.

JOHNSTON, ERIC. *See* U. S. International Development Advisory Board.

KERR, CLARK, J. T. DUNLOP, F. C. HARBISON, and C. A. MYERS. *Industrialism and Industrial Man: The Problems of Labor and Management in Economic Growth*. Cambridge: Harvard University Press, 1960. 331 p.

KUZNETS, SIMON S. *Six Lectures on Economic Growth*. Glencoe, Ill.: Free Press, 1959. 122 p.

LEE, DOUGLAS H. K. *Climate and Economic Development in the Tropics*. New York: Harper, for the Council on Foreign Relations, 1957. 182 p.

LEWIS, W. ARTHUR. *The Theory of Economic Growth*. Homewood, Ill.: Irwin, 1955. 453 p.

LISKA, GEORGE. *The New Statecraft: Foreign Aid in American Foreign Policy*. University of Chicago Press, 1960. 246 p.

MASON, EDWARD S. *Economic Planning in Underdeveloped Areas: Government and Business*. New York: Fordham University Press, 1958. 87 p.

——. *See also* American Assembly.

MEIER, G. M., and R. E. BALDWIN. *Economic Development: Theory, History, Policy*. New York: Wiley, 1957. 588 p.

MEIER, RICHARD L. *Science and Economic Development: New Patterns of Living*. Cambridge: Technology Press, M.I.T., 1956. 266 p.

MIKESELL, RAYMOND F. *Promoting United States Private Investment Abroad*. Washington: National Planning Association, 1957. 87 p.

MILLIKAN, MAX F., and W. W. ROSTOW. *A Proposal: Key to an Effective Foreign Policy*. New York: Harper, 1957. 170 p.

MOORE, WILBERT E. *Industrialization and Labor: Social Aspects of Economic Development*. Ithaca: Cornell University Press, 1951. 410 p.

——, and ARNOLD S. FELDMAN, eds. *Labor Commitment and Social Change in Developing Areas*. New York: Social Science Research Council, 1960. 378 p.

MYRDAL, GUNNAR. *An International Economy: Problems and Prospects*. New York: Harper, 1956. 381 p.

——. *Rich Lands and Poor: The Road to World Prosperity*. New York: Harper, 1957. 168 p. (Also published in England as *Economic Theory and Under-developed Regions*. London: Duckworth, 1957.)

NATIONAL BUREAU OF ECONOMIC RESEARCH. *Capital Formation and Economic Growth*. Princeton University Press, 1955. 677 p.

NATIONAL PLANNING ASSOCIATION. *Technical Cooperation in Latin America,* a series of case studies and reports for the Special

Policy Committee on Technical Cooperation, 1955–1957. Washington: National Planning Association; Chicago: University of Chicago Press.

———. *United States Business Performance Abroad,* a series of case studies on operations of U. S. firms in a number of countries: Sears, Roebuck (Mexico), W. R. Grace (Peru), Creole Petroleum (Venezuela), Firestone Tire & Rubber (Liberia), Standard-Vacuum Oil (Indonesia), United Fruit (Latin America), Trans World Airlines (Ethiopia), General Electric (Brazil). Washington: Author, 1953–1961.

NURKSE, RAGNAR. *Patterns of Trade and Development.* Stockholm: Almqvist and Wiksell, 1959. 62 p.

———. *Problems of Capital Formation in Underdeveloped Countries.* New York: Oxford University Press, 1953. 163 p.

PAPANEK, GUSTAV F. *Framing a Development Program. International Conciliation.* New York: Carnegie Endowment for International Peace, 1960. Pp. 307–372.

PENTONY, DEVERE E., ed. *The Underdeveloped Lands: A Dilemma of the International Economy.* San Francisco: Chandler, 1960. 196 p.

———. *United States Foreign Aid: Readings in the Problem Area of Wealth.* San Francisco: Chandler, 1960. 148 p.

ROCKEFELLER, NELSON. *See* U. S. International Development Advisory Board.

ROCKEFELLER BROTHERS FUND. *Prospect for America.* The Rockefeller Panel Report III, Pt. IV, "Special Problems of the Economic Development of Less Developed Countries." Garden City, N.Y.: Doubleday, 1961. Pp. 205–247.

ROSTOW, W. W. *The Stages of Economic Growth: A Non-Communist Manifesto.* Cambridge University Press, 1960. 178 p.

SCHELLING, THOMAS C. *See* American Assembly.

SHANNON, LYLE W., ed. *Underdeveloped Areas: A Book of Readings and Research.* New York: Harper, 1957. 496 p.

SHONFIELD, ANDREW. *The Attack on World Poverty.* New York: Random House, 1960. 269 p.

STALEY, EUGENE. *World Economic Development: Effects on Advanced Industrial Countries.* Studies and Reports, Series B, no. 36. Montreal: International Labor Office, 1944. 218 p.

———, and DAVID C. FULTON. *Scientific Research and Progress in Newly Developing Countries: An Exploration of Ways in Which Basic and Applied Research Can Be Used More Effectively to Speed Socio-Economic Development in Africa, Asia, and Latin America.* Menlo Park, Calif.: Stanford Research Institute, 1961. 48 p.

STANFORD RESEARCH INSTITUTE. *Significant Issues in Economic Aid to Newly Developing Countries.* Menlo Park, Calif.: Author, 1960. 75 p.

STRAUS, RALPH I. *See* U. S. Department of State.

TEAF, HOWARD M., JR., and PETER G. FRANCK, eds. *Hands across Frontiers: Case Studies in Technical Cooperation.* Ithaca: Cornell University Press, 1955. 579 p.

TINBERGEN, JAN. *The Design of Development.* Baltimore: Johns Hopkins Press, 1958. 99 p.

U. S. CONGRESS. Joint Economic Committee. *Comparisons of the United States and Soviet Economies,* papers submitted by panelists appearing before the Subcommittee on Economic Statistics. 86th Cong., 1st sess. Washington: GPO, 1959. 616 p.

U. S. DEPARTMENT OF STATE. *Expanding Private Investment for Free World Economic Growth,* by Ralph I. Straus. Washington: Department of State, 1959. 72 p.

U. S. INTERNATIONAL DEVELOPMENT ADVISORY BOARD. *Partners in Progress.* Washington: GPO, 1951. 120 p. Also subsequent reports. The Board reported initially under the chairmanship of Nelson Rockefeller, and later under the chairmanship of Eric Johnston.

U. S. PRESIDENT. *Report to the President on Foreign Economic Policies,* by Gordon Gray. Washington: GPO, 1950. 131 p.

U. S. PRESIDENT'S COMMITTEE TO STUDY THE UNITED STATES MILITARY ASSISTANCE PROGRAM (Draper Committee). V. 1, *Composite Report.* Washington: GPO, 1959. 197 p. V. 2, *Annexes,* a series of eight studies. Washington: GPO, 1959. 355 p.

U. S. SENATE. Committee on Foreign Relations. *United States Foreign Policy.* 86th Cong., 2d sess. Washington: GPO, 1960. Of the thirteen studies prepared for the Committee, three were particularly concerned with economic development:

    2. "Science and Underdeveloped Countries," Ch. 4 of "Possible Nonmilitary Scientific Developments and Their Potential Impact on Foreign Policy Problems of the United States," by the Stanford Research Institute. Pp. 139–147.

    6. "The Operational Aspects of United States Foreign Policy," by the Maxwell Graduate School of Citizenship and Public Affairs, Syracuse University. Pp. 555–633.

    12. "Economic, Social, and Political Change in the Underdeveloped Countries and Its Implications for United States Policy," by the Center for International Studies, Massachusetts Institute of Technology. Pp. 1165–1268.

U. S. SENATE. Special Committee to Study the Foreign Aid Program. *Foreign Aid Program,* a compilation of studies and surveys. 85th Cong., 1st sess. Washington: GPO, 1957. (In addition to the studies listed here, there were ten country and area surveys prepared for the Committee.)

1. "The Objectives of United States Economic Assistance Programs," by the Center for International Studies, Massachusetts Institute of Technology. Pp. 1–73.

2. "Personnel for the Mutual Security Program," by Louis J. Kroeger & Associates. Pp. 75–148.

3. "The Role of Foreign Aid in the Development of Other Countries," by the Research Center in Economic Development and Cultural Change, University of Chicago. Pp. 149–246.

4. "The Use of Private Contractors in Foreign Aid Programs," by Jerome Jacobson Associates. Pp. 247–355.

5. "Agricultural Surplus Disposal and Foreign Aid," by the National Planning Association. Pp. 357–405.

6. "Administrative Aspects of United States Foreign Assistance Programs," by the Brookings Institution. Pp. 407–538.

7. "American Private Enterprise, Foreign Economic Development, and the Aid Programs," by the American Enterprise Association, Inc. Pp. 539–618.

8. "Foreign Assistance Activities of the Communist Bloc and Their Implications for the United States," by the Council for Economic and Industry Research, Inc. Pp. 619–766.

9. "The Foreign Aid Programs and the United States Economy," by the National Planning Association. Pp. 767–879.

10. "The Military Assistance Program of the United States: Two Studies and a Report," by a Special Civilian-Military Review Panel, the Institute of War and Peace Studies of Columbia University, and the Systems Analysis Corporation. Pp. 881–1056.

11. "Foreign Aid Activities of Other Free Nations," by Stuart Rice Associates, Inc. Pp. 1057–1161.

VINER, JACOB. *International Trade and Economic Development.* Glencoe, Ill.: Free Press, 1952. 154 p.

WOLF, CHARLES. *Foreign Aid: Theory and Practice in Southern Asia.* Princeton University Press, 1960. 442 p.

WOOD, C. TYLER. *See* American Economic Association.

Bibliographies

Hald, Marjorie. *A Selected Bibliography on Economic Development and Foreign Aid.* Santa Monica, Calif.: RAND Corporation, 1957. 93 p.

Hazlewood, Arthur. *The Economics of "Under-developed" Areas: An Annotated Reading List of Books, Articles, and Official*

Publications. London: Oxford University Press, 1959; 2d ed. 156 p.

Talbot, Phillips, ed. *A Select Bibliography: Asia, Africa, Eastern Europe, Latin America.* New York: American Universities Field Staff, 1960. 534 p.

Trager, Frank N. "A Selected and Annotated Bibliography on Economic Development, 1953–1957," *Economic Development and Cultural Change,* July 1958, pp. 257–329.

United Nations. Library. *Bibliography on Industrialization in Under-developed Countries.* 1956.II.B.2. New York: Author, 1956. 216 p.

INDEX

Acheson, Dean, 39, 256–257
Act for International Development (1950), 27, 32, 43
Africa, colonialism, 115, 321, 323–324; Communist activity in, 131, 132, 320, 407, 409; development in the 1950's, 397–398, 399, 402; nationalism, 132, 182; population growth, 275, 424; U. S. policy in, 416; U. S. public opinion on aid, 436–437; *see also* individual countries
Agrarian reform, 186, 251–259, 361–362; Communist programs in underdeveloped countries, 134–136, 146, 157–160; political aspects, 254–255; and U. S. policy, 186, 256–259, 361–362
Agriculture, and industrialization, 300–304, 420–421; growth in China and India, 406; productivity, 301–304; *see also* agrarian reform
Albania, Communist activity in, 156; industrial output, 165; Soviet projects in, 409
American Institute of Public Opinion, 438
Anglo-Iranian Oil Co., 288, 299, 363, 365 n.
Anti-imperialism, Communist theme, 132–134, 154, 319, 411–413; *see also* imperialism
Arab Development Bank, 419–420
Arabian American Oil Co., 148, 288
Argentina, 403
Asia, capital investment, 260–262; colonialism, 278–280, 323; Communist activity in, 147, 176, 407, 409–410; development in the 1950's, 237, 398, 402; nationalism, 182; population growth, 275, 424; U. S. public opinion on aid, 436–437; Western aid programs, 381–382, 416–417, 418, 419; *see also* individ-

ual countries, Soviet Central Asia
Ataturk, Mustapha Kemal, 22, 217, 226
Aubrey, Henry G., 412
Australia, 48, 68, 416–417

Becker, Carl L., 61
Belgian Congo, 399
Belgium, 69, 323–324, 403
Berg, Paal, 168 n.
Bhutan, 397
Bilateral aid policies, 351–352, 414, 432, 447–451
Birth control, *see* population
Blasier, S. Cole, 291
Bolivia, 328; agrarian reform, 252; labor legislation, 246; nationalization of tin mines, 293, 338; technical assistance, 237, 352–356
Bowles, Chester, 191
Brandt, Conrad, 143
Brazil, economic development, 242, 308, 309, 403; Soviet propaganda, 148, 151; technical assistance, 237
Bulgaria, Communist activity in, 156; economic growth, 405; industrial output, 165; Soviet projects in, 409
Burma, 218; Communist activity in, 137, 176; government revenue, 269; growth in output, 403; investment in, 462; Japanese reparations, 417; refusal of U. S. aid, 24; self-government, 321, 323; technical assistance, 237, 407
Butler, Harold, 19
Byelorussian S.S.R., 413

Cambodia, 407
Canada, 44, 48, 116, 308; economic development, 68, 262, 403, 404; foreign aid programs, 335, 413–414, 415, 416–417, 418; source of raw